LAU

Community and Revolution in Modern Vietnam

MODERN VIETNAM

Community and Revolution in Modern Vietnam

Alexander B. Woodside
East Asian Research Center
Harvard University

Houghton Mifflin Company · Boston

Atlanta   Dallas   Geneva, Illinois
Hopewell, New Jersey   Palo Alto   London

Map drawn by Dick Sanderson.

Printed in the U.S.A.

Library of Congress Catalog Card Number: 75-18429

ISBN: 0-395-20367-8

For John Fairbank

Contents

Preface

Despite the two harrowing Indochina wars of the past three decades, and despite the fact that in population, resources, and cultural achievements it is the equal of many important European countries, Vietnam has never received much serious attention at universities in the Western world. In the spring of 1969, Harvard University asked me to teach a course introducing American students to modern Vietnamese history and culture since 1802. I have taught this course every year since then and have learned a great deal, although not nearly enough, both from the challenges of my students and colleagues and from the research I was forced to do to bring out some of the immense, if tragic, intellectual interest of the recent Vietnamese experience. This book-length essay is to a large extent the result of my first five years of teaching history at Harvard.

A small freemasonry of scholars around the world has just begun to address itself to the challenges and opportunities that the study of Vietnamese civilization offers. In such a poorly researched field, where political controversies become stale before even the most rudimentary tools of understanding (such as translations of Vietnamese literature) have become available, it is probably dangerous to assume a general awareness (if not a precise knowledge) of Vietnamese history in one's readers, and to go on from there to place the Vietnamese experience in a framework of comparative analysis. Yet, at a number of points in this book I have done precisely that. This book does not pretend to be a comprehensive narrative of twentieth-century Vietnamese history. Instead, I have thought it worthwhile to anticipate comparative study of the recent histories of the countries that once belonged to what we loosely call the "Confucian civilization" in East Asia—Vietnam, China, Japan, and Korea. I have flirted with this interest of mine in the comparative study of Confucian and formerly Confucian societies in writing both this book and its predecessor, *Vietnam and the Chinese Model*.

Of course, the reader will soon see that I have wavered between embracing and rejecting an unconditionally East Asian approach to the study of the Vietnamese revolution. I have not resolved the unresolvable (and perhaps infertile) dilemma of deciding whether Vietnam belongs more to East Asia or Southeast Asia. For what is remarkable about traditional

Vietnam is the way in which classical East Asian themes have been employed to dramatize purely Vietnamese political concerns. An example might be the famous eighteenth-century poem written by the Vietnamese scholar-patriarch Nguyen Nghiem—"Confucius Dreams of the Duke of Chou"—which was almost certainly intended as an idealized lament for the decaying power of the Vietnamese Le emperors of the mid-1700s rather than a celebration of the ancient legitimacy of the Chinese Chou rulers of the fifth century B.C. What is also remarkable about traditional Vietnam is the way in which Vietnamese Confucian scholars could, in one mood, write strait-laced disquisitions on Chinese philosophy in flawless classical Chinese and, in another mood, concoct homiletic, playful, or even politically subversive poetry on purely Vietnamese problems in a writing script that was a strange mixture of Chinese and privately invented Vietnamese characters. The most "Confucian" of all eighteenth-century Vietnamese philosophers, Le Qui Don, a brilliant star of debates with Chinese and Korean scholars at the Peking court itself, seems to have divided his time between composing Chinese-language analyses of the Chinese classics and preparing practical instructions for Vietnamese brides in the private Vietnamese script. Even among the Vietnamese elite, therefore, imported political and philosophical doctrines had to be balanced with the more popular and indigenous side of Vietnamese culture.

As William Blake once made clear, every age is a Canterbury pilgrimage, with a repetition of certain kinds of general human types. It is not unlikely, therefore, that we will meet new versions of Le Qui Don among twentieth-century Vietnamese revolutionaries—even communist ones. And if we do, our ruinous ignorance of Vietnamese, East Asian, and Southeast Asian history may prevent us from fully recognizing them. The men who made the American and French revolutions are very familiar deities or demons to us, in contrast to the men who made and are making the Vietnamese one.

According to one count, more than four hundred important journals and newspapers appeared and disappeared in Vietnam between 1932 and 1945 alone; more than two hundred Vietnamese journals and newspapers covered the events of the Ngo Dinh Diem reign in the south between 1954 and 1963. The exploration of this archival treasurehouse of Vietnamese journalism alone is necessary to any serious study of the revolution. Yet so far the task has barely been begun. The generalizations that are made in this book therefore rest upon much more fragile foundations than those the reader will find in comparable books on revolutions in the West. Availability and reliability of documentation pose as much of a problem as quantity. In writing about the August Revolution of 1945, for example, I did not have access to the basic "Party Documents" (*Van kien Dang*) that exist on this subject. I had to rely on the detailed series of articles based on them, which appeared in the Hanoi newspaper *Nhan dan* at the end of August 1970. And even if I had had access to the original documents, I would then have had to remember that published documents are not the last word. In the case of the Vietnamese communists—to say nothing of other political movements and governments—publications often present only finished pictures or abstractions of controversies, and not very much in the way of informal exceptions to rules. The reader may perhaps begin to gather from all of this a sense of the stimulating, but almost inexhaustible complexities of Vietnamese studies.

Community and Revolution in Modern Vietnam was originally contracted as part of a series under the general editorship of Robert I. Rotberg, Massachusetts Institute of Technology.

My thanks are also due to a number of friends who have read and commented upon this manuscript. I am grateful, too, to all my colleagues and mentors at Harvard's East Asian Research Center—especially to the center's two directors, Professor John K. Fairbank and Professor Ezra Vogel—for providing me with support and inspiration during the writing of this book.

Alexander B. Woodside

1

Colonialism and the Vietnamese Community

The Setting and the Meaning of the Vietnamese Revolution

As a society, Vietnam is older than either France or the United States. It possesses more than twenty centuries of recorded history, and Vietnamese nationalists would claim much more: Ho Chi Minh wrote a polemical history of Vietnam, in 1942, which dated its origins to 2879 B.C. If a visitor from Saturn had arrived on earth sometime toward the end of the eleventh century A.D., he might have found little more than forests and swamps in the vicinity of present-day Washington. Had he then traveled across the Pacific to the neighborhood of modern Hanoi, he would have found a thriving city named Thang-long ("Ascending Dragon"), the capital of the Vietnamese state of the eleventh and twelfth century Ly dynasty. There he would have become enveloped in a world of temples and of Buddhist philosophers, as the guest of a cosmopolitan Buddhist society which had survived in the Red River delta for more than two centuries after a similar kind of society had disappeared in China during the T'ang dynasty persecutions of Buddhism.

The depth of the Vietnamese people's consciousness of their own history and literature would astonish the far less imaginative nationalists and relic-worshippers of North America and of western Europe. In 1964, Hanoi children were shown animated film cartoons which attempted to depict life in the legendary Vietnamese kingdom of Van-lang, a kingdom which was supposed to have come to an end, after being ruled by eighteen glorious sovereigns, in the third century B.C. The purpose of these car-

1

toons was to show that in this kingdom even a heroic child had once
managed to defeat a seemingly invincible invader king who "wore nothing
but black, and whose sleeves were too big for him; he scooped up everything, chickens, geese, pigs, all small children, handfuls of bananas and
coconuts, and all were stuffed into his two sleeves."[1] Not every society in
the world would have prepared for what turned out to be years of warfare
and of American bombing by encouraging its children to think of myth-
events that had supposedly occurred some three thousand years before the
invention of national flags or of "socialist realism."

The Vietnamese consciousness of literature is equally likely to over-
whelm Western citizens whose command of their own literary heritages is
often a fragile thing. The textbook on modern Vietnamese literature
(principally of the 1800s and early 1900s) which middle school students
in Saigon were using in 1963 was 1,400 pages long and resembled a small
telephone book. Little of the literature which it covered has ever been
translated into English or French. For more humble evidence of the fact
that Vietnam is and always has been one of the most intensely literary
civilizations on the face of the planet, Western visitors to Vietnam need
only have glanced at the conical hats which peasants wear, or used to wear,
in the Hue area in central Vietnam. These hats are called "poetry hats" in
Vietnamese because they have poems inscribed inside their brims, and the
poems can be read when the hats are held up to the sunlight.

No amount of statistics, rhetoric, or social science theory can explain the
Vietnamese revolution adequately if its properties of acute historical
consciousness and cultural pride are insufficiently considered. These
properties were not so much destroyed as psychologically enlarged by the
shock of French colonialism. In the middle of the nineteenth century,
Vietnam, which was then ruled by the emperors of the Nguyen dynasty
(1802–1945) from their capital at Hue, was temporarily overcome by
French military pressure and by its own internal weaknesses and forced to
subside into the humiliating position of being a French colony. The six
southern provinces of "Cochin China" around Saigon were conquered by
the French between 1859 and 1867, and central Vietnam (Annam) and
northern Vietnam (Tonkin) were converted into "protectorates," after a
number of French military forays there and a French war with China, in
1883–1884–1885. In the medieval period, northern and central Vietnam
had functioned as separate and riyal political societies for several centuries.
But this formal three-way division of Vietnam into Cochin China, Annam,
and Tonkin was unprecedented and was regarded by many Vietnamese as
the deliberate magnification of Vietnamese regionalism by a foreign power.
The term "protectorate," applied to the center and to the north, became
something of a fiction. From 1887 all three regions, Tonkin, Annam, and
Cochin China, as well as Cambodia and Laos, were brought under the
ultimate authority of a single French governor-general, the overlord of all
Indochina, whose headquarters were in Hanoi. Yet more ordinary admin-

istrative barriers between the regions, sanctioned by this fiction, remained to interrupt and impede Vietnamese national life.

The French presence in Vietnam was a "modern" one only in the most limited and ambiguous ways. New institutions coexisted with old ones under a colonial policy known as "association." Cochin China, the full colony, was of course ruled by a French governor at Saigon, by French and by Gallicized Vietnamese officials under this governor, and by French law courts. No significant Vietnamese institutions of the traditional period survived here. But elsewhere the situation was more complex. Annam and Tonkin, the two protectorates, were governed by the Hanoi governor-general and by two French "resident superiors," one in Hanoi and one in Hue. Yet the Vietnamese monarchy at Hue and the premodern Vietnamese bureaucracy were allowed to survive in Annam and Tonkin, in circumscribed and subordinate positions, as traumatized, moldering tokens of the classical past. Each province in Annam and Tonkin had two parallel administrations, one led by a French province chief, who governed Europeans and Vietnamese who had become French citizens, and the other led by a Vietnamese governor who ruled all other Vietnamese, and who was appointed to his position, subject to French approval, by the old-fashioned Vietnamese emperor at Hue. Even the civil service examination system which recruited the members of the Vietnamese provincial bureaucracy—a system which had been in existence for more than eight centuries, and whose abolition had been proposed by Vietnamese reformers in the 1860s—was preserved by the colonial regime, in the north and the center, until 1919. Thanks to the embalming agency of colonialism, it actually managed to outlive its Chinese counterpart by fourteen years.

Behind this increasingly anachronistic, contradictory, pasteboard framework of new and old institutions, Vietnamese society itself between 1884 and 1945 produced a host of changes. Some of them were revolutionary in nature—the beginning of the breakdown of the great family and of the traditional patrilineage, the wearing of Western clothes, the rise of the concept of romantic love between the sexes, nationalist demonstrations, labor strikes, and the domestication of Western political thought from Rousseau to Trotsky. With the collapse of some of the old civilization's values, even the classical Sino-Vietnamese aesthetic sense betrayed signs of change. Paintings of flying cranes, for example, became less acceptable, because the old mandarin superstition that cranes symbolized longevity was being discarded, together with the placing of such a high value on old age and longevity themselves. Such a prosaic act as swimming suddenly became a popular revolutionary cult, in Vietnam as in China. And it became popular if only because it indicated a change in style, in cultural procedure, from that of the long-nailed scholar who practiced calligraphy and rituals to that of the physically vigorous soldier or social engineer.

Change of this kind was possible, at least for the sons of the upper class, because the colonial cocoon was never hermetically sealed against escape, either into Vietnamese history or across the world to Europe. More than 100,000 Vietnamese were transported to Europe to serve the French cause during World War I. Especially after 1930, Vietnamese student travel to France became almost commonplace. The contrast between the metropolis and the colony became one of the most important of all revolutionary stimuli; and it could be justly observed that the Vietnamese revolution was not a revolution against France so much as against the brutalizing colonial environment which Frenchmen had created in Vietnam which had in turn corrupted its creators. The second and third generations of French residents who were born in Vietnam, and who were guaranteed positions at the top of the colonial administrative and economic hierarchies by race rather than by talent, grew up assuming that their superiority over the Vietnamese was some kind of natural law. But once they departed from the colony their ancestors had conquered, this psychological self-mystification process lost its force, for the rulers as well as for the ruled. Nobody described more sardonically this strange evaporation of the psychological complexes upon which colonialism thrived, once the colony itself was subtracted, than Nhat Linh, the famous Vietnamese novelist. Journeying to France by ship for the first time in 1927, in the company of French colonial officers, Nhat Linh observed that:

> . . . the farther the ship got from Vietnam and the closer it got to France, to the same degree the more decently the people aboard the ship treated me. In the China Sea they did not care to look at me. By the Gulf of Siam they were looking at me with scornful apprehension, the way they would look at a mosquito carrying malaria germs to Europe. When we entered the Indian Ocean, their eyes began to become infected with expressions of gentleness and compassion . . . and when we crossed the Mediterranean, suddenly they viewed me as being civilized like themselves, and began to entertain ideas of respecting me. At that time I was very elated. But I still worried about the time when I was going to return home![2]

The spread of the Vietnamese revolution, far more so than that of the Chinese revolution, depended upon the demystification of the claims and illusions of colonialism. Nhat Linh's statement is a clear revelation of the importance of the discovery, by intellectuals of his generation, that the inequities and the reciprocal social and ethnic antagonisms of colonial Vietnam were associated with the idiosyncratic conventions and laws of one specific setting, not with any universal biological or technological or ideological determinisms that could never be challenged. Vietnam was not a society that had been colonized in the interests of a universal spirit of modernity. Quite the contrary, it was a forcing-house of irrational growths that a single ocean voyage could dissolve.

Travel of this kind also confirmed Vietnamese intellectuals of the 1920s and 1930s in their sense that they were being denied rights to which they were entitled elsewhere—even in, or especially in, France. And enjoyment of these rights depended upon the removal of the barriers and partitions that had proliferated in Vietnam under the influence of colonial adminis- trative and stratification policies. In the summer of 1938, a coterie of frustrated Vietnamese intellectuals produced a famous litany of reform proposals which indicated the extent of the fragmentation which colonial strategies had encouraged in Vietnamese political, social, and economic life. These proposals demanded the creation of *one* united representatives' group for all of Indochina with the power to advise the colonial govern- ment; the admission of Vietnamese representatives to ethnically mixed councils and commissions, like municipal councils, chambers of commerce, and agricultural councils, on an *equal* basis with Frenchmen; the reform of law codes, so that there would be *one* unified legal system for the colony rather than different sets of special laws for Frenchmen, Vietnamese, over- seas Chinese, Chams, and highland minorities; the unification of all measuring systems within the colony; the abolition of multiple, parallel tax-collecting and fiscal systems; and the reform of the private schools, which were creating a segregated caste of Vietnamese Catholics with an educational background different from that of the rest of the population. Not entirely as an afterthought, the reformers also requested freedom of assembly, freedom of speech, freedom of publication, and full freedom to go abroad.[3]

To find a single cultural or psychological "key" to the explanation of modern Vietnam would be as difficult as it would be to find such a key for explaining modern France or modern America. There are, for example, a number of different, highly complex Vietnamese value systems—including the semitraditional bureaucratic one, the romantic individualist one, the Buddhist contemplative one, and the modern communist one—through which Vietnamese cultural interests and political inclinations are constantly being refracted. Yet one theme does seem to have united many Vietnamese of a great variety of political loyalties and ideological outlooks in the twentieth century. To put it crudely, this theme is the search for better collective organization or for more effective "organized communities" and "organized groups" (*doan the*) with which to overcome the fragmentation of the colonial period and those structural weaknesses of traditional Viet- namese society which the very fact of colonialism itself had exposed. For decades there has been a powerful chorus of voices in Vietnam, both on the right and on the left, on the subject of the need for more cohesive *doan the*.

The Vietnamese search for methods of organizing communities more effectively, including the community of the nation itself, obviously draws part of its strength from the importance of communal instincts—represented especially by the family, the lineage, and the village—in traditional Viet- nam. And here, of course, Vietnam is far from unique among Southeast Asian societies. As far away as Java, by no means a neighboring society to the Vietnamese, villages were regarded as communal reflections of the cosmic order, in which social and religious obligations blended with each other. Nativist nostalgia for those harmonies of precolonial communities, real or imagined, which had been shaken by the European presence, could express itself in twentieth-century Java even in such vital cultural and educational modernization currents as the Taman Siswa movement of the 1920s and 1930s, which significantly saw its whole association as one spiritual family. The Vietnamese people have shared this type of nativist nostalgia, combined with reformism, in full measure. Yet it might be possible to argue that their quest for entirely new organizational formulas that could be profitably introduced into the ancient communal atmosphere of Vietnamese culture has been much more intense than that of many other Southeast Asian peoples. Even peasant religious revivals in Vietnam, after 1920, rarely rejected Western organizational procedures completely. And among the intellectuals, a spreading contempt for the weakness of existing protective organizational principles in Vietnamese life became a very part of the tinder of revolution.

Writing in the Hanoi newspaper "The Ancient Lantern General Report" (*Dang Co tung bao*) in the summer of 1907, the pioneering journalist Nguyen Van Vinh accused the Vietnamese people of being slavish, spendthrift consumers of Chinese goods, both commercial and cultural, and traced this shortcoming to their lack of enough sense of "organized community" to resist foreign influences and produce their own goods.[4] In 1925 the writer and politician Pham Quynh, regarded by many Vietnamese as an excessively Gallicized mandarin apologist for French rule, declared passionately that in an age of "violent" international relations each national people must strengthen their own "natural" organized community in order to preserve their race and culture, the Vietnamese people being no exception.[5] At times when it appeared that the Vietnamese nation as a whole could not achieve independence and a modern coherence, a profusion of religious and social movements—Cao Dai, Hoa Hao, revived Buddhism, the Tonkin Scouting Association, labor unions, and even the Saigon shoeshine boys—have attempted to develop new resources of organizational power on a smaller scale, as part of their effort to capture or recapture an ideal spirit of collective action. In 1947, at the outset of a seven years' war with France, and at a time when the Indochina Communist Party was no longer supposed formally to exist, Ho Chi Minh wrote a book of instructions for his party cadres in which he suppressed any reference to the now illicit term for "party" (*dang*) but invoked, instead, a far from casually chosen substitute term, "organized community" (*doan the*).[6] A Catholic intellectual in Saigon, Nguyen Van Trung, writing in the 1960s, asserted that the "fundamental political question" in Vietnam was "the question of changing a psychology: how can we sit with each other, live alongside each other, and accept each other." According to Nguyen Van Trung, foreign interventions in Vietnamese affairs had only been encouraged by Vietnamese internal disunity.[7] As he wrote, thousands of nameless communist cadres in northern villages were denouncing, with a fervor that would have seemed abnormal in European communist circles, the individualistic "small producer mentality" among Vietnamese peasants which stood in the way of more dynamic agricultural organization. More examples could be added indefinitely.

The search for contemporary patterns of cohesion and organization that would be worthy of Vietnamese civilization's brilliant past runs through the Vietnamese revolution. Although not its only characteristic, it is one of its most perdurable, and deserves more than one book-length examination. The quest for cohesion has been more intense, if possible, in Vietnam than in modern China. In China, too, disgruntled revolutionaries like Sun Yat-sen were forced to speak of the need for overcoming a traditional society that was like a "heap of loose sand." But China never really knew the community-smashing consequences of full colonialism which the Vietnamese people experienced, particularly the rise of a plantation system which played havoc with old families and neighborhoods, or a full-fledged sectarian educational system linked to a proselytizing European religion which was protected (if tepidly at times) by an omnipotent colonial government. Furthermore, Chinese society had possessed a more vigorous associational life before its contact with the West had begun. And many of these traditional Chinese associations and organizations had been strong enough to soften the consequences, on the local level, of the Chinese dynastic state's growing subordination to foreign powers. Good examples are the redoubtable Shanghai and Hankow tea guilds which humiliated and successfully boycotted Western tea-dealer merchants in the late nineteenth century. In Vietnam, the lack of meaningful organizations outside the imperial court had always been much more extreme, and had been qualified only by spasmodic gentry and peasant protest movements. The search for "organization," by Vietnamese revolutionaries and by their enemies, has been correspondingly more acute.

The Vietnamese search for organization has also, perhaps, been more prosaic, without being enlivened by the real and synthetic tempests of publicly orchestrated "cultural revolutions" such as those China staged in 1966—or in 1919. (This does not mean, of course, that Vietnam has not experienced a cultural revolution.) The Chinese tradition of utopian thought is perhaps the richest in the world. Its monuments have ranged from Mo-tzu's state of universal love and the equal field system to nineteenth-century Taiping visions of the abolition of familism. Its compulsions have often made Chinese history resemble a series of gigantic pulsations toward, and then away from, certain recurrent utopian schemes. Vietnamese society has never known a utopian tradition of similar power and durability, perhaps because historically Vietnam was too frequently beleaguered by foreign attackers to be able to afford one.

In both China and Vietnam, however, the crusade for cohesion, within a

modern framework of progress, has been a defensive one. A Japanese
political scientist, comparing the experiences of Japan and of China within
the past century, has suggested that in Japan the term "nation" has
acquired the mystical importance, and that sense of being a permanent
natural given, that the term "revolution" has acquired more than any
other in China. To most Japanese, "revolution" means an unnatural,
violent outbreak that might destroy the "nation"; to most Chinese,
"revolution," because it has been associated for decades with resistance to
outside pressures and incursions, conveys the flavor of legitimacy, referring
to a permanent process that is also an everyday occurrence. The poignancy
of the comparison lies in the fact that these terms are written the same way
in both the Chinese and the Japanese languages.[8] In Vietnam, the symbolic
importance of the term "revolution," which is extravagantly used in the
1970s by both communists and conservatives, matches very closely the
symbolic content of the term in China. And Vietnamese attempts to
develop strong "organized communities" that will both support revolution
and be sufficient evidence of the triumph of revolution are not just conditioned by nostalgic nationalist memories or mythologies of precolonial
collectivities which deserve to be restored. They are also conditioned by a
Hobbesian realization that the strength of all new organized communities
in Vietnam, economic, social, and political, will be determined by reference to various enemies—colonialism, or even a simple inability to flourish
effectively in the modern industrial world.

The Social Revolutionism of the Early Colonialists

From the 1860s to the 1890s, French colonial rulers set in motion the
beginnings of a transformation of the traditional distribution of power
among social classes in Vietnam. This transformation was not wholly
intended—and it was never completed—but it created the tensions and
uncertainties which haunted the early revolutionaries' organization-building
activities. The French protectorate in Tonkin, and the French colony in
Cochin China, were established at the very high cost of the debasement
and moral effacement of many members of the traditional Vietnamese
scholar-gentry class. This was the era when former fish vendors and
militiamen like Tran Ba Loc could replace cultivated scholar-officials as
the administrators of whole districts, prefectures, or provinces in Vietnam,
provided that they displayed a proper friendship for the French army or
navy. As early as 1863, as Milton Osborne has shown, the aide-de-camp of
the French governor of Cochin China was talking of French intervention
in Vietnamese life to redeem the Vietnamese peasantry from the rule of an
"aristocracy of scholars"—a task that became almost unnecessary in the
south, since most Vietnamese degree-holding bureaucrats there voluntarily
withdrew from the colony, refusing to serve the invaders under degrading
circumstances.[9] In northern Vietnam, French military officers publicly
humbled and terrorized high-ranking Vietnamese mandarins. Nothing

demonstrates this better than the incident of 1884 in which a French general's staff officer sent three envoys from the Vietnamese court up in dirigibles, and then brought the terrified, groveling courtiers down to earth again, amid the laughter of an assembled audience.[10]

In the vastly different circumstances of the 1930s, when the French colonial government was, on the contrary, attempting to freeze the Vietnamese social structure into inert tranquillity, the minor social revolution of the later 1800s was itself one reason why such attempts were doomed to failure. What the seventeenth-century English philosopher James Harrington referred to as "violent revolution"—foreign conquest followed by a confiscation of the various properties of the preconquest elite—is not an inappropriate description of the events of the early years of Vietnamese colonial society.

First of all, the colonial regime created new social groups among the Vietnamese population to serve as middlemen between the rulers and the ruled. Vietnamese students were recruited, often from the Vietnamese Catholic community; they were given Western shoes, hats, shirts, and trousers, and trained to be interpreters. As the new linchpin occupation of interpreters grew in numbers, it became indispensable to French officials. More important, this new group, abruptly raised to great heights by a new kind of social mobility which involved the arbitrary redistribution of influence and power by the alien French—became both a symbol and a source of oppression to Vietnamese who were less thoroughly Westernized. Saigon residents of the 1870s, if the popular literature of the period is a guide, thought the new interpreters were "as pompous as bandits, having a braggadocio that fills the heavens, being more menacing than a children's bogey."[11] Jules Boissière, the Provençal novelist who lived in Indochina in the early 1890s, considered the interpreters produced by the College Chasseloup-Laubat in Saigon to be "pillaging, rich, insolent" people.[12]

To Western observers, it might have seemed that the French, by creating a new Vietnamese middle class of interpreters and also of government secretaries, were bravely and progressively manufacturing a host of new professional positions that could be filled on the supposedly modern, "non-ascriptive" basis of which applicant possessed the most personal merit and talent. For Vietnamese, however, the French had merely made the traditional stratification system more arbitrary. Status no longer depended upon a hard-earned knowledge of the Chinese classics, the prerequisite for advancement in the precolonial civil service examinations. Now it depended upon the capricious patronage of foreign militarists. And because those French military officers who served so frequently as colonial administrators in Vietnam in the late 1800s rarely spoke Vietnamese, the fate of Vietnamese involved in lawsuits, at least in the south, depended upon the good will of the interpreters. An untalented or malevolent interpreter was regarded as a certain guarantee of jail, or even of a death sentence. The introduction of "impersonal" or "universalistic" Western law courts simply broadened the scope of particularistic behavior and corruption. A Saigon popular ballad put the matter succinctly: "As for anyone from the rural villages, by the time they have arrived at the palace to wait for French officials on business, their spirits have already left them. Whether you succeed or not depends upon the words of the interpreters. When you have business to be raised, you don't care how much money you use to bribe them."[13]

The modestly trained interpreters did not monopolize the necessary middleman role. The French presence inevitably created another distinctive new social group, the Vietnamese women who served as wives, mistresses, and prostitutes to French soldiers and administrators. Known to the Vietnamese as "French mothers" (*me Tay*), these women also became potent intermediaries between their own people and those Frenchmen who spoke no Vietnamese. The Saigon ballads of this period provide us with sensitive barometers of the currents of opinion in the early colony, expounding a disenchanted sociology of subservience which centered upon the peculiar positions the "French mothers" occupied in conquered Vietnam: "If you get into trouble, you depend upon Miss Hai [a prostitute] escorting you in to report to their honors [French officials], for only then is the case settled. And when she looks at you and sees that you do not have any money . . . she ignores you, and does not report your business to their honors so that your village can be grateful to you. Even if you possess the family status of a senior uncle, and get into trouble, she bullies you and calls you *may* ['sonny'] and throws your application away quickly." Or: "In one night you do not know how many husbands she has. Malays and Filipinos both possess her. . . . The doors of authority [that is, the French] are always open to anyone who reports obsequiously to her. She regards anyone who is poor . . . and who greets her in a hurry without looking openly respectful as an opportunity for saying, 'I shall whisper in the officials' ears about you. You, sonny, are my enemy, imprisonment for life for you' . . . ."[14]

Of course the sudden, random rise of a few poor Vietnamese to levels of manipulative power and influence as interpreters and "French mothers" did not represent the upward ascent of a class, but merely the windfall promotion of a small minority of the members of the lower classes. And since it was a social elevation which usually implied both dependency upon foreigners and a repudiation of traditional moral and social codes, it engendered its own psychological crises. Louis Peytral, another French observer of this complicated, volcanic social scene, noted in 1897 that Tonkinese interpreters felt inferior to Saigon interpreters, because the latter were farther removed from the censure of the traditional Vietnamese gentry class and were treated much more generously by the French. Tormented by this sense of inferiority, the northern interpreters thereupon behaved all the more ruthlessly toward their own people.[15] The uneven, unpredictable, transitory nature of these social elevations made many of their beneficiaries more miserable than happy.

But what counted was that the early colonialists' diffusion of these windfall privileges—under the banner of a shoddy populism whose main target was the Vietnamese elite resistance leaders—mocked and diminished the traditional order of the Vietnamese gentry. Of all the groups of lower class Vietnamese who were suddenly flung into menial but influential positions by the French conquest, none was more flamboyant than the Vietnamese who worked as household servants in French colonial homes, and who became known to other Vietnamese as the "boy" (*boi*) group. These kitchen boys frequently roamed the streets of Saigon in marauding bands, in the first few decades after the colony was founded. They engaged in street fights, in which knives and oxhide whips were used, with other bands of young Vietnamese males whose occupational specialty was to blow the trumpets at French military posts.

The "boy" group imitated, and, in agreement with each other, parasitically adopted the ranks of their French officer masters. But at the same time, in a carnival of publicly released envy and disrespect, the "boy" group might ape the costumes and manners of precolonial Vietnamese bureaucrats.[16] Their pathetic usurpation of the symbols of high status, which would have been severely punished by Vietnamese dynasties, blended the old and the new but did not really contain any prospects of social advancement. Yet the license of the "boys" and the interpreters, as a pollution of the old society's privileges and rituals, deeply antagonized those members of the still proud Vietnamese scholar elite who remained in the cities and towns. For still others imitated the "boys," as another sonorously critical nineteenty-century Saigon ballad reveals: "With their red silk, their shoes and socks, showing their spit-and-polish off to the world, poor people imitate them in order to fill themselves with importance . . . only when you examine them carefully do you realize they're merely boys who serve rice."[17]

It is clear that members of the previously segregated Vietnamese Catholic community played conspicuous parts in this quasi-revolutionary reshuffling of the precolonial social order. What had made French imperialism in Asia superficially distinctive from that of other Western countries was its heavy institutionalization of the desire to expand Catholic Christianity. From the 1820s to 1884 the slogan "freedom of religion" had been the ideological lance-point of the French campaign against the traditional Vietnamese state, which had been executing European missionaries and their Vietnamese converts for their presumed "seditious" opposition to the dynasty and to state Confucianism. Undeniable schisms and discontents within traditional Vietnamese society had permitted the Vietnamese Catholic community to grow despite cruel persecutions. Furthermore, the positive appeal of Catholic Christianity to Asian peasants—like those of the

Philippines—could also be a potent one at times, and deserves consideration in its own right. In western Tonkin alone, which had an estimated Catholic population of some 140,000 people by 1855, the annual rate of conversions fluctuated between 500 and 1,300 adults per year between 1846 and 1855. Le Duy Phung, an opponent of the Nguyen dynasty who launched a large insurrection in Quang Yen province in 1861, was served by a Vietnamese Christian general. By 1892, the total of Vietnamese Catholics may have risen to some 570,000, perhaps one-twentieth of the population.[18]

But by the time of the final consummation of the French conquest, in 1884, the Nguyen dynasty's numerous edicts of proscription of Christianity had also taken their toll. They had led to a general and progressive pauperization of the indigenous Catholic community. This pauperization, combined with a much stronger Vietnamese upper class association of the Christian religion with French aggression, had meant that by the 1880s most new Vietnamese Catholic converts were being drawn from the "most inferior and most ignorant classes of the population," as a future French governor-general of Indochina put it.[19] They were being drawn from among "the boys, the cooks, even lower again, and from among the floating and questionable populations of the markets of the great cities."

Prominent portions of the new wealth created by the colonial regime drifted into the hands of such men, who naturally made efforts to escape their pauperization. Le Phat Dat, an interpreter to the French who had studied at a Penang mission school, is a good example: he rapidly transformed himself into one of the most powerful landowners of the Saigon area. Tran Ba Loc, whose penniless father had been imprisoned by the Nguyen court for his Christian beliefs, became a humble auxiliary militiaman to the French invaders and died as a rich provincial governor-general in 1899. The warfare which attended the French conquest, especially of the south, forced Vietnamese peasants and the landowners above them to abandon their lands. The land records and maps which French colonial administrators subsequently drew up did not recognize the property claims of these refugees; and Vietnamese land speculators like Le Phat Dat, by linking themselves to the "land committees" of the newly created colonial municipal councils, were able to appropriate the lands of past property-owners who had fled from the war zone. In southern Vietnam, even today, the morally explosive legacies of this Harringtonian "violent revolution" simmer in many subterranean channels. Popular gossip surges disrespectfully around the imposing edifices of nineteenth-century Catholic churches and cathedrals: they were all built, it is claimed, upon landed estates that had been stolen from preconquest owners.

Is it useful to mourn this moral and economic disestablishment of part of the traditional elite? It would be irrelevant and romantic to do so: the traditional elite had never presided over a social paradise. But it is important to remember that when the colonial regime resorted to policies of social conservatism, as it soon did, its earlier attacks upon the social status quo made its later conservatism look highly self-serving rather than morally principled. Not only that, its disestablishment of part of the traditional elite contributed to the inability of Vietnamese opponents of a revolution on the left to develop convincing conservative ideologies that could win the support of many people in the twentieth century, unlike their conservative counterparts in China. For such opponents, if they were newly rich, found it difficult to harmonize their own morally suspect property interests with their right to invoke prestigious cultural traditions from the uncontaminated precolonial past.)

The conquerors' intentional and unintentional revisions of the social structure even affected the rate of social and cultural Westernization in Vietnam, making the politics of such Westernization highly individualistic.(Comparisons between Vietnam and Japan, an East Asian society with a noncolonial history, are instructive even in such simple (but symptomatic) aspects of acculturation as the adoption of Western clothing.

By preserving their independence, the Japanese were able to adopt Western clothes in stages, as part of a comprehensive, conscious national debate. Western clothing first entered Japanese life on a controlled basis (like the rest of Western civilization) as a military necessity. Western uniforms were needed to facilitate the performance of the Western-style drills of the new Japanese army. Japanese governments, however, attempted to confine "barbarian costume" strictly to soldiering. As late as 1870, Japanese university regulations rather innocently stipulated that students were forbidden to wear strangely skirtless, swordless Western clothes while they were studying new subjects like rhetoric, logic, and Western philosophy. In 1872, a pivotal year in Japanese clothing history, the Japanese elite changed course and deliberately chose Western clothes for nonmilitary reasons, accepting them even for public ceremonial dress. In 1887, indeed, after the Japanese upper classes had actually begun to flaunt their Western clothes as manifestations of their precocious "civilization and enlightenment," an influential journal, "The Friend of the National People" (*Kokumin no tomo*) delivered a populist attack upon Western clothing styles, arguing that they were being used to exalt the power and panache of the aristocracy at the expense of the common people.[20]

In Vietnam(on the other hand) there was no wide-ranging national debate or coherent series of elite decisions about the utility of foreign clothes. The brusque social compulsions which followed the redistributions of power under the early colonial regime insured that Western clothes would be adopted by many Vietnamese in the late 1800s as symbols of various degrees of individual membership in the colonialists' universe. A folk saying of the early colonial period explained that wearing Western clothes not too subtly improved a Vietnamese man's position in a colonial law court: "The man who wears a Western suitcoat kills people and is let off as if nothing had happened. The man who just wears a Western undershirt runs to stand next to the man who wears the Western suitcoat."[21]

How many patron-client relationships were forged between Vietnamese who could afford much Western clothing and Vietnamese who could afford only a little, as the saying suggests, is difficult to say. Before 1900, however, cultural change in Vietnam was linked to the scramble by individuals for arbitrarily offered social rewards(much more than in Japan, where it was one ingredient in a carefully planned and discussed program of revitalization for the whole national community.) This individualistic pattern hardly disappeared after 1900. Encouraged by colonialism, it remained one of the cardinal disintegrative forces against which Vietnamese revolutionaries were forced to muster their energies.

The Decline of the Bureaucracy's Power to Summarize National Life

The structure of the traditional Vietnamese state, and the modified survival of important elements of this structure under colonialism, also dominated the issues of integration and disintegration and the nationalist-revolutionary search for new organizational formulas.

At the time of the French conquest, Vietnam was undoubtedly the paramount bureaucratic society in Southeast Asia. Under the Nguyen emperors, the traditional Vietnamese civil service had become remarkably complex. Thousands of written rules governed its communications, its formalized procedures of promotion and demotion, the circulation of its officials in office, and the periodic ratings of its officials by higher officials. The hierarchical salary structure of this bureaucracy was divided into eighteen separate levels. Bureaucrats themselves were recruited by means of a nation-wide civil service examination system which had originated in Vietnam in 1075 A.D. as a copy of the even older Chinese civil service examinations. To become a member of the bureaucratic elite, scholars had to pass regional examinations in the provinces and, if they wished to win truly powerful and prestigious positions, further metropolitan and palace examinations at the capital city of Hue. Success in the examinations demanded a pedantic knowledge of the Chinese Confucian classics, especially those texts which the twelfth-century Chinese philosopher Chu Hsi had first called the "Four Books"—The Analects of Confucius, Mencius, the Great Learning, and the Doctrine of the Mean. Hundreds or even thousands of candidates would assemble every three years for the examinations in great rectangular fields, which were patrolled by soldiers riding elephants. Here they would be asked to write poems with complicated conventions and strict rhyme schemes, essays upon Chinese Confucian philosophy, and disquisitions upon the public policies of past dynasties, Vietnamese and Chinese.

Behind this examination system stood a long tradition of Vietnamese cultural borrowing from China, a tradition which nevertheless coexisted with an equally important determination to resist and defeat invading

Chinese armies—as in A.D. 1406–1427 and again in 1788–1789. Unlike North Americans—who take their language from England, their paper, tea, and printing from China, their numerical system from India, their alphabet from the Phoenicians, and their tobacco from the New World Indians—the Vietnamese were conscious of borrowing mainly from the culture of one civilization, instead of many.

When Hue, in central Vietnam, was built as a walled capital city for the Vietnamese emperor after 1802, it was constructed as a deliberate copy of the Chinese capital at Peking. Its walls, gates, and palaces were all designed to imitate specific walls, gates, and palaces in the capital city of China. The Vietnamese emperor, in moving about his capital, performed the same movements and conducted the same rituals that the Chinese emperor performed and conducted in Peking. From his own diplomats and from Chinese merchants he obtained Chinese court records which enabled him consciously to do so. As in China, the emperor bore a colossal political burden. Confucian political theory emphasized government not by law but by "worthy men"— that is, government through hierarchical moral elitism, in which the removal of competent emperors from the political scene was regarded as an almost certain guarantee of chaos. As in China, politics and ethics were considered inseparable—as inseparable as politics and economics are thought to be in the modern West. But ethical canons were defended not so much by a deeply permeative legal-judicial system which constantly identified and punished offences as by a plethoric ritualism in politics and in family relations—by an abundance of carefully worked out rituals which sought to eliminate immoral conduct ahead of time.

Unlike his Chinese counterpart, the Vietnamese emperor bore an added burden as a symbol of "Vietnameseness" and as the direct protector of his people against foreign attack. It would have been impossible to imagine a foreigner ever occupying the Vietnamese throne. In the early 1900s, Chinese nationalist scholar patriots, looking back into Chinese history for models to inspire their nationalism, chose a gallery of seventeenth-century Chinese intellectuals who had opposed the Manchu invasion of China— Huang Tsung-hsi, Wang Fu-chih, and others. Vietnamese scholar-patriots of the same generation were much more inclined to find their historical models in Vietnamese emperors: especially Le Loi, subsequently the Le Thai-to emperor, who had overthrown two decades of Chinese rule in Vietnam in 1427, and the Tay-son Quang-trung emperor of 1788–1792, who had gloriously defeated another Chinese invasion. On the other hand, there was never any Japanese-style celebration of an unbroken imperial line in Vietnam. This meant that dynastic change remained a prominent factor in Vietnamese politics and history, and was, if possible, even more traumatic than in China.

But what was the relationship of the traditional monarchy to organized communities? This was one of the first questions early Vietnamese revolutionaries, lamenting the dearth of effective organization and of community sentiment in Vietnamese politics, were forced to ask. It might not be too disastrous an oversimplification to state that whereas European kings had frequently built up (or at least permitted) the growth of associations in order to increase their own power, Chinese and Vietnamese rulers had prevented their formation in order to preserve theirs. Roman law, especially as it was expanded by medieval European political theorists, had permitted a distinction between the ruler as a public institution and the ruler as a person. Lawyers like Edmund Plowden in Tudor England spoke of the king of England as having two "bodies," his "body natural" and his "body politic"—the latter meaning the government as a whole, including representative assemblies like Parliament, which were supposed to strengthen the king's authority. In Vietnam, as in China, any distinction between the person of the emperor—whose role was supposed to be that of a moral teacher whom the whole society revered and imitated—and a "body politic" was unheard of and would have been regarded as destructive of Confucian kingship, whose boundaries could not be delimited or subdivided practically.

Between the bureaucracy and the villages, therefore, no independent or semi-independent associations or intermediate bodies were allowed to exist. Guilds were small and controlled. There were no equivalents of modern chambers of commerce. Towns and cities had neither municipal charters nor municipal governments. Traditional Vietnamese towns, in fact, were merely units in the national administrative hierarchy—again, as in China—rather than being self-governing entities with mayors and municipal councils. There was a Buddhist ecclesiastical hierarchy, but it lacked a pan-Vietnamese framework that high-ranking Buddhists could direct or manipulate themselves; the first national Vietnamese Buddhist congress did not materialize until 1951. The Vietnamese court granted "ordination certificates" to Buddhist monks and did lavishly patronize the larger temples. But it did this more to control them than to facilitate their increase, since the political prestige of the monarchy was linked to Confucianism, not to Buddhism. In neighboring Thailand, where royal power did not rest upon Confucianism, a king like Mongkut (ruled 1851–1868) might answer the attacks upon Buddhism which appeared in the foreign missionary press in his country by writing spirited rejoinders to the criticisms, in which he signed himself "Buddhist champion." No Vietnamese emperor ever had the slightest incentive publicly to adopt a similar position. As a result, at the time of the French conquest, Vietnamese Buddhism was without the institutional or organizational coherence necessary to permit it the slightest independence or political vigor.

The Confucian bureaucracy, for all these reasons, remained the most important organized segment of traditional Vietnamese society to feel the full impact of colonialism. And the decay of the traditional bureaucracy after 1884 was a crucial aspect of that communal disintegration which haunted the psychology of so many Vietnamese patriots.

According to the treaties of the 1880s (between France and the Viet-namese court) which imposed "protectorates" upon Tonkin and Annam, Frenchmen could not formally govern directly the Vietnamese population outside Cochin China. Pham Quynh, the most illustrious member of the Vietnamese intelligentsia to defend French colonialism, nevertheless went so far as to charge in 1926 that these treaties were a "hollow and empty indulgence of convenience." French province heads in Tonkin and Annam controlled the political situations there in times of crisis, and the Vietnam-ese emperor at Hue, who continued to preside over the indigenous bureaucracy, was guided by the wishes of the French governor-general of Indochina as well as by the French resident superiors of the north and center.[22] Vietnamese provincial governors-general, governors, prefects, and district magistrates, constrained by their marriage with French officials in a biracial dyarchy, still remained the chief visible manifestation of govern-ment in the everyday lives of northern and central peasants. Nevertheless, the peasants did not misunderstand the new connection between the old indigenous bureaucratic forms and the rule of foreigners. In March 1908 in Dien Ban prefecture in Quang Nam province more than eight thousand Vietnamese demonstrators, protesting against colonial taxes, stormed into the prefecture capital, seized the Vietnamese prefect, and announced that they would carry him bodily to the provincial capital to "give him back" to the French province head.[23]

By this time, the "degeneracy" of the Vietnamese provincial bureaucracy had become a major issue among the elite. Pham Quynh himself was fond of quoting Jules Boissière, the French critic of the 1890s of the Indochina colonial government who had warmly idealized the precolonial Vietnamese state. Boissière had complained, correctly, that Frenchmen did not under-stand the psychology of public service of traditional Vietnamese mandarins; and he had also stated, almost certainly incorrectly, that before the French conquest it would have been impossible to find as many as ten government officials in Vietnam who owned as many as one hundred acres (*mau*) of land. Basing himself upon Boissière, Pham Quynh concluded that the colonized civil service of 1926 was only a "caricature" of the traditional one.[24]

Despite these romanticizations, the traditional Vietnamese political system had plainly begun to decay long before national independence had been lost. By 1840, for instance, it was apparently riddled with opium addicts. An imperial edict of that year, prescribing punishments for offi-cials who smoked opium, threatened hoarders of less than one hundred catties of opium with one hundred lashes, hoarders of more than one hundred catties with total confiscation of their properties. Indeed the crisis was thought to be so great that the edict overrode considerations of status, by meting out the same punishments to high mandarins and to lowly underlings alike, and suspended Confucian ethics, by rewarding sons who publicly reported opium-smoking fathers.[25]

But the process of decay within the civil service dramatically accelerated under colonialism. What a sociologist might call the internal "goal consensus" of the bureaucracy weakened, that is, the sense of professional mission, founded upon classical ideals, to which all its members subscribed. Such a trend was fatal, because it was this sense of mission which supposedly inoculated bureaucrats against the temptations of selfishness, encouraging them to refuse bribes or to agree to serve in troublesome bailiwicks. To some extent, the loss of a sense of common mission within the civil service was caused by the expanding intellectual and ideological heterogeneity of Vietnamese society as a whole. By the 1930s, Vietnamese who read Confucius and Mencius had to live side by side with Vietnamese who read Rousseau and Zola. But whether actively serving officials belonged to "old studies" (*cuu hoc*) circles or possessed a Western-oriented "new studies" (*tan hoc*) background, in their professional lives they now became trapped in a general climate of demoralization.

As evidence, in 1926 the results of an investigation of prefectural and district officials in Tonkin—those officials who were the crucial intermediaries between the government and the people, and upon whom the success or failure of rural administration depended—were published in a famous Hanoi periodical. The survey divided northern prefects and district magistrates into three age categories. It found that the majority of them were elderly bureaucrats, past the age of retirement, who had risen and fallen many times in the "sea of officialdom" and whose chief concern now was to accumulate funds for their remaining days. The second group were middle-aged French-speaking men who had come from the ranks of civil service clerks. They were as corrupt as their elders, but less capable of establishing rapport with the villagers in their jurisdictions. When one district magistrate of this kind in Hai Duong province lay dying in a provincial hospital in 1924, his provincial governor-general publicly acknowledged the bitter, ominous fact that not a single person from his district had come to visit him on his deathbed. The third group of local officials, the youngest group, had acquired training in modern European law and administration and had arrived in their posts talking of freedom and equality. After a few months in their districts they were physically abusing the villagers and extorting money from them, or imprisoning village functionaries who were one day late in coming to report to them, and then releasing these functionaries only for a price.[26] In sum, styles of local government that were remarkably uniform in their decadence could issue from a civil service with diverse educational backgrounds and an unprecedented inability to cherish common ethical and professional objectives.

Of course the decline of the bureaucracy's collective sense of identity was provoked not just by the growing heterogeneity of the society in which it worked, but by the fact that in the 1920s and 1930s new recruits to this bureaucracy were no longer heavily indoctrinated for professional service by ritualized classical examinations. The traditional bureaucracy's sense of mission had actually been created among its members—or inculcated in them—before they received their first appointments. In 1919, however, the Confucian civil service examination system was abolished, as a hopeless anachronism. Significantly, no equivalently rigorous but more modern method for choosing officials ever replaced it. A few "examinations for district magistrates" were held sporadically between 1919 and World War II. But these had little value, being merely a disguising formula to permit people to intrigue to gain positions. At times when these tests were not administered, higher officials were simply given the power to make "exceptional appointments," which meant the unrestricted right to confer bureaucratic commissions upon anyone they chose. Given the loss of real power by the Vietnamese throne, it was inevitable that the precolonial censorate—that part of the bureaucracy which inspected, critically, the behavior of the other parts, and made recommendations for impeachments to the emperor—would atrophy, as it did. In the 1930s, the air was accordingly filled with proposals for new formulas of control and inspection of bureaucrats, but few were ever institutionalized.

In addition to the multiplying divisions of Vietnamese society and the disappearance of classical moral indoctrination as a preliminary to official service, the whole power setting of the civil service had changed. The psychological repercussions of this were profound. The French monopoly of most of the meaningful positions of authority in Vietnam diminished the significance of bureaucratic promotions, and Vietnamese officials turned to forms of local aggrandizement in compensation. Corruption—or what Westerners call corruption—changed its nature, arising from different motives. In traditional Vietnam, the ethical basis of a human relationship was lost if the relationship was not particularistic. Extensions of kinship models (including the brother-brother relationship) were employed to organize relationships in secret societies and even in early political parties. Men who had to do business with complete strangers commonly sought out go-betweens who would create relationships for them with such strangers. School teachers in rural Vietnam received no salaries from the Vietnamese court, for they were expected to receive sustenance and presents from the local community as evidence that they had properly earned local trust. Ideally, the more support they received from the local community, the more of an accepted insider they could claim to be, and the better a broker between the village and the society at large. To a limited extent, this was also true of local officials.

But corruption among Vietnamese bureaucrats increased in the colonial period. After 1884, Vietnamese bureaucrats confronted the entirely new problem of maintaining "face" in their relations with the French civil servants working near them who were paid far more than they. (For southern officials, this characteristically colonial problem was renewed by the American presence of the 1960s.) In 1930, a former governor-general of Indochina speculated that the monthly salary of a Vietnamese governor of a large province in central or northern Vietnam was less than that of a young French traffic policeman. Acceptance of bribes, apparently, became a common enough act for mandarins who wished to maintain dignified official living styles in this strangely competitive colonial situation.

The conversion of what had been the proudest bureaucracy in Southeast Asia into a stuffy sanatorium for victims of inferiority complexes did not occur overnight. But comparisons were always being made, not just between the salary standards of the colonial state's French and Vietnamese administrative components, but between their educational standards as well. Pham Quynh warned the French, in 1926, that the "dignity of the old bureaucracy"—the Vietnamese one—would be lost forever if its members did not receive the blessings and, above all, the prestige, of a modern administrative education. If the situation were to be saved, all provincial prefects would henceforth have to be "doctors of law."[27] But this shrewd warning went unheeded. By the 1930s, the provincial civil service had sunk into a condition of stagnation—a stagnation that was curiously self-conscious. For its higher-ranking members, aware of their inferiority even to the new Vietnamese administrative clerks in the towns, defiantly turned their infrequent tests for the recruitment of district magistrates into isolation-preserving esoteric games. Bright young men, in consequence, clung to urban careers as law court clerks and turned their backs upon rural administration—a bad omen for the future of the colony. One of the characters in Khai Hung's great novel "The Family" (*Gia Dinh*), published in 1938, gave a particularly caustic assessment of the reason why careers as administrative middlemen in the countryside no longer seemed attractive:

.... Examinations for district magistrate are much more difficult than examinations for legal clerk. In the correcting of examinations for legal clerk, the examiners are merely professors and law court judges, but in the district magistrate examinations there are also Vietnamese mandarin examiners. And these Vietnamese mandarin examiners are not regional or doctoral degree-holders in any branch of studies or in any language . . . Because of that, these gentlemen are extremely severe, and ask extremely difficult questions. Moreover each year they only pass two people . . . but even if you pass the examinations your salary will be about two hundred piasters less [than that of a law clerk] . . . . These district magistrates of today are very cheap, and they have acquired very bad reputations. If I were to abandon a highly paid position, and go out and beg for the privilege of being a mandarin in order to be paid ninety piasters a month, how greatly people would disparage me. . . .[28]

Almost certainly the Vietnamese provincial bureaucracy in Tonkin and Annam became less representative of the population at large in these years than it had been before the French conquest. To the lower classes, once the turmoil of the 1880s and 1890s had died down, the bureaucracy was still in effect if not in theory a closed world. To the sons of the urban upper classes there were now other ladders to climb. The availability of more modern careers in the towns was not the only cause behind the bureaucracy's impoverishment of talent and of representativeness. Achievement in colonial Vietnam was governed to at least some degree by racial distinctions or by the possession of appropriate citizenship symbols, as much as it was by Confucian theories of graded degrees of knowledge; and this placed the indigenous civil service at a further disadvantage. Vietnam was now a dual society. "Structural dualism," under colonial circumstances, conventionally refers to the contrasts between urban areas and the hinterlands, the former with high income, high occupational mobility, and great concentration of newspapers and book publishers, and the latter with low income, low mobility, little industrialization, and few modern instruments of mass communications. Julio Cotler, speaking of Latin America, has proposed that the more modern sector of such a society may gradually incorporate segments of the population of the less modern sector into its system, but do so in such a limited and gradual way that the system of domination is actually strengthened as it expands. Instead of dissolving the dualisms, it "neutralizes" the activities of the people in the less modern sectors it absorbs by alienating them from others in those sectors who are not absorbed. The basic situation of structural dualism remains.[29] The phenomenon Cotler describes may be as true in the psychological realm as in the institutional one: colonial Vietnam suggests as much.

The legal framework of the colony artificially preserved into the 1930s the tendentious conquerors' distinction of the 1880s between France as the bearer of modern civilization and Vietnamese culture as the prisoner of the past. Instead of permitting the Vietnamese to modernize their own laws, the colonial government specified that Vietnamese appetites for modernity could be satisfied only by licensed movement from the Vietnamese legal sphere, whose customs were to be kept relatively unbroken, to the French legal sphere. In other words, Vietnamese who wished to escape from the jurisdiction of the premodern Vietnamese law code of 1812–1815 had to become French citizens. Once they had acquired French citizenship, they could expect both better professional opportunities and better treatment in the colonial law courts. Even the terminology of the colonial naturalization laws was evocative: "accession" to French citizenship was permitted upper-class Vietnamese who possessed diplomas of higher education, and who therefore appeared "to have attained a sufficient degree of Western culture."[30] This perpetuation of competing legal and cultural citizenships, and the politically dominant citizenship's incorporations of ambitious but only mildly nationalistic Vietnamese into its circle, also helped to prevent the Vietnamese civil service, or any other Vietnamese organization, from building a fully representative, socially synoptic clientele. It is certain at least that the colonial naturalization laws, as showy embodiments of structural dualism, encouraged an atmosphere of sycophancy at the higher reaches of Vietnamese society, even though only a very small number of Vietnamese ever acquired French citizenship.[31] One of the leading Vietnamese journalists in the period after World War I, Lang Nhan, wrote a column entitled "Irrational Tales" in the Vietnamese language journal "Indochina Magazine" (*Dong Duong tap chi*) which was regularly filled with pungent commentaries and funereal sarcasms about the irrationalities of colonial life. Looking at the citizenship question, Lang Nhan satirically described its peculiar psychologies:

> No period in Vietnamese history has been as strange as this current French and Chinese period [in which Vietnam was governed both by French civil servants and by Chinese-style mandarins]. In the "mating of the writing brush and the fountain pen," if the results have mostly been favorable pregnancies, it doesn't mean there haven't also been some strange abortions. When East and West unexpectedly meet, if the meeting follows Heaven's way it gives birth to a group of Franco-Vietnamese people, whose noses may be long but whose hair is usually black, whose eyes may be blue but whose skins will still be flaming yellow. But if the meeting goes against Heaven's will, it produces a group of "Annamese Frenchmen," whose appearances are completely Vietnamese but . . . who, when they give speeches, use Frenchified Vietnamese. . . . Two gentlemen . . . who are Vietnamese in origin, 100 percent Vietnamese, decided to request that they be admitted to French citizenship, because they had made their own determination that they were French. The court referred them to a doctor for examination. The doctor reported that the two gentlemen did not have a single drop of French blood in their blood vessels. The two gentlemen did not accept this (naturally) so they asked the court to appoint another doctor to reexamine them. This doctor concluded: although the two gentlemen are Vietnamese in appearance, their flesh and skin [i.e., under the skin color] are French. . . . Only now, thanks to that doctor, do we understand that there is such a thing as Vietnamese flesh and skin and such a thing as French flesh and skin. . . . But I imagine that French skin, especially French skin that is under colonial skies, has a special characteristic that establishes its superiority to our skin, a special characteristic that is limitlessly precious: whoever lays a finger on it is imprisoned. On the other hand, our skin is thick, you can thrash it with oxhide, or slap it with fingers that are as large as bananas . . . and in court these things are still placed in the category of "acquitted as usual."[32]

Social Change and the Sterile Seedtime of Modern Law

The institutional changes and social upheavals that did take place in Vietnam under the colonial regime, between 1884 and 1939—the construction of roads and railways, the growth of population, an increased economic dependence upon world markets—were not accompanied by any pervasive expansion of modern law. Running through the high colonial era was the general assumption that the moral order which had protected the traditional community would continue to be a sufficiently talismanic force for social cohesion, and that the moral norms of traditional Vietnam would continue to enjoy an automatic collective respect and enforcement, even at a time of economic reorientation, dual zones of citizenship, arbitrary interpreters, and kitchen boy mandarins.

But the traditional Confucian norms, which presupposed the social centrality of families and lineages, did inevitably contract. And as the void they left was not adequately filled by modern legal codes, the stability and predictability of social relationships in Vietnamese society began to decline—at least in the eyes of the Vietnamese intellectuals who wrote about it. Pham Quynh, friendly to the colonial government but also under the influence of French law professors like Gaston May, observed in 1921 that Westerners had "stable attitudes" but that Vietnamese generally were characterized by "anxious attitudes." The reason for this was that citizens of Western countries could assume two things that members of the Vietnamese population could not: first, that their societies would protect their individual rights, and second, that everyone in their societies would be treated equally.[33] Just how quickly what Pham Quynh called "anxious attitudes" and "blurred" notions of individual rights and responsibilities in Vietnam could be translated into episodic violence which made violent revolution itself almost a serenely awaited climax—in the growing gulf between receding norms and weakly extending laws—is a difficult question. But certainly the colonial phenomenon of underdevelopment of the laws played its part in the urban intelligentsia's obsession with the lack of enough organization in Vietnamese life.

Moral norms had been especially crucial in traditional Vietnam because the Vietnamese court, fearful of being at the mercy of too large a bureaucracy, had tried to minimize the amount of formal litigation that occurred within the purview of bureaucratically appointed territorial administrators, partly in order to keep their numbers, and the demand for their services, small. An imperial edict of 1833–1834, for example, had ordered that "fine and petty miscellaneous litigation" should first be "orally analyzed and orally decided" by the village chiefs. Only if the village chiefs could not decide these matters should their circumstances be reported to district and prefectural officials. The goal of this edict was the reduction of litigation and the stimulation of methods of "mutual peacemaking" among the villagers. "Penal-judicial offices" in every Vietnamese province were specifically ordered not to deal with disturbances concerning "maltreatment and verbal abuse," "debt money," or "physical brawling" in the villages. Village chiefs and village notables were actually compelled to make "oral judgments" in these matters. If their judgments were so brazenly inequitable that prefectural and district officials were nonetheless required to intervene to satisfy public opinion, the court ordered these officials to solve all issues "at once." And the court emphasized this behest by forbidding such officials to engage in literary correspondence over these affairs in order to prolong them. According to court records, there were less than one thousand people in jail in Vietnam at the end of 1825—proof of the success of the dynasty's deliberate localization of justice in the informal sanctions of the lineages and villages.[34]

Under the French colonial government, the judicial system became infinitely more complicated and ornate without acquiring any foundations in the popular consciousness. There was a regional potpourri of law courts. In Cochin China, there were no indigenous law courts, only French ones, where people of all races were judged. This situation also prevailed in the French "concessions" in the cities of Hanoi, Haiphong, and Tourane (Da Nang), all outside Cochin China. Elsewhere in Vietnam—in the north and in the center—both French and Vietnamese legal tribunals existed. The Vietnamese tribunals could try only cases in which everyone involved was a Vientamese who was not a French citizen. Litigation between a Vietnamese and a Chinese merchant, for example, had to be tried in a French court. The second Chamber of the Court of Appeal of Hanoi could annul or revise the judgments of "indigenous" courts. Even the juridical status of the regions from which legal institutions took their form and content was unclear. As late as 1939, some French writers spoke of Tonkin as a hybrid "colony-protectorate," but others suggested that Tonkin did not really belong to any known juridical category.[35] And even the French courts in Vietnam employed a mixture of law codes: sometimes French law, sometimes special edict laws devised for Indochina, and sometimes traditional Vietnamese law, depending upon the race of the people involved.

This incredibly piebald judicial system was nonetheless designed to accommodate traditional moralities, no matter how desiccated they might have become by the 1930s. The Gia-long legal code of 1812–1815, which had punished children who used family property without permission from their elders with one hundred strokes of the bamboo, remained a disguised or undisguised authority on family law throughout the colonial period. Essentially, this code had been designed to punish malefactors who had strayed beyond the moral code of their families and villages, not to define the rights and duties of the individual in society.

According to the Gia-long code, when a husband died his widow, no matter how old, remained in sole possession of the family property until her death. By the 1930s, members of the Vietnamese urban upper classes were protesting this anachronistic legal legacy on the grounds that it inhibited commercial development, since children could not administer their own property so long as one senile parent survived. Yet the Tonkin civil code which was belatedly promulgated in 1931 and the Annam civil code which appeared even later both upheld the Gia-long law code's ancient restriction on the division of family property. In keeping with the post-World War I colonial view of Vietnam as a social (or at least moral) museum, in which the big, hierarchical, patriarchal traditional family was a palladium of stability, even the new Tonkin and Annam civil codes of the 1930s said little on such subjects as the financial relations between two marriage partners. The French civil law code itself, which did not need to protect the Confucian patrilineage, had 195 articles on this subject; the Annam civil law code had only 13 articles on it, and the Tonkin code only 12.

The Vietnamese revolution of the 1930s and 1940s therefore took place in a context in which Confucian family conventions existed but had lost much of their vitality and in which whatever new laws existed were far too complex, and far too feebly developed, to be popularly known. As world revolutions go, this was very much the opposite, obviously, of the English revolution of the seventeenth century—to make an arbitrary but instructive comparison. In the English revolution, the law, and lawyers, were central elements. Litigation was universally popular and had fostered certain habits of debate. The common law guarded the property rights of landowners who were in opposition to the crown, and this made defense of the law, by lawyers like Sir Edward Coke, a prime rallying cry in the campaign against Charles I, who was accused of royal manipulation of the law. Radicals like the Levellers sought the simplification and popularization of the law so that it would cease to protect only the gentry. But the Vietnamese revolution developed in an environment virtually free of laws, as far as the lower classes were concerned. Hence it was probably preceded, at least in the countryside, not so much by a series of sharp, easily identifiable political confrontations and turning points as much as by the gradual rise of innocent disorders which, when combined with the national tradition of resistance to foreign rule, made all higher stages of violent rejection of the existing government less of a Rubicon crossing when they came. At least Hoang Dao, a brilliant but frustrated graduate of the Indochina Law School in Hanoi and onetime clerk to French colonial tribunals, suggested as much in an important 1934 essay, entitled "The Countryside People and The Law." This essay, which appeared in a renowned journal, gives an authentic picture of tensions and information gaps in village life about a decade before the August Revolution:

> The people of the countryside have absolutely no knowledge of the tortuous complexities of the laws. They're not clear about what matters and things are not forbidden; they do not understand how one thing is a serious crime, and another thing is a light crime. And indeed there's no one who teaches them so that they will know. Books of laws and official documents that are sent to the villages merely pile up in the cabinet of the council of notables, and never see the light of the sun any more. At most only a few old-style clerks are still inquisitive enough, because of their profession, to pay

attention to the laws. Outside them, free from the canton chief and the village chief down to the lowest man in the village, all are ignorant. And as soon as there is any business that has to be taken up to the mandarin, all of them become as fearful as if they had committed manslaughter. Is such a situation any different from the situation of a dim-sighted man riding a blind horse at midnight into a deep pond?

In the past, even though our emperors did make laws, their laws were designed exclusively for the bureaucrats to enforce, while the people were forbidden to look at them or read them, on the pretext that if the people clearly understood the laws this would produce a great many lawsuits. Moreover, at that time there wasn't a village or a hamlet that didn't have a degree holder to expound and teach the laws as they were associated with orthodox morality. Now, circumstances have changed; the law goes off on its own path, morality goes off on its own path, they are no longer jumbled together in confusion as they were before, so the old tradition can no longer hold its ground any more. We must know the laws! In Western countries, such a principle has been obvious for a long time. In our country, thieves steal and refuse to acknowledge their crime, rationalizing that taking property that is abandoned on the streets is a legitimate thing. People who have to report births and deaths, and who are going to be punished because they have not made their reports, further argue that they are guiltless. How many other daily occurrences make us realize that the laws, in their relationship to our people, are like a mysterious field of philosophy. . . . But to know the law to its utmost limits is not an easy matter, especially in our country, where the laws of the Hue court must also be carried out completely.[36]

In other words, the abnormal structural complexity of the colonial legal order (which juxtaposed French law and traditional Vietnamese law) combined with the effects of the disappearance of the old examination system and the slow withdrawal of a degree-holding elite from the countryside to produce an atmosphere of volatile ambiguities and uncertainties. The withdrawal of the degree holders meant, at the same time, the withdrawal of those people from the villages who had had the greatest tendency to exhibit a high degree of conformity to the moral injunctions of the premodern state.

Of course the situation, like all Vietnamese situations, defies a perfectly dogmatic analysis. It could be asserted that much of the politics of rebellion in the precolonial society itself had stemmed from the abusive, corrupt exploitation of court laws by self-aggrandizing sub-bureaucrats. When Huynh Thuc Khang, a well-known mandarin journalist, made a fiery statement of grievances against the French colonial regime in 1928, he singled out the unfair and unpredictable administration of criminal law as one of his three major complaints—the other two being the proliferation of rural taxes and the lack of adequate schooling. Khang painted a grim picture of innocent people being accused, arrested, and jailed without formal investigation, as a result of which "hidden injustices" accumulated. He argued that fraudulent evidence was commonly used, criminal charges were rarely made explicit, the term "suspect" was widely used to "assassinate" many individuals and households, and that as a result of these "fabrications" small affairs became large ones, leading to resistance and rebellion.[37] This meant, in effect, that the causes of rural ferment had not really changed since before 1884: none of these things had ever really been absent from traditional Vietnam, and generations of peasant rebels had sustained their movements by attacking local government rackets.

What did come in with the colonial period was the decline of a reasonably homogeneous elite of prefects, district magistrates, and village degree holders who were irrevocably wedded to publicly recognizable moral patterns. The unprecedentedly heterogeneous educational backgrounds of colonial local officials ultimately facilitated the disappearance of unequivocal social and moral standards in the villages under their sway; and no new, dynamic, publicly recognizable network of modern laws ever filled the void or inculcated alternatives to the ancient community patterns which were beginning to disappear. This was not the famous situation discussed by Max Weber of a competing plurality of systems of conduct, in which men could recognize the validity of two different systems and observe both, as in the case of the man who fought an illegal duel in order to satisfy his code of honor and then turned himself in to the police. In Vietnamese terms, both the "code of honor" and the laws which governed the police now failed to exhibit sufficient magnetism in widening areas of social life.

The famous Javanese princess, Kartini, observed how "humble crowds" of Javanese would "burst out laughing" behind the backs of Dutch assistant residents in Java when these Dutch colonial officials appeared in public under the shade of gold unbrellas, which were part of the formal regalia of traditional Javanese princes.[38] French behavior was fatally similar in Vietnam. When the governor-general of Indochina visited a Vietnamese provincial town, Vietnamese households were required to place incense altars in front of their doors and light incense candles in his honor. The smoke from their incense was supposed to be wafted respectfully toward the long-nosed European barbarian who now claimed preeminent political powers in Vietnam.[39] Parasitic political styles or culturally bastardized charades like these, even when reinforced by a ubiquitous secret police, simply lacked the strength either to halt the disintegration of the old community moralities or to prevent Vietnamese nationalists from looking for new formulas of reintegration and reconciliation that would exclude and resist colonialism.

2

The Early Nationalists' Search for a New Community

The Traditional Heritage and the Dilemmas of Activists

Looking for anticolonial formulas of reintegration, however, did not mean quickly finding them. Hindsight, that treacherous ally of the historian, has made the litany of grievances and of breakdowns just described much more schematic than it should be. Furthermore, inherent in Vietnamese society, were serious obstacles to any rapid mobilization of large groups or communities under a nationalist banner. Any underestimation of these obstacles is, by logical extension, an underestimation as well of the revolutionaries who eventually overcame them.

In 1932, just thirteen years before the August Revolution, a front-page article in the most influential newspaper in the city of Hue complained that the Vietnamese people lacked a "national perspective" and a capacity to organize themselves on a national scale, for three reasons. First, everything was subordinated to the family and to familism in Vietnamese culture, including the concept of the nation. Emperors were interested primarily in the founding and maintenance of their own dynastic house. Mandarins worked for the state, but essentially in order to further family glory. The people themselves did not regard anyone outside their families and lineages as being "intimate" (*than ai*) enough to make sacrifices for. Lineages would fight with other lineages over rank in the village, and outside the family, cooperation was difficult to arrange. It was impossible to talk about "society" in a country where no indigenous business firm had more than three members and no indigenous factory had more than five employees. (This was of course an exaggeration.) "Our East Asian society," the newspaper fulminated, "is nothing but a society of children inside their families." Second, the work of the "nation" and the concerns of "society" were dissociated from each other. The emperor and his mandarins paid little attention to the livelihood of the people, apart from collecting taxes and compiling elementary statistics; and the people for their part knew nothing about the inner business of the imperial bureaucracy. Third, "learning" and "government" were also dissociated from each other. Education served purely individualistic purposes—it was the road to individual advancement as a mandarin or government secretary—and revolved around imported Chinese or French texts, rather than Vietnamese ones, while keeping its content relatively uncontaminated by national themes, problems, or traditions. Because of these three dissociations—between family and society, between national business and general social concerns, and between education and national politics—it was impossible for the Vietnamese people to develop a national spirit.[1]

In fact, of course, a national spirit or "proto-nationalistic" spirit had existed in Vietnam for centuries, its trophies being the victories over Chinese invasions which have already been cited. Moreover, this spirit had burned with an especially bright flame from the earliest moments of the French conquest in the nineteenth century. In Cochin China it had been expressed by local military commanders like Truong Cong Dinh (1820–1864), who refused to accept the Hue court's decision to cede three southern provinces to France, and by literati like the great poet Nguyen Dinh Chieu. He wrote of the peasants who had been killed fighting the French near Saigon in 1861: "You are dead, but temples and shrines have been erected for your cult, and your name shall be cherished by thousands of generations to come."[2] In the north, this ancient spirit could be seen especially clearly in the "righteous uprisings" (*khoi nghia*) of the scholars and patriotic provincial gentry which began in 1885 and which are commonly known, at least at their beginning, as the royalist or "aid the king" movement. The flight of the Ham-nghi boy emperor from Hue in July 1885, and the decree issued in his name calling for resistance to the French presence, precipitated the uprisings. They were unlike anything in China in the 1800s, for the Vietnamese scholar-gentry had never been so scrupulously and so fastidiously separated from contact with practical military knowledge and affairs as their counterparts to the north. The uprisings produced particularly famous demonstrations of elite determination to fight the French in Thanh Hoa (where the Ba Dinh uprising of 1885–1887 was led by two provincial military commanders and a superintendent of education), in Ha Tinh (where Phan Dinh Phung led the longest "aid the king" insurrection of all, the Huong Khe uprising, from 1885 to 1896), and in the Bai Say region on the borders of Hai Duong and Hung Yen provinces. In Bac Giang province in the north, in an uprising of a much more lower-class nature, Hoang Hoa Tham led the Yen The region peasants from 1887 to 1913.

But the contradiction here between newspaper lamentations about the absence of a national spirit and the mystique of the nineteenth-century resistance movements is not so burdensome as it might seem. The lamentations would not have arisen in the first place if there had not been some kind of national spirit, albeit a mightily frustrated and dissatisfied one. David Marr, indeed, makes the cogent point that it was precisely the imperfection and incompleteness of elite resistance to the French in the 1880s and afterward—the fact that *some* Vietnamese mandarins were willing to serve the colonial regime rather than to rebel and recapture their country from the invaders—which inspired the others to greater and greater efforts against colonial rule.[3] A much more difficult problem is the relationship between the Vietnamese revolution and the East Asian classical heritage. For the burdens of the traditional high philosophies under which most early Vietnamese revolutionaries labored, the centuries-old metaphysical apparitions which drove them, offered a considerable variety of proper courses of action, including personal withdrawal from politics into what could be regarded as either an irresponsibly arcadian by-world or the true center of the moral stage, depending upon the precedents being respected as well as upon personal point of view. Even the central Confucian doctrine of "doing what is known to be unachievable" (*chih pu k'o erh wei*), uppermost in the minds of many Chinese and Vietnamese intellectuals in the early 1900s, had its limits. On the one hand it exalted moral ardor and perseverance against great odds, which were useful in a revolution, but on the other hand it discouraged even the most rudimentary utilitarian calculations, political and economic.[4]

More specifically, the Confucian tradition embraced both the possibility of working for world salvation and the possibility of practicing personal self-cultivation, a much more introverted form of behavior. In theory, both possibilities were supposed to belong to the same moral progression of actions, with self-cultivation leading ultimately to world salvation through a number of intermediate steps. In practice, many Chinese and Vietnamese scholars tended to develop fitful biases toward either the social salvation of others, or intense personal cultivation, but not both. For the social salvationists, there was the illustrious example of the eleventh-century Chinese philosopher politician Fan Chung-yen, who had issued the ringing maxim that the scholar ought to be the first in worrying about the world's troubles and the last in enjoying its pleasures. The polar opposite of Fan Chung-yen's ideal was not perhaps really Confucian self-cultivation at all, but the ideal of "non-action" which had originated with Taoist philosophers. Votaries of nonaction as a political guide, of whom there were a number in Vietnam, were opposed to organized elites of any kind because they encouraged people to compete. "Action" presupposed struggle, and struggle caused chaos: to eliminate chaos, action or organized activism must be avoided.

For anti-French members of the Vietnamese intelligentsia, in the 1880s, a chief enemy within was the intellectual tendency on the part of some scholars to make personal cultivation, and even non-action, ends in themselves. One Vietnamese provincial ruler, Nguyen Khuyen, wrote a bitter poem at about this time about "stone statue" bureaucrats who preferred to commune with nature, in the extreme Taoist non-action manner, instead of fighting the French:

> Seeing this bizarre stone statue, I want to ask, For what reason did you jostle your way through crowds to this place? Are you eternally admiring the flowers and the herbs of this homeland of ours, to the point of being about to join hands and enter into this self-indulgent orgy? . . . Let us leave the small knapsack of the universe for the people who come after us to shoulder. Rare enjoyments that are out of this world are the enjoyments of old age. A drink for you, a drink for him, a drink for me, and a drink for you over there. . . .[5]

Khuyen resigned his position rather than collaborate with colonialism. And he was obsessed by the fear that quietist parodies of the ancient self-cultivation theme, extended into Taoist non-action, could acquire such importance in the minds of members of his own class that national and world affairs would indeed dwindle, for them, to the proportions of a "small knapsack."

Elite Nationalism and Lower-Class Organizations

Even if the "world salvation" theme prevailed over the tendencies of self-cultivation (as an end in itself) and non-action in the minds of Vietnamese scholars, what forms of political communion could the upper classes share with the peasants? After the failure of the "aid the king" movement, a gulf seemed to open between the two social worlds. Hopeful intermediaries and messengers crossed this gulf repeatedly, but with disappointing results.

That dissociation in Vietnamese life between national business and social concerns which the Hue newspaper article of 1932 execrated was far from complete among peasants, handicraft workers, coolies, and porters. But the problems of "national business" easily became colored and transformed by the reflexes and traditions of the two lower-class forces most likely to fight the French: religious sects and secret societies.[6]

Most Vietnamese religious sects of the early twentieth century appear to have been inspired by the centuries-old Chinese White Lotus sectarian tradition, which had hundreds of branches. The Phan Xich Long movement of 1911–1913 in the Mekong delta certainly represented a partial transfer to Vietnam of White Lotus practices. This tradition might offer the peasantry benign descending Buddhas, prescriptions for invulnerability, and a wide range of salvationist pageantry. Sects which issued from the tradition usually possessed dual leaderships, religious and political, with one man playing the role of the messiah Buddha and another man, the political manager of the Buddha, allowing his followers to proclaim him king or emperor. The structure of such a religious sect, in both China and Vietnam, tended to be hierarchical and autocratic, although among the ordinary members themselves there could be a real spirit of fraternal egalitarianism. Ordinary followers were not permitted to participate in all the activities of the different sets of leaders, the appointment of successors and the transmission of duties among the leaders were severely restricted and guarded, and it was not uncommon to find octogenarians monopolizing the right to teach. Such sects commonly expounded the doctrine of the descent to earth of the Maitreya Buddha—the messiah Buddha of the future, who was believed to be living in the "heaven of the satisfied gods" before his incarnation on earth—and the arrival with the messiah Buddha, after some cosmic convulsions, of a politically, economically, and religiously reordered universe. This doctrine was not the creed of any band of professional revolutionaries. Most of the time it remained no more than the undeveloped core of a religion of individual and familial happiness-seeking. But it *could* also coexist with an ideological commitment to the appearance of a descendant of a vanquished dynasty, who supposedly suddenly manifested himself in order to overthrow the corrupt established order. When such a "supplement" was added to the doctrine, the messiah Buddha quickly became the god of bloody rebellions.[7]

Phan Xich Long, a Cochin China mystic, launched a White Lotus-style movement in the south in 1911 by claiming to be a descendant of the Ham-nghi boy emperor, much as the White Lotus rebellion of 1796 in west China had revolved around men who claimed to be descended from the Chinese Ming emperors. And just as Chinese White Lotus uprisings always began with the discovery of a latter-day incarnation of the Buddha, so too the Phan Xich Long movement paid homage to a "living Buddha" in a village near Cholon. In March 1913, leaflets scattered throughout the Mekong delta signed by the "emperor Phan Xich Long" appealed to Vietnamese peasants to drive out the French. On the night of March 28, Phan Xich Long's army—hundreds of peasants wearing white turbans and white tunics—invaded the city of Cholon. Undisciplined and outgunned, this small peasant army was speedily defeated. Superficially, the whole episode was an amazing repetition of the famous attack by white-robed Chinese peasants of the White Lotus-flavored "Heavenly Principles Religion" upon the palaces of Peking exactly one century earlier, in 1813. The White Lotus sectarian underground, employing a confusingly kaleidoscopic nomenclature, had spread throughout East Asia long before the arrival of the West.

In different East Asian societies, however, even the White Lotus sects reflected different levels of social development. The Japanese peasant movements which had invoked the name of the messiah Buddha back in the 1860s in silk-producing areas of Japan (like Nagano and Gumma prefectures) had also advanced practical demands—such as the reduction of taxes, the right to free sale of agricultural produce, and the remission of rural debts. The Phan Xich Long affair showed that in early colonial Vietnam, on the other hand, religious sects animated by messianic Buddhism did not embody a substantial interest in practical distributive justice or in social and economic reforms. The poor Japanese peasants who had marched against the Japanese government with flags bearing the salvationist slogan of "the Brahma Heavens" in the 1860s did have much in common with the members of Phan Xich Long's army. Both were relying upon messianic Buddhism to save them from traumas caused by contact with the West. But the Vietnamese religious sects were not led by the disciples of wealthy well-educated farmers, as some similar Japanese movements apparently had been. Their leaders lacked a comparable educational foundation to guide them in framing programs, as well as being obsessed by the need simply to drive out foreigners. They had insufficient premises in common with upper-class revolutionaries (because of the weaker diffusion of education to Vietnamese peasants than to Japanese peasants in the traditional period).[8]

What about secret societies, a very different organizational type? Secret societies like the Triads were also present in both China and Vietnam: there had been a Triad uprising in northern Vietnam as early as 1807. They were more egalitarian in structure than the religious sects. Instead of using the organizational model of a religious hierarchy, with graded degrees of possession of the inner secrets of the religion, the Triads invoked the very different organizational formula of the fraternal compact. All the members of the movement were sworn brothers who could participate in its mysteries. The power of the Triads, being more democratically distributed inside the organization than that of the White Lotus groups, often could spread more quickly, with younger men finding it easier to work their way up to the top of the leadership.[9] The other side of the coin was that the potential for internal schisms within the Triads was at least as great, if not greater, than it was among the religious sectarians. Every Triad brother felt himself qualified to interpret the purposes of the movement. Sometimes Triad schisms were deliberate devices of controlled metamorphosis. A bloc of Triad members would secede from an existing Triad organization, infiltrate a local army which was attempting to repress the Triads, adopt a new name, and in time subvert the army they had joined. The history of the activities of the "Elder Brother Society" within the Chinese Hunan army in the 1800s offers one clear demonstration.

Popular novels, rather than religious visions, prefigured and underwrote the careers of the secret societies. To the Triads, their concept of a fraternal compact originated as the "spirit of right conduct of the peach garden," or the "peach garden compact of Liu and Kuan and Chang." Here they genuflected to the memories of the three heroes of the medieval Chinese novel "Romance of the Three Kingdoms" (*San kuo chih yen-i*). This novel, and others like it, undoubtedly suggested methods of organization to real life rebels which permitted them to circumvent the need for a religious hierarchy. The "Romance of the Three Kingdoms" eventually became so popular among the Vietnamese people—even more popular in Vietnam, if possible, than in China—that it became known among them simply by the adoring shorthand title "Three Kingdoms" (*Tam Quoc*). Apart from the obvious connections between the organizations of lower-class political insurrections and those of the novel's heroes, the impact of this novel upon mass psychologies in China and Vietnam was profound but is still unexplored. What is plain is that the novel's influence, and that of the Triads, was not confined to the countryside but spread as well to the poorer populations of the towns, by means of card games as well as through storytellers.

In Cochin China, the Triad society (known there by its original Hokkien title of "Heaven and Earth Society," *Thien dia hoi*) had been imported by Chinese immigrants. Vietnamese began to join the organization in substantial numbers after 1900. Once the Vietnamese component of the society had become strong enough, it broke away from the overseas Chinese Triads to which it had first belonged and created a private Vietnamese "Heaven and Earth Society." (This very act was, to some extent, a Vietnamese variation of standard Triad metamorphosis devices.) The Vietnamese Triads then abandoned the faded political slogan of the overseas Chinese Triad organization—"oppose the Ch'ing and restore the Ming"—in favor of more timely slogans with a more potent indigenous meaning: "oppose the French, and corrupt officials, and revive the Vietnamese homeland." But they kept the Chinese society's principles of having private symbols and passwords, esoteric cant, and secret assemblies. The organs of the Vietnamese Triads were especially strong in Gia Dinh, Cholon, Bien Hoa, Thu Dau Mot, Ben Tre, and Chau Doc. They were repeatedly repressed by the colonial police but never eliminated: they simply kept reappearing decade after decade in bewilderingly different guises.[10] Limited by their lack of access to modern education, and unable to break away from the archetypal conventions of the old society, they sponsored mutual assistance efforts among destitute members of the lower classes. Repeatedly, Vietnamese elite nationalists asked themselves a question which remained bafflingly unanswerable: could these secret societies make a significant contribution to the revolutionary revitalization of the national community?

Elite revolutionaries faced two difficulties in attempting to exploit the solidarity-creating achievements of lower-class secret societies. First, the secret societies lacked the coherent vision of the world outside Vietnam which the elite nationalists were beginning to acquire. They were, therefore, less capable of comparing the situation inside Vietnam with those situations outside which suggested and inspired improvement and nationalistic self-assertion. Second, their past history aimed the secret societies almost as much against the self-confident habits and values of the Vietnamese elite itself as against colonialism. Because peasants and urban coolies had not been able to measure up to the criteria for achieving success which prevailed in the elite world, they had created their own organizations, like the Triads, where they could award and obtain status and prestige on a more realistic basis. In the secret societies a simple-minded pugnacity, rather than classical scholarship, could be exalted as a true leadership quality; and the political myths which the secret societies cherished could be invoked to dignify acquisition of the most easily obtainable spoils and plunder, which were rarely to be found in the realm of high politics. The secret societies might be regarded as informal lower-class compensations for the fact that there was only one real ladder of success in Vietnam for all social classes—the examination system, until 1919. The Vietnamese social system had run in one channel, without having an officially permitted variety of social achievement outlets for members of each social class, like the special socialist organizations to which urban workers in modern Europe often belong. Patriotic upper class scholars found it difficult—but not impossible—to convert these illegitimate lower-class compensatory organizations to their own purposes.

The intellectual who made the most spectacular early attempt to wed the secret societies to his own formulation of the nationalist cause was Nguyen An Ninh, a French-educated journalist and translator of Rousseau who became one of the chief celebrities of anticolonial politics in the Saigon area in the 1920s and 1930s. Ninh came from Hoc Mon district in Gia Dinh province, a hotbed of secret society activity. Even more fittingly, he had a patriotic father who had translated the "Romance of the Three Kingdoms" into romanized Vietnamese. But Ninh himself was more familiar with French law schools than with Triad oaths when he began. He simply created his own secret society. It was known commonly as the "Nguyen An Ninh Society" (*Hoi Nguyen An Ninh*), but its more formal title was the "High Expectations Youth Party" (*Cao-vong thanh nien dang*). Deeply intrigued by the secretive styles of the Triads, whose members he hoped to recruit, Ninh made himself the "generalissimo" (*chu soai*) of his own organization yet cautiously permitted only a few of the people who joined to know the "personal name and lineage name and the face and eyebrows" of their "chief." He "borrowed" sacrificial rites from other societies for his own meetings.

In an effort to blend more completely the lower class drive for socio-economic compensations and upper class anticolonialism, Ninh's program included both plans for an attack upon all the Frenchmen in Cochin China and a scheme to "borrow forcibly" the properties of rich households and to redistribute them among the poor. Ninh does not, however, ever appear to have been able to supply any truly serviceable ideological or emotional link between modern nationalism and the traditional consumers' communism of the older secret societies. He himself remained a Western-trained intellectual to the end. In a deposition to the Saigon appeals court in 1929, he even explained that inspirations and precedents for cultivating a secret society in Cochin China had come to him from a French book, Georges Coulet's *Les sociétés secrètes en terre d'Annam* (published in Saigon in 1926) as much as from personal familiarity with Vietnamese secret society traditions.[11]

For the other intellectuals who supported the "Nguyen An Ninh Society," its organizational deficiencies could be attributed to its stress upon empty show and to the variety of motives of the apparent charlatans who were attracted to it: people who "merely searched for a livelihood and for notoriety in the profession of barking at the shadows of the moon and of flapping bragging lips," as Phan Van Hum, an associate of Ninh's, acidly described them.[12] The point, of course, is that searching for a livelihood within the compensatory confines of a secret society had long been a legitimate lower-class activity, no matter how much the elite might denigrate it. There was a gap between what might be called the "natural self" activities of secret society members, concerned with their daily problems, and the "transcendental self" dreams of revolution of Ninh and Hum and other leaders of this kind: yet both groups of men felt themselves to be psychologically and morally complete.

The Confucian Elitism of Phan Boi Chau and Phan Chu Trinh

By the time Nguyen An Ninh had begun his experimentation with the secret society traditions of eastern Cochin China, the first generation of Vietnamese elite nationalism had almost come to an end. The two most dogged and preeminent paladins of this first-generation nationalism were Phan Chu Trinh (1872–1926) and Phan Boi Chau (1867–1940). Both of them belonged to families which had participated in the "aid the king" movement, and both of them were heavily influenced by the ideas of the 1898 reform movement in China. Neither of them was ever an uncompromising opponent of every aspect of the status quo in Vietnam. Chau wished to expel the French but was for at least much of his life a monarchist, whereas Trinh became a more dedicated enemy of Vietnam's puppet monarchy than he was of the French.

Phan Chu Trinh was born to a respected upper-class lineage in Quang Nam province. He was a younger son, like many other East Asian revolutionaries, such as Ho Chi Minh, Sun Yat-sen, Liu Shao-ch'i, and Luong Ngoc Quyen. His family was briefly pauperized by the "aid the king" fighting, which drove Trinh into the mountains with his resisting father. But Trinh still managed to acquire a classical education, to pass the regional civil service examinations in 1900, and to earn a lowly position as a clerical manager at the Hue Board of Rites. At this time he avidly read books by the two architects of the 1898 reforms in China, K'ang Yu-wei and Liang Ch'i-ch'ao, which spoke of the sources of strength of the Western countries and which now began to circulate in Hue. He severed his relationship with the colonial mandarinate, visited Hong Kong and Japan (1906), traveled through the provinces of Vietnam reviling classical studies and the examination system of which he was a product, and then was imprisoned for life on Poulo Condore prison island (1908) as part of a general French campaign of suppression of dissident scholar-gentry. Released in 1911 at the behest of the French League for the Rights of Man, he spent the next fourteen years (1911–1925) in France. His death in Saigon in 1926 precipitated demonstrations of mourning all over Vietnam which became a landmark in the evolution of revolutionary politics.

Phan Boi Chau, who was actually a more important progenitor of revolution, was born to a scholar-gentry family in Nghe An province in north central Vietnam. A precocious boy who practiced writing the Analects of Confucius on banana tree leaves at the age of five,[13] he also passed regional civil service examinations in 1900 and then began to read "with passion" the books and newspaper articles of Liang Ch'i-ch'ao, who was then living in exile from China in Yokohama, Japan.[14] Chau immediately began to plot measures for restoring Vietnam's independence. He wrote an emotional allegorical tract about Japan's seizure of the Ryukyu Islands which really dealt with the French in Vietnam, made propagandizing pilgrimages through Cochin China, and created an organization known as the *Duy Tan Hoi* ("Renovation Society"). The title of the "Renovation Society," when written in Chinese characters, was the same as the term for "Restoration" (*ishin*) which the Japanese had employed in their talismanic phrase "Meiji Restoration," which had inaugurated Japan's national revival in 1868.

In sum, Chau dreamed of a Japanese-style ebullition of modernizing nationalism in Vietnam that could keep the centuries-old Vietnamese monarchy as its symbolic centerpiece. Realizing that Vietnamese nationalists required external aid, Chau went to Japan itself in 1905, as the leader of what was to become an "Eastern Travel" (*Dong du*) movement of several hundred Vietnamese students. There he became the apprentice of Liang Ch'i-ch'ao in Yokohama. He solicited aid for Vietnamese nationalists from top-ranking Japanese politicians like Okuma Shigenobu (who told him that he thought Vietnam was more backward than such other occupied countries as India, Poland, and Egypt), wrote a history of Vietnam's loss of independence, and obtained several interviews with Sun Yat-sen, the leader of China's republican revolutionaries.

Phan Boi Chau's dream of a Meiji-style "renovation" in Vietnam had vanished by 1911. Japan had expelled Vietnamese revolutionaries by this time; and the superficial success of the 1911 "Double Ten" revolution in China made an unimpeachably republican revolution along Sun Yat-sen's lines almost irresistible to the Vietnamese nationalist zealots whom Phan Boi Chau led. In the spring of 1912, consequently, a rally of Vietnamese exiles in south China replaced the Renovation Society with a new organization, the "Society for the Restoration of Vietnam" (*Viet Nam Quang Phuc*

Hoi), which soon received sporadic financial assistance from the Chinese Koumintang or Nationalist Party. At this rally, Chau publicly pronounced himself in favor of a democratic republic rather than a monarchy. He had by then (as he tells us in his memoirs) read Rousseau and Montesquieu and enjoyed numerous contacts with republican-minded "Chinese comrades." However, Chau also vainly hoped for the construction of a vast, apocalyptic alliance between China and Japan, one potent enough to drive Western invaders out of all Asia.[15] He did not perceive how explosively the interests in Asia of Chinese and Japanese governments would diverge after 1912. To some extent, indeed, his classically trained mind remained anachronistic-ally captivated, even until his death in 1940, by the possibility of applying to modern East Asia those famous "horizontal alliances" and "vertical combinations" of states which had enlivened the elitist politics of China in the Warring States period (403–221 B.C.)

The ideals and the organizational precepts which Phan Boi Chau and Phan Chu Trinh explored and loved could never have been democratic in the Western sense. The first generation of Vietnamese nationalists, which was also to a large extent a generation of examination system degree-holders, naturally saw the problems of building organized communities more in Confucian terms than in those that a John Stuart Mill or an A.D. Lindsay would have welcomed. To put it far too generally, the Confucian political tradition in East Asia enshrined the notion that the people were the foundation of government but not the masters of government. Govern-ment, it was accepted, should be "for the people" but it should not be at all "by the people." When the Chinese philosopher Mencius, whom centuries of Vietnamese intellectuals studied and revered, wrote in a famous passage that in the ideal polity the people were the most important element, the gods of the soil and grain came next, and the prince himself was to be the most lightly regarded of the three, he was espousing these notions, not democratic ones. Government, for its part, should be conducted by worthy men, by members of a morally transcendental elite, by paragons of self-cultivation who, when they spoke, won the trust of everyone and, when they acted, won the pleased agreement of the people (as another famous passage from the Chinese classics, from the *Li-chi* or "Record of Rituals," stipulated.)

Early Vietnamese revolutionaries took events in Western history like the American Revolution and altered them to fit this context of Confucian elitism. During the early years of his exile in France, probably between 1913 and 1915, Phan Chu Trinh wrote an epic poem nearly four thousand lines long in which he attempted to expound the modern revolutionary history of Europe and America for the benefit of Vietnamese audiences. The title of his poem was, significantly, "Rare Encounters with Beautiful Personages" (*Giai nhan ky ngo*). Trinh was in effect serving as a cultural broker, attempting to introduce the thought and action of Western revolu-tions to Vietnam in ways that the Vietnamese upper classes could comprehend. The work also proved the lingering potency of Japanese thought and fashions in the minds of first generation Vietnamese nationalists, for it was really a poetic adaptation of a Japanese novel written about 1885 by Shiba Shiro (also known by the pseudonym of Tokai Sanshi), a bureaucrat and Osaka newspaper entrepreneur who had graduated from the University of Pennsylvania.

Trinh's epic opens in the same way as Shiba Shiro's novel, with its Japanese hero, a "scholar of determination," inspecting the State House in the city of Philadelphia and there encountering two female activists, one Spanish and one Irish. His hero listens to these two women describing the American revolutionary war:

> In the past, when the American people first flocked together, they initiated liberty here, in group discussions. Heroes were leaving their impress on the rivers and mountains of their homeland, it was truly the year 1774. Irresolute and anxious, the Americans cast their glances north and south: there was the De-thuy [Delaware] River, and over there was the Tao-khe [Erie?] Lake. The State House drafted proclamations in those rooms, and from that point freedom was increasingly engraved on the hearts of the people. Far and near the clouds clustered, and bees drifted down from the skies . . . . Old mothers forgot their hardships, and shedding tears, they urged their sons to charge directly onto the battlefield. . . . Washington had to endure a period of bitterness, remnants of his soldiers formed an army and deployed themselves at Erie, the weather was brutally cold. . . . Rolling up his flags, and holding his mandarin's badge of office in his mouth, Washington cut through the Delaware River and destroyed the English in a frightful battle. From that point on his military prestige echoed like thunder on all four sides.
>
> The more you think about that situation of hundreds of officers enduring hardship and poverty, the more you sympathize with them: with decaying shoes and torn sandals they wandered about. . . . Alas! How exhausting and deplorable life could be! . . . For what reason did they renounce their bodies? Concerned with repaying the debt of their nation, they regarded themselves as if they were nothing! When you think about it your feelings are increasingly inflamed and aroused; how commendable are the Americans, who truly are a civilized race. For that reason they opposed the oppressive English, improved their schools, developed industry and commerce, and built a rich and powerful country. Everywhere on the four horizons the words peace and serenity were radiant. . . .[16]

The American Revolution, as interpreted by Phan Chu Trinh about 1913, began with the appearance of properly cultivated individual heroes like George Washington and ended with a peaceful, utopian universe, rather in the manner of the progression from individual moral purification to a pacified world which had been laid down in the Chinese classic "The Great Learning" (*Ta Hsüeh*) some twenty-one centuries earlier. The individual hero remained the key to revolution, not more impersonal social and economic forces or even a political assembly like the Congress, which is hardly mentioned. Trinh, moreover, could not accept the idea of a nationalist crusade that ended merely in the rise of one rich and powerful nation-state. If such a crusade was to end to everyone's ethical satisfaction, it had to do so in a kind of utopian universal tranquillity, a "great peace," that was beyond the nation-state. No matter how many nationalist theories were imported from the West, moral goals rather than purely utilitarian goals had to be their object, at least for Vietnamese nationalists with one foot in the old classical tradition. Desirable nationalist revolutions could not revolve around riches and power as ends in themselves. They had to revolve around acts of social reciprocity ("repaying the debt of their nation") which would lead to an ethically serene world. The separation of politics and ethics, pervasive in the West since the time of Machiavelli, could not be formally reenacted here—not yet.

Between 1913 and 1925, Phan Chu Trinh's views changed: they became increasingly receptive both to the idea of socialism as a dynamic mode of collective action and to social Darwinist criticisms of existing institutions. When he returned to Saigon in 1925, Trinh gave an important public speech in which he discussed "the ideology of monarchical rule and the ideology of rule by the people." Under the obvious influence of Rousseau's comments upon primitive societies in *The Social Contract,* he observed that a society ruled by a monarchy was no different from a "herd of goats" which starved or were well fed depending upon the whims of their shepherd. Then, mixing Rousseau with Darwinism, Trinh suggested that in "far antiquity and middle antiquity," when people were still feeble and ignorant, all races of people needed monarchies to "envelop" them and "protect" them. In the 1920s, however, less than ten percent of the world's population was ruled by monarchs, Trinh calculated, and (he ignored Canada) there were none at all in the Americas. Republics based upon people's rights were now in the front wave of civilization.

But where had these newfangled popular republics come from? In answering this crucial question, Trinh said nothing at all about the historical importance of Europe's relatively autonomous cities or of the international expansion of the European merchant classes. Instead, he reverted to the ideals of the Chinese classics to find honest scholarly demiurges for his beloved republics: in Europe in the seventeenth and eighteenth centuries, "worthy philosophers" had sprung upon the world "the ideology of the people's rights," with apparently little more motive power than their own inclinations to personal sagehood.[17] Trinh's classicism, with its elitist values, remained intact to the end. He even absolved Confucius and Mencius of any blame for having ever justified the monarchical absolutism he hated. He informed his Saigon audiences that at the time these great Chinese philosophers had lived, the golden age emperors they remembered vividly and fondly had been really relatively powerless figures—indeed, no more autocratic than the "general manager of the League of Nations of this age."[18]

Given this classical elitism in the mind of a nationalist intellectual like Trinh, and given the fact that lower-class secret societies existed to solve prosaic daily life problems as much as to further the cause of the reintegration of the Vietnamese nation, where could the nationalist movement find a suitably powerful collective spirit or impulse?

Elitism ruled out effective organized populism, but it certainly did not mean a total separation between the intelligentsia and the people. Moreover, elitism was being qualified in Vietnamese life in many visible and invisible ways. The embodiment of what was perhaps the last major nonviolent strategy of the truly irrevocably committed Vietnamese revolutionaries was the "Tonkin Free School" (*Dong Kinh nghia thuc*), which flourished for less than a year in Hanoi in 1907. Financed by patriotic Tonkin scholar-gentry families, the Tonkin Free School aimed at undermining the hegemony of Confucian classical studies in Vietnam by bringing the modern education which some Vietnamese students were receiving in Japan, to Hanoi itself. The nationalist intellectuals who taught the school's classes and poetry sessions emphasized such causes as the use of romanized Vietnamese rather than the more cumbersome traditional Chinese and Vietnamese characters; the development of factories and of agricultural cooperatives; the domestication of the ideas of European political and educational theorists; the domestication of the ideas of the 1898 Chinese reformers; and even the abandonment of traditional clothing styles. A badly frightened colonial government soon closed the school's doors.

One of the many things which made the Tonkin Free School something of a watershed in the organization of the Vietnamese revolution was its fragile first attempt to reverse the classical tradition of one-way class imitability. This tradition—that the common people should imitate the educated elite but that the educated elite should not imitate the people—went back at least to the Analects of Confucius, to the dictum that the virtue of the gentleman acted upon the virtue of petty people as the wind acted upon grass. One of the Tonkin's Free School's most popular musical instructions, or songs urging Vietnamese upper-class students in Hanoi to reform their behavior, exhorted: "Let's avoid all wine, let's avoid the scent of opium, let's avoid the Chinese shops that sell expensive black fabrics and satins for Western dames. Let's avoid the occupations of gambling and plaguing the people, let's avoid the occupation to which we've been accustomed for so long of being 'clever at home but stupid in the market' [that is, cheating your own people and being docile to foreigners]. Avoid taking advantage of your position and . . . avoid big sleeves and flowing robes. . . ."[19] "Big sleeves and flowing robes" was a reference to the traditional ostentatious costumes of the elite: one message of the song was that all patriotic students should now wear the clothes of commoners.

From such messages—and their indirect acknowledgments that gentlemen could no longer flaunt expensive, separatist styles of consumption in the faces of commoners without any reference to the commoners' own desires or conditions—enormous consequences were to come in the decades after 1907. But rejection of the emblems of class differentiation did not mean real egalitarianism. Nor did it mean unconditional acceptance of lower-class participants in the leaderships of revolutionary organizations. And in fact, many Vietnamese nationalists of the generation of Phan Boi Chau were more concerned by the lack of cohesion of the elite itself than they were by their own isolation from the common people. From their point of view, far too many members of the traditional upper classes, instead of fighting the French, were continuing to seek offices and bureaucratic titles under the aegis of colonialism. Phan Boi Chau himself was obsessed by the need to launch a war against the fatally distracting upper-class appetite for the "honors of office" (*cong danh*), which he called "empty names" (*hu danh*). Believing the mystique of public service among Vietnamese elite families to be the secret of French colonial control, Chau produced a typically vigorous diatribe against it:

> Some people . . . still do not know what a nation is. . . . Their own positions are firmly anchored. For several thousand years examination system degree holders have caused the earth to overflow with straw dogs [that is, dogs woven out of straw which guarded the graves of rich people, but which could not really bite or bark] while administrators and councillors have filled their walls with pictures of dragons [that is, more unreal symbols of pomp]. From young people to adults, our people are all competing for names and reputations. . . . A baby which has not yet been separated from its cradle already desires a French medallion and a gold belt. Its mouth is not yet dry of its mother's milk and yet it already jabbers with desire for the badge of a colonial elected representative or the insignia of a mandarin. Alas! Is that glory . . . ?
>
> Why don't you people reflect, all these things are just like giving coconut-sheath hats to monkeys and paper shirts to ghosts. These types of things are exactly the types of things that people use to deceive and flatter us . . . the whole nation has become surfeited with its fate of being a horse or a water buffalo, its knees are tired and its feet ache, the very trees and grass are tired of playing the parts of servants, so why are you still after degrees and certificates? Why do you still covet bureaucratic grades? . . . Where is our wisdom? Where is our spirit?[20]

To readers familiar only with the history of Western revolutions, the hatred which Vietnamese (and, to a lesser extent, Chinese) revolutionaries expressed for the civil service examinations and bureaucratic recruitment systems in their societies deserves additional explanation. One famous Chinese historian may well be at least partly right—but no more than partly right—when he suggests that because the Confucian examination system gave, *in theory*, almost all Chinese (and Vietnamese) access to positions of power, it furtively undermined the historic prospects of a genuine "democratic revolution" in China (and Vietnam) in the traditional period. For such evolutions had occurred in Europe in reaction to *theoretically* much more closed, exclusivist, frustration-creating oligarchical political systems. Because the Chinese and Vietnamese traditional polities already encompassed the theoretical (but only the theoretical) elements of a classless upward mobility—that is, they lacked permanent aristocracies, in spite of their elitist political ideologies—they were harder to uproot, even though they could not be converted to modern political purposes.[21]

It is obvious that this line of analysis would not be excessively congenial to, say, a Marxist; and the fact that a peasant had the right to become a mandarin in traditional China or Vietnam if only he could afford the considerable time and money needed to become a classical scholar should not obscure the fact that few peasants ever did. But an alien colonial government, superimposed upon the vestiges of such a political system, could exploit its lingering degree-hunting psychology even after the foundations of the system—the civil service examinations themselves—had been destroyed, as they were in Vietnam by 1919. Enough "coconut-sheath hats"—positions in the law courts and on colonial councils and in the increasingly discredited provincial bureaucracy—still remained to be dispensed as patronage to the "monkeys" who clamored after them.

Revolution and Organization as Seen by the Chinese Reformers of 1898

China and Japan were indeed fountainheads of revolutionary ideas for Vietnamese in this period, but the flow of inspiration and information did move both ways. On the Vietnamese side, it was not just a matter of Phan Boi Chau's pilgrimages to Yokohama and Tokyo and Canton, or Phan Chu Trinh's literary debts to early Meiji novelists who wrote about the American Revolution. Chau and Trinh actually thought in terms of one East Asian universe or laboratory of revolution. They hoped that the tides which coursed through this universe would engulf Vietnam. In haranguing Saigon audiences in 1925 about the disadvantages of monarchy and the advantages of democratic republics, Trinh could think of no better way of introducing his lesson than by glorifying the Korean youth movement of 1919 and the Chinese strikes and boycotts against imperialism of 1925. More than that, he traced the poverty and weakness of China, Korea, and Vietnam to a conspicuous common factor: two-thirds of their upper and middle classes had been recruited from what Trinh called, facetiously, the "eight-legged group"—examination system scholars who could write tortuous "eight-legged essays" but who could not understand the irrepressible force of Western civilization.[22] Trinh saw monarchism, and bogus and genuine forms of Confucianism, not as Vietnamese problems but as East Asian ones.

To end the discussion here, however, would be to foster the usual creeping Sinocentric fallacies. *Bilateral* exchanges of experiences and watchwords were much more common in the East Asian revolutionaries' world than is usually supposed. This was an era (to choose one simple example) when the peasants of north China learned about the financial burdens of Vietnamese peasants, and learned also to use them as a reference point for evaluating their own difficulties. Probably as a result of discussions between Chinese and Vietnamese revolutionaries, the Chinese revolutionary organization the *T'ung-meng hui* ("United League") issued a summons to the people of the north China province of Honan, some time before 1911, asking them to rebel against China's Manchu rulers. The summons listed all the salt taxes that Honanese farmers paid and then asked these farmers rhetorically if the salt taxes they paid were really any lighter than the notorious salt taxes Vietnamese peasants were being forced to pay to the French.[23]

Sun Yat-sen (1866–1925), the Cantonese who led the *T'ung-meng hui* and who most courageously advanced the claims of the Chinese revolution before 1911, visited Hanoi in 1902 and in 1907. He succeeded in establishing branches of the *T'ung-meng hui* in Hanoi, Haiphong, and Saigon. In line with his strategy of identifying and winning over the "great men" (*chü-tzu*) of the overseas Chinese communities in Southeast Asia, rather than appealing directly to these communities as wholes, he shrewdly made the secretary of the Hanoi Cantonese merchant guild the general manager of his party's affairs in Hanoi.[24] Admittedly, Sun Yat-sen's influence over Vietnamese revolutionaries was less impressive than it was over the Chinese residents of Vietnam. Phan Boi Chau did imitate certain organizational features of the *T'ung-meng hui*, in creating his own "Society For The Restoration Of Vietnam" in 1912. But he also ignored most of the seminal socialist ideas of the *T'ung-meng hui* political program, especially Sun's controversial plans for state intervention and public control of future increases in the land values of China's agrarian economy.[25] Quite apart from the fact that Sun Yat-sen was perceptibly more radical than most of his contemporaries in the Vietnamese revolutionary movement, he was insufficiently competent as an East Asian classical scholar to dramatize the politics of revolution and cultural confrontation in ways that would be as persuasive to Vietnamese mandarin intellectuals as they were to Saigon Chinese businessmen.

But two Chinese reformers did impress Vietnamese mandarins with the breadth of their explanations of the sources and nature of Western imperialism and of the kinds of antidotes the East Asian world should be searching for. They were the leaders of the 1898 reform movement already mentioned, K'ang Yu-wei (1858–1927) and Liang Ch'i-ch'ao (1873–1929). Both of them were the scions of Cantonese scholar-gentry families. Both

K'ang and Liang hunted for the secrets of the strength and weakness of political societies. K'ang alone published studies of the reforms of Meiji Japan, and of Peter the Great in Russia, a chronicle of the political decline of Turkey, and a tract on the tragic division of Poland. Both of them heavily influenced the stumbling approaches which Vietnamese thinkers now made to the questions of national organization and disintegration. Indeed, however primitive their fusions of classical traditions and Western political and economic nostrums may seem now, up to the 1920s their ideas provided a rich, almost inexhaustible source of inspiration to both the Chinese and Vietnamese upper classes. Here, undeniably, is one of the starting points of the Vietnamese—as well as the Chinese—revolutions.

Like early Vietnamese nationalists, K'ang Yu-wei desired a maximization of organized solidarity in his society. To accomplish this, he wanted the "lower feelings" (*hsia-ch'ing*) of the masses to reach the "upper polity" (*shang-t'i*) of the elite more frequently. Like the early Vietnamese nationalists, K'ang also did not perceive any debilitating contradiction between the two principles of solidarity and hierarchy. With this in mind it is easier to understand the significance of K'ang Yu-wei's requesting the Ch'ing emperor, during the 1898 reform movement in Peking, to establish a constitution and a parliament or "national assembly" in order to "stabilize" China. K'ang declared that the foundation of the "strength" of Western countries was their constitutions and their parliaments. But he was interested in constitutions and parliaments not because they were the apparatus of democracy, but because he saw them as the apparatus of greater political mobilization. He conceived of parliaments as places where "the prince and the national people" discussed the government and laws of a country, not as places where party representatives of the people decided policy and presented it to a constitutional monarch as an accomplished fact, awaiting only a perfunctory royal signature. With a parliament, China's political troubles would become the concern of the prince and of millions of people, not just the concern of the prince and of a few great ministers.[26]

K'ang informed the emperor in 1898 that there were many precedents for parliaments in East Asian history. The Yellow Emperor had asked questions of the common people; and Mencius had said in the fourth century B.C. that all the people of a country should talk. A "constitution" had actually been established in China during the Spring and Autumn Period (722–481 B.C.) but, unfortunately, no national assemblies had ever come into existence to support it. Now all the Western countries were busily practicing the statecraft of China's first sages—they were relying upon parliaments and constitutions in order to make themselves strong— while China herself had all the blueprints of this statecraft in her classical literature, and was simply not applying them.

What motive did K'ang Yu-wei have for developing this plaintive myth about the existence of proto-parliaments in China at the time of the legendary Yellow Emperor? Parliaments to him meant strength—not so much increased economic power as the strength of a more luxuriant, more intense, more dependable moral and political consensus. Never, of course, did K'ang dream of a pluralistic society in which power was finely distributed among different social groups. And at no point did K'ang connect parliaments with anything like a legal structure of civil liberties for the individual. An expansion of political participation in China, an expansion of political activism, but within the context of an autocratic system of power holding: this was the idyllic synthesis which K'ang felt could hold out the West. Very significantly, K'ang Yu-wei—and the Vietnamese revolutionaries and writers whom he held in thrall—did not recognize as one of the secrets of Western might the libertarian strand (such as it was) in Western political institutions and political theories. Many Westerners themselves at that time (and later) would perhaps have argued that pluralism was the bulwark of the western European and American societies, and that their solidarity really came from the coexistence of different churches, different political parties, and different ethnic groups within the framework of one polity, with upward mobility not inevitably depending upon a narrow, preordained membership in one church or party. Looking at the West from his Chinese vantage point, K'ang Yu-wei made the fascinating decision that it was not pluralism that was the key to Western power at all. One way or another, the next seven or eight decades of Chinese and Vietnamese revolutionaries were to agree with this historic intellectual decision. But what, then, *was* the key?

Ignoring Western pluralism, K'ang cherished instead an admiration for what he thought was the well-drilled, robot-like nature of Western religious monotheism. (The social and cultural uniformity of Western peoples was as much exaggerated by K'ang Yu-wei and his generation as the uniformity of the Chinese people is exaggerated by Westerners—in both cases, because of the unnatural simplifications of intercultural observations.) In 1898, K'ang went much further than urging a parliament upon an embattled emperor of China. He also asked that the Peking emperor make Confucianism into a national religion at least as efficient as Presbyterianism, with an organized nationwide Confucian congregation or "synod" and a full-fledged Ministry of Religion to direct it. The proliferation of folk religious cults in China—some Chinese worshiped the god of wealth, some who were artisans worshiped the god of carpenters, some worshiped the chief star of the Dipper (regarded as the god of literature), while some made sacrifices to the dragon king or the monkey king or the king of the oxen—represented a perilous dissipation of popular religious energies which weakened the nation-state, K'ang argued in 1898. The extravagant multiplicity of such cults below the district governments interrupted and limited the power of the rulers to condition and lead the people morally. In addition, it allowed European and American travellers in China to ridicule Chinese customs and to place them on the same "barbarian" level with those of

India, Africa, and Java. The proposed antidote to this liability should be the disciplined popularization of all the ceremonies in Confucian state temples, which in 1898 permitted only the participation of male bureaucrats and examination system students. Women and the lower classes should now be welcomed at such state temples. In the West, K'ang ruminated, prayers were offered exclusively to heavenly gods, temple sacrifices were conducted only in the name of one religious founder, and people purified themselves regularly by bowing and singing together and by chanting their religious classics. What the Chinese peasantry, and even the Chinese elite, now required, was a common religious focal point similar to the Sundays of Western peoples, when they could gather together to worship the founder of a national religion.[27]

The main features of this argument—the desire for nationally organized congregations which reached below the district level and which had no ideological competitors there, however tattered—could be modified, by future generations of East Asian revolutionaries less impressed by pious Western church-going habits, to justify the creation of much more secular "congregations," such as those of a Leninist party. K'ang's 1898 proposals, therefore, point the way into the twentieth century for both China and Vietnam, yet K'ang himself was conservative. The beauty of converting Confucius into a kind of posthumous Chinese Christ, as K'ang saw it, was that Confucianism as a state religion could coexist with the ages-old monarchy.

In the long run, K'ang Yu-wei's definition of the problem—China's lack of a social cement, like monotheism and congregational worship, strong enough to permit her to resist Western attack—was much more significant than his solution. Even in 1898, large numbers of the Chinese intelligentsia could not share K'ang's extremely idiosyncratic vision of Confucius and of Confucianism. In Vietnam, the influence of K'ang Yu-wei ran in many diverse channels. K'ang's hope of rehabilitating traditional Chinese religion and making it competitive with Western belief systems, by introducing Western-style congregational organization into it, was partly translated into action in Cochin China in the late 1920s by the Cao Dai movement. The aggressive new associationism which K'ang's reform proposals stimulated among Chinese intellectuals was particularly marked in the southwest province of Kwangsi, across the border from Tonkin. "Sagely studies societies" were organized in the towns of Kweilin and Wuchow to hold regular Sunday-style readings of the Confucian classics, and a large "free school" was also opened in Kweilin.[28] It is probable that the Tonkin Free School in Hanoi was aware of its vastly more Confucian forerunner in Kweilin; but the model it publicly acknowledged was Keio University in Tokyo.

To Vietnamese nationalists, engaged in their own quest for the talismans of national organization, K'ang Yu-wei's specific ideas were only of limited use. The reason for this was that K'ang had not deeply understood the new patterns of cohesion (and conflict) of Western industrial civilization and had never read the works of such proprietorial apostles of the new industrial society as Saint Simon and Comte. Phan Chu Trinh, after spending more than a decade in France, did acquire an insight into Western industrialization, but—as proof that K'ang's thought had harbored elaborations of permanent anxieties and wishes among its eccentricities—he still never escaped completely from K'ang's spell. (In 1925, in Saigon, he publicly blamed the failure of the 1898 reform movement in China not upon K'ang's ideas or lack of power but upon the fact that a "one-time imperial concubine," the empress dowager, had disliked change.[29]) Following K'ang, Trinh agreed that the touchstone of fundamental Confucian philosophy was "benevolence" or "selflessness" (jen). But he and K'ang recast the normal Confucian progression of moral and social development, from oneself to one's family to one's nation to the world, in different ways. K'ang gave his recasting a Buddhist flavor: with the possession of benevolence he believed, one "body" could become a "group," the group could become a "great group," and the great group could universalize itself into the dharma world, the world of the laws of the Buddha.[30] Admiring this pattern of expanding associationism based upon a pure moral ethic, Trinh nonetheless rejected the dharma world as the ultimate goal of the cultivation of benevolence. Having lived in Europe, he was prepared to make a portentous substitution for it: socialism.[31] He had long since rejected K'ang Yu-wei's love of monarchy, of course, and he had reduced K'ang Yu-wei's passionate Confucian salvationism, based upon benevolence, from a universal context, in which there was "no need to speak of nations," to a sharply nationalistic one.

In the last analysis, Vietnamese nationalists of the early 1900s offered completely uncritical adulation to no Chinese ideologues, even though they inhabited the same intellectual community. Neither Phan Boi Chau nor Phan Chu Trinh could accept the T'ung-meng hui conception of revolution, which was that of an unembroidered Darwinist struggle among ethnic groups, with Chinese fighting Manchus for the right to rule themselves. This conception lacked a sufficiently powerful moral atmosphere.

Yet perhaps the most serious divergence which a Vietnamese revolutionary like Phan Boi Chau made from his Chinese patron, Liang Ch'i-ch'ao, came over the issue of the utility of revolution itself. Both K'ang Yu-wei and Liang Ch'i-ch'ao were dogmatically opposed to the transposition of Western revolutionary methods to East Asia. Sun Yat-sen and his T'ung-meng hui believed in the efficacy of a universal methodology of revolution, including the lavish use of assassinations, and tended to assume that either American constitutionalism or Russian anarchism, both of which had numerous admirers in the T'ung-meng hui, could be applied in China with as much carefree appropriateness as they could be applied in America and Russia. Their Tokyo newspaper, Min-pao ("The People Report"), for which a number of Phan Boi Chau's Vietnamese students worked, reflected this viewpoint. For K'ang and Liang, on the other hand, and for Liang's Yokohama newspaper "The New Citizen Journal" (*Hsin-min ts'ung-pao*), cultural relativity determined the success or failure of revolutions; and China could not yet afford to become the scene of a revolutionary carnival imported from other societies. K'ang Yu-wei made this very clear in his painstaking but tendentious history of the French Revolution, which was published in Japan in 1906 and immediately denounced by Sun Yat-sen's party.

According to K'ang Yu-wei, when the French Revolution had first broken out, the leaders of what K'ang called "the people's party," including the eminent general Lafayette, had not intended to do much more than reform the existing system and create a constitution. Unfortunately Lafayette, who had helped the Americans secure their independence, wished to apply American formulas to France. He did not realize that French circumstances and social patterns were dissimilar from the ones he had known in the thirteen colonies. As a result, formulas that had produced "government" in America had produced "rebellion" in France. Lafayette had been like a doctor attempting to cure a sick patient, K'ang wrote: he had not carefully studied his patient beforehand. His recommendations had been effective for the particular symptoms of the illness on the surface, but not for the more general problems of the illness on the inside. Putting the finishing touches upon this elaborate picture of Lafayette as a devastatingly Americanized universal revolutionary ignorantly returning to a France from which he had long been absent, K'ang thunderously concluded that Lafayette's "American medicine" had done great, poisonous damage to the French people.[32] This 1906 picture of Lafayette was not, of course, intended to be very complimentary to Sun Yat-sen—who had spent much of his life in America, Hawaii, and Hong Kong, and who was not deeply immersed in Chinese classical knowledge.

But in this floating East Asian intellectuals' freemasonry to which Vietnamese revolutionaries belonged as well as Chinese, it was Liang Ch'i-ch'ao who presented the most serious challenge to the proposition that revolutions had a facile universal character. His black, pessimistic vision of the revolutionary process in a country like China or Vietnam was published in his Yokohama newspaper in 1904, about a year before Vietnamese revolutionaries began their migration to Japan to study with him and with other Chinese political exiles. It can be assumed that the Vietnamese were familiar with it, since copies of "The New Citizen Journal" reached Vietnam before 1905 and its arguments were to be many times restated by Liang after 1904. Liang's frightening thesis had considerable prophetic power. Since many of its cruelest premonitions were to come true in both China and Vietnam in the next fifty years, any study of twentieth-century East Asian revolutions must pay it conscientious attention. Liang denied that revolutions possessed any casual ecumenicity of beneficial social results. To him, they functioned as a kind of madman's clearinghouse of national historical and cultural peculiarities. Specifically, he suggested that there were seven special features differentiating Chinese revolutions, and Chinese revolutionary history, from revolutions in the West. (Liang defined "revolution" broadly but superficially—and conceded that he did so—as the use of military force to overthrow existing governments.) What were these seven features?

First of all, whereas Western revolutions had commonly tended to be "revolutions by corporate groups" (*tuan-t'i ko-ming*), in China, violent political change had customarily expressed itself in "revolutions by private individuals" (*ssu-jen ko-ming*). (Significantly, Liang raises the "organized community" theme at the very outset of his thesis.) The parliamentary army which spearheaded the English revolution in the 1640s, the congress and assemblies which managed the American Revolution, the assemblymen who had led French revolutions, and the "upper level corporate groups" which had sponsored the revolutions of 1848 in central Europe were all examples of the successful group organization of political change in the West. But no genuine "revolutionary corporate group" could be discerned in several thousand years of Chinese history, according to Liang. The White Lotus movement and the Taiping movement had acquired transient mass followings, but the fates of these movements had depended upon the power manipulations of one or two private individuals, not upon the consensual spirit of "right conduct" of the full membership. Because of their fissiparous individualism, Chinese political organizations like the Triads could not make revolutions on the basis of their own strength.

Liang's second point was related to his first one. Historically, he argued, China had produced "wild ambition revolutions" (*yeh-hsin ti ko-ming*) but had never produced "self-protection revolutions" (*tzu-wei ti ko-ming*). For a revolution to succeed, it must appear to the public that the would-be revolutionaries were trapped in a situation where they had to resort to violence simply to protect legitimate interests, as a matter of obeying "no alternative" moral demands. In the West, defense of legitimate interests had plausibly been associated with revolutionary advances; but in China, defense of legitimate interests had usually meant retreating into conservatism. Traditional Chinese revolutionaries, like the founder of the Han dynasty, had carried out violent political change merely to serve personal ambition. In his contempt for "wild ambition revolutions," Liang appears to have been complaining that it was preternaturally difficult to develop a political posture in China that could visibly symbolize, on a national scale, the defense of legitimate group interests reather than personal ambition.

Liang's third point was that "upper stratum of society revolutions" and "lower stratum of society revolutions" had appeared historically in China, but that "middle stratum of society revolutions" had never done so. Why was this important? The "master force" of Western revolutions had generally been located in the middle stratum of society. Liang now presented an intricate four-part chart of revolutions in China, with twenty-two examples, ranging from the founder of the T'ang dynasty (an upper stratum revolutionary who succeeded) to Koxinga on Taiwan (an upper stratum revolutionary who failed) to the founder of the Ming dynasty (a lower stratum revolutionary who had succeeded) to the leader of the Taipings (a lower stratum revolutionary who had failed). Because there had never been middle stratum of society revolutions in China, violent political change had never been connected with realistic economic reforms. Liang's obvious implication, in advancing this argument, was that upper-class political leaders had little incentive to change the economy, lower-class leaders thrown up by society-wide disasters were too poorly educated to look for anything but utopias, and middle-class leaders with more limited, realistic ambitions for economic improvement, ready to respond to even moderate economic decline, did not exist.

Fourth, Liang thought that China typically produced "complicated revolutions," whereas the West was the home of "simple revolutions." This distinction was less mysterious than it seemed: Liang simply meant that Chinese political change was always distorted and prolonged by factionalism. He observed bitterly that in America in the 1770s there had been no other revolutionary armies besides Washington's, that in England in the 1640s there had been no other revolutionary armies besides Cromwell's, but that in China any "revolutionary situation" automatically summoned forth dozens of revolutionary armies at the same time, like the twenty odd factions or components of factions which struggled for precedence in the "revolutions" at the end of the Eastern Han or Sui dynasties. Consequently, Western countries suffered limited damage in a revolution, and gained considerable benefits. But China suffered vast destruction—because of the many competing armies—and won very few national gains. Here Liang clearly was concerned by the lack of national focal points in Chinese political life under the old regime, i.e., by the lack of places where a united opposition could crystallize coherently rather than sporadically and with great disunity. He did not directly mention the fact that unlike France or America or England in their prerevolutionary periods, China had not developed national or regional consultative institutions (or assemblies) which, no matter how weak, would permit opposition to grow in a relatively focused way.

Fifth, Liang feared that the period of time consumed in China by revolutions—that is, by political change through military means—was much longer than it was in Western countries. In China, old regimes could not be overthrown without years of ferment within the dynasty and the rise of many "heroes" to oppose the dynasty; and after a new government was installed, it required more years to repress the losing heroes and to calm the ferment. The whole process took decades. By the standards of Chinese politics, Liang commented sardonically, the "reign of terror" era in the French Revolution had really been rather brief. Introducing a horrifying simile, Liang wrote that the task of political stabilization in China at the time of a revolution could only be compared to the tedious bouts of mutual annihilation of fighting crickets. If one hundred fighting crickets were placed in a cage, half would be found dead after a few days, 60 to 70 percent would be found dead after a few more days, 80 to 90 percent would be found dead after some days more, and only when all the crickets except one were dead would the fighting in the cage finally come to an end. This "fighting crickets" world of postrevolutionary politics in China had always had a disastrous effect upon the evolution of Chinese society. It had even caused a decline in population at the end of every dynasty. (Liang had a social Darwinist fear of a declining Chinese population.) What Liang was demonstrating with his fighting crickets simile was trite, but not necessarily untrue: Chinese politicians, all attempting to be the one "Son of Heaven," would not accept a pluralistic power structure, with a legitimized opposition, on a long-term basis.

In an elaboration of this, Liang made his sixth point that while revolutionaries in the West cooperated with each other against publicly recognized common enemies (he conceded that the French Revolution had provided exceptions to this rule), Chinese revolutionaries attempted to exterminate each other as well as destroy the old government. The homicidal turmoil of the various kings of the Taiping movement in the 1800s was only the most recent demonstration. In a society dominated by models of moral hierarchy which had come down from the past, Liang implied, there was no reliable way of artificially creating or electing new leaders whom everyone would instantly respect and accept.

Seventh, and last in his litany of the horrors of revolution, Liang declared that foreign military intervention to annul revolutions was more likely to happen in China than it was in the West. He then cited five types of foreign involvement in Chinese revolutions, ranging from the interventions of Turks and Tibetans in the Sui and T'ang periods to the intervention of the British and Americans in the Taiping Revolution in the 1860s.[33]

Western readers may smile at Liang's oversimplifications of Western history, or even at his arbitrary treatment of the Chinese past. Those Chinese citizens who had to experience the full fury of the pestilence of fighting crickets which visited China during the long warlord period of the 1910s and 1920s (and even of the 1930s and 1940s) would, on the other hand, have to commend Liang's prescience in 1904, even if they still believed, unlike Liang, that the goals of the revolution made the preliminaries worth it.

The real question, however, was why Liang Ch'i-ch'ao's Vietnamese disciples, beginning with Phan Boi Chau, did not adopt his fighting crickets in a cage view of revolution, given the fact that this view also generally seemed to fit Vietnam, with its Chinese-style bureaucracy, its Confucian monarchy, its social polarization between gentry and peasants, and its lack of national representative and deliberative bodies. The Vietnamese revolutionaries refused to absorb Liang's pessimism. This refusal did not, of course, affect their intense loyalty to Liang as a preceptor. For this was an era in both China and Vietnam when revolutionaries and reformers won their followings not so much by their specific programs and views as by offering their disciples inspiring examples of selfless dedication to great enterprises of "right conduct." The young Mao Tse-tung, for example, at the time a middle school student in Changsha, Hunan, proposed in 1911 that a Chinese republic be established with Sun Yat-sen as its president, K'ang Yu-wei as its premier, and Liang Ch'i-ch'ao as its foreign minister.[34] The fact that Sun was a republican and K'ang and Liang, Sun's ememies, were monarchists, did not disturb him; and Vietnamese political allegiances in this period also seem to have centered more upon "beautiful personages" than upon ideas.

But the Vietnamese revolutionaries' invulnerability to Liang's eloquent distrust of revolutions as magic solvents for all problems probably had more important origins than a vague loyalty to strong moral personalities which transcended concern for those personalities' outlooks. Even at this stage the Vietnamese revolution had an optimistic toughness running through it which the Chinese revolution often lacked. And the explanation was simple: while Chinese revolutionaries could only look back in history to the sporadic insurrections of folk religions and secret societies, or to those seventeenth-century scholars who had refused to collaborate with China's Manchu invaders, Vietnamese revolutionaries had a much more impressive pantheon of historical heroes to inspire them. This pantheon was not just filled with noble losers, like the Trung Sisters, who had fought a Chinese invasion of Vietnam of A.D. 43 and about whom Phan Boi Chau wrote a play during an early period of exile in Siam;[35] or like Phan Dinh Phung, who had resisted the French in the late 1800s and about whom Phan Boi Chau wrote memorial biographies.[36] It also included valiant winners—Ly Thuong Kiet, Le Loi, and Quang-trung among others—who had defeated Chinese invaders in the eleventh, fifteenth, and eighteenth centuries respectively. To assert that Vietnamese revolutionaries like Phan Boi Chau (and later, Ho Chi Minh) always had models of wholly successful historical resistance movements in their minds that their Chinese counterparts could not share would be going too far. But it was true that there was no equivalent of Le Loi or of Quang-trung in Chinese history, and the existence of these two precedents in Vietnamese history—of upper-class and lower-class leaders both who had triumphed over Chinese colonialism—gave twentieth-century Vietnamese nationalists a stronger sense of informed optimism than their Chinese colleagues and, possibly, a greater reluctance to experiment with unnecessarily radical forms of social reorganization.

The Problem of Social Units and Their Conceptualization

When the leading Hue newspaper charged in 1932 that Vietnamese nationalism was handicapped by the lack of enough dynamic interpenetration of family concerns and society concerns, or of national business and social life, or of education and national politics, it stirred up a host of anxieties about traditional Vietnamese civilization which had always been present— if only in submerged or oblique forms—in the work of the revolutionary movement. The first dissociation the newspaper mentioned, that which existed between family and society, had in fact received the attention of a variety of intellectuals right across East Asia. Here is another realm where it is entirely appropriate to speak of the one East Asian revolutionary universe.

In traditional Chinese, Japanese, and Vietnamese thought and language, there had in fact been no concept completely equivalent to the Western concept of "society." Confucian thought essentially stressed the arrangement of *relationships* between people and people, but it paid far less attention to the *combinations* of different sets of people. It did not acknowledge the power and influence of any abstract entity like "society" separate from individual existences, even though it did believe in a general moral climate which could degenerate, and in a moral and physical environment. The European practice of talking about all Chinese constituting one figurative "association" or epiphanic social gathering of some kind seemed very strange. But the growing interest in Western political theories, and in their application to East Asia, demanded that this conceptual void, exposed by acculturation, be filled. Liang Ch'i-ch'ao's own solution was the idea of "grouping" (*ch'ün*). But his idea remained vague and ambiguous,[37] even though Herbert Spencer's work *A Study of Sociology* was translated into Chinese in this period as "A Study of Groups" (*Ch'ün hsüeh*).

It was Japanese philosophers who took the initiative in coining the term for "society" which is employed in Japan, China, and Vietnam today. After 1868, Japanese intellectuals had used about thirty different terms in a desperate effort to simulate the foreign notion of "society": the terms with which they experimented included terms which later came to mean "fellow" or "fraternity" (*nakama*), "business company" (*kaisha*), and "friendly association" (*kōsai*). The philosopher Nishi Amane (1829–1906) resolved the vexing issue by borrowing an expression which had once been used by the Chinese Sung dynasty philosopher Ch'eng Yi (1033–1107) to refer to "communal religious meetings." Having borrowed it, he then arbitrarily imposed the sense of the European concept of "society" upon it. The resulting product of this extraordinary demonstration of Westernization through innovative classicism—*shakai* in Japanese, *she-hui* when the Chinese borrowed it back from the Japanese, and *xa-hoi* when the Vietnamese then borrowed it from the Chinese—now permitted East Asian revolutionaries and reformers to begin to express notions of masses of people interacting with each other symbolically if not literally.[38] Acceptance of these notions at social levels below the intelligentsia in turn became crucial.

No sooner had East Asian revolutionaries domesticated the idea of society than they were forced to begin breaking it down. Which elements of society would promote or cooperate with change, and which elements of society would resist change, according to Western theorists? Since the time of its own revolutions at the end of the eighteenth century, the Western world had made social classes an object of supposedly scientific study and of political organization. For the Chinese and the Vietnamese, however, social classes were at first a puzzle. How could a system of social rank and membership be determined almost exclusively by economic criteria (and, with Marx, by the system of production)? Before the 1917 revolution in Russia, Marxist thought penetrated the minds of Chinese and Vietnamese thinkers only feebly. They received its influences more from Japan than directly from the West. A book on "modern socialism" by a Japanese writer (Fukui Junzō) was translated into Chinese, which of course Vietnamese students could read, in 1903: the Chinese translator of the book complimented Marxism not so much by conceding its self-claimed "scientific" nature as by stating that it was rich in "principles of scholarship." The first Chinese writer really to discuss Marx, again rather distantly, was Liang Ch'i-ch'ao himself, in a 1902 newspaper article.

Significantly, however, Liang at this time was far less interested in Marx than he was interested in the theories of the American social evolutionist Benjamin Kidd (1858–1916). Kidd was a minor Darwinist author of books on the "principles of Western civilization" who had made a rather exhibitionistic career out of being attacked by Victorian clergymen. In the course of a long discussion of Benjamin Kidd's work, which seemed more portentous then than it does now, Liang casually mentioned that Marxism was one of two great currents of thought in contemporary Germany. He noted that it attributed society's weakness to the domination of a majority of weaklings by a minority of strong people. Liang's incomprehension of Marxist social class analysis is clear enough, but there is more to be observed here. To Chinese eyes in 1902, and to the Vietnamese who studied with Chinese scholars like Liang, nineteenth-century Western thinkers lacked the hierarchy of importance that seems obvious to citizens of the West in the late twentieth century, with Marx and Freud and Darwin reigning above all the others in influence. Before 1917, only Darwin was fashionably understood in China and Vietnam.

Purely as a system of ideas, Marxism was simply not strong enough to cast a great spell over the Chinese and Vietnamese intelligentsias on its own. It remained buried in secondary layers of the acculturation process, eclipsed by the thought of since-forgotten writers like Benjamin Kidd, until the huge political shock of the events in Russia in 1917 gave it a strange new meaning. As early as 1906, a writer (Chu Chih-hsin) for the newspaper *Min-pao,* published by Sun Yat-sen's organization, had offered Chinese and Vietnamese readers biographies of Marx, Lassalle, Engels, and others, as well as a partial summary of the Communist Manifesto. But an article about world socialist parties by another writer for this newspaper, also in 1906, used the Chinese term "rich gentry" as an equivalent for the Western term "bourgeoisie," and the Chinese term "common people" as an equivalent for the Western term "proletariat."[39] In other words, the stress by European socialists upon the importance of the newfangled social structures that had emerged only with the rise of industrialized societies in the West was ignored. "Bourgeoisie" and "proletariat" were comfortably associated with social groups that had existed for centuries in the traditional Chinese agrarian-bureaucratic society.

On the whole, Vietnamese thinkers were even slower to grasp the new social and economic realities that were purported to be behind this language. The notion of social classes was introduced into Vietnam long after the Vietnamese revolution itself was under way, and was regarded as being "extremely new" even in the late 1920s. In 1930, writing for educated Saigon readers, one Vietnamese journalist explained that the exotic new term "upper class" (*thuong luu*) really meant "the intellectual cream" (*tinh hoa tri thuc*) of a nation, but that for convenience he would use the term "private property owners" (*tu san*) interchangeably with it.[40]

In their search for the true principles of "organized communities" or *doan the*, therefore, Vietnamese revolutionaries of the first two decades of the century found it difficult to think in terms of units as large as social classes. Here they were no different from Chinese revolutionaries before 1917. Where Chinese and Vietnamese revolutionaries of this generation did diverge was in the amount of ideological prediction and lower class emphasis they brought to their work as they schematically divided their societies into a multitude of social groups and then arranged these groups according to a scale of revolutionary potentialities. In this work, the Vietnamese revolutionaries tended to be more conservative. Or, more precisely, they tended to be less inclined to make ideological predictions about given social groups and less interested in the lower reaches of their society. The most obvious comparison here is the one between Chang Ping-lin's theoretical division of Chinese society, published in 1906, and Phan Boi Chau's speculative anatomization of Vietnamese society, published in 1907.

Chang Ping-lin was one of the major intellectual luminaries of Sun Yat-sen's *T'ung-meng hui.* He was also a notable friend to Vietnamese exiles in Japan. He wrote his famous 1906 essay upon "revolutionary morality" with the assumption that Chinese society could be most conveniently divided into sixteen different occupational groups, and that these sixteen different occupations reflected sixteen different levels of political morality. People who lacked morality, Chang argued, could not make a revolution. Significantly, Chang ranked the Chinese peasant highest on the scale of occupational (and therefore revolutionary) morality, on the grounds that the peasant, hard-working but frugal, was innocent of all the artful schemes and immoral plots in the world. The peasant, Chang said, was capable of both respectful obedience and of rebellion, depending upon which was more appropriate, and, when he died, the peasant courageously treated death like a sweetmeat. The Chinese worker was ranked second. Chang credited workers with the same unsubmissive courage as the peasants, but because workers were more guileful, and occasionally cheated townspeople, their morality was not so high as that of the peasants. Next to peasants and workers came four other occupations whose intrinsic moral codes, Chang believed, qualified their practitioners to be good revolutionaries: small traders or itinerant peddlers (brave and tough, like classical wandering knights); immobile shopkeepers (who were more artful, but who generally lived simple lives and had to preserve an honest credibility with the public); scholastic pedants (who were poor, but who did possess a basic "clash with barbarians" spirit, and who were too faithful to their narrow classical interests to be immoral opportunists); and self-sufficient "artists," hard-working calligraphers, sculptors, and engravers. The ethics of these upper six occupational groups should be the ethics of the ideal revolutionary party in China, Chang wrote. But instead, the actual promoters of the revolution were coming from the lower ten occupations, including opportunistic "men of the world" scholars, whose behavior was usually immoral.[41]

This essay was almost the closest the mainstream 1911 revolutionaries in China came to analyzing the political behavior of different social classes. European Marxist writings might point to the greater revolutionary potential of dissatisfied landless peasants, whom they called a rural proletariat. Chang Ping-lin for his part wanted to base his revolution upon the people who were most morally pure and uncontaminated by their environment—the frugal but satisfied land-owning peasants. In other words, he did not really associate revolution with the socioeconomic grievances of various social groups. Grievances, from his perspective, were often what made men cunning and devious, and thus unfit to display any transcendental "right conduct" in the pursuit of political change. The Russian Revolution of 1917, and the failure of the Chinese revolution of 1911, began to fracture this Confucian view of revolutions, in which morality, not material interests, served as the touchstone used in predicting the behavior of social groups.

But for Phan Boi Chau, Chang's most illustrious Vietnamese counterpart, the peasantry, instead of being ranked first, was not regarded as being capable of playing any role at all. Following the practice common among Chinese revolutionaries and reformers, Chau divided the Vietnamese population into ten different groups, exclaiming that common action among the members of each of these ten groups was necessary to save Vietnam. What were these ten groups? In order, they included rich households; bureaucrats in office; the children of the powerful and respected families; the Vietnamese Catholics; Vietnamese serving in military forces; members of various parties and associations; the interpreters, secretaries, and kitchen boys; women; the children of families who had had members killed by the enemy; and last, the overseas students.

In one respect—his selection of women as one of the ten decisive groups—

Chau was more radical than Chang Ping-lin, or other Chinese revolutionary dissecters of society of that time. It would be tempting to see in Chau's acceptance of women, as an important activist category, a reflection of the more prominent roles which women had played in Vietnamese life throughout history, compared to the roles Chinese women had played in China. In general, however, Phan Boi Chau was more conservative and more elitist (if also more practical) than Chang Ping-lin. With the exception of the kitchen boys, his view of the history-changing elements of society was confined to the upper and middle social strata. He exalted the Trung sisters, Le Loi, and the thirteenth-century general Tran Hung Dao, all of them upper-class heroes who had fought invaders from China. But unlike what the communists were to do after 1940, he did not venerate the memory of Vietnamese peasant uprisings. In the study of Vietnam's national history which he wrote and then circulated among Vietnamese revolutionaries in 1909, Chau assumed that Vietnamese peasants were stupid, selfish, and divided, more willing to quarrel among themselves than to fight outsiders.[42] He did concede that "tens of thousands, hundreds of thousands of nameless heroes must already be in existence before there will be heroes with names." But this statement virtually represented the apogee of his positive evaluation of Vietnamese villagers as an historic force.

In sum, Phan Boi Chau was immune to much of the populist flavoring of the Chinese and Japanese traditions of political theory to which he attached himself. In a famous 1906 manifesto, for instance, he transferred his theme of a famous hero surrounded by nameless heroes to Japanese history, declaring that at the beginning of Japan's nineteenth-century regeneration, there had been only one Yoshida Shōin, but that later, tens of thousands of other unregarded Yoshida Shōins had assembled to "clap their hands and shout," giving the Meiji Restoration mass support. Yet in depicting Yoshida Shōin (1830–1859), a Chōshu warrior who had been executed for his implacable political opposition to the decaying Japanese shogunate, as a Japanese version of Le Loi, Chau carefully ignored Yoshida's fevered populist dream of an alliance between warriors and peasants against the Japanese aristocracy, or Yoshida's belief that only "grass clump heroes" or patriotic peasants could save Japan, that the Japanese elite was bankrupt.

Added to this, the working environment of the early Vietnamese revolutionaries was considerably less lower class than the working environments of Chinese revolutionaries at the same time. No Vietnamese politician enjoyed a constituency remotely comparable to that made up by the Chinese laborers of Vancouver, San Francisco, and Honolulu who were so faithfully financing Sun Yat-sen. But the relatively greater elitism of Chau and his followers was not just a matter of constituency influences. Upper-class heroes in Vietnamese history whose names and exploits could be plausibly associated with the survival of the Vietnamese nation were much more plentiful, and much more compelling, than equivalent upper-class prodigies of resistance to foreign conquest in Chinese history. History itself—or perhaps more precisely, the lean oracular romanticism of Vietnamese elite historiography down through the centuries—was probably the factor most responsible for the early Vietnamese revolutionaries' more complacently limited view of the social scope of the ideal revolutionary society. Despite its own undeniably traditionalistic elements, the earth-shaking populism of the later Vietnamese revolution is, in this perspective, all the more remarkable and fascinating.

The Vietnamese Nationalist Party and Its Problems of Integration

Vietnamese revolutionism began to mature about the middle of the 1920s. The kidnapping, trial, and condemnation of Phan Boi Chau by the colonial government in 1925 produced an explosion among Vietnamese students, journalists, and the Vietnamese community in France. Its repercussions were enough to persuade the regime to grant Chau amnesty. The popular demonstrations of mourning, again heavily involving the students and journalists but also including landowners and some workers, which broke out all over the country in 1926, when Phan Chu Trinh died in Saigon, were another portent. By 1927 the Chinese Kuomintang, or Nationalist Party, the successor of the *T'ung-meng hui,* was sweeping to political power in China, and to the construction of a national Chinese government at Nanking, under the leadership of Chiang Kai-shek. Vietnamese revolutionaries fervently hoped the Kuomintang would support a pan-Asian movement of confrontation with Western colonialism. In the early nineteenth century, Vietnamese emperors had built, at Hue, a replica of the Chinese capital of Peking. Now, in 1927, Vietnamese revolutionaries were to build a replica of the Chinese Nationalist Party, in a new elaboration of the old Vietnamese pattern of controlled cultural borrowing from China.

The Vietnamese Nationalist Party (*Viet Nam Quoc Dan Dang,* known as the VNQDD) even had the same name (when written in Chinese characters) as the Chinese Kuomintang. It evolved out of a Hanoi book club and was created in great secrecy in a village within the ambit of Hanoi on Christmas night, 1927. Christmas was chosen with conscious calculation: the founding members of the party had Christ in mind as well as Chiang Kai-shek, and intended to emulate what they regarded as the self-sacrificial pilgrimage of Jesus.[43] The Nationalist Party of 1927 is especially important because it represented a new, and higher, stage in Vietnamese revolutionaries' efforts to forge new forms of integration, embracing a wider variety of social groups. The fearsome estrangement between the "nation" and "society" which Hue journalists were to make an almost exaggerated issue of debate in 1932 had, to some extent, been courageously reduced by the Vietnamese Nationalist Party, before it was brutally suppressed in 1930.

Nguyen Thai Hoc, the chairman and chief architect of the party, was born to a small peasant family in Vinh Yen province northwest of Hanoi. Unlike the first-generation leaders of the communist movement, he did not have mandarin antecedents. Unlike Ho Chi Minh, he was not well enough educated or experienced to maintain the old Vietnamese elite tradition of contact with foreign models: he and his associates admired the Chinese Kuomintang, but from afar, not having or being proper mandarin "men of talent" who could visit Nanking and ask for assistance.[44] Hoc did learn some Chinese characters from a village schoolteacher. He attended a Franco-Vietnamese primary school in the prefectural town nearest to his village, and reached the climax of his education when he managed to get enrolled in the superior school of commerce in Hanoi in the 1920s. He was enthralled by the French Revolution.[45]

The French Revolution was more a reinforcement than a cause of his own political ideas, however. Hoc told a companion-in-arms that "revolutionary thoughts" had first flowered in his mind at the age of ten, not because of economic discontents or because of contact with Western books, but because of close contact with villagers who had been involved in previous acts of resistance to French rule. His family's water buffaloes, which he was obligated to look after when he was not in school, had habitually wandered to a nearby village which had once been the native place of a man, now dead, who had fought the French; and the aged, half-mad mother of this man, still living herself, had hugged Hoc and other children and had piteously implored them to revenge her son's death by overthrowing the colonial regime.[46] Nothing, perhaps, could summarize the origins of the Vietnamese revolutionary spirit more simply than this tale of a cult of the dead with its stormy patriotic imaginings. By 1926 Hoc was sending letters proposing reforms in the colony (free schools for peasants, the development of Vietnamese industries) to French governors-general and resident superiors, who complacently ignored them.

What was noteworthy about the Vietnamese Nationalist Party, led by Hoc, was that it was not a coterie of one or two dominating, autocratic, "beautiful personage" leaders who overshadowed all the hero-worshiping followers within their orbit. It sincerely groped for methods of efficient egalitarianism which had eluded earlier Vietnamese nationalist attempts to build new "organized communities." Styles of participation were broader. The Hanoi delegates to the founding meeting in 1927 selected the party's name. Delegates from Thanh Hoa proposed, successfully, that the party adopt a secret-society-style oath, which meant requiring new members to swear "absolute secrecy concerning the party, and absolute loyalty to the party" in front of an altar (comparable to those of ancestor worship) that was called the "altar of the ancestral land." Another Thanh Hoa delegate to the founding meeting, a man (Hoang Van Tung) closely linked to the "New Vietnam Revolution Party" (*Tan Viet Cach-menh dang*) of central Vietnam, insisted that the VNQDD combine its rococo secret society membership oath with the modern structure of a Leninist political organization. As a result of this advocacy, one "central committee" was installed at the top of the party to preside over a many-tiered edifice which included regional committees, then provincial committees, and then local party cells, which themselves were divided into four subcommittees dedicated to finances, propaganda, spying, and organization.[47] Each level elected representatives to the next highest level, ultimate decision-making power belonged to the top level, and, in ironic conformity to the colonial law banning public assemblies of more than nineteen people anywhere in Vietnam without government permission, each party cell had a maximum of nineteen members. The VNQDD represented, in 1927, an unprecedented triumph of organized associationism for Vietnamese revolutionaries, both in the elaborateness of its organizational structure—its cells, committees, subcommittees, and elected chairmen—and in the diversity of regional and individual political initiatives it enshrined and sheltered, relatively harmoniously.

Party programs and activities themselves were, of course, failures. The party had pledged itself to transcend social and religious divisions in order to win independence through military means. But one of its leading intellectuals, Nhuong Tong, produced a treatise entitled "The Harbinger of Revolution" (*Cach-menh tien-thanh*) in the late 1920s which outlined the crimes of the colonial regime. The treatise appears to have assumed that the act of revolution was very little more than a reaction to these crimes.[48] Party plans lacked any image of a desired future, based upon specific social and economic reforms, for the period after colonialism had been defeated. In the first year of the party's existence, its leaders spoke of a three-stage program which included the "embryonic" period of recruitment of new members, a "strategy preparation" period, and a "destruction" period for carrying out the armed overthrow of the Indochina government. A fourth stage was casually added to the first three only in December 1928. It was a "construction" period which would bring to Vietnam Sun Yat-sen's vague "three people's principles" of nationalism, democracy, and a limited socialism that would nationalize hypothetical increases of wealth. But it was clear that the planned violence of the "destruction" period still governed the VNQDD's thoughts and ambitions.[49]

The party, however, suffered the harsh fate of destruction itself a quarter century before colonialism did. Members of the VNQDD who worked for French firms like Poinsard-Veyret and Denis Frères, especially in the south, had been pressing their central committee to strike against the French recruitment of ignorant northern Vietnamese peasants for debilitating, underpaid labor on southern plantations. This internal coolie trade, which had included kidnapping and bribery and the death and suffering of many peasants, had become a scandal to Vietnamese nationalists. In February 1929 VNQDD activists assassinated Bazin, a chief French administrator of the plantation coolie trade, in Hanoi. The French response was a reign of terror. More than two hundred members of the party were arrested and most of its cells were liquidated. At a meeting of surviving senior party members at Lac Dao, on the border of Bac Ninh and Hung Yen provinces, in September 1929, the romantic Nguyen Thai Hoc declared that the party still had functioning cells in four northern provinces (Thai Binh, Ninh Binh, Hung Yen, and Tuyen Quang) and that as a result of the French campaign of repression it must now launch the armed uprising of its destruction stage, not because it expected to win but in order to exploit what military strength it had left to it. Hoc's proposal was supported by a majority vote after a turbulent debate. This made the Lac Dao conference a turning point in Vietnamese history.[50]

Armed uprisings were planned for cities, towns, and French-occupied military centers. Party members serving in the colonial militia were counted upon to function as a fifth column. At the end of 1929, colonial authorities discovered most of the party's caches of weapons: these included nearly six hundred homemade bombs, resembling World War I European grenades, which had been secreted in a number of northern villages. Hoc, at another meeting of the party in a Hai Duong village in January 1930, told his audience that life was a gamble and that they could at least make an impression upon the Vietnamese people: he was still committed to the use of force. Two companies of Vietnamese militiamen stationed at the northern town of Yen Bai, and loyal to the VNQDD, revolted prematurely in February 1930. The French reaction decimated the VNQDD, for the colonial government captured and guillotined its most active leaders, including Nguyen Thai Hoc himself. Their removal from the scene was to leave little middle ground, in turn, between the colonial regime and the growing Vietnamese communist movement.

To end the story here would be to do less than justice to the VNQDD as a revolutionary movement. Both its successes and failures are illuminating. Its conception of the postcolonial future was confused and imprecise. Nevertheless, here was a party which did reach out to groups and to sub-communities within the Vietnamese nation which had previously not been well enough represented in nationalist movements. Following Phan Boi Chau's 1907 identification of women as one of the ten decisive groups into which the nation could be broken down, the VNQDD, in 1927, gave women as much freedom as men to enter the party. (At first women were compelled to form their own separate cells: only at the time of the tense preparations for revolt in 1930 did the party abolish all distinctions between male and female members in its organization.) Equally important, the party was virtually unique, as Vietnamese political movements went in the 1920s, in its bold attempts to win over the Vietnamese soldiers serving in the colonial militia. In order to make rebellion among these soldiers more secret and more convenient, the VNQDD created a separate branch of the party exclusively for party members who were soldiers; and this special branch elected its representatives directly to the party's central committee, bypassing the normal intermediate levels. In other words, the party placed the immediate recruitment of strategic social groups above consistent obedience to Leninist organizational imperatives.[51]

Who were the militiamen? The Vietnamese colonial militia had been created in 1886, as an imitation of the Bengal police force which the British had brought into existence in India. Its members were recruited by Vietnamese canton chiefs, proportionately to the number of adult male taxpayers per village. The villages were responsible for the men whom they furnished. As of 1931, for all of Indochina outside Cochin China, the "indigenous guard" possessed 15,220 Vietnamese soldiers, commanded by 388 Frenchmen.[52] The militia conscription system drafted peasant boys who were paid miserable wages and who were, moreover, effectively uprooted from their farming environments by their three-year terms of service. Although (according to one newspaper's estimate) only about four percent of the village youths who were eligible for the military rolls were actually forced to serve as soldiers every year,[53] the socially deracinated quality of their lives made it easier for revolutionaries to reach them. At the end of just its first year of existence, the VNQDD had recruited nearly 400 of these militiamen in Tonkin and 256 in Cochin China, according to one leader's recollection. And of the 229 VNQDD members who were arrested by the French in early 1929, 40 were militiamen.[54] The party concentrated especially upon the recruitment of noncommissioned or petty officers.

If we return to the paramount theme of the revolutionary search for better ways of organizing Vietnamese political life, we must ask how extensively the VNQDD represented an advance in structure from the old position of the hierarchical religious sects or of the more egalitarian fraternal secret societies organized upon a basis of pseudokinship. The question obviously goes beyond the matter of mere factionalism. Of course it must be noted that the VNQDD did possess factions: Nguyen Thai Hoc's insistence upon armed uprisings, at the Lac Dao conference in 1929, was unsuccessfully opposed within the party by a group which ominously called itself the "reorganization clique" (*phai cai to*).[55]

At his trial in Hanoi in the summer of 1929, Nguyen The Nghiep, a captured party leader, informed the tribunal that no one was the real head of the VNQDD, "because we wish to treat each other in an egalitarian manner"[56] —a fascinating explanation. Whether or not he made this state- ment partly to deceive the French police—Nguyen Thai Hoc, who had actually been elected party chairman several times, was still at large—his public assumption that there was an inevitable contradiction between egalitarianism and a clearly defined leadership structure was revealing. What it revealed, perhaps, was a fear that in Vietnam in 1929 clearly defined leadership structures were still far too likely to bear the obstinate psychological and cultural impress of traditional family and lineage hier- archies, to which "modern" revolutionaries were becoming increasingly opposed. The VNQDD, in brief, failed to absorb very deeply the Leninist approach to revolution. For Lenin, revolutions had to be made by small, specialized, autocratic professional elites, who directed and came from mass organizations but whose membership was restricted in the interests of fighting efficiently the equally restricted and autocratic Russian state. The VNQDD leaders appear to have been aware of this organizational theory but not of the sharply focused political vision behind it: they were uncertain of what connections existed between traditional undesirable social forms and the undesirable colonial state, and therefore they were unwilling to imitate any of the things to which they were opposed for the sake of victory against the colonial state. VNQDD members were too fearful of confusing the symbols of an autocratic revolutionary leadership with the symbols of authority of the old culture to embrace "democratic centralism" unreservedly.

In moments of crisis, however, the VNQDD did not escape from the authority patterns of traditional Vietnamese organizations. In 1927 the bookish Nhuong Tong, a close associate of Hoc, proposed that their budding revolutionary movement follow the inspiration not of Sun Yat-sen and Chiang Kai-shek, but of Gandhi. He wanted their group to conduct a peaceful revolution, climaxed by a six-month general strike against the Indochina colonial government if it refused to concede self-rule to the Vietnamese. This general strike could be preceded by six years' work building cooperatives among students, workers, soldiers, civil servants, and kitchen boys—that is, among all those who had contact with the French. The hope was that these cooperatives could accumulate enough capital to finance the general strike when it came. This idea of a "peaceful revolution" was debated for two nights among the future VNQDD leaders. Hoc himself condemned it vigorously on the grounds that it was "utopian." But the issue was resolved only when the group realized that Nhuong Tong, Gandhi's putative disciple, was slightly younger than the members of the group who had espoused greater violence. Nhuong Tong was then sternly told that it was the duty of younger revolutionaries to obey the older ones.[57] The age criteria which determined the distribution of power in the traditional lineage, in brief, were unabashedly invoked to determine history-making choices of revolutionary policy.

Despite the desire "to treat each other in an egalitarian manner," despite the desire on the part of many VNQDD members to make conscious breaks with the old culture, traditional forms of hierarchy and ascribed status (age) did continue to flourish unpredictably behind the scenes. Probably they were part of the explanation for the weak diffusion of the VNQDD's platform and objectives even among its own members (who numbered perhaps fifteen hundred by 1929). Quite apart from the party leaders' natural fear of police infiltration, their view of younger, less experienced members of the party as subordinates in an invisible hierarchy more shaped by the past than by Leninist canons gave them little incentive to disclose their own thoughts and personalities. A legal court clerk in the border province of Tuyen Quang who was arrested as a VNQDD member in 1929 told the Hanoi tribunal that "the programs and laws of the party, the majority of the people in the party cannot read." He was not referring to illiteracy. A Bac Kan province telegraph office worker who had been arrested for being a member of a Lang Son province party cell explained at the same tribunal that it was possible to attend meetings of the party's central committee council without having even sworn the party oath—for he had done so. But when he asked to see the ordinary regulations of the party, he could not.[58]

The combination of these two facts suggests that fear of police infiltration was not the only reason for the party's poor capacity to communicate information about its ambitions to its followers. Had it been, such access to the central committee council would have been less casually granted. And given the mystery about the party's projected destiny, given the fact that its internal "self-disclosure" practices were not great enough to keep a coherent movement together indefinitely, not all of its members could have been held together in the late 1920s by a communal anticipation of heroic disaster and of inevitable martyrdom. On the fringes of the party lurked people like the quavering nineteen-year-old chauffeur, charged by the French with being both a VNQDD member and a provincial secretary of Ho Chi Minh's Revolutionary Youth League, who described himself as being "the child of a worker household" who "did not know what revolution was" but who was unemployed and hungry and who had been hired by the VNQDD to work as a paid courier for it.[59] The odds that this teenager was lying may not have been overwhelming.

Above all, the minds of the VNQDD leaders almost certainly wrestled with peculiar tensions between the new political theories which were being laboriously imported into Vietnam—especially theories which focused upon class conflict, and which artificially equated the VNQDD itself with the Russian Populists or Narodniki[60] —and the urgent needs of national and social integration in Vietnam which patently were not solved by these theories. The difficulties of the VNQDD were less simple than the problem just of escaping from outmoded structural and cultural heritages of the past.

As cities and towns grew in colonial Vietnam, they grew as clustering collections of inward-looking village-style communities. The ethnic heterogeneity of the urban populations—French, Vietnamese, Chinese, Indian—which now lived side by side, but in relatively self-contained cultural enclaves, did not necessarily lead to a greater cosmopolitanism of outlook. Instead, these various ethnic groups mingled with each other but did not combine, in a classic manifestation of the patterns of the Southeast Asian "plural society." Western theories of revolution, which assumed the growth of an increasingly cosmopolitan international community and which could therefore afford the luxury of regarding economic conflict entirely as a matter of conflict between social classes, now had to permeate a society where conflicts among ethnic groups had become almost a daily occurrence. The Vietnamese plural society produced its most spectacular eruption of violence in the colonial period in the summer of 1927, in the northern port city of Haiphong. It is worth noting that the scene of what the Chinese were to call, for decades afterward, the "August 17 massacre" was a city where ethnic differences were least reinforced or exacerbated by economic gaps or by a conjunction of ethnicity with class. Haiphong Chinese tended to be workers, sailors, and shop employees, unlike the richer Chinese rice mill owners and businessmen of the more peaceful southern urban complex of Saigon-Cholon.

The Chinese community in Haiphong in 1927 numbered an estimated 15,000 people in a total city population of perhaps 120,000. It did not even have a Chinese-language newspaper to sustain its sense of separateness. The China Merchants' Guild, the focal point of this community, (which was divided into a Kwangtung "congregation" and a Fukien "congregation," each with its own elected headman) did maintain five schools, a library, and a clinic; but it would not be unfair to describe this as a relatively underdeveloped cradle of communal institutions. The "massacre" of August 1927 originated in a street fight between two female water carriers, one Chinese, one Vietnamese. Neighbors joined the fight, the battle lines were drawn along purely ethnic lines, the Vietnamese policemen sent by French municipal authorities to quell the riot instead attacked the Chinese, a number of Chinese were killed, and many Chinese shops and houses were burned during ten days or more of disorder. At the height of the violence, the China Merchants' Guild even sent telegrams to China imploring the Chinese government to send a warship to Vietnam to protect the Haiphong Chinese.[61] Chinese chambers of commerce and fraternal organizations in places as far away as Burma, the Philippines, and Cuba organized campaigns of assistance for their compatriots in Vietnam. The Nanking government did go so far as to send investigators to Tonkin.

By the leaders of the VNQDD—which was just on the verge of being formally launched—the Haiphong massacre was regarded as a disaster of the first magnitude. The suspicion ran deep, not without justice, that the colonial government had deliberately encouraged Vietnamese hoodlums and policemen to attack the local Chinese, in the hope that such an outrage would deter the Chinese Kuomintang government from giving succor to Vietnamese revolutionaries. Nguyen Thai Hoc personally visited Haiphong to study the disturbances, while his associates in Hanoi, fearing that the violence would spread, spent scarce funds to hire Vietnamese roughnecks to guard the Chinese restaurants in the city.[62] This was an intelligent precaution, but it was also a futile way to begin a revolution: the VNQDD leaders were in effect seeking to restrain the "collective mentality" of the crowd, instead of exploiting it and building it up into a Bastille-storming frenzy, like the more successful French revolutionaries of 1789. The truth was that the explosive undercurrents of the plural society represented another major challenge to nationalist, revolutionary community builders and to the imported Western theoretical literature upon which they depended. In the end, the problem was solved by being circumvented, when the revolution moved to the countryside in the 1940s.

3

The Intellectuals and the Problem of Social Organization

Social and Cultural Barriers in the World of the Intellectuals

Some of the obstacles to a greater cohesion and integration of Vietnamese life which have just been mentioned—the "nonaction" option within the Confucian tradition, the greater belief in the history-making powers of individual heroes than of democratic collectivities, the diploma-hunting individualism (or diploma hunting for family reasons) encouraged by the examination system—were obstacles which raised basic questions about the world of the intellectuals.

And in the 1920s and 1930s, Vietnamese intellectuals, like Chinese intellectuals, were perfectly willing to turn the spotlight upon themselves as a group or social class, and ask penetrating, critical questions about their own situation. What were the patterns of the social interaction of the intelligentsia? What kinds of questions about the world were Vietnamese, and Chinese, intellectuals predisposed to ask? What was the nature of Vietnamese, and Chinese, "intellectual culture" and the sociology of intellectual life? And what was the relationship between all these things and the current decadence of East Asian societies? The May Fourth Movement of 1919 in Peking and Shanghai and other Chinese cities was the matrix of modern self-criticism by the Chinese intelligentsia. Unlike many of the stereotyped self-criticisms by Chinese intellectuals which emerged with machine-like regularity on the command of omnipotent politicians in the 1960s, the criticisms and self-criticisms of the intellectuals of the 1910s and 1920s were often brilliant and provocative, even if they were also written with unjustified pessimism and with diagrammatic exaggeration. Vietnamese intellectuals, without having any formal May Fourth Movement of their own, nonetheless participated in their own way in what was a general East Asian tendency.

In traditional Vietnam, as in traditional China, dynasties had carefully prevented the formation of nationwide communities of interdependent intellectuals, for political reasons, by preventing the growth of large scholar associations outside the imperial bureaucracy. Emperors were fearfully aware of the fact that the civil service examination system itself created important networks of social relations among scholars: between teachers and students, between examiners and successful candidates, among students who had passed examinations in the same year at the same site. Even Vietnamese intellectuals who rebelled against the Chinese-style scholasticism of the Vietnamese examination system deeply cherished the social ties which the system bred among its participants. The most flamboyant nineteenth-century rebel of this kind, Cao Ba Quat (executed in 1854), once wrote a noticeably sentimental poem on the subject of "taking leave of my students, outside the wall of the provincial capital, in order to journey to the metropolitan examinations at Hue." He was quite frank about the social needs which scholarship satisfied: "My students have come to see me off on my travels. They step along behind me, and do not have the heart to leave me. Is that really manhood?. . . When I entered life, only literature existed. So I used it as a means of helping myself to have fun. I give my thanks to all you young men, My feelings of attachment will never fade."[1]

To prevent the easy transformation of such "feelings of attachment" into concerted political activities by cliques of scholars against the court, the movements of the scholar class were strictly observed and controlled. Court statutes stipulated, for example, that when Hue scholar-officials were sent out to the provinces on official duty, even their seating arrangements at banquets, and their conversations with provincial scholar-officials with whom they might be dangerously well acquainted, had to follow certain meticulously prescribed forms. When an imperial commissioner was received by a provincial governor, the commissioner had to sit on the eastern side of the room and the governor had to sit on the western side; the two men were then permitted only to discuss "the business of government and the health of court officials," a general prohibition being applied to "private items" of conversation. These rules, designed to prevent plotting and the emergence of private understandings between two scholar-officials in a province far from the court, came under the bureaucratic rubric of "the etiquette of confrontations" (*dich the le*). The term for the evil against which they were aimed—*dang,* meaning "factions"—rather unhappily became the term for "political parties" in twentieth-century Vietnam.

Traditional scholars were well aware of the significance of these forms of control. But they were less well aware, before the present century, of other opportunities which the imperial bureaucratic system had denied them. Fukuzawa Yukichi, the great Japanese reformer, pointed out in 1873 that there was no equivalent in the Japanese language, at that time, for the English word "speeches." In other words, Japan had no concept of public speaking in which one man presented his own ideas publicly to a large audience. Methods of large-scale oral communication which had existed in premodern Japan had included the "question and answer" form of teaching at Buddhist temples, in which disciples and teacher-priests exchanged questions and answers for the enlightenment of others, a little like a modern panel discussion; and they had included Buddhist hymns of praise and "advocacy" recitations, designed to dramatize religious doctrines. In Fukuzawa's opinion, the long absence of less stereotyped forms of public speaking in Japan was such a critical bar to democracy and to Westernization that he himself was driven to found one of Japan's first modern lecture halls.[2] Vietnamese intellectuals were in not too different a position. In the traditional period they had been accustomed to expressing their thoughts publicly mainly in funeral orations, or in verse novels, or in relatively predictable, ornamental expositions of morality at village meeting houses. Now they too had to make a sudden transition to more secularized, Western-style forms of public communication. And they had to do so under the eyes of colonial police and censors.

Increasingly large numbers of intellectuals now chose to stay outside the politically tainted government service. But in the middle of a revolution, what public role could the intellectuals claim? This controversial question has never been resolved to everyone's satisfaction in modern Vietnam. Many intellectuals themselves, emancipated from the old bureaucratic constraints, advanced sweeping, totalistic definitions of their mission as a group. Duong Ba Trac (1884–1944), a former member of the Tonkin Free School, defined the "scholar class" in 1925 as consisting of those people who "had scholarship" and who "had thought," those people who were "luckier" than ordinary people, those people who had a "natural disposition toward quickness of apprehension and discernment," those people who had a more complete degree of education than ordinary people, those people who were respected by emperors above and revered by the people from below. The functions of the intellectuals, as Trac put it, included building nations, transmitting customs, maintaining the teachings of the ages, upholding the obligations of morality, nourishing men of talent, and guiding the "backward." The intellectuals were the "first knowers" and the "first perceivers" of a society: if the people who were "after knowers" and "after perceivers" could not depend upon the intellectuals, upon whom could they depend? When intellectuals "advanced," they became civil servants. When they "withdrew" they became teachers. But whichever pole of action they clustered around they were compelled to "help those in danger," to bring order out of chaos, and in general to work "to save the age" (*cuu the*).

Little in this definition, up to this point, would have surprised a traditional Vietnamese scholar. It was essentially a grandiose summary of the "world salvation" inclination in the Confucian tradition, as opposed to the Taoist-Confucian "nonaction" one. However, in his definition of 1925, Trac added some new elaborations. He argued both that intellectuals ranked first among the four categories of people (ahead of peasants, artisans, and merchants, the traditional Confucian formulation) and that the "ancestrally transmitted" or hereditary "customs" of the Vietnamese nation were precisely the customs of the high scholar-officials, not of the less Sinicized masses. In the past, scholars had been regarded as the transmitters (and embodiments) of moral teachings. Now, under the pressures of Darwinism and of colonial conquest, Trac had seen fit to broaden their role: they became the social class which transmitted and embodied not just moral teachings, but all the desirable national habits. Indeed, Trac appears to have assumed a kind of biological continuity among the intellectuals from generation to generation, as suggested by his references to their luck, to their natural quickness of apprehension, and to their function of preserving national customs (which presumably would have been modified by great social turnovers among the elite).

The importance of all this for the Vietnamese revolution should be clear enough. Nationalism by itself did not make it inevitable that the intellectuals would abandon their elitist qualities and make common cause with the lower classes. In Trac's perspective—and Trac was by no means an extreme conservative—there seems to have been a perceived need for a permanent social "quintessence" (*tinh-hoa*), the intelligentsia, to "symbolize" the nation against the oppressive outside world. The recognition of such a need could only mean that the new sensitivities of nationalism had a capacity to harden class lines as well as to dissolve them.[3]

Of course the intellectuals, as the "first perceivers" of the facts of Vietnam's fragmentation, were acutely conscious that they did not constitute a single organized community themselves. Here the analyses of Chinese and Vietnamese intellectuals in the precommunist period—their analyses of their own kinds of people in their own societies—showed remarkable similarities. They deserve to be compared, if only to illustrate the thesis that Vietnamese concern over the lack of cohesive national communities was even stronger than the Chinese. The critiques of Fu Ssu-nien for China (1918) and of Phan Khoi for Vietnam (1930) are as cogent as any that could be used for this purpose. I have no evidence that Phan Khoi had read any of Fu Ssu-nien's famous essays before he produced his own.

Fu Ssu-nien, who had been elected marshal of the Peking student marchers and demonstrators of May 4, 1919, had already become one of the leaders of May Fourth period journalism in China. He asserted in 1918 that the first failure of Chinese intellectuals was the domination of their world by personal cliques. Fu pointed to a dichotomy between "the study of laws and categories" (*k'o-hsüeh* in Chinese, *khoa-hoc* in Vietnamese, the general East Asian term for what Westerners call "science") and its Chinese antithesis, "family studies" (*chia-hsüeh*). Western science, or "studies of laws and categories," took branches of learning as its pivot; Chinese "family studies," on the other hand, took people as their pivot. Fu did not trouble to conceal the fact, as is obvious, that the very concept of "science" had acquired a polemical, culturally dividing flavor in China after 1911, and that, in the minds of the May Fourth thinkers, there was a sense of brooding warfare between intellectuals whose world revolved around intellectual categories and those whose world revolved around intellectual families.

Extending his distinction, Fu argued that Chinese intellectual groups were not accustomed to differentiating themselves on the basis of dis-similar subjects of investigation, or on the basis of the separation of courses of study. Instead, they differentiated themselves most unconditionally upon the basis of loyalties to different teachers. Disciples followed their teachers very closely: what the teachers did not study, the disciples usually did not study either. Literature that was unfamiliar to the teachers remained unfamiliar to their disciples. As a result of this, most Chinese scholars' groups decayed after a few generations of personal "transmission" of studies of this kind, whereas Western scholars, oriented much more toward categories of study than toward people, could keep building and advancing.

A separate facet of the persistence of family studies among Chinese intel-lectuals which retarded their progress—according to Fu Ssu-nien—was that the Chinese scholarly world, instead of developing into a pluralistic world of specialists, had become instead a world of morally polarized, non-specializing dilettantes and polymaths. Chinese scholars could never agree upon mutually cooperative divisions and subdivisions of labor—regarding intellectual concerns—because all schools of thought in China sanctified their own existence by the salvationist belief that "one school of thought could change the world." Hence few if any schools of thought ever tried to narrow the scope of their inquiries to proportions that would permit the really dynamic accumulation of specialized knowledge.

What existed instead were social fragment groups of intellectuals, each attempting to establish thought monopolies, each seeking to "combine their light with that of the sun and the moon." Each Chinese school of intellectuals typically tried to encompass *all* intellectual concerns, and this ambitious totalism had prevented the growth of scientific subdivisions: thought and ethics, like politics and ethics, had become so tightly inter-woven that intellectual rivals were actually regarded by their competitors as being morally illegitimate. In Fu Ssu-nien's opinion, a number of eighteenth-century Chinese intellectuals (Ch'ien Ta-hsin, Hui Tung) had been the equals of any philosopher or scientist in the West in intellectual endowment, but "there was not a branch of studies they did not practice."

Their inability to find a specializing focus had doomed both them and China. To summarize the problem in words Fu Ssu-nien did not use, Chinese intellectuals, entering the 1900s, were still at the Leonardo da Vinci stage, capable of producing dilettante geniuses but not the sustained growth of specialized scientific disciplines whose practitioners could positively cooperate with each other.

It would be unfair not to note, once again, the excessive pessimism of Chinese self-criticizers of the May Fourth era, and the gloomy self-deprecation which underlay their pleas for reform. It would be misleading not to observe also that the poverty of the disciplined intellectual interaction of Chinese scholars was not the only thing which deeply worried Fu Ssu-nien. For example, he also pointed (and this also had relevance for the Vietnamese) to the historical decline of the popularity of logic and of logical methods in Chinese thought. This meant that Chinese scholarship and thinking could be used less conveniently as a "tool" for making breakthroughs into new areas: it lacked enough instrumental power to generate many theoretical revolutions on its own. Chinese intellectual history had produced fewer logicians than Western intellectual history, according to Fu Ssu-nien, and most of these Chinese logicians had made their appearance no later than the sixth or seventh century A.D. Chinese thought was relatively rich in imagination and relatively poor in experimentation, relatively rich in analogy building but relatively poor in deductive reasoning. And analogies tended to be used, in Chinese thought, not in the service of deductive reasoning, but in the service of preordained ideological demonstrations. For Fu Ssu-nien, the most vividly characteristic example of this situation was the well-known Chinese maxim "the heavens do not have two suns, and the people do not have two kings." The expression "the heavens do not have two suns" was the premise, and the expression "the people do not have two kings" was the conclusion, but the connection between them was a political and moral vision, not a Western-style logical deduction.[4]

The main thrust of Fu Ssu-nien's criticism, nevertheless, was directed at what he regarded as the poor social organization and the unspecialized, undelimited cognitive ambitions of Chinese intellectuals, which made it difficult for them to combine with each other. What was at issue here, to some extent, was the lack of functional specificity in human relationships in China, of which the teacher-disciple relationship was one. Human relationships were far from being superficial in the interests of an unknown efficiency: they tended to encompass the total personality. Just as shop apprentices had to kowtow to their masters, the social structures of the shops in which the apprentices worked being modeled upon the family (with the master of the shop functioning as the father), so too in the scholarly world disciples kowtowed to their teachers; and the price of deviation from their teachers' precepts could be the most psychologically shattering forms of personal conflict.

In the eyes of Phan Khoi (1887–1959), one of the brightest stars of the Vietnamese intellectual and journalistic scene in the 1920s and 1930s, the situation which Fu Ssu-nien had analyzed for China was really much worse in Vietnam. Partisan personal coteries among Vietnamese intellectuals had become such a barrier to a free exchange of ideas about Vietnam's problems, in his opinion, that he was prepared noisily and publicly to denounce these coteries as "scholar cliques" (*hoc phiet*), a coinage which he hoped would remind his readers of the contemporary "warlord cliques" in China—those selfish, self-aggrandizing military factions of Yen Hsi-shan, Wu P'ei-fu, Chang Hsüeh-liang, and other Chinese warlords.

What particularly troubled Phan Khoi about the proliferation of such scholar cliques among Vietnamese intellectuals was that the self-contained, particularistic cocoons they created made it impossible to foster intellectual debates on a national scale. Whenever the ideas of the scholar cliques were criticized, their leaders simply retreated into an offended silence, leaving the air full of suspended, unresolved questions. Phan Khoi of course went much further than Fu Ssu-nien in converting a general anxiety about the social relations of the intellectuals into the demonic incarnation he called scholar cliques. His own explanation for his extremism attributed it to his personal concern about the difference between the quality of the intellectual struggle over the future of Confucianism in China and the quality of that struggle in Vietnam, both contests raging as he wrote in 1930.

In traditional Vietnam, Confucianism as a formal philosophy—or as a number of formal philosophies—had never flourished outside the court and government bureaucracy to as great an extent, even proportionately, as it had flourished in private schools and academies in prerevolutionary China. This had obvious consequences. When the May Fourth generation of intellectuals in China, finding Confucianism to be antiscientific and antidemocratic, "put Confucius on trial" in the 1920s, they precipitated a vigorous battle between themselves and Confucian loyalists. In Vietnam, on the other hand, the trial of Confucius had evoked largely "indifference," according to Phan Khoi: Confucian intellectuals "dried their tears" when they learned that they could still become mandarins by going to the new French schools. Phan Khoi exclaimed that he did not weep for the dissolution of Confucianism in Vietnam so much as he wept for the ingratitude and superficiality of Vietnamese intellectuals in not probing and protesting this dissolution more. Could the dark hegemony of the scholar cliques, who blocked systematic national discussion, be the cause? And how could a revolution—either in thought or in politics—proceed in a society of inward-looking clusters of intellectuals who refused to adopt Western scientific methods? With these methods, "truth" was arrived at by verification, and the process of scientific verification would cause such prejudices and partialities and "haughtinesses" magically to disappear.[5]

In order to develop a Vietnamese national community, in sum, Phan

Khoi wished to abolish the old conceptions of social space which divided such space into qualitatively differentiated spheres, with traditionalistic social aggregates of one kind or another—families, lineages, or "scholar cliques"—occupying these spheres with a truculent ritualism. As substitutes for these spheres and social aggregates, he wanted to install the universal rules suggested by modern science, universal rules applicable to everyone in the one undifferentiated social space. And he was by no means the only Vietnamese intellectual who regarded the old particularistic social and psychological barriers as enemies of the newer, better organized sense of community the Vietnamese people required.

Nguyen Van Vinh (1882–1936), a famous interpreter, also attacked the socially and psychologically partitioned traditional society whose intelligentsia (about whom he was really writing) were reluctant to share information and opinions. In the 1910s, in a quaint but deadly serious essay, he had written:

> Our Vietnam has a strange habit, which is to laugh at everything.
> If people praise us, we laugh, but if people criticize us, we also
> laugh. . . . Many times our laughter is unintentionally cruel. It has a
> way of insolently despising people . . . it has the meaning that you
> self-assuredly are paying no attention to the words of other people
> but have already mentally slandered their thoughts beforehand; it
> has the meaning that you are not looking carefully at the things
> other people do but have already mentally criticized their work. . . .
> We must understand that when people talk to us, it is in order to ask
> us how we are thinking. No matter who it is who speaks with us, we
> must reply. Following our will, if we want to express our feelings so
> that other people will know them, we must speak the truth. If we do
> not understand, we must ask them to repeat their question. But if we
> do not wish to speak our thoughts . . . we must subtly employ polite,
> elegant words to make other people understand that their questions
> violate our privacy a little too much.[6]

In many areas of life, however, the new behavior Vinh was recommending—free exchanges of questions and answers, rather than the old distance-preserving laughter—depended upon the acceptance of a depersonalized view of the world, in which knowledge and information could be clearly separated from the personalities of the people who disseminated them. And there were two difficulties here. First, it was not easy to "depersonalize" knowledge with powerful political implications, in a society which was colonized and undergoing a revolution. Second, as intellectuals like Phan Khoi recognized, the Vietnamese language in the 1920s and 1930s still had far too many ways of implying personal social distinctions and far too few ways of discussing impersonal actions and enterprises.

Indeed, the language issue affected the nationalists' drive for a revolutionary reintegration of Vietnamese society in a variety of ways. Some nationalists clung to the extreme position that the Vietnamese people should not "steal" vocabulary from the Chinese and French languages, the two sources of linguistic borrowing in the 1920s and 1930s, but should carefully invent all their own words, even if the invention process led to ungrammatical grotesqueries like *doi linh* for "revolution" instead of the popular Chinese import, *cach-mang*. To these patriots, the Vietnamese people suffered from a "hereditary sickness," which was the disease of scorning their own mother tongue. This sickness could renew itself through changing circumstances. Before the colonial period Vietnamese intellectuals who suffered from it had written their public documents in classical Chinese, and had deprecated the Vietnamese spoken language as "rustic." Now, under colonialism, such intellectuals were brandishing a new epithet for the Vietnamese language (they called it a patois) and were producing politicians like Bui Quang Chieu, the leader of the Constitutionalist Party, who was notorious to nationalists for writing and speaking in French. Most ominous of all, the coexistence of two languages under the colonial regime, Vietnamese and French, helped to create new partitions and barriers to understanding in Vietnamese society, and therefore helped to move it even farther away from achieving the ideal of a single national community. As one Vietnamese student put it, Vietnamese judges in colonial law courts gave their decisions in esoteric French (French that was esoteric to Vietnamese plaintiffs and defendants) precisely the way conniving buffalo dealers used a peculiar slang language with each other in order to deceive their customers.[7]

On the other hand, if Vietnamese intellectuals confined themselves to the Vietnamese language as it then existed, placing a limit upon the distracting foreign influences which it had incorporated, they could not easily adopt those tendencies in the depersonalized world view of post-Renaissance western Europe which some of them felt they urgently needed, in order to stop the schismatic sterility of the scholar cliques. The traditional Vietnamese language, enriched by its historical Chinese importations, abounded in terms which described moral doctrines, or social distinctions, or aesthetic qualities. It was, in fact, probably richer than many Western languages in these respects. But, as Phan Khoi observed, it lacked flexible variety in describing time, which had been less important in the precolonial society: for a diversity of subtly different Western time words like "often," "always," "ordinarily," and "usually," it could provide only one covering word of its own (*thuong*). Not having experienced a chaos of stimuli from an industrial environment, the Vietnamese language lacked enough pragmatic abstractions of completed or incompleted action. As Phan Khoi further observed, concepts like "fact," "matter," "affair," "thing," and "deed," which were expressed in many words in Western languages like English or French, all had to be matched by one crude, undiscriminating indigenous word (*viec*) in the 1930s.

Generally speaking, traditional linguistic borrowing from China had commonly served the explicit purposes of bureaucratic centralization and of hierarchy building in Vietnamese life. The combination of Chinese and non-Chinese words in the Vietnamese language had often been exploited to achieve ever more delicately, finely shaded degrees of etiquette and hierarchical consciousness. Indeed, mixtures of Chinese and non-Chinese words permitted the Vietnamese to convey fastidious hierarchical distinctions that were impossible in China: to choose an example from the 1920s, this might mean addressing an ordinary intellectual by the native term for "teacher," (*thay*) and addressing a less ordinary intellectual, like Phan Chu Trinh, by the Sino-Vietnamese term for "teacher" (*tien-sinh*).[8] With such a rich armory of hierarchical nuances at their disposal—a richer armory than the Chinese possessed—and without any counteracting importation of Western vocabularies which reflected declining social distinctions and expanding machine production processes, most Vietnamese intellectuals could epitomize with a vengeance the ancient Confucian definition of the educated gentleman, as the man who "is at peace with everyone but is distinctive from them." And "peace," in practical terms, would continue to mean the noncommunication and the mutual indifference of scholar cliques addicted to "family studies."

Linguistic isolation, therefore, was no more the proper recipe for a dynamic national community than the Gallicized, class-conscious linguistic atmosphere of the law courts could ever be. Yet the continued existence of linguistic politics in colonial Vietnam, with their contending parties and spokesmen, was a prominent factor in the disunity of the intelligentsia. This was another problem which revolutionaries could begin to resolve, as it turned out, only after they had come to power.

The Intelligentsia and Mass Communications

Familistic organizational styles and divisions over language policy were one kind of communications difficulty which affected the revolutionary history of Vietnamese nationalist intellectuals. Quite a different kind was provided by the fact that although the intellectuals were living in a society with a large degree of illiteracy in the rural areas, they were nonetheless compelled to rely heavily upon the printed word in order to reach their audiences. Books and newspapers were their instruments—and, when possible, oral poetry.

Film-making, a revolutionary form of mass communication, was virtually denied Vietnamese nationalists before 1945. A group of French businessmen began to invest in Vietnamese films as early as 1923: with the help of several famous Vietnamese stage actresses, they made a movie version of the most important work in Vietnamese literature, Nguyen Du's *Truyen Kieu*, "The Story of Kieu," written in the early 1800s. But before the year 1930—when Hanoi audiences saw their first talking film, "All Quiet On the Western Front"—watching films was barely considered to be even an esoteric form of amusement in Vietnamese cities. After 1930, French businessmen in Indochina did begin to build movie theaters in Hanoi, Haiphong, Hai Duong, Nam Dinh, Lang Son, and Bac Ninh, as well as in the south. The first feature-length Vietnamese sound films, made by Vietnamese producers (like Dam Quang Thien, a student at the Hanoi Medical School) and with Vietnamese actors, did not appear until the year 1937, relatively late in the colonial period. And these first Vietnamese films, made in the late 1930s, were normally financed by overseas Chinese businessmen. Such businessmen exercised a tyrannical management over them and typically filmed them, with Vietnamese actors, in Hong Kong rather than in Vietnam. (One Vietnamese film made in 1937, entitled "The Wind Storm," even portrayed double-decker streetcars of the Hong Kong variety running through the streets of a city that was supposed to be Hanoi.) In any case, colonial censorship, as well as a dependence upon overseas Chinese investment capital, prevented Vietnamese films made in the colonial period from presenting serious nationalistic themes.

The revolutionary film industry in Vietnam dates only from the year 1947, when the Viet Minh resistance army established film-making units that were attached to the political offices of several Viet Minh war zone commands. Viet Minh film makers slipped through the French lines into Saigon, bought film, printing frames, and film-rinsing equipment, slipped back into the forest to rejoin the guerrillas, and produced a succession of films about the war, with titles like "The Battle of Ben Tre" and "The Printing House of the Resistance."[9] In this way the war of 1946–1954 became the first episode in the history of modern Vietnamese nationalism to be anchored in the popular Vietnamese consciousness of politics by twentieth-century electronic technology. If it is true that film conveys information and political themes more rapidly, and in greater quantity, than books and newspapers, this may be a factor of some importance in the evolution of modern Vietnam.

Until the late 1940s, at any rate, nationalist propaganda had to be carried entirely by personal contact, by poetry oral and written, and (despite the fierce censorship) by urban newspapers. The French colonial regime itself sponsored the appearance of the first newspaper in Vietnam, a Saigon government gazette known as the "Gia Dinh Report" (*Gia Dinh bao*) which emerged in April 1865.[10] What especially distinguished this gazette was that it was written, not in Chinese characters, but in romanized Vietnamese. Romanized Vietnamese (known as *quoc ngu,* the "national language") originated in the seventeenth century. It was based upon Portuguese phonetics, and had been given its first systematic presentation in the Vietnamese-Portuguese-Latin dictionary of the Jesuit missionary Alexander of Rhodes, which had been published in Rome in 1651. From the colonial government's point of view, romanized Vietnamese, if it were really capable of supplanting the use of Chinese characters by Vietnamese intellectuals, might prove to be a useful weapon: it could remove these intellectuals from their membership in the ancient East Asian cultural universe and bring them closer to unquestioning membership in the French Christian one. The more such intellectuals read the "Gia Dinh Report" and other works of romanized Vietnamese, it was hoped, the more the Chinese philosophical treatises, histories, and religious sutras to which they long had been addicted would become transformed into unintelligible classical bric-a-brac, imprisoned in a writing system that could no longer be comprehended.

Not too surprisingly, this grand design failed. Romanized Vietnamese became, not a weapon of the colonialists, but a weapon of Vietnamese reformers and revolutionaries. From the outset, it had strong potentialities for serving the purposes of an unprecedented new populism. For one thing, it could be more quickly taught to Vietnamese peasants than the traditional cumbersome writing systems. For another, it helped to remove stylistic barriers between the intellectuals and the common people, barriers belonging to the old Confucian hierarchy, by freeing upper-class writers from some of the philosophical abstractions and aristocratic brevities of written classical Chinese or Sino-Vietnamese. By 1907, Saigon had acquired its first daily newspaper (not a government gazette) in romanized Vietnamese. And by 1915 Hanoi had one as well.

The newspapers and journals which nationalist intellectuals and reform-minded interest groups produced in Vietnamese cities in the 1920s and 1930s did have certain non-Western idiosyncrasies. Because precolonial Vietnam lacked any tradition of a daily press, the very idea of a daily newspaper itself was borrowed from the West. In cultural borrowing, however, as most social historians are well aware, borrowed ideas are usually married in some way to existing prototype institutions in the society that is doing the borrowing. It might not be too farfetched to suggest that most Vietnamese newspaper publishing companies of this period were the offspring of a marriage between the Western organizational tradition of joint stockholding companies and the Vietnamese tradition of small groups of mandarins combining to form select poetry-writing clubs.

Vietnamese newspapers certainly reflected the individualism of traditional mandarin poetry clubs, updated by western joint stock company methods. Newspaper publishing companies, mostly operating on a shoe-string financial basis, proliferated with an almost unchecked fertility in the cities, partly because they permitted Western-style entrepreneurship to be subsumed under the traditional literary bias of the Vietnamese elite. And poetry club individualism, combined with censorship, complex government regulations, and extensive illiteracy, meant a newspaper industry with swarms of daily and weekly journals that served only tiny, fragmented, essentially urban clienteles. In the year 1929, for example, the circulation of the most important Vietnamese language newspaper in the city of Hue, "Voice of the People" (*Tieng dan*), which was published twice a week, was 336,331 copies *per year*;[11] and the fact that it had to compute its circulation rates on a yearly rather than on a daily or weekly basis suggested the size of the mass audience for newspapers in central Vietnam. The newspaper which occupied the storm center of Saigon nationalism at the time of Phan Chu Trinh's funeral in 1926, the "French Indochina Times" (*Dong Phap thoi bao*), prided itself at that time on having just raised its publication rate from 2,300 copies per issue (in 1924) to 11,000 copies per issue.[12]

To measure the ties which the intellectuals were able to develop with other members of their society purely by the size of the circulation rates of their journals would be to work a rather primitive kind of historian's mischief. All over East Asia, revolution preceded the appearance of fully grown newspaper-oriented societies by a clearly discernible time margin. At the outbreak of the 1911 Revolution in China, for example, there were only about 650 newspapers and journals in China (of which only about 150 were well known)—as compared to the more than 3,700 newspapers and journals which existed in the United States, a considerably smaller society, on the eve of the American Civil War in 1860. Yet some Chinese, at the time, still called the 1911 Revolution the "black color revolution" because they were extravagantly impressed by the number of journals (with messy black print) which were promoting it.[13] In Vietnam, in fact, the true golden age of journalism is not presumed to have begun before 1932, when the iconoclastic journal "Customs" (*Phong Hoa*), the most famous of all literary organs of reform under French colonialism, began to appear in Hanoi. In the thirteen years between 1932 and 1945, some 428 significant new journals and newspapers are estimated to have appeared and disappeared in Vietnamese cities and towns, as opposed to a grand total of only 97 in the nearly seven decades between 1865 and 1932.[14]

Yet the tiny circulation rates of the journals sponsored by Vietnamese intellectuals are not totally irrelevant as indicators of certain characteristic weaknesses in the background of upper class writers. And these weaknesses had to be overcome before such writers could mobilize their fellow countrymen. The degree of the popular impact of new methods of communication like newspapers naturally was influenced by patterns in the traditional social structure, as elsewhere in East Asia. After the Meiji Restoration of 1868, Japan had known two different newspaper traditions, associated with two different social classes and indeed with two different cities. Early Japanese newspapers which appeared in Tokyo were called "political discussion newspapers." They were published by members of the old feudal warrior class who tended to be rivals of the Satsuma-Choshū warrior factions which had gained power in Japan in 1868, and they were concerned almost entirely with political controversies whose appeal was confined to the elite. Newspapers which appeared in the commercial city of Osaka, on the other hand, were called "small newspapers." They were published by Osaka merchants as money-making activities, they contained gossip and novels as well as news, they reached tens of thousands of readers, and they represented a counter-trend to the Tokyo political discussion journals.[15] (In China too, in the 1910s, there was a distinction between "big newspapers," written in classical Chinese for mandarins, and commercial "small newspapers," which were written in colloquial Chinese.)

In Japan, in 1868, there was already in existence a merchant class strong enough and well enough educated to produce commercial newspapers which could break down anachronistic elitist approaches to journalism. But in Vietnam the "small newspaper" phenomenon, a forerunner of mass newspapers, was slower to appear, partly because of the absence of a significant indigenous merchant class. And denied any substantial confrontation with the innovative spirit of an indigenous commercial class, even Vietnamese revolutionaries, as unconscious upholders of mandarin tendencies, clung inordinately to the old classical communications psychology.

What was this psychology? Enshrined at the heart of it was the belief that "the purpose of literature is to carry doctrine." As Fukuzawa Yukichi had noted, unfettered, unconstrained, unstereotyped public "speeches" were relatively alien to East Asia. The dissemination of free-floating information and facts, detached from moral indoctrination, lacked strong support from Vietnamese tradition. A writer in the revolutionary journal "Customs" pointed to this factor, in 1933, as an obstacle to the development of popular Vietnamese journalism:

> In the old days, stories in our country, by obligation, had to have the full combination of loyalty, filial piety, purity, and right conduct in them before people were permitted to read them. If they did not have these things, even though the story might be most interesting, and corresponded with the actual facts to a great degree, not only could no one read it, but our people would regard it as something that should be banned. The elders of our country in the old days wanted transmitted writings to be lessons. Therefore, it had to be, that people in the stories who did good things always reaped good results, and cruel people always came to cruel ends.
>
> At the time that newspapers in romanized script made their appearance, our people further decided that newspapers could only be organs for maintaining the moral principles and customs of our society, and could only be that, nothing more. . . if you want to teach morality, there are already whole books on moral principles; there's no need for stories and newspaper articles. A book of stories or a newspaper is the same, if you want to get people to enjoy reading them you must make people happy, or move them. And if you want them to be happy or moved, you need writings that correspond to reality. The situation of the times, things that the ears hear and the eyes see, are all living lessons, influencing people and making them ponder. For example, if you want to teach a person to be a filial child, you employ a scene of a mother raising children, with

tenderness and hardship and sacrifice, in order to move him. Isn't
this better than "weeping hard enough to ripen the bamboo shoots
and call up the fish from under the ice," as in *The Twenty-Four
Stories Of Filial Piety?* Journalism is an occupation that, in the West,
people have understood for a long time. Never in the West do they
use newspapers to expound moral principles . . . newspapers are only
organs for disseminating thought and general information. It is only
in our country that moralists still have the belief that our people
should be fascinated by stories of morality, and should like to read
them as if they were novels.[16]

The Education of the Intellectuals and Their Search
for New Public Personalities

Colonial educational policy was characterized by a tension between cultural expansionism and racial elitism. The colonial regime certainly wished
to bring comprehensive French cultural influences to bear upon Vietnamese youth. School holidays in colonial schools commemorated episodes in French history rather than in Vietnamese history, and there are
many Vietnamese intellectuals alive today who can ruefully remember
childhood school days when they were compelled to sing "We are the
descendants of the Gauls," on the anniversary of Joan of Arc. Yet the
colonial regime—or, more properly, the Frenchmen resident in Vietnam
who were its chief support—also feared that the colonial schools might
produce an unmanageable army of French-speaking Vietnamese intellectuals who could compete with native Frenchmen living in the colony for
positions in the colonial administration. A Frenchified elite did appear,
therefore, but it was one sufficiently restricted in size so that it would not
upset the apparatus of alien rule. According to statistics that are now
famous, or infamous, higher education (university level) in all of Indochina
in 1939 ministered to the needs of just 732 students.[17]

Did the weakness of colonial education hinder or stimulate revolution?
The forces of anticolonialism naturally made it one of their most hotly
pressed issues. From the standpoint of the need for stronger forms and
reflexes of organized associationism in Vietnam, the poverty and the confusion of colonial educational institutions were damaging—if there is any
validity in the old axiom, never completely proved perhaps, that the higher
a person's level of education, the greater the rate of his participation in
voluntary associations.

During much of the colonial period, the educational system in metropolitan France itself had two tiers or series of grades. One series of grades
was reserved for a minority of brilliant pupils, with the purpose of transporting them through primary schools, middle schools, and university, and
the other series of grades was reserved for the majority of the population,
with the purpose of giving them primary school training. The first series

was the home of the *lycée,* an elitist super middle school with an abundance of resources. The second series included primary schools and
"complementary" or superior primary schools: the latter added perhaps
four years to the regular primary school education but did not in any sense
function as middle schools. Essentially, it was this second kind of education which was imported into Vietnam, and given the ambiguous title of
"Franco-Vietnamese" education.

"Franco-Vietnamese" primary schools consisted of six grades, divided
into two levels. To their six years' worth of education could be added
another four years of "superior primary school" education, acquired in the
cities which possessed such schools—Hanoi, Nam Dinh, Haiphong, Hue,
Vinh, Qui Nhon, Saigon, Can Tho, and My Tho, for example. Only a select
handful of Vietnamese pupils ever penetrated the three or four French
lycées which functioned on Vietnamese soil. For most Vietnamese students, especially from the lower classes, extended primary school education
was offered as a forlorn substitute for real middle school education. Some
"colleges" for Vietnamese—such as the National Studies College at Hue, or
the Protectorate College at Hanoi—eventually offered an abbreviated form
of *lycée* education.

To say that this educational system lacked rational arrangement, and
that it was filled with occult or meretricious barriers and roadblocks, is to
miss the point. Vietnamese intellectuals grew up in a world in which, as
the conservative reformer Pham Quynh publicly observed in 1926—and
he is a good witness—educational powers were all in the hands of foreigners, racial factors abounded, and educational questions quickly became
political questions.[18] The insensitive juxtaposition of various modes of
ascent in society, educational and cultural, sharpened social schisms but
also sharpened a nationalistic consciousness of those schisms. Schools like
the Chasseloup-Laubat school in Saigon actually combined under the same
roof "Franco-Vietnamese" education for less advantaged Vietnamese
children with *lycée* education for the sons of French colonists and for the
sons of privileged Vietnamese upper class families. But the hothouse Vietnamese children, usually Catholic, who attended the *lycée* section of such
an amalgamated school, rather than the "Franco-Vietnamese" section, did
not necessarily learn to love their French schoolmates. As one of them
later testified, bitterly:

> Living in the French world [of the Taberd School in Saigon in the
> 1940s] and yet unable to become truly French, I felt myself to be
> "superior" to other Vietnamese because I was allowed to be close to
> the French, yet at the same time I felt myself still "inferior" to the
> French on some point or other. The psychological makeup of the
> Vietnamese people who lived in the one French world was truly
> complicated. To speak the truth, we were not "inferior," but, on the
> contrary, were better than the French on many points, especially in
> academic studies. All through my secondary school years, there was

not a single French boy who could stand at the top of the class. . . .
One time, I heard two French monks discussing with each other the
phenomenon of French students being inferior to Vietnamese
students, and one of them blamed it on the hot climate of the region.
We were not inferior but we still *felt* ourselves to be inferior, because
living in the French world meant that we were compelled to wish for
things for ourselves that we could not have: how could we have
protruding noses and curly hair like the French, how could we be
regarded as real Frenchmen. . . . In order to compensate for this
inferiority complex, we in turn began to despise the gang of French
children, attributing to them stupidity and slow-wittedness, teaching
them obscene Vietnamese words and then bursting out laughing
every time they repeated those words without comprehending
them. . . .[19]

The educated intellectuals who did emerge from this complex but underdeveloped school system then had to turn around and make their appeals
for national cohesion and necessary cultural change to a society which had
missed the revolution in primary school education which was occurring
elsewhere in East Asia.

Japan, in 1929, was spending almost 70 percent of its total educational
budget upon primary school education. In China, in the 1920s and 1930s,
university and middle school education in the cities and towns expanded
much more rapidly than primary school education in the villages, which
provincial governments were required to finance.[20] Incomplete Ministry of
Education statistics for China for 1935 suggest that only about 30 percent
of the Chinese children who were eligible for primary school education (15
million out of 49.4 million) were actually being accommodated in the
schools.[21] Even so, however, these Chinese statistics, reflecting a relatively
stagnant village educational world, indicate a much superior performance
to that revealed in statistics published for the rice-rich colony of Cochin
China a year later, in 1936. Of some 600,000 Vietnamese children eligible
for elementary schooling in Cochin China in 1936, only 136,432 were
apparently enrolled in school—or less than 25 percent.[22] Moreover, even
the Vietnamese primary schools were linguistically stratified. It was
impossible to find a homogeneous educational community even here. The
schools were subdivided into two ranks or categories. Teachers in the lower
rank taught their pupils in Vietnamese, while teachers in the upper category taught their pupils in French, "filling their brains" with "blurred"
French phrases which the pupils could not understand (as Pham Quynh
put it), at the same time making it difficult for pupils from the lower
halves of the schools to move into their upper halves.[23]

The educated intellectuals themselves, at the top of this society, were of
course anything but a homogeneous group. Force-marched into a laboratory of colonialism and acculturation which they could not control, they
produced their own unprecedented diversity of new cultural and personal-

ity types. And on a more conscious level, the intellectuals engaged in a rather poignant search for ideal personality types which they hoped would be useful in any reconstruction of Vietnamese society, personality types which were not so much an "internalization" of Vietnamese society as it actually existed in the 1920s and 1930s as they were individualized projections of the desired national community of the future. As the intellectuals' range of choices expanded, problems of organization grew even greater.

Attempts to import and domesticate Western behavior—and Western personality types—began fairly early. The leading Vietnamese architect of colonial primary school education, Tran Trong Kim (d. 1953), began writing primary school textbooks after he became a teacher at the Hanoi Pedagogical School in 1911. By 1924 he had become chief of the commission for drafting primary school textbooks. Although he was himself a rather eccentric devotee of Confucian philosophy, Kim inaugurated the social demystification of traditional Confucian ethics in Vietnam. He did this more by means of their tactical circumscription than by their abolition. He published a controversial "Primer of Ethics" in 1913, for use in the "Franco-Vietnamese" primary schools, which treated ethics as a specialized part of the educational curriculum, separable from other parts, rather than as a subject which exercised a diffuse but unchallengeable domination over the entire educational process, as it had when education meant the memorization of the Confucian classics. The primer overflowed with terms which Kim had translated into romanized Vietnamese from French—"conscience," "tolerance," "obligations," "personal responsibility"—none of which had had fully exact counterparts in traditional Vietnamese.

Furthermore, Kim's rather dull, matter-of-fact definitions of these terms continued to reduce the majesty of classical ethics in Vietnamese life. His primer declared, with really rather revolutionary bathos, that "conscience" was a "court of law dwelling within one's own feelings. When one does something good, it rewards one, and makes one feel satisfied and happy; when one does something evil, it punishes one, and makes one regretful and worried." No stolidly judicial, mechanically reacting "conscience" of this kind had ever been expounded by Confucius and his disciples. Obligations to oneself were described in Kim's primer as physical training and washing oneself; obligations to others were represented as offering respect to their property, dignity, and freedom; and obligations to society were described as patriotism and paying taxes. Kim's primer did not completely reject traditional ethics: it recommended the maintenance of ancestor worship "in order to recall the favors of one's ancestors, expending all their feelings and strength creating a home and a country for one." But by giving such traditional virtues as filial piety a limited, specialized role under "family ethics," instead of treating them as absolute, unlimited principles which applied to national politics too, Kim did introduce into primary school education in Vietnam after 1913 a slightly altered vision of the role of the individual in society.[24]

The next stage in the campaign by certain intellectuals to domesticate Western personality types in Vietnam was characterized by outright translations. Translations are, indeed, one of the truly important but unstudied pivots of East-West relations. The preeminent early translator of Western literary works into Vietnamese, Nguyen Van Vinh, was a friend of Tran Trong Kim and a fellow Tonkinese graduate of the Hanoi Interpreters' School. Having gone through the interpreters' school rather than the Confucian examination system, which was still functioning when he graduated in 1898, Vinh became a partisan of romanized colloquial Vietnamese and a vociferous opponent of the use of Chinese and of Chinese characters. He translated into Vietnamese for the first time selected writings by Plutarch, Balzac, Dumas, Jonathan Swift, and Victor Hugo. His Vietnamese translation of Molière's great seventeenth-century comedy of manners, *Le bourgeois gentilhomme* ("The Bourgeois Nobleman") which had first been performed in France in 1670, became one of the triumphant early productions of the modernizing Hanoi theatrical profession.

Le bourgeois gentilhomme, as Molière wrote it, satirized a rich, vulgar shopkeeper, Monsieur Jourdain, who led the life of a stupid but determined social climber. Monsieur Jourdain paid out vast sums of money to parasitic dancing instructors, music teachers, and philosophy professors: he wanted these men to teach him gentility, gallantry, and all the other presumed arts of frequenting the aristocracy, so that he might avoid having to hobnob with his fellow shopkeepers. His employees, however, laughed at him behind his back. In Nguyen Van Vinh's hands, the French "bourgeois nobleman" was metamorphosed into an erratic Vietnamese mandarin who was uncertain when he could properly wear his tunic. In Molière's play, the socially incompetent Monsieur Jourdain, trying to prove his cultural worth, made a silly attempt at writing a courtly love song about a cruel mistress who spurned her lovers. In the French text, the sense of the bourgeois nobleman's song went roughly: "I believed that Jeanneton/Was as sweet as she was beautiful./I believed that Jeanneton/Was sweeter than a sheep./ Alas! Alas! She is a hundred times,/ A thousand times more cruel/ Than the tiger of the woods." Vinh's translation of this song, however, converted Jeanneton into a rather improbable Vietnamese seductress: "I used to think of Miss Thieu/As being both kind and pretty./I used to think of Miss Thieu/As being as meek as a sheep./I did not suspect that Miss Thieu was corrupt,/In corruption not very different from/The tiger living in the jungle."[25]

Nevertheless, despite the crucial and obvious fact that the Western ideas and institutions which were being transferred to Vietnam were being changed at their point and time of entry by a handful of cultural brokers like Nguyen Van Vinh, the very act of bringing a seventeenth-century French comedy to the Hanoi stage, and crudely Vietnamizing it, was significant. Perhaps the theatrical spectacle of a floundering bourgeois nobleman (or his Vietnamese mandarin alter ego) attempting to learn more cosmopolitan ways tallied with anxieties and ambitions common to many Vietnamese intellectuals at that time. At least it may have satisfied their common intuition that even the antics of Molière's Monsieur Jourdain might provide clues about how to acquire, or how *not* to acquire, more "modern"—and perhaps more effective—reflexes of behavior. Nguyen Van Vinh, however, was not the most aggressive spokesman for the cause of Vietnamese adoption of the qualities and conventions of Western middle class personalities.

Vietnamese intellectuals had been searching for a technique—or for methods of expression—which could most satisfactorily propagandize the need for social change. By the early 1930s, their search had ended. The answer to their prayers had materialized, in the form of the modern Vietnamese novel. It is almost impossible to convey to Westerners the importance of the novel as a force for social revolution in twentieth-century East Asia. In Vietnam, political ideologues ranging from Catholic conservatives to communist guerrillas have written novels to dramatize and demonstrate the sources of decadence in their society that must be eliminated, and the ideal types of behavior that must replace them. The great novels of Vietnam (and China) in this century have often served roughly the same purpose that, let us say, pamphlets and sermons served in the English Revolution of the 1600s or in New England just before the American Revolution.

There were a number of reasons for this celebration of the novel by reformers and revolutionaries. For one thing, political views placed in the mouths of characters in novels were not so likely to be censored or suppressed by the colonial regime as political views expressed more directly in undisguised tracts and polemics. For another, social change could be seen most simply and conveniently as a dialectic between two opposing sets of forces, one in favor of change and the other opposed; and it was easier to present this dialectic in a novel, where different characters could be created to represent the different forces, than in an ordinary, one-dimensional exhortation. Then, too, the iconoclasm of every revolution has its cultural limitations: that is, revolutions have limitations imposed upon them by the cultural traditions of the societies in which they arise. In Vietnam, as in China and Japan, the term for "novel" literally meant "small tales." It was a deprecatory expression at least twenty centuries old which referred, as far back as Han dynasty China, to street-corner storytellers and to what were considered to be their morally dubious stories. Novels, in sum, were an art form officially despised in the traditional period (but very popular and influential) which revolutionaries in this century could nonetheless inherit without having to invent, and could then exploit in a new way while staying firmly within the context of the cultural history of their own people.

No group of writers used the novel more brilliantly as a platform for social change than the "Self-Reliance Literature Group" (*Tu luc van doan*).

This was the most influential coterie of writers in Vietnam in the 1930s, and it deserves a vastly more detailed exploration than can be made here. The presiding genius of the group, Nhat Linh, was born in 1906 in Hai Duong province in the north, to a father who had served as a district magistrate and as a colonial clerk in Laos. Nhat Linh himself languished as a clerk and as a middle school teacher in Hanoi before he began to dazzle the Vietnamese literary firmament. The other central members of the "pleiad" of this group included Khai Hung, Tu Mo, The Lu, Hoang Dao, Thach Lam, and Nguyen Gia Tri, an artist. The manifesto of the group, published in the eighty-seventh issue of its journal, "Customs," in March 1933, called in effect for a social revolution in Vietnam without considering very closely the relationship between such a revolution and political power: an omission that was reminiscent of American-educated Chinese intellectuals like Hu Shih in the same period. The manifesto proposed the preparation or translation of books that stressed "social thought" and were egalitarian; it demanded the use of easily comprehensible writing styles with a minimum of Chinese words; it exalted the new and the "progressive"; it emphasized individual freedom; it condemned Confucianism; and it advocated the application of Western "scientific methods" to Vietnamese literature.

Hoang Dao published a political-cultural guide for Vietnamese youth a few years later which crystallized the political outlook of the Self-Reliance Literature Group more explicitly, while still avoiding the subject of political power. This guide suggested that the Vietnamese people in the 1930s most needed a commitment to the new; a belief in progress; a life based upon idealism; the performance of work for society; the development of character; the emancipation of women; the cultivation of the scientific mind; participation in politics for national rather than for individual purposes; physical training; and, most crucial, a willingness to submit to organizational methods. Vietnamese conservatives regarded his book as a gospel of "extremism," more ultracritical of the past than any other document of the 1930s.

With the marked exceptions of Khai Hung and Thach Lam, the authors of the Self-Reliance Literature Group all too frequently depicted in their novels a medley of ideal personality types which were acutely and aggressively Western—personality types which had floated so far ahead of Vietnamese realities that they seemed "outside society," as one critic of Nhat Linh wrote. Their difficulty was that only a minority of Vietnamese intellectuals were ardently willing to embrace science and organization and individualism without showing even the slightest deference to what might be called the familiar plots of Vietnamese culture and of Vietnamese personality development. To some extent, Nhat Linh, as an urban, European-educated writer, was struggling to transfer the values of industrial Europe to colonial Vietnam without being able to transfer their social environment to Vietnam along with them.

A number of examples could be cited of the Self-Reliance Literature Group's creation of industrial society folklore which imitated the industrial society folklore of western Europe and North America, long before there was any real industrialization in Indochina. Perhaps the most extreme examples were the detective stories of The Lu. Some analysts have suggested that Western detective story heroes like Sherlock Holmes could not have appeared in the literature of preindustrial Europe. The prototype, Sherlock Holmes himself, was an individualistic superman detective whose distinguishing characteristics included intense specialization of knowledge and a capacity to work scientifically. The poet The Lu, admiring such a hero, created his own Vietnamese Sherlock Holmes. Naming him Le Phong, he made him (in a series of stories) the leader of specialized empirical investigations of crime, conducted within a framework of objective laws; and he endowed Le Phong with the same Promethean urge to collect and unravel scientific data as his British counterpart. The Vietnamese Sherlock Holmes even had a Vietnamese Lestrade as a foil:

Mr. T. Phung worked in the Hanoi secret police office; he was a young man who did his work very carefully and clear-sightedly. He usually met Le Phong during secret happenings that they both discovered very quickly. Seldom would he go against the opinions of Le Phong. Le Phong never concealed the secrets of his trade. He skilfully expounded his judgments in a modest manner, thereby allowing the detectives of the secret police office never to lose face. . . .[26]

Needless to say, the rise of such parasitic industrial society folklore corresponded to very little that was real in Vietnam in the 1930s, being stimulated by an alien social system that was thousands of miles away. In one of these Vietnamese Sherlock Holmes stories, the private detective Le Phong talks to himself about the nature of the suspicious mystery woman, Mai Huong, whom he is investigating. His creator The Lu's barely repressed desire to transfer the phenomena of Western industrial societies to colonial Hanoi leaps right out of the detective's reasonings:

Mai Huong, Henriette Mai Huong . . . a Vietnamese girl who has become a French citizen . . . a person who is extraordinarily clever, what's more a person very well educated . . . one possibility is that she is the chief plotter of this affair, and a second possibility is that she's a clever agent of the assassins. A group of assassins whose activities are very quiet, very perfectly handled, very secret, no different from a very skilful party of organized crime in the Western countries. And this young girl is just like that. As strange, as dangerous, and with the same unusual gestures as those of a female gangster in America or in England. Who would have thought that in our Vietnam, abominable monsters like that would have appeared.[27]

Literature like this was too superorganic and unreal to supply either an ideology, or a set of realistically adoptable model personalities, capable of regenerating and reorganizing Vietnamese society. Yet appropriate new public personalities were desperately sought by Vietnamese intellectuals, almost as if they were magic-bearing masks. If such personalities could not be fabricated from unabashed Western stereotypes, could they be fabricated from previously unnoticed bedrock elements in the East Asian classical culture of the past? To move from the first part of this question to the second is to move from the atmosphere of alienated, Westernizing intellectuals like Nhat Linh and The Lu to the atmosphere of Pham Quynh. Pham Quynh was a journalist and politician who accepted the concept of French-Vietnamese collaboration yet, paradoxically, regarded himself as a nationalist who was also searching for the secrets of a better organized national community. The answers, for Pham Quynh, could not be found in the characters of Western playwrights or in Vietnamese simulations of the adventures of Sherlock Holmes.

As Pham Quynh saw it in 1925, Vietnam's first need was an "ideology" or a "mass of thought" which could serve as a "master-spring" for national reconstruction. "Ideology" he defined as meaning a fusion of intelligence with idealism: he gave the term a positive, East Asian classical flavor which it lacked in Western languages. To Pham Quynh, the reason for Vietnam's "instability" and "crudity" was the fact that its people had good thoughts but did not know how to combine them and assemble them into an ideology; the task of Vietnamese intellectuals now was to "organize thought," in order to develop a basic spiritual strength. And the only ideology that could cope with the "ten thousand difficulties" of the Vietnamese people's situation was nationalism: the nation had to be worshiped the way saints and gods had been worshiped in the past.

Western romanticism and science of the Sherlock Holmes kind had little place in Pham Quynh's scheme, nor did social and sexual egalitarianism. (Once again, it is necessary to stress that the link between nationalism and egalitarianism or populism which the communists were later to make so fashionable was far from inevitable.) In the course of a characteristically tortuous argument Pham Quynh clumsily differentiated "nationalism" from "patriotism." Patriotism was a "sentiment," and sentiments wavered and wandered and could not be verified: they were the property of "little girls." Nationalism, on the other hand, was a means of thought; it was exact and specific, and was the property of "male heroes." In creating a nationalist ideology, the Vietnamese people would have to "tolerate" Western culture, in the interests of self-preservation. But Confucianism was the spiritual "quintessence" of Vietnam. It taught familism, and filial piety, and the ideal of the "gentleman" who knew how to live in a "whole" manner, without blaming other people for his misfortunes or behaving passionately in small matters. The Vietnamese people, indeed, would now have to regard Confucian doctrines as an "ancient citadel wall" which could still resist the currents of depravity outside the country.

This approach to the question of a national ideology avoided the trap of importing artificial industrial society values from the West. But it fell into the equally dangerous trap—from the nationalist point of view—of rummaging in a compost heap of ideas and narcotic West-defying formulas to which the Vietnamese nation did not have a clear private title: it stressed those elements in Vietnamese culture, mainly upper class, which had originally been imported from China. To protect their own traditional elitist culture on nationalist grounds, Vietnamese conservatives now were forced to minimize China's hegemonic role in the East Asian classical world. Pham Quynh stipulated sharply that those aspects of Vietnamese culture which had been transmitted from China were not the "private property" of the Chinese nation, but were the common property of all East Asia, including Japan and Korea as well as Vietnam. But this was still not very satisfying to nationalists in quest of national uniqueness.

Moreover, a national ideology required the existence of an ideal national character. Pham Quynh unhesitatingly identified the ideal Vietnamese national character, in 1925, as that of the "wind-and-stream" man, the imperturbable intellectual who tranquilly offered wine to his friends.[28] But this was a tradition which the Vietnamese shared unmistakably with the Chinese. The "wind-and-stream" man (Chinese: *feng-liu;* Vietnamese: *phong-luu*) was usually a Taoist romantic whose spirit was supposed to transcend petty distinctions of poverty and wealth, or of high rank and low rank, and who was supposed to live according to his own canons and standards rather than according to those of others. He could not be conquered by an army or seduced by a large salary; he prized spontaneity and naturalness, would not accept external constraints, but never behaved excessively. Chinese neo-Taoist philosophers in the fifth century A.D. had been particularly famous for their expositions of the qualities of the "wind-and-stream" romantic tradition.

Now the search for serviceable or for politically sanctifying personality types and their antecedents is a common feature of revolutions and of nationalist movements both. Revolutionaries, in particular, often invoke specious but useful models from the past to give legitimacy and coherence to their own innovations and departures in wholly different historical contexts. The cult of things Roman during the French Revolution offers examples—like that of Babeuf, who signed himself "Gracchus." Pham Quynh's apotheosis of the "wind-and-stream" man was not a bizarre contribution to this search; and it would be dangerous to deny that imperfect versions of the "wind-and-stream" man are a reality in twentieth-century Vietnam. (Some of them have played an indisputable part in preventing any easy transfer of Western political party behavior to Vietnamese soil.) But there were two reasons why Pham Quynh's position was doomed to win few adherents. First of all, his longing for a tighter ideological organization of Vietnamese society, which he was hardly the only Vietnamese to express, could not be implemented by the "wind-and-stream" romantics whom he exalted, since these genteel mavericks could not, by definition, enjoy organization or allow themselves to be organized. Second, the "wind-and-stream" man was unsatisfactory to other Vietnamese nationalists as the key to a revitalized society, even more unsatisfactory than a Western-style detective investigator. As an ideal it suggested moral toughness but also passivity. Unscrupulous men might even be able to use it to rationalize the reflex of "nonaction," and to imply that lack of violent resistance to French colonialism was a cultural predisposition, molded by centuries-old virtues, rather than the temporary result of successful French repression. In addition, the ideal was too Chinese, and reflected too much a set of class characteristics rather than genuinely national characteristics. It was not a conspicuous peasant tradition: most Vietnamese peasants could not afford to be permanent "wind-and-stream" men.

Most members of the small educated class of lawyers and doctors and absentee landlords who appeared in Vietnamese cities in the 1920s and 1930s did not adopt either the innovative individualism of the characters in "Self-Reliance Literature Group" novels or the complacent, old-fashioned ritualism of the mandarins of the past whom Pham Quynh admired. In a manner reminiscent of the deprived children in the famous psychological experiment who overestimated much more than rich children the sizes of designated coins in drawings they were asked to make of them, because of their greater need for such coins, this small urban middle class placed an exaggerated emphasis upon the material possessions it was able to acquire, also perhaps as a way of salving its sense of subordination to French administrators. But its materialism did not embrace any confident love of the new, as might be found in industrial societies. Society was actually seen metaphorically as a pond in which the water levels rose and fell in a way beyond the control of the pond's inhabitants: it was the colonial power which "made the wind and the rain." The only way to survive in such a pond was to imitate one's peers and to duplicate, without much thought, the role performances of one's ancestors. Le Van Truong, the most prolific writer in Indochina in the decade 1935–1945, (and perhaps the most popular), commented in one of his novels upon the behavioral sterility of the Vietnamese town dwellers as they lived in their "pond":

> The salons of the high society families in Vietnam do not have any individual characteristics of their own. Just by closing our eyes and sitting at home, we can guess fairly exactly how the salons of Mister X and Mister Y are decorated, and what's in them, if someone informs us first how many rice fields Mixter X and Mister Y have, how many houses, and how much yearly income. They may differ in petty details, but in general they all have cupboards set up close to the wall, a carved plank bed just in front of the cupboard, and in the front part of the house, near the doorway where you go in and out,

four chairs and a Chinese-style table with a tea set, with a pair of antique vases, with some ceramic ware and chinaware scattered about, and with a few carved wood tablets with parallel verses inscribed upon them hanging here and there. . . . If in the minds of every high society Vietnamese there are a mandarin, a row of houses, and a few landed estates, then in the salons of these people there will also invariably be a cupboard, a carved bed, a tea set, a table and chairs made in the Chinese style, a pair of antique vases, and a few carved wood tablets. . . . "The Vietnamese people are good at being imitative," that's what people say. In other words, because our people are intellectually lazy and lack individuality they do not possess any special initiatives. . . . In the stagnant pond of high society squirm the catfish and the perch, wallowing in the stinking mud in the hope of obtaining some extra fat for themselves.[29]

What was missing in Vietnam, far more than in China before World War II, was a middle class confident enough of its own position to gamble on the most moderate kind of noncommunist revolution without fearing for its own survival. The imitation-prone urban society which Le Van Truong described, with its static view of the world, could never have qualified. Even the psychology of its children was confined to an imitative conformism which sheltered neither East Asian values nor Western values sufficiently honestly, if the writings of disgruntled representatives of this age group are to be believed. One normal school student, later famous as a revolutionary politician, charged in 1925 that Vietnamese youths had converted pleasure itself into the talismanic ideology that so many Vietnamese sought, and that their only concerns were food, clothing, the mouthing of French poetry, and the upper class quest for jobs in government service. Many people were talking of the "disease of melancholia" of Vietnamese youth. But, this student wrote, their sadness was really just another surface illusion, or imitative fad, comparable to the fads of ordinary people who wore silk tunics in order to look like mandarins; it was not the ultimate, desirable, exemplary sadness of a proud Napoleon humbled by exile to the island of Elba.[30]

Vietnamese reformers and revolutionaries, anxious to change and strengthen their society, continued their experimental parade of promoted and demoted ideal personality types. The appearance of the first communist cadres, in the late 1920s, in a sense climaxed the parade. But even if the more activist intellectuals had not been frustrated by the constrictions of colonial education, and by the pedestrian apathies of the "stagnant pond" of educated Vietnamese urban dwellers, there were times when they were also checkmated by forces within themselves. Their selection of new personalities could be governed by a fatalistic historicism as well as by the desire to create a more powerful, cohesive nation. Not all Vietnamese intellectuals of the period before World War II saw French colonialism the way the communists were to see it—as the capitalistic exploitation of Vietnam by a small European elite, aided by Vietnamese compradors and most notoriously represented by financial machines like the French Bank of Indochina. This was, after all, a borrowed vision, made originally in the West.

For some intellectuals, the French conquest of Vietnam could be seen in terms of the Buddhist law of cause and effect. This law proposed that men were rewarded or punished for deeds committed in earlier existences. According to this perspective, Vietnam was suffering from the imperial ravages of France because the Vietnamese state which the French destroyed had itself been a cruel colonial power: it had conquered the Cham people of central Vietnam in the 1400s. Nearly five centuries later, the Vietnamese people were paying for the unprincipled aggression of their ancestors. One of the "Self-Reliance Literature Group" novelists dramatized this theme, with yet another shuffling of personalities, in a famous short story, full of a kind of sensuous despair, which he published in 1941. In this tale by Hoang Dao, a young Vietnamese man found himself in a small boat on the river outside the walls of the city of Hue, being paddled by a ferry boat girl who was singing a song of lamentation as she paddled:

> Xuan trembled and closed his eyes again. Within the two rows of dark trees quietly reflecting their own shadows in the mirror of the river, he suddenly caught sight of strange figures, undulating above an ancient capital city whose architecture was that of the Cham people. . . . He saw materializing before his eyes the landscape of the country of Champa as it had just been destroyed, and he naturally assured himself that Huyen [the Vietnamese ferry boat girl] was a Cham princess, forced by the victorious Vietnamese to serve them wine and sing them songs that they had never heard. The princess would have been as cold as Huyen was now, but her innermost feelings would have been numb with shame. . . . The Vietnamese soldiers would have been self-confident and boastful, but when they heard her sad lament they would all have stared, half haunted and half respectful. . . . At that moment he did not find in his veins the passions and character of a victorious person any more. He only saw that inside himself he was numb like a defeated person because he suddenly realized that Huyen was a fellow countryman of his, and that the song she had sung a while ago was a song of lament of the period in which he was presently living. A kind of vast sadness and resignation overflowed his soul. . . . Was it that this influence of the song about the loss of one's country affected him because of a situation of emotional weakness, or was it that inside him he already carried the strings of a mournful musical instrument, which, when slightly touched, vibrated into sound?[31]

The Ambiguities of Familism as a Source of Organizational Power

All this tentative exploration of the modern uses and meanings of different personalities—whether they were the "wind-and-stream" romantic kind, or fifteenth-century Vietnamese conquerors of Champa, or Western individualists—raised the question of the family, which remained the nursing-ground of all the real personalities which existed in Vietnam in the 1920s and 1930s.

The endlessly repeated truism about the Vietnamese family is not unjust: the family was the undisputed foundation of traditional Vietnamese society, economically, politically, and judicially. Groups outside the family, ranging from craft guilds to secret societies, were organized on various pseudofamilial bases. People derived their personal status from their family status; people were controlled through their families; and people constantly determined their own behavior by assessments of how it would reflect upon their families. The kinship system, whose form (if not always its informal substance) deliberately resembled the Chinese kinship system, was patrilineal. In such a formally male-centered world, marriages, which were arranged, required the bride to go live with the family of the groom—a rather different pattern from the marriages of the modern West, in which bride and groom both leave the families into which they were born and set up their own third household. The traditional Vietnamese family was a little like a modern business corporation: it survived the deaths of its individual members or "shareholders" at any one point in time. It was designed, in other words, to be a permanent corporate group. Since the survival of the family depended upon a supply of male heirs, who brought in the daughters-in-law and maintained the ancestor worship cults, a variety of devices—concubinage, or even adoption—were sanctioned to rescue a family from the consequences of the infertility of any of its members. One such adopted son, in Thanh Hoa province in the early nineteenth century, became such a celebrated paragon of filial devotion to his adopted parents, after changing his surname, that he was chosen to serve as a village chief and a canton head for more than twenty years on the strength of this reputation. He even earned an encomium in the official court biographies of the Nguyen dynasty.[32]

The strategic relationship within the family was not the relationship between husband and wife. Rather, it was the relationship between father and son. Filial piety dominated the core of the Vietnamese ethical system. In order to prevent the disruption of the family, the father-son relationship was maintained after the death of the father, by means of ancestor worship. Even the most austerely rational Confucian intellectuals regarded this as a necessary ethical discipline which could help to uphold proper group standards of behavior, through the "acknowledgment of one's origins." Ancestor worship required the installation of an altar table in the home and the performance of sacrifices on important anniversaries, on lunar New Year's, and on the first and fifteenth days of every month. New brides were presented to the ancestors, at this table, as the climax of their wedding ceremonies. As early as 1682, at a synod of missionaries and their followers at Hoi An in central Vietnam, Vietnamese Catholics debated the issue of whether ancestor worship was a "religion" or merely a communal ritual in which they too could legitimately participate. Ultimately, many of them compromised by not installing altar tables for ancestor worship in their homes but employing altars to Christ for the same purpose, praying for the souls of relatives who had departed on the anniversaries of their deaths. Ancestor worship also integrated Vietnamese lineages, those collections of families which were genealogically linked to each other by the male heads of each family to a common ancestor, and which had developed residential proximity and important social ties. Rites were conducted at the graves of the founders of lineages and, if they existed, in the lineage ancestral halls. Many families and lineages kept written genealogies of their lines of descent. In the precolonial period, the entire economy of the village of Yen Thai on the edge of the West Lake at Hanoi centered upon the specialized handicraft production of the thick dark gold paper which was used exclusively for the compilation of these genealogies.

From the point of view of Vietnamese revolutionaries, this traditional family system was undemocratic; it was inegalitarian; it suppressed youthful initiatives; and it demanded the investment of so much emotional and social energy and loyalty that it blocked the emergence of badly needed organizations outside, and above, the family. At the same time, however, the family remained the primary source of whatever cohesion did exist in Vietnamese society. Even Vietnamese students in France, as late as 1929, could nostalgically praise the "closeness" and the "profound affection" of the Vietnamese family, where everyone ate in common "from a single food tray," and could denounce with corresponding vigor the coldness and the lack of solidarity of what they disdainfully called the "each person one room, each person one plate" French family system.[33]

By the 1930s, reformers and revolutionaries had a new fear. They feared the possibility that Vietnamese conservatives, ardent to preserve traditional institutions like the family, were becoming de facto supporters of French colonialism in order to do so. Such an attitude on the part of cultural conservatives represented a striking about-face from the position of their nineteenth-century mandarin ancestors, who had linked their conservatism to resistance to colonialism, partly because they had seen colonialism entirely as the agent of destruction of the nation's institutional heritage, not of its preservation. But by the 1930s the colonial power was no longer so disruptively awarding mandarins' positions to Catholic outcasts, or to coolies and interpreters. It was, on the contrary, hoping for a museum-like calm to fall over the remnants of the old Vietnamese hierarchical order. In his most famous novel, "A Severance of Ties" (*Doan tuyet*), published in

1935, Nhat Linh pits his independence-minded Vietnamese heroine against a conservative court prosecutor. And he makes the prosecutor admit the growing identification of interests between the colonial government and the devotees of the hierarchical Confucian family:

> Who can count the young girls who have been whirled giddily about because of that gust of romanticism which I have just mentioned, who have completely forgotten the Heavenly-appointed offices of the pious daughter-in-law and the virtuous wife, who have forgotten how to be the pillar of the family like the virtuous wives of the old Vietnamese society. . . . Up until now the French have served to maintain the social foundations of the people of the protectorate. We ourselves cannot be broadminded in this matter, because broadmindedness is actually weakness. Bringing about the demolition of the family, the demolition of the society, are faults that lie with us. . . .[34]

The situation of course was very complex. To the extent that it stayed intact, the autocratic, hierarchical nature of the family furnished the colonial government with an inexpensive source of social control and political stability—*unless,* indeed, the family in question had a tradition of resistance to French rule, as many did, in which case the old family values—especially the duty of the children to follow their fathers—worked decisively against the colonial regime. The father-son relationship was really one of symmetrical interdependence. The son owed his father obedience, respect, the provision of grandsons, career success, and the proper services of burial and mourning; but the father owed his son moral and intellectual training, material support in his immaturity, the provision of a wife, and the provision too of resources with which a successful career could be built. The father's authoritarianism, which Western writers of books about China and Vietnam are far too fond of emphasizing, was really an incidental characteristic of his all-important teaching function. The belief was common (if not universal) that if the father showed his children too much kindness and love when they were young, or fondled them instead of being "severe" and making them regard him the way "they would look at the faces of demons and gods," his children would become persons "difficult to teach."[35] In sum, the relationship between father and son was intense but not necessarily cold or intimidating, or resented by the sons, consciously or subconsciously. The voluminous writings about the family by premodern intellectual rebels in China and in Vietnam rarely treated the father-son relationship as a subject of controversy or as a symbol of oppression. Family solidarity tended to be undermined not by the tensions of this relationship, but by the tensions of the relationships among brothers—or by the tensions of the relationship between mother-in-law and daughter-in-law.

Following the patterns of the Chinese-style marriage, which had been domesticated in Vietnam for centuries, women were incorporated into alien patrilineal families, which bought the rights to their fertility, their sexual services, and their domestic labor by the payment of a bride-price. The politics of marriages were tortuous: marriages were after all inter-lineage alliances. Exchanges of gifts, and the payment of the bride-price, gave both the families involved a strong ritual and financial stake in the marriage. This, rather than the compatibility of the bride and groom, was supposed to guarantee the marriage's success. In theory, men could divorce their wives for seven reasons—the famous "seven grounds for expulsion" which had become established in Chinese law during the T'ang dynasty, when northern Vietnam was still a conquered Chinese protectorate. These seven reasons were: infertility, lustfulness, jealousy, talkativeness, thieving, disobedience to her husband's parents, and leprosy. Few of these shortcomings were regarded as shortcomings because they were damaging to the husband's private happiness or interests. As a Chinese scholar in the Ming dynasty (1368–1644) pointed out, in an essay defending the "seven grounds for expulsion," a leprous woman could not take part in the family sacrifices and thus was not upholding family traditions; an infertile woman was guilty of creating a situation which would lead to the discontinuation of the family sacrifices; a woman who was lustful was causing turmoil in the lineage; a woman who was jealous was causing turmoil in the family; a woman who talked too much was sowing discord; a woman who thieved violated right conduct; and a disobedient woman rebelled against morality.[36] What was really at issue in most of these reasons was family and lineage solidarity, not the ties between husband and wife.

Because Vietnam was not China, and because beneath most imported Chinese institutions in Vietnam there usually flowed indigenous undercurrents that are difficult to plumb, it would be dangerous to assume that the "seven grounds for expulsion" ever enjoyed a consistent sovereignty in Vietnamese life. Most of the time they were probably dead letters. Women, on the whole, held greater informal rights in Vietnamese society than they did in China. Even in Vietnam, however, the daughter-in-law owed her mother-in-law the same obligations that a son owed his father, but could expect much less in return. The relationship was lethally unbalanced. The main check upon the autocratic domination of the mother-in-law was her need to preserve the health of her daughter-in-law so that she could bear sons. The bride's adaptability within her new household certainly depended upon her submissiveness. The great fifteenth-century Vietnamese statesman Nguyen Trai (1380–1442), in the magisterial poetic moral code "Songs of Family Exhortation" (*Gia huan ca*) which he wrote especially for female audiences of the medieval period, made the ideal woman in his poem say about her marriage:

> Books have the expression "when you enter a household you
> inquire about its prohibitions," so when I speak I must become

skilled in self-restraint. Being graceful and soft in my words in order to satisfy the household, I must realize that only when I follow the instructions of my husband will the household be at peace. I should not rely unduly upon my beauty and my talent, and then belittle and scold what things my husband says. If I speak inconsiderately as if I belonged to a superior social station, it will echo up to the ears of the ancestors more than it should.[37]

The words "the instructions of my husband" concealed the fact that husbands, to satisfy the demands of filial piety, had unflinchingly to obey their mothers. It was upon this principle that the mother-in-law's autocracy rested.

By the 1930s, all these anachronistic patterns of human relationships had come to be regarded by intellectuals both reformist and revolutionary as crucial obstacles to the development of new (and anticolonial) political and social commitments by the Vietnamese population. Such intellectuals were searching for new forms of organized communities; and the irony here was that while they were responding, in this search, to what they regarded as the disintegration and lack of organization in Vietnamese life, in one vital realm—the realm of the traditional family—they were now forced to believe that disintegration had not gone far enough.

Familism, indeed, may even have undergone a certain psychological intensification in Vietnam after the 1880s in reaction to the decline of other institutions. At least in the short run, the old family system was not destroyed by, but could actually accommodate, many of the meagre early results of modernization. In the cities, for example, Vietnamese women received more education than they had in the past. But their greater level of education did not always lead them into more individualistic marriages in which the public competition for "face" among their mothers and family elders could be avoided. As Thuy An, a woman novelist and poetess, noted sardonically in a 1933 Hanoi journal article, the greater educational qualifications of these women were simply absorbed into the mercantile ferment of the old-style family's marriage politics:

Let's go into a middle-class family that has a daughter about to be given in marriage. We see her mother and the madame go-between in an uproar, the former saying to the latter: "The 300 piasters cash that the mother of the groom has given us is too little, clothes and shopping for my daughter have already consumed almost 200 piasters, and there is still the banquet that will come in a few more days. We fear that 500 moon rice cakes, and 500 earth rice cakes, will not be enough, we must make up the extras ourselves because we know many people. As for automobiles, I have decided upon eight automobiles, I have to maintain face with the people of the village, four or five automobiles would be awkward and inconvenient." The go-between bargains, the mother persists, and the daughter is no different from an article of merchandise displayed in a market, with sellers and buyers agreeing on a price.

Such a custom of giving your daughter away by sale seems to change day by day according to the degree of evolution of the girls, but who would suspect that it daily gets worse. For girls who have some learning, and a capacity to seek ways of making their own living, the "price" gets increasingly expensive. At the time they are married their mothers, in addition to computing the value of their own efforts at raising their daughters and giving them moral instruction, count in addition the efforts expended giving them an education. . . . Adding together all these efforts, it amounts to a formidable sum of money, and causes the grooms to be terrified when they hear it. Hence many men sigh and say: "I would much rather marry an ignorant peasant."[38]

The assumption behind all this haggling was that married daughters, because they no longer contributed to the family into which they had been born, were a net gain for the family they married into. Against this assumption Westernized romantics protested in vain.

Being the bedrock of the society, family patterns were the most difficult to change. Yet, if they were not changed, they could survive obtrusively enough to negate the effects of changes elsewhere. The dilemma of reformist revolutionary intellectuals with regard to the old family may be summarized this way: if the Confucian family suddenly disappeared, existing forms of social discipline might disappear with it, undesirable psychological aberrations and social deviations might take their place, and Vietnamese society would become even more difficult to organize. On the other hand, as long as the fortress of the Confucian family remained perfectly impregnable, genuinely new patterns of political socialization and behavior would be slower to emerge. The ultimate destiny of the family quickly became, therefore, one of the truly cardinal questions of the Vietnamese revolution.

But conservative intellectuals were equally incapable of unanimity on the subject of the family, and this is worth noting too. Even conservatives were not immune to the attractions of Western-style individualism as a possible rejuvenating force in Vietnamese life. But the more important point is that traditional Vietnamese thought harbored its own tensions between associationism and individualist tendencies, making the conservatives of the 1920s and 1930s the heirs to an ambiguous heritage. Something of its ambiguity appeared in one of the most definitive statements made about the family by a conservative before World War II, the famous essay on "Family Education" written by Bui Quang Huy, a teacher at the Hanoi Protectorate School. Huy first published his essay in 1925.

In the traditional Vietnamese family, according to Huy, the father and the older brother were the "pillars" of the household, the models for their children and younger brothers. The hierarchical standards of this family were exemplified by the classical slogan "the upper act, the lower imitate." Family members sacrificed themselves for the happiness of the whole family community (the *doan the* theme again) "like ants with regard to their swarm, like bees with regard to their beehive." Now, however, the world esteemed individualism. Blood relationships that once bound people to their kinsmen had changed into feelings of selfishness, and older and younger brothers no longer "wrapped up and sheltered" each other. With such loneliness and ingratitude, how could there be a community? Men were shaped by three forces: the environment, the society, and the family. Vietnam's environment was not now causing any harm: it remained the environment which had produced the heroes of the past (Le Loi, Quang-trung, Nguyen Du). Reforming the family was easier than reforming the national society, because, as Huy now observed significantly, "the powers of building and changing reside with us" in the case of the family. If it was impossible to reconstruct the ideal (and semimythical) "crowded family" of the past, with many generations of people living under one roof, it might be possible at least to make blood relationships count again, and to revive mutual help among blood relatives.

Obviously, Huy emphasized family reform rather than reform of the society because the ancient Confucian principle of beginning with the "inner invigoration" of the family and working outward to the world coincided all too clearly with the situation that colonialism had robbed the Vietnamese people of control of their own national community, leaving the family as the only community they could reconstruct on their own. This conception of the family as a small but potentially self-maintaining institution in a generally decaying society was undoubtedly contradicted by the facts. Yet the substance of this conception, dictated by both Confucianism and colonialism—confidence in the efficacy of the small group as the only starting point in an unpromising social milieu—was to reappear in many other Vietnamese contexts, including those of the early communist party cells. Conservative thinkers hardly monopolized it.

What were Huy's plans for reforming the family? He argued that children should be taught to know two things—"self-government" and "community." And the most suitable recipe for reform would be nothing less than a grandiose Vietnamese revival of the styles of classical group play that had been practiced by the sons of "Chinese nobles" back in the "ancient period." Briefly, to Huy this meant the cultivation of play arrangements among carefully chosen blocs of elite households. Under supervision, the children of these households would all be assembled at one of the households one day and at another one another day, and encouraged, under the Olympian management of their elders, to eat and play with each other, to practice their literary lessons, and to make ceremonious visits to temples and scenic sites together. What this amounted to was the resurrection of a kind of Neo-Confucian mutual guarantee system, but at the level of children, in which parents calculatingly chose their children's friends, served as hosts for the children's group play sessions, and promised to regard the children of the other parents temporarily under their roofs as their own. These introverted household arrangements, Huy hoped, would create a "community ethic" among the children.[39] He did not point out that this classical community ethic would also serve to insulate upper-class children from the increasingly heterogeneous social relations of the cities and towns, where there was now more mixing of social classes and more casual interclass exchanging of patterns of behavior.

Yet Huy's desire for new demonstrations of manipulated communalism in Vietnamese life was modified by his admiration of egotistical, individualistic Western heroes like Napoleon. The arrival of such a hero was the panacea of panaceas: Napoleon's "heroic spirit," Huy believed, inflamed the hearts of Frenchmen even after he was dead. The resolution of such heroes "flowed over the surface of the waters" and "lingered in the branches of trees and on the tips of the grass." On the other hand, it was not likely that such heroes, whom Vietnam badly needed, could be comfortably produced in the atmospheres of conformism which characterized the traditional family and the group play procedures Huy was championing. Here was a conflict in conservative thought, between individual heroism and associationism—and it was an old conflict. Despite Huy's celebration of Napoleon, the conflict in his mind was not so much a conflict between Western romanticism and Vietnamese Confucianism as it was a conflict between the traditional belief in the importance of education ("an untaught child is not a person") and the equally traditional belief in the possibility of sudden, natural sagehood or Buddhahood. Who, after all, had taught Confucius to be a sage? Who had taught Shakyamuni to be a Buddha?

Like many early revolutionaries, therefore, Bui Quang Huy, an apostle of conservatism, could not completely make up his mind. Was organized associationism, or the short-cut solution of the partly predestined appearance of unconstrained individual heroes, more likely to save the country? Praying for the latter, he denounced the tyrannical Vietnamese fathers of the past who had treated their sons like "machine people," so that it was as if a "current of electricity" had to pass from the father to the son before the son could make any decisions or movements. There were, in brief, two poles in his thought. One was that of Confucian associationism in defense of old values; the other was that of sagehood-style individualism which possessed inspirational leadership qualities. Something was missing: the possibility of an associationism that could work for sweeping national reforms.

Conservative Intellectuals and the Prestige of Confucian Methods

In the final analysis, the old family—and that partial restoration of all its somewhat mythical cohesive magic that Bui Quang Huy recommended in 1925—could be defended intellectually against the voices of revolution only if Confucianism itself could be defended intellectually. And here, among all the East Asian peoples, the Vietnamese were at a marked disadvantage.

In 1930 the editor of one ephemeral Vietnamese periodical ("East-West Weekly Report," *Dong-Tay tuan bao*) made the observation that of the three East Asian countries of Japan, China, and Vietnam, Japan had understood Confucianism most wisely, as a result of which it had managed to survive as an equal of the West; China had understood and applied Confucianism less wisely; and Vietnam had understood it and applied it least wisely of all. Nostalgic eccentricities lurked behind this observation; yet it possessed enough validity, in a curious and unintended way, to doom an entire generation of Vietnamese conservatives before World War II.

The outstanding monument to what might be called "Confucian nationalism" among Vietnamese intellectuals was a sprawling 804-page book by Tran Trong Kim entitled "The Confucian Teaching" (*Nho giao*). In preparation since 1920, it reached its first completed form about 1930. Like other members of the group of writers which sponsored and wrote for the Hanoi journal *Nam Phong* (roughly, "The Vietnamese Ethos") between 1917 and 1934, Kim wanted to find values in the Vietnamese past that could be preserved even while he himself was modifying the teaching of ethics in Vietnamese primary schools, as has already been discussed (see page 85). "The Confucian Teaching" was written as a mammoth work of apology and praise for Confucianism—which was to be cherished not just because of its intrinsic values but because it was such an inseparable part of the Vietnamese past. And even Phan Khoi, the most pertinacious critic of Kim's book, admitted with considerable emotion in his review of it that "not to know Confucianism is not to be Vietnamese."[40]

Kim, of course, went much farther than this admission: in his view the "Confucian teaching" had produced worthy fathers, filial sons, enlightened rulers, and loyal bureaucrats for centuries in Vietnam, and had brought unparalleled advances in public enlightenment. It had, he conceded, brought less welcome things, like the materialism and opportunism of the civil service examinations. But that was because it had been misunderstood. The teachings of the sages had not been properly implemented. Confucianism had never been hostile to new currents of thought, and was quite compatible with the scientific perspectives of the modern age. The Vietnamese people should, therefore, "follow the times" by studying economics, physics, chemistry, and other Western sciences. But they should, at the same time, compromise between East and West by using the "Confucian teaching" as the foundation of moral education, adopting its centuries-old doctrines for the purpose of creating and maintaining "a special personality." Once again, the question of personality types, and the part they played in fostering national cohesion, had returned to torment the intellectuals.[41]

Just in the realm of political and economic change, Kim's espousal of harmonious combinations of Confucianism and science, and of Confucianism and democracy, was bound to be as clouded as similar programs had been in China. What about science and Confucianism, first of all? The hegemony of the Neo-Confucian doctrine of the "investigation of things," which had been a basic element in the thought of many Vietnamese philosophers before the colonial period, dated back to the impact of the Chinese philosopher Chu Hsi in the twelfth century. It looked scientific; but its love of research and classification had been applied in fact mainly to humanistic and historical studies, not to nature in any methodical way. (Le Qui Don, the eighteenth-century philosopher, was a notable Vietnamese practitioner.) Confucian philosophical doctrines, moreover, were much more concerned with natural laws than with laws of causation, more inclined to tell men that they must behave in certain ways than to explain to them why they behaved in a certain way.

What about democracy and Confucianism? The problem here was that the Western term "sovereignty," when first translated into Vietnamese in the early part of the century, became extremely ambiguous. Kim argued that Vietnam could make a comfortable transition from monarchy to democracy (with a monarch) without sacrificing anything of value in Confucianism, because the Confucian precept of loyalty to the prince actually meant loyalty to the "princely rights" (*quan quyen*) which were being exercised by the ruler, not loyalty to the man who was ruler himself; and every form of government possessed a collection of princely rights. This dubious reinterpretation of the Confucian canon—which did, however, contain ironic echoes of a Vietnamese past when monarchs unable to defend their kingdoms had been abandoned—was assailed by Kim's critics. They declared that what every form of government possessed was "owner rights" (*chu quyen*), not princely rights. (Both these terms were being freely used in Vietnam then to translate the Western concept of sovereignty.) Furthermore, the critics asserted, owner rights resided in constitutions. It was constitutions to which people were loyal, not the powers of kings or presidents, and this meant that Kim had seriously misunderstood the focus of loyalties in Western democracies.[42] Confucian loyalties, in sum, could not be modernized or mildly reformulated to satisfy the needs of a democratic society.

However, it was not in the realm of political and economic change that the distinctively Vietnamese flavor of the pathos of Kim's book, "The Confucian Teaching," was to be found. In the past, Confucianism had been regarded in Vietnam more as an all-permeating ethical system than as a formal philosophical tradition. Now, Kim attempted to establish it as a philosophy, equal to any Western philosophy. To do so, he described the metaphysical speculations of a host of different Chinese thinkers (including the controversial Wang Yang-ming, whom he claimed belonged to the direct, orthodox succession to Confucius and Mencius) and suggested that the original thought of the historical Confucius himself had evolved from a profound metaphysical curiosity, like that of a good Western philosopher, rather than from more prosaic social and political interests. The trouble was that many of the less prominent Chinese philosophers whom Kim so painstakingly described in his book had played no role whatsoever in *Vietnamese* life. Most of Vietnam's history in the early modern period had been dominated by a limited, relatively recent form of Confucianism—essentially, a narrow, simulated version of the state Neo-Confucian orthodoxy which had developed in China no earlier than the eleventh and twelfth centuries. And the link between Vietnam's imitative state Neo-Confucianism and those parts of the Vietnamese past which were most useful to twentieth-century Vietnamese patriots—for example, the tradition of heroes who had fought Chinese invaders—was tenuous. Much more than in China, the historical inspirations of Vietnamese nationalism could be detached from the history of Confucianism—if not from informal Confucian virtues and ideals. Kim had great difficulty identifying specifically the positive role that Confucianism had played in Vietnamese history, as opposed to Chinese history. His difficulty was reflected only too clearly in the fact that in the 804 pages of his book, he devoted only 15 pages to the subject of Confucianism in Vietnam itself.

The consequences of this difficulty significantly affected the Vietnamese revolution, intellectually and socially. For they affected the intellectual prestige of the conservative opposition to the revolution. Conservative nationalists were unable to defend, plausibly enough, the *Vietnamese* role of the formal ideology which had, for centuries, reinforced and legitimized the "big family," for example. Until Japan was crushingly defeated in 1945, the Japanese political elite were much more successful than their Vietnamese counterparts at rationalizing the continuing role of Confucianism in Japanese life, for at least three reasons.

First, the Japanese had an historical tradition of having had a multiplicity of their own Confucian philosophical schools, which meant that for centuries they had been "intellectualizing" the differences between themselves and China. As a result of this indigenous tradition, in the 1920s Japanese intellectual contemporaries of Tran Trong Kim, like Hattori Unokichi, could make a distinction pleasing to nationalists between the teachings of Chinese Confucian scholars of the past few centuries, which were wholly "Chinese" and "unsuited" to other peoples, and the original teachings of Confucius, which were universal, and to which modern Japanese philosophers, not Chinese ones, were really (Hattori claimed) the most faithful and appropriate heirs. The Vietnamese, in contrast, had a tradition of political and military resistance to China but not the same kind of well-defined tradition of philosophical separateness within the East Asian classical world, going back centuries, to which intellectual nationalists could appeal.

Second, after 1868 Confucianism in Japan became more extensively blended with the indigenous Shintō religion. Indeed, it became part of the ideological underpinnings of an emperor system whose legitimacy depended more upon its unbroken permanence through time than upon the virtue of individual emperors, as it would have in China and Vietnam. The Confucian virtues of loyalty and filial piety *were* successfully converted into loyalty to a modern nation-state in Japan; but this occurred at the cost of accepting heavily mythological Shintō perspectives on the question of a ruler's legitimacy which Chinese and Vietnamese Confucian intellectuals would have rejected as wholly alien to Confucian teachings.

Third, in Japan before the coming of the West, Confucianism had served as the status ethics of the ruling warrior class. It had been linked to "the way of the warrior" (*bushidō*), the bellicose, self-sacrificial behavioral code of the Japanese military aristocracy. In Vietnam and China, on the other hand—admittedly, much more so in China—Confucianism, as the philosophy of scholar-bureaucrats rather than of warriors, had reflected very different elite orientations. It had come to imply the civilized man's deprecation of fighting and soldiering. And Vietnamese and Chinese nationalists, concerned with repelling Western aggression, were in no mood now to admire a creed which they associated with pacificism and military weakness.[43]

But even the contrast between Vietnamese and Chinese Confucian nationalism is striking. The Vietnamese variety was weaker than the Chinese, simply because it lacked enough discernible native philosophic roots. Chinese Confucian nationalists could make Confucius, or Mencius, a national culture hero, even though this might destroy the old Confucian spirit of universality. Vietnamese Confucian nationalists were unable to do so. Because Vietnamese Confucianism had been, in formal terms, a borrowed bureaucratic ideology, it had not produced many figures of its own who could be reinterpreted or apotheosized, or fertile varieties of thought that could be reinterpreted to serve patriotic ends. What were the results of the relative weakness, compared to China, of the Confucian element in Vietnamese conservative nationalism? For one thing, conservative patriots who wished to reconcile Western industrialism with traditional East Asian social behavior and intellectual tendencies—that is, reconcile the individualistic, "materialistic" West with the supposedly more "spiritual" East—had to borrow their rationalizations much more from Western thinkers themselves than from the East Asian classical past. In 1918, Pham Quynh supplied an interesting example of this:

> Our own ancient civilization was a civilization that was purely
> quality, the quantity part had shrunk to nothing. Therefore for a
> long time we only revered the spiritual dimensions of things and
> neglected the structural elements. For this reason we do not possess
> adequate qualifications for struggling in this world of today which is
> purely quantity-oriented.... Thus ... we must be clever in recon-
> ciling the two dimensions of quality and quantity so that we balance
> them equally, only then will our progress be steadfast. On the quan-
> tity side we must study the cunning professions, the tricks of compe-

tition today, in order to seize sovereign rights in the sphere of economics . . . we must develop our entrepreneurial abilities to the full. . . . On the quality side we must gather up the new thoughts and spirit in order to add strength to the roots of our old civilization. We must expand our knowledge, train our behavior, preserve the good customs and habits of the past, and not be infected by the perverse, clamorous customs of today, but protect our national essence and nourish our national soul.[44]

The intellectual (as opposed to cultural) weakness of Vietnamese conservatism revealed itself in all its awkwardness in this rather famous essay, read by several generations of Vietnamese school students. For Pham Quynh had to acquire his entire scheme—of a "struggle between quality and quantity"—from a minor Italian historian, Guglielmo Ferrero. Ferrero had just published a book, *Europe's Fateful Hour*, in which he attacked Western civilization, but especially that of America, for adopting a "quantitative" approach to life and for believing that the main purpose of humanity was the production of the greatest possible quantity of wealth in the shortest possible time. To this he opposed the former interest in "quality" of Europeans, which he feared was being lost. Rather than doing as so many Chinese conservatives had done with the same thing in mind—invoke the ancient East Asian classical distinction between "substance" and "function" in order to justify the coexistence of Chinese ethics with Western science—Pham Quynh was driven to exploit a modern Italian distinction between the civilizations of America and Europe, and then recast it to suggest the bigger difference he felt existed between the West and East Asia.

This situation continued into the second half of the twentieth century. In the era of American intervention in Vietnam, Americans frequently asked (hardly in a disinterested way) why opponents of revolution in Vietnam had no ideology, effective or otherwise. There were many reasons: one of them, at least, could be found in Vietnamese Confucianism's peculiar inadequacies as an intellectual quarry for nationalists. Conservatives like Ngo Dinh Diem were forced to borrow soporific Western doctrines like "personalism" in order to buttress their intellectual respectability; Chinese conservatives, even ones like Chiang Kai-shek, needed fewer Western ideological reinforcements of this kind. (Paradoxically and ironically, Vietnamese conservatism's lack of sufficient philosophic roots in the Vietnamese past occasionally permitted Vietnamese communist revolutionaries to be more publicly traditionalistic than their Chinese communist counterparts. For they were, and are, less encumbered by any need to explain that they were not accidentally paying homage to well-known intellectual traditions, associated with specific national philosophers, which contradicted Marxism and belonged to their political enemies.)

The relative weakness of Confucianism as a national ideology in twentieth century Vietnam, compared to Japan and China, obviously had less dire consequences for Vietnamese revolutionaries than it did for Vietnamese conservatives. Certain surviving Confucian reflexes did prevent the intellectuals within the revolutionary groups from formulating, more quickly than they did, alternatives to the situations in which they found themselves. But the continuing strength of archaic Confucian philosophies among even some of the revolutionary intelligentsia, while it deserves the attention it has received, was surely not the most important factor in retarding the growth of a new politics in Vietnam. The most important factor was also the most highly visible one: the failure of colonial educational facilities to expand sufficiently, or sufficiently uniformly. The smallness of these facilities was no bar to revolution. But it did insure that much of the revolution would be fought rather blindly—and with an unusual dependence upon the visions of a small group of Vietnamese revolutionaries who had managed to educate themselves outside Vietnam.

4

Colonialism and Premonitions
of Revolution in the
Countryside

Historical Stabilities and Instabilities in Rural Society

As corporate bodies managing their own communal resources, European villages underwent a certain decline between the eighteenth and the twentieth centuries. During this period it was not unusual to encounter European historians who regarded the disintegration of the ancient rural communal institutions as a tragedy, arguing that they had long represented equality and happiness.[1] Not surprisingly, the temptation to mourn the ideal village community of a bygone age has been much more acute in twentieth-century Vietnam than it ever was in Europe. The suddenness of the impact of colonialism, combined with the large scale of the forced cultural changes that occurred, made this virtually inevitable. Even Vietnamese revolutionaries have been inclined to concede that the premodern Vietnamese village was the home of a communal resourcefulness whose surviving reflexes cannot be ignored, given the national need for organization of all kinds in order to hold off the West. But what was this communal resourcefulness, if it existed? And if it did exist, how was it affected by French colonial rule?

First, there is the question of Vietnamese images of the village and of rural people. After World War I, Vietnamese writers, like Chinese writers, wrote a significant number of works describing the miseries of rural poverty and, in some instances, glorifying the eternal values of the countryside, proposing that the countryside could still breed people of a daring creativity who could never be found living in the towns. Such literature was not controlled or sponsored only by the communists. Nguyen Tuan, a superb short-story writer, was in some respects a good example. He published an immensely popular story entitled "The Calligraphy of the Man Who Was Condemned to Die," about 1940. The theme of the story was one of prophetic romanticism: rural rebels did not enjoy political power, yet, but they were still capable of conquering the pride of decadent urban bureaucrats and their agents, by means of the purity and the boldness of their talents and insights. Nguyen Tuan's hero was a well-educated but unchastened rural outlaw, famous for his excellent calligraphy, who had been captured and condemned to be executed. The jailer in charge of the prison where the illustrious outlaw was confined was haunted by the knowledge that if he could only entice his prisoner into writing some Chinese phrases on ten squares of white silk that he had bought, and then hang the silk for display, he would have a precious art object that the whole world would covet. Eventually, he did persuade the condemned outlaw to write something for him. But after the outlaw had finished writing on the silk, he turned to the gratified but startled jailer and said to him, with blunt regality:

> "Life here [in the provincial town] is mixed up. We advise you officials to move your residences away from here. This place is not the sort of place where you should hang a piece of pure white silk with such clear, incisive calligraphy. We don't know where you found this [Chinese] ink but it's very good and very fragrant. Can you detect the fragrance emanating from the inkbowl? We advise you truly: you must find your way back to the countryside . . . only then should you let your thoughts turn to the enjoyment of calligraphy. Living here, it is difficult for you to preserve your natural goodness intact, and sooner or later, your originally good and righteous life becomes all soiled and besmirched. . . ."
>
> The prison official was moved. He bowed once to his prisoner, and spoke a sentence which the tears falling into his mouth caused to be choked off: "Please give me your instructions."[2]

For at least three decades, many educated Vietnamese have learned this story almost by heart. But what about its underlying premise? That countryside outlaws could triumph over the hirelings of urban administrations, not in economic or in athletic-military terms, as in Western "underdog" stories, but on a cultural basis, by means of the fact that the countryside permitted them both a legitimate rebelliousness and a right to use the high culture as a weapon against urban elites? Such a premise raises questions about the traditional patterns of integration of Vietnamese rural life, which in turn were crucial factors in the emergence of agrarian revolutions.

To begin with, Vietnamese rulers constantly feared the rich, unpredictable creativity of village cultural and religious life. Therefore they tried to control it. In A.D. 1663 the Le Huyen-ton emperor issued a forty-seven-article code of instructions for Vietnamese villagers. His code was reissued about a century later, in 1760, and may be regarded as a reliable index to the moral atmosphere of rural life which dynasties desired, and the social tensions in rural life which dynasties deplored, in the seventeenth and eighteenth centuries. All the articles of the code were to be read and expounded in each village on various "rites" days, such as the lunar New Year's and the various days of prayers for wealth and good harvests. The thirty-fifth regulation in the code made it very clear that there was, in fact, a gap between the orthodox, approved high culture of the Vietnamese court and the cultural interests of the villages. For this article stipulated that villagers were not allowed to "cut printing blocks and to engrave and print" Buddhist and Taoist visionary writings (which were food for religious sects), or "national tales" (which were food for secret societies) and ballads and poems "which are associated with profligacy." Only the "classics, histories, philosophy, belles-lettres, and essays" could be printed and circulated in the villages. Most of these were imported from China or written by Vietnamese scholars who obeyed the most orthodox (and most politically harmless) Chinese literary modes.[3] In the nineteenth century, only a few decades before the French conquest, the Sinicized Vietnamese court's futile determination to eliminate the emblems as much as the realities of a discordant village cultural life reached a new severity with the emperor Minh-mang's petty struggle to persuade Vietnamese rural women to wear trousers (in the Chinese style) rather than skirts.[4]

Efforts to enforce an orthodox culture in the villages were related to efforts to enforce respect for one orthodox system of political symbols. And such a system of symbols did run from the capital city to the villages. Concern with the maintenance of various village rites, one of the preoccupations of the Le dynasty village regulations, included exhortations to the villagers to respect the temples and graves of "meritorious ministers" and soldiers of the past which the dynasties themselves had built in the villages. These shrines now remained as motionless hostages of masonry, protected by the court but located in the villages, whose preservation and inviolability were an important test of the court's continuing power at the grass-roots level. Far from all being tokens of popular causes, some of these dynasty-sponsored village monuments were even sharp affronts to local pride. The Nguyen dynasty, for instance, built an "honoring of fidelity shrine" to the memory of its general Tong Nhat Phuc in Binh Dinh province. Binh Dinh had been a hotbed of hostility to the Nguyen cause before 1802, and Phuc had noisily promised that if he ever conquered it he would "obliterate even its grasses without a trace."[5] He did not completely keep this promise. But Binh Dinh peasants preserved his shrine with little enthusiasm.

Despite these tensions between court and village over the politics of culture, it is noteworthy that Nguyen Tuan's brilliant calligrapher outlaw who shamed his urban jailers did not come from the lower classes in the village. Rural revolts usually required educated leadership. And few peasants ever acquired a comprehensive classical education or won degrees in the civil service examination system. Education did integrate the village directly at one social level. Students of a particular teacher formed a "same disciples' association" which solicited subscriptions from the villagers to finance their school. If their teacher died, the members of this association had to march in his funeral procession to his grave, wearing white turbans and tunics, and then mourn him for three years, as if he had been their father. Teachers, consequently, were enabled to play powerful roles in village life and politics, given the fact that they could draw upon an organized constituency. But this constituency did not—in normal times—reach deeply into the peasantry.

Nevertheless, traditional Vietnamese society was much better integrated than many Western accounts would suggest, and one reason for this was the social breadth and consistency of its values. Most peasants did share and uphold, as much as they could financially afford to, the ideals and spirit of the traditional family system and of ancestor worship. Furthermore, the traditional family system was rather unfairly attacked in the 1930s by urban critics for the isolation and selfishness it bred: in fact, it had spawned customs in the traditional period which not only reinforced the solidarity of blood relatives but also reinforced village solidarity. Intense family loyalties were by no means always the enemy of the growth of better village community loyalties.

Many examples could be chosen to prove this: one important one was the custom, especially widespread in the north in the precolonial period, of "buying posterity." Villagers who did not have children of their own to maintain "incense and fires" sacrificial cults to them after they were dead might purchase the performance of such cults, from the village, by contributing money to the village public funds and, in addition, donating portions of their rice fields to the village so that the villagers could use the income from these fields to keep the sacrifices going. Some people bought posterity merely for themselves and for their wives. Others bought posterity for parents on both sides of the family. As for the village which had received money and land from people who were buying posterity, it had to draw up a signed document of agreement and afterwards erect a stone stele confirming the agreement in the village meeting house. Upon this stele were engraved the lineage and personal names of the person who had bought posterity, the names of the prefecture, district, canton, and village where he lived, the amount of money the people in the village had received from him and how it was to be spent, the amount of "contracted for posterity" land that he had set aside and where it was located, and the days of the months of the year upon which the people of the village were to offer sacrifices for him.

In practice, buying posterity often had little to do with the biological fertility or infertility of the gentry. Rich householders in the village who possessed both property *and* many children nonetheless might buy posterity. They might do this to help the village's funds and also to increase their own prestige, by getting the whole village, rather than just their own lineage, to hold sacrifices to them on the anniversaries of their deaths. As for people who had landed possessions but no children, buying posterity encouraged them to contribute some of their possessions to the village, where they could be used for the common advantage.[6] Short of an exhaustive investigation of nineteenth-century Vietnamese village land records (which no one has ever carried out), it is impossible to say precisely how deeply this custom influenced village history on the eve of French colonialism. The point is that a tradition like ancestor worship worked both ways, as far as village stability was concerned: it could encourage customs leading to the modification of individual family fortunes as well as produce a psychology which caused individual families to try to keep their wealth to themselves.

Moreover, the values which Vietnamese peasantry and elite shared with each other were not exclusively the values of a repressed harmony which offered no emotional release. Within the precolonial village, it was possible to find organizational models and archetypes, shared by nearly all, which stressed (or mimed) conflict rather than harmonious integration. Therefore it is profitable to look at the Vietnamese village as a complex world with a multitude of highly shared values and customs whose potentialities could work either for or against order and harmony, depending upon changing social and economic circumstances.

The Duke of Wellington's famous reported remark that the battle of Waterloo was won on "the playing fields of Eton" meant, presumably, that experience in competitive team sports paved the way for an easier psychological acceptance of the coordination and discipline that were required in a modern military officer corps. Vietnamese peasant rebels, trying to build rebel armies, of course had no "playing fields of Eton" in their backgrounds to help them develop their organizational proficiencies. Formally regulated competitive team sports were relatively underdeveloped in traditional East Asia, which lacked both the psychological need of modern machine age societies to rehabilitate the importance of physical skills, and the impetus to new forms of collective action which industrialism provided. But Vietnamese peasant rebel leaders could draw upon a fund of games-playing experiences of a very different kind: for example, the "human chess" (*co nguoi*) games that were played incessantly in the larger villages. (In smaller villages, a smaller-scale game known as "paper lamp chess" was substituted.)

In traditional "human chess" in rural Vietnam, the chessboard itself was drawn or painted upon the courtyard of the village meeting house. The two players who were opposing each other sat upon small platforms elevated above the courtyard, so that they could direct the movements of their chessmen; before they ascended their platforms, they had to make prayers to the village deities. Each player directed sixteen chessman: one "general," two "scholars," two "elephants," two "chariots," two "cannons," two "horses," and five "soldiers." To become one of these two players directing the game from the elevated platform, villagers fought each other in preliminary chess elimination tests. The "chessmen" themselves were teen-aged boys and girls of the village, who sat upon chairs placed on the courtyard chessboard, carrying placards with the names of their positions written upon them. The sixteen chessmen on one side were all boys, those on the other side were all girls, and sexual titillation was not absent from this arrangement: elderly village rakes who played chess enjoyed the idea of trading boy chessmen for girl chessmen during the course of a game. When the players had decided upon their moves, they waved small flags from their platforms at their chessmen seated below; and the chessmen had to obey the flags. Several small children clutching drums and cymbals were installed upon the platforms to urge the players on: if a player took too long to wave his flag, the children were instructed to harass him by pounding the cymbals and the drums right beside his head. Inside the village meeting house, the rest of the villagers were gathered to register every move in the game. If a player made one wrong move, he was defeated.

Winners of these human chess games in the villages received rewards. But losers had their footsteps dogged around the village by people beating drums and blowing bugles, simulating the behavior of the followers of a funeral procession. The idea, of course, was publicly to shame the losers. Because many villagers participated in these human chess games, and many villagers lost them, the outcomes of the games created such enmities and resentments that some villages were even forced to supply armed patrolmen to accompany the victors back to their homes.[7] One point here is that the games played in Vietnamese villages did not shy away from the institutionalizing of competition. Another point—equally crucial to the politics of revolution—is that Vietnamese villages indulged in a sport which gave great training in the planning of tactical and strategic gambits, and in which players who did not plan their moves rapidly enough were publicly shamed by small children. Peasant insurrections (and their attempted repression) took place in this context.

Beyond their mixtures of widely shared customs and ideals, which were more ambiguous from the standpoint of political tranquility than is sometimes supposed, Vietnamese villages harbored tensions between cultural-ethical ideals and social realities. These tensions could be exacerbated in times of economic turmoil. The dynastic code of instructions for the villages of A.D. 1663 indicates very clearly both the nature of these tensions and their relationship to class warfare. For example, one article of the code warns villagers that the ordering principle of village life must be that of age over youth, and that young men of the village must treat all village elders like their fathers and must not be disrespectful to these elders

because of an inclination to "presume upon their great wealth." Another
article of the code declares that men who assist the village chiefs are to be
chosen by the chiefs on the basis of their age and qualifications being
"respected by the masses," not on the basis of their being younger men
who come from wealthy families.[8] In other words, there was a continuing
tension between the ideal leadership of the elderly, which was justified by
Confucian ideology, and the real leadership of the rich and powerful, who
were not necessarily so old. The traditional Vietnamese order, like the
traditional Chinese order, never successfully resolved this tension.

By Confucian standards, the eldest males in the village should automatically have occupied leadership positions. In fact, however, if they were
poor and illiterate, they were compelled to defer to younger gentry
family members, who possessed enough literacy and managerial knowledge
to keep the village records and to manage its communal resources, enough
classical education to perform the village rituals, and enough social prestige
to secure favors for the village from the bureaucrats—members of their
own kind—who administered the district government above the village.
Village families with some property and with classical educations also
definitely possessed what Westerners would call "class consciousness." Or
at least they possessed a sense that they were distinct from the rest of the
population: those families whose sons' names had appeared on the rolls of
winning candidates in the civil service examinations for more than one
generation could even raise flags on poles in front of their houses (or
simply hang silk banners from their houses) with phrases in Chinese characters advertising their glory. Families with money alone struggled to
acquire a special community prestige by holding ostentatious marriages and
funerals. As the 1663 code of instructions for the villages observed: "Rich
men want to maintain their advantage over others through these things,
while poor people, wanting to achieve rich men's standards, are thereby
driven to the point of selling all their lands" in order to finance the staging
of showy rituals too.[9]

What all this meant was that at moments of economic decline or disruption, this piquant contradiction between cultural ideals and social realities,
as one of the more poorly disguised fault lines of Vietnamese society,
could help to suggest a set of easily defined grievances to disadvantaged or
dissident groups within the village. For the rule of the rich was never
legitimized by the official value system, let alone by peasant outlooks and
wishes. What, then, was the secret of the village elite's habitual political
survival and even prosperity?

There was one substantial difference between leadership in Vietnamese
lineages and leadership in Vietnamese villages. Lineages, like villages,
harbored both rich and poor families. And lineages, like villages, could be
torn by tensions between two different sets of leadership criteria: the
Confucian set which emphasized age, sex, and generation (the lineage head
should be the oldest male of the senior generation in the lineage, no mat-

ter how poor); and the less ideal, more practical set which emphasized education, wealth, and social power. The difference was that leadership in the village might involve menial administrative chores as well as the more general, and much more desired, controlling power over village rituals and properties. As a result, there was usually a further division in Vietnamese village life between the formal village leadership—of the village chief, who performed the administrative chores—and the informal village leadership, of the councils of notables, who possessed the real power, and who came from the real socioeconomic elite.

The modern term for "village" in Vietnam (*xa*) was in use at least as early as the tenth century A.D., when Vietnam was just beginning to break away from Chinese rule. It is by far the most enduring term in the whole history of Vietnamese territorial nomenclature. The modern term for the "hamlets" into which Vietnamese villages are subdivided (*thon*) did not become common until the fifteenth century. In the early medieval period, village chiefs were members of the court bureaucracy, appointed by the emperor, who were temporarily stationed in the villages as a phase of their professional bureaucratic careers. From the late 1400s, some historians have argued, the nature of Vietnamese village chiefs underwent a dramatic change: the chiefs became villagers chosen by their fellow villagers, rather than continuing to be centrally appointed local officials.[10] Other scholars have asserted that this metamorphosis did not really occur until the early eighteenth century, at least in the north.[11]

Whatever the date of this change, at the time of the French conquest the village chiefs were chosen by the villagers but—in theory—had to be approved by the court. They served specific three-year or five-year terms, carried out court orders and collected taxes, functioned as intermediaries between the bureaucracy and the village, and actually enjoyed greater prestige when they retired from their positions and became members of the council of notables, whose servants they also had been. The notables themselves were not the agents of the central government. They held their positions for life as a permanent elite. They chose the village chiefs, and ran the private business of the village—temple sacrifices, crop patrols, the disposition of public lands. As the natural rulers of the village, they could still be a heterogeneous group: they included men of high scholarly or bureaucratic rank, retired canton and village chiefs, and, perhaps, rich landlords who had a modicum of literacy and who were too powerful to be kept out. At times of unrest—in the late 1700s and again in the late 1800s— village notables were quite capable of conscripting their own small armies.

It would be very hard to deny the stability of the traditional Vietnamese village hierarchy, overall. This is true despite the fact, previously noted, that the qualifications of some of the notables did not always conform to the public Confucian esteem for age and for scholarly attainment. The traditional village hierarchy was so strong, indeed, that it survived the revolutionary convulsions of Vietnamese society in the late 1700s and was in robust form a century later on the eve of French colonialism. And a clue to the explanation of this peculiarity is that the target of the Tay-son revolutionaries—the three peasant brothers from Binh Dinh province in south central Vietnam who overthrew the Vietnamese political order between 1771 and 1788—was not the power of the village notables at all. As in other, smaller peasant uprisings in Vietnamese history, the main target of the Tay-sons was the racketeering corruption of local officials and sub-bureaucrats from outside the villages who were collecting an increasingly diverse, back-breaking range of fees and taxes from Vietnamese peasants, including "offer and bow money," "paddy remittance money," "granary indemnity money," "lamp oil money," "betel and areca money," lacquer taxes, cotton cloth taxes, and of course the omnipresent land tax.[12]

Father Diego de Jumilla, a Spanish Franciscan missionary active in central Vietnam in 1773, was one of the first Western eyewitnesses of a Vietnamese peasant rebellion. He observed that squads from the Tay-son peasant army publicly burned the government tax registers in even "the smallest hamlet" that they entered, attacked and disarmed government tax collectors, and announced that they were abolishing most of the previous government's taxes. Yet the Tay-sons did not expend great energies attacking directly the ruling elites inside the villages, with the exception of their random assassination of village chiefs who proved to be conspicuously "refractory."[13] The village notables, in other words, enjoyed a much greater capacity than local bureaucrats and sub-bureaucrats to ride out the storms of a peasant rebellion. The autocracy they exercised, no matter how onerous, was not inevitably associated, by the peasant mind, with the tax-levying exploitations of a dynasty or the dynasty's commissioned bureaucratic agents. This was the crux of the matter. The famous "independence" of Vietnamese villages from central government control, which was hardly completely true, was still taken seriously enough by Vietnamese villagers to guarantee the security through nonimplication of village elites, at times when central governments themselves were incurring great odium. Moreover, unlike Japanese peasant rebellions—which reflected such a procrustean sense of village solidarity that successful rebel armies in Japan often demanded the active participation of one man from every family in the villages they controlled[14]—Vietnamese peasant rebels usually tolerated the existence of village notables who refused to join them and who merely showed no overt hostility to their ardent crusade against the tax collectors beyond the village gate.

All this made the task of Vietnamese revolutionaries who wished to bring change to their entire society, including the villages, a difficult one. It was one thing to mount a revolution against the colonially manipulated national political system. But as long as the semimyth of village "autonomy" was preserved during the colonial period, conservative Vietnamese village notables could wrap themselves inside it, disclaiming responsibility for French outrages or for the indignities of the decaying Vietnamese court and provincial bureaucracies. At the same time, such notables were in a position to hinder critically any thorough recruitment or mobilization of Vietnamese villagers for revolutionary purposes.

The Village under Colonialism: Landlordism and Changes in Class Relations

How deeply did the Indochina colonial government penetrate Vietnamese rural society between the 1880s and 1954, and how much did the Vietnamese revolution owe to the stimulations or provocations of this penetration? Extreme penetration versus superficial penetration: the case can be argued either way, and has been.

By the late 1930s, the appearance in Indochina of certain visible features of an unprecedented modernization process—nearly 3,000 kilometers of railways, nearly 28,000 kilometers of roads, nearly 18,000 motor vehicles—suggested cataclysmic transformation, or at least the probability that with the new roads and cars Vietnamese villages were receiving more visitors, more often, than they had ever received before. The mobility of peasants themselves certainly increased. Just within Tonkin, up to fifty thousand peasants (a majority coming from the two provinces of Nam Dinh and Thai Binh) left their villages for brutalizing drudgery in the colonial mining industry. Within Indochina, some ten thousand or more Vietnamese peasants migrated to Laos, where they became miners or petty merchants in Luang Prabang and Vientiane. External peasant migration also took place, to destinations as far away as New Caledonia and Tahiti: between 1926 and 1934 some ten thousand peasants from Tonkin traveled as coolies, voluntarily or involuntarily, to French colonies in the Pacific.[15] The first Vietnamese peasant character ever to be strongly represented in the American theater was one of these coolie migrants, the irrepressible "Bloody Mary" in the James Michener-Rodgers and Hammerstein musical "South Pacific" (1949). She was identified in the play as a Tonkinese woman who preferred betel nuts to Pepsodent, and who had once worked for a French planter but now spent her time making grass skirts and selling shrunken human heads to the impressionable American marines.

Despite the railways, the roads, the cars, and the peasant migrations, however, as late as 1936 it was not too difficult to find large villages even in Cochin China, not too far removed from the towns, whose young children had never seen a single European face and in which no French administrators had ever set foot since the beginning of the colonial period.[16] To some extent it was reformist and revolutionary intellectuals, not peasants, who had become significantly more mobile. Taking advantage of the new railways and roads, they undertook brief fact-finding journeys into the rural areas. Then they wrote expositions of the decay of Vietnamese agrarian society under colonial rule which were promptly suppressed, to reappear in urban bookstores only after 1954. Having discovered the existence, in the West, of labor-saving machinery and modern medicine, many of these new intellectuals found the continuing social and cultural status quo in the countryside shameful, rather than poetic as some of their more Taoist forefathers might have believed it to be. With a greater proportion of Vietnamese intellectuals being both more mobile and more dedicated social pathologists than their ancestors, it was not surprising that they discovered more social diseases. How much of the decay was real, and how much of it was just a matter of changed perception?

Obviously, the colonial government's introduction of heavier and more pervasive forms of taxation, especially in the countryside, was enough to make the taxes the Tay-son armies had fought against in the eighteenth century seem almost like a pleasant memory. They became an issue early in the Vietnamese revolution. The famous "Asia Ballad," which apparently circulated in Vietnamese nationalist circles at the time of the Tonkin Free School around 1907, complained eloquently about oxen taxes, taxes on "chattering pigs," salt taxes, rice field taxes, ferry boat taxes, bicycle or conveyance taxes, taxes on betel and areca nuts, tea and drug taxes, commercial license taxes, water taxes, lamp taxes, housing taxes, temple taxes, bamboo and timber taxes, taxes on peddlers' boats, tallow taxes, lacquer taxes, rice and vegetable taxes, taxes on cotton and silk, iron taxes, fishing taxes, bird taxes, and copper taxes.[17] Colonial wine taxes and salt taxes were regarded by the villagers as particularly offensive innovations. Previous Vietnamese dynasties had taxed large rice wine distillers and merchants, but had not dared to tax peasants who made their own household rice wine. The colonial authorities, however, created a government wine monopoly by decree in 1893 and 1902, forcing even the humblest wine producers to sell their wine to the government at prices the government fixed. The government then resold the wine to the villages, at a profit. To Vietnamese peasants, the rice wine tax simply resembled a second land tax, since rice wine production was a natural extension of the yearly rice harvesting.

Then there was the Indochina government salt monopoly, which dated from 1903. It quickly became, in the next four decades, the all-too-familiar symbol of the divorce between the political standards of the colonial metropolis and the lower standards of the colony itself. The reason for this was clear: the government salt monopoly in France had been condemned and overthrown permanently a century before, during the French Revolution. For many Vietnamese families living along the seacoast, salt making had been a reliable, moderately profitable handicraft industry. Forced now to sell their salt at fixed low prices to the colonial government, which resold the salt to consumers at a profit to itself, the salt-making families soon faced the constant prospect of bankruptcy. Salt making became concentrated in the hands of a few large companies. Fishermen who had once bought salt to preserve their fish from the coastal salt-making people now had to buy it from the government at much higher prices. Their own impoverishment appears to have followed inevitably—although the subject does deserve much more research.[18]

Yet were these taxes and monopolies really the causes not just of humanitarian concern, but of revolution? Were they even factors in that dissolution of the sense of community which Vietnamese revolutionaries lamented? As a recurrent symbol of the wall of double standards which stood between France and her Asian colonies, the salt monopoly could hardly have been bettered. And acquiring an appreciation of these double standards was indeed an important step forward in the development of a nationalist or nationalist-revolutionary consciousness. This occurred among the intellectuals. Peasant demonstrations against colonial taxation, as in central Vietnam in 1908, were impressive but did not develop spontaneously from below entirely, being encouraged by nationalist mandarins. Colonial taxation can perhaps be linked to the explosion of rural revolution more directly only in Tonkin in the period 1943–1945, when—as will be shown—the colonial government was forced to adopt wartime tax policies in the villages which were so socially insupportable that they brought down much of the existing social structure, as well as the existing government.

The fate of the sense of community was the key, even if it was more real as an idea than as a fact. What happened to the relations among social groups and social classes in the Vietnamese countryside under colonialism? Did their circumstances change, significantly and irrevocably?

Speaking very generally, under French rule Cochin China became a society of plantations, particularly rice and rubber plantations. The north, on the other hand, became a society of increasingly fragmented small agricultural plots, supplemented by some straggling, undercapitalized plantations up in the Tonkin highlands. Speculation about colonial Vietnam's agricultural economy still remains based upon the unchanging foundation of the research of Yves Henry, Pierre Gourou, and others; and each one of their superb pioneering books of the 1930s and 1940s is, to some extent, a house of cards standing undisturbed in a windless world, at least as far as the description of long-range trends is concerned, since the precolonial economy remains a virtual mystery. But the French, clearly, did not invent the big rice plantation system in southern Vietnam.

A kind of monster private landlordism, and a scarcity of village communal lands (compared to the north and to the center) had characterized Cochin China before the French conquest. The acting financial commissioner of Vinh Long province, southwest of Saigon, reported to the emperor Minh-mang in early 1840 that 70 percent or 80 percent of the villagers in his province were landless, and that a small minority of landlords selfishly dominated lands they could not possibly cultivate themselves.[19] The Mekong delta was still a frontier land in the nineteenth century. The Nguyen courts had encouraged the growth of large-scale landlordism in the south, as well as plantations manned by soldiers and prisoners, both for economic reasons (the cheap development of a vast agricultural frontier) and for political ones (the permanent Vietnamization of the south against lingering Cambodian influences.)

What French colonial governments did do was to expand the plantation system, especially into the western, "back river" region, into such provinces as Rach Gia, Bac Lieu, Soc Trang, and Can Tho. They also promoted a very lucrative rice export trade from the south, with Cochin China rice being sold eventually to more than thirty different countries, not just in East Asia and in Europe but even in South America (Chile, Peru, Uruguay) as well. As early as 1864 the Cochin China government sold land publicly—at a rate of two hundred francs per hectare, with three years to pay—to its French and Vietnamese supporters. Much of this land, as already noted, had previously been occupied by Vietnamese peasants who had fled from French soldiers. By 1943 more than half the cultivated acreage of Cochin China was controlled by the owners of a mere 150,920 estates. The number of Cochin China landowners who owned more than fifty hectares of land were less than 3 percent of all landowners in the region, yet they occupied more than 45 percent of all the cultivated land. Land concentration rates in the south were more rapid than elsewhere in Vietnam. The acreage owned by small peasant landholders (five hectares of land or less) was small and continued to shrink, being less than 13 percent of all cultivated land in Cochin China at the time of the world depression. The potential political incubus of landless peasants also seems to have been greatest in Cochin China: it has been estimated that in 1930 more than one-half the farm families of Tonkin owned land, as opposed to only about one-third of all the farm families in Cochin China.[20] Precise estimates are impossible, however. Statistical analysis of Vietnamese economic history all too often leads directly into a quagmire of illusions. For example, a plausible argument has been made that landlessness in Tonkin was really only better disguised, that many peasants there who were officially recognized as landowners were really "fronting" for landlords who controlled them and who wished to avoid taxes.[21]

Nevertheless, the social structure of Cochin China in the 1930s did appear to be much more polarized, and to have an entirely different nature, from that of Tonkin and Annam. In 1930, Cochin China had almost 6,300 landowners with 50 hectares of land or more, as compared to 51 in Annam and a few hundred in the north. Such an unequal distribution of indigenous economic power, favoring the south, represented a reversal of the pattern of the unequal distribution of political power in the precolonial period, which had favored the north and the center. In 1860, the Vietnamese dynastic state had had stronger vested interests supporting it in Tonkin and Annam than in the south, where the civil service examination system had worked poorly and where few southerners had managed to convert classical educations into bureaucratic power. In 1930, the colonial state had stronger vested interests supporting it in the south. When loyalty to a temporizing monarchy and to the Confucian political ideology it tried to represent faded in the north and center, and hundreds of out-at-the-elbows, culturally proud mandarin families began to look to revolution as an answer, there was no army of six thousand or more big landowners there to help arrest the contagion of revolt.

Of course, to depict all these thousands of Cochin China landlords as complacent, highly solvent champions of the French governor in Saigon would be going much too far. If the social psychology which lurked behind the Cochin China rice economy is carefully examined, what is quickly noted is that insecurities permeated the entire structure, from top to bottom. The south was not the home of a highly satisfied landowner class sitting on top of a social volcano. On the eve of World War II, Cochin China probably knew a very different situation—one in which disillusionment with the rice plantation export system was general, so general in fact that it was not sharply differentiated enough along class lines to produce widespread, mature class warfare.

The world depression had naturally devastated the system. In 1929, one hundred kilograms of rice had sold on the Saigon market for 11.56 piasters; by 1933, one hundred kilograms of rice was selling on the same market for 3.86 piasters.[22] The exportation of rice did not significantly diminish. But the social results of the sharp decline in prices—rice prices in 1933 being no more than one-third of what they had been in 1929—could easily be imagined. By converting southern rice into a cash crop designed for export, the colonial regime had created at the same time a vulnerability to world price fluctuations, in such commodities as rice, which had not existed in traditional Vietnam. It has been a commonplace in much Southeast Asian historiography, perhaps never scrutinized as much as it should be, that nationalism became a force in rural areas only when peasants were compelled to change from subsistence farming to the cultivation of cash crops, or when subsistence farming ceased to yield a subsistence. (The origins of Vietnamese peasant nationalism, however, precede this.) Certainly the diffusion of a heavily commercialized rice economy throughout the south had victimized lower-class members of the population who had not assimilated as much French culture as the big landowners. For this economy rested much more decisively than the precolonial one upon esoteric (to the peasant) legal formulas and institutions. Only in 1939, for example, after decades of bitter land wars in western Cochin China, did the Saigon government issue a code of provisions which tried to help small peasants understand the proper legal methods for submitting applications requesting permission to claim and clear parcels of land of under ten Vietnamese acres. Until 1939 there was no legal machinery in the south that an ordinary peasant could comfortably operate to claim ownership of the small plots of land which he himself had cultivated. And even after 1939, peasant applications to clear such land had to be "recognized by" village functionaries, had to be filed at the province chief's office, had to

include the peasant's poll tax papers, and had to contain extensive information about his occupations and ethnic membership.[23] Here was a situation
where the inequitable complexities of colonialism were presented to land-
hungry peasants very directly.

Then came the depression, as an added burden. Its impact caused
peasants to desert large portions of land in such western provinces as Rach
Gia and Bac Lieu. In eastern Cochin China, after 1931, peasants began to
plant corn, peanuts, sweet potatoes, and manioc in a desperate experimentation with supplementary crops that might allay their fatal dependence
upon rice. In 1937, one writer publicly divided the really poor peasants in
the south into three different categories, according to diet: those who lived
on bran and vegetables, like the pigs of a rich household; those who lived
on bran and water, like the pigs of a poor household; and those who could
only steal a taste of animal feed, while pretending to bargain, in rural
markets.[24] Even sweet potatoes had become too expensive.

Yet a real collision between these pathetic bran eaters and the big landlords did not occur before World War II, and the military power of the
colonial government may not have been the only reason. In the summer of
1931, French and Vietnamese landowners met in Saigon to form an
association for the protection of the "private privileges" of Cochin China
landlords—the *Syndicat des Riziculteurs de Cochinchine.* One indication of
the mood of its members (all of whom had to possess a minimum of
twenty Vietnamese acres of land) can be found in its statement to the
colonial government that it sought a law postponing the payment of all
landlords' debts, in order to keep its members from committing suicide—as
one bankrupt French landowner, Pierret, had recently done.[25] By the
1930s, in other words, the plantation economy had an abundance of woes
for everyone, no matter how unevenly they were distributed. By 1934 a
majority of the big landowners in western Cochin China were in debt.
More precisely, they were both debtors and creditors. To satisfy their own
creditors, they had to pawn their estates. Their debtors were, of course,
their tenant farmers, who had rented fields from them but now could not
pay their rents. The tenant farmers tried to flee to other lands. The
creditor-debtor landlords themselves, looking both ways in their credit
relationships, like the Janus-headed prisoners of a crumbling economy,
faced lawsuits and the forced auctioning of their estates. In a petition
which the "back river" landowners presented to an incoming French
governor of Cochin China in the summer of 1934, these landlords revealed
more of their psychology. They would, they said, tolerate being arrested
and sent to jail for not meeting their tax obligations. The reason for this
was that they feared debts much more than taxes: debts were what bankrupted them. And as the price of rice kept falling, their chances of repaying
their debts dwindled.[26]

On the eve of World War II, the Cochin China plantation owners faced
the further nightmare of a shrinking rice export market. Their plight was

publicly assessed by Bui Quang Chieu. Chieu was a major landowner himself, a member of colonial councils, and a leader of the Constitutionalist Party. He referred to the "heart-rending" facts that the China market was now almost closed to Vietnamese rice producers, the Japanese market had been lost for a long time, French African colonies bought very little rice, and now (1939) the French wheat surplus and the selfish clamor of French wheat farmers were threatening to restrict the access of "colonial rice" to the market of the mother country itself. One domestic solution—the industrialization of Tonkin, which might permit currently undernourished northern peasants to buy more southern rice—was (Chieu said) desirable but remote. Chieu, who was regarded as a pro-French conservative by many Vietnamese revolutionaries, candidly explained that the psychological aspects of the Indochina economy's crisis were especially grave. They were dangerous because this economy had been established in a manner which did not take into account "the legitimate rights of a people of twenty-two millions," the Vietnamese people were now conscious of their inability to organize their economy in order to protect their own interests, and if this situation were not changed the alternatives would be too terrible to contemplate. Reactions would be so serious that "we do not want to think about them."[27] With these dark forebodings hanging over it, and placed over it by none other than a member of the Vietnamese upper class who was presumed to own some fifteen thousand hectares of land, Cochin China society entered upon its last fifteen years of French rule. Marxist revolutionaries were not alone in condemning Vietnam's economic subservience to French interests: Vietnamese landlords themselves could hardly conceal their anxieties.

Of course, if insecurities did pervade the entire rural social structure, from landlords to landless peasants, their postcolonial impact was not so confused as their colonial one had been: by the late 1960s, the memories of this history of insecurities had made the southern landlord class one of the most conservative, and one of the least conciliatory, landlord classes in Asia. (They strenuously resisted land reform schemes that were much more modest than those which had been accepted by Taiwan landlords.) The question is, what psychological germs of revolution existed in the 1930s? Alexis de Tocqueville wrote of the "spiritual estrangement" which took place between landowners and tenants in France before the French Revolution, as more and more members of the French nobility ceased to live in the countryside. It would not be difficult to discover the same process at work in Vietnam in the 1930s, despite the miseries and fears which landlords and peasants genuinely (if differentially) shared. The social bonds which had joined peasants to local elites tended to break down all over Southeast Asia during the colonial period, for a variety of reasons.[28] Although its growth was limited, Western education in the cities and towns enveloped some landlords' sons in a world which peasants never experienced, giving specialized, elitist training, patterned upon Western values and history, to these men but at the same time robbing them of any ability to supply effective leadership back in the countryside.

Typically, the sons of landowning families—and indeed the sons of all urban upper-class families—learned about their own countryside through Vietnamese translations of French books. A work like M.A. Coquerel's *Paddys et riz de Cochinchine* was serialized in Saigon Vietnamese-language newspapers before World War I, accompanied by large maps of provinces like Rach Gia. At the same time, the southern landlord class was increasingly cut off from traditional Vietnamese scholarship on the countryside, like that represented by Trinh Hoai Duc. The views of Vietnamese peasants themselves on this estrangement process are almost impossible to obtain, except through ballads. There are no regional lists of grievances for Vietnamese provinces in the 1940s similar to those which existed for French provinces in 1789, and to which Jean Jaurès, writing his socialist history of the French Revolution, complained that he could get only limited access. One landowner's grandson, however, has described this kind of estrangement very vividly:

> The more deeply I entered the French world, the more frustrated I became at the Vietnamese world in which I was forced to participate, the more I could see only the coarse yokel uglinesses of people with yellow skins and flat noses, to whom I used to feel I was connected because I also had a flat nose and yellow skin. On school vacations when I went home, I liked to argue with older relatives. But they were "country people," and so I didn't consider anyone of them to have any weight at all. My grandparents had the custom of inviting tenant farmers to remain and eat with us whenever they came at meal times, those times when they came to visit. Previously, I had paid no attention to this at all, but now I felt uncomfortable at having to eat communally with these simple-minded, good-natured farmers. Their especially "yokel" gestures, like swallowing rice wine fast and then hissing, like noisily sucking down their soup, like picking their teeth and then gurgling water in their mouth, etcetera . . . made me break out all over in goose pimples.[29]

There is no point in falsely romanticizing the old examination system or its social legacies. But it is not too preposterous to link part of the dehumanization of landlord-tenant relations to the decline of the classically educated gentry landlord class, indoctrinated in Confucian ethics, either. In the 1920s and 1930s the landlords' financial interest in their lands expanded, but their interest in supplying rural services as part of the duties of "gentleman" bureaucrats diminished. The culture of town-based absentee landlords became more Westernized. Yet, paradoxically, these landlords retained the traditional elitist concept of the separation of manual labor, which was for peasants, from intellectual labor, which they reserved for themselves, the upper class. In sum, the new Western-educated

absentee-landlord class issued from a curious marriage between Western
capitalism and traditional East Asian cultural elitism. Idealistic sons
of this class who very rarely and very exceptionally did decide to leave
the towns and become practicing commercial farmers on their own
lands, working side by side with their tenant farmers, were usually
prevented from doing so by parents or by elderly relatives. The theme was
important enough to attract the attention of writers. In a memorable scene
from one of Khai Hung's famous novels, written in the 1930s, a Vietnamese
family elder rebukes the young hero of the novel for preferring farming to
the life of a district magistrate:

> You young men to-day are very stupid. You think that in doing so
> [becoming a farmer] what you are doing follows the model of Euro-
> peans and Americans. Ha! Returning to the land! But if you live in
> our country, to work in the fields means to have your feet and hands
> dirty with mud, to be miserable, to be overpowered by superiors, to
> be bullied, to suffer demands and requisitions, to be overtaxed, to be
> sued, to be summoned to court, to be done in by eighty-five differ-
> ent kinds of bogeys, but never to have happiness similar to the kind
> they have living in Europe and America. I have always known that
> scholars come first, peasant second. . . . [30]

Nowhere was the problem of the separation of the intelligentsia, and of
intellectual youths, from agricultural problems more acute than in Tonkin.
Here, of course, traditional cultural elitism was stronger than in the south,
and Western capitalism was a bit weaker. Moreover, complicated tenancy,
subtenancy, renting and subrenting patterns had developed in the north,
and the average size of family holdings was declining. The colonial
Forestry Service, once wanting to rent 2.5 hectares of rice lands for
scientific purposes, had to deal with seventy-six different owners and had
to sign seventy-six different rental contracts.[31] But one famous Vietnamese
researcher estimated in the year 1943 that of all the landlords in the north,
70 percent regarded their properties merely as places of retirement, where
they could relax after their government and business careers, and as relatively invulnerable forms of wealth which they could leave to their
children. Another 20 percent of all northern landlords regarded their lands
merely as convenient "safety deposit places," rather like outdoor banks,
where they could invest money and receive interest in the form of rents.
And no more than 10 percent of all northern landowners were conversant
with farming methods, actually visited their fields themselves, and
inspected the work of their tenant farmers.[32]

Within Tonkinese villages, an astonishingly small percentage of the
educated village population was engaged in agriculture. Yet farming
remained the villages' basic economic pastime. The village elders and Confucian scholars—and every ambitious man still wanted to be an elder or a
scholar—owned land, but delegated farm work to women, children, and

male farm hands. Unschooled women not only had to spread the fertilizer but to make decisions about such technical issues as how much sunlight various crops needed. Farm hands and children were the ones concerned about the health of the village oxen and water buffaloes. The economic duties of educated male villagers were confined to paying the household taxes, preparing a fifth lunar month field inspection calendar, and supervising the reaping of the tenth month harvest.

This regressive division of labor in northern villages antedated colonialism. But it acquired new qualities of irresponsibility in the 1920s and 1930s. For one thing, the sons of the village elite, admiring the newfangled foreign goods which were reaching even rural areas (candles, soap, milk, cotton and silk goods) found a new reason for despising village economic life: not only were the peasants engaged in the manual labor of the "petty man," but the manual labor in which they were engaged was economically backward by Western standards. Such youths deserted the villages as quickly as they could, participating in a general flight from the countryside which received the title of the "going out to the provincial capital movement."[33] For another thing, the older gentry who remained in the villages became deeply frustrated by the Western cultural challenge; as a result, they often withdrew into self-designed cocoons, into the most introverted kinds of traditionalism. They lavished their attention upon orchids and metaphysical contemplation rather than upon new fertilizers and expanded rice yields. The enjoyment of an economic surplus might make no difference: instead of investing this surplus in agricultural innovations as eighteenth-century gentlemen farmers in England would have done, Tonkin village elite families tended to spend it upon defiantly classical leisure pursuits. A famous Vietnamese story of the early 1940s, by Nguyen Tuan, describes the inner exile of a Tonkin village patriarch:

> Old man Kep was a man who liked to drink wine, chant poetry, and collect orchids. He had reached the age where he could have complete leisure . . . because now in his family they had a surplus number of rice bowls [that is, they were well off]. In the past, he had also wanted a flower garden so that he could go out into it morning and afternoon in order to savor his own feelings. But he ruminated that he was merely a Confucian scholar living in a perverse French-Chinese period which had debauched all the old ways of thinking, and dissipated so many spiritual values. He was merely one individual who had chosen the wrong century and whose hands were empty of the new tools, so that he could not ensure his own personal survival, let alone talk about the enjoyment of collecting flowers. Old man Kep commonly said with his own friends that having a flower garden was an easy matter but that having enough time to care for the flowers was difficult. What he wanted to say was that a person who grows flowers must many times use perfect sincerity

and perfect devotion in his treatment of all these beauties which can never raise their voices and speak. Only in that fashion does one follow the Way, the Way of the man of talent. . . .[34]

In this story, the two sons of "old man Kep" have abandoned their village "to go to do French jobs" in the provincial town. Such migration from the villages, and from the peasants with "black faces and muddy hands" whom the new urban life styles mocked, became really significant only about 1928, according to Nghiem Xuan Yem, the most profound observer of change in the Tonkinese countryside. The exodus included even marginally educated males with token literacy. Yem estimated that of every ten men in the villages there were as many as seven or eight "plowers of clods" who would have liked to leave for the towns, where those who did come usually became trapped in menial employment of some form. For "French jobs" could mean anything from working for merchants to serving as messenger boys, or as foremen or watchmen, or as mailmen, or as railway station coolies.[35] The problems of agricultural development, meanwhile, continued to be the unwanted monopoly of the skirted village women with their carrying poles, of the illiterate short-trousered farm hands, and perhaps of a very small minority of literate men.

In early 1944, as the Pacific War reached a crisis, a mild effort was made to reverse the hemorrhage of talent from the villages—but in the interests of protecting urban populations from Allied bombs. The inhabitants of northern cities and towns, in an ironic foretaste of the more massive planned population dispersions that were to occur when American bombing began in 1965, were ordered to move to more peaceful rural areas. All Hanoi primary schools were moved to the countryside. All superior primary schools and Franco-Vietnamese middle schools were subdivided and moved into village havens in the three provinces of Ha Dong, Ninh Binh, and Thanh Hoa.[36] However, this withdrawal of some members of the educated upper classes from the cities—a "de-urbanization of the intelligentsia" or at least of their children—never reached the same scale, even proportionately, of the Chinese intelligentsia's wartime retreat from Peking and Tientsin and Shanghai and Nanking after 1937. Nor did it lead to anything like the Chinese intelligentsia's forced discovery of its own peasantry in Yenan or in southwestern China. Such a return to the countryside was too small, and came too late, to reduce in a meaningful way the gap between educated landowners and uneducated peasants which had been growing ominously for decades.

Village Reforms and the Twilight of the Village Oligarchs

As social change and its premonitions began to filter into the villages—in the form of Western soap, or the gaudy lure of "French jobs" in the towns, or the French-speaking landlord's son who was suddenly embarrassed by the eating habits of peasants—the village hierarchy itself felt acute stresses and strains. The relationship between the local village hierarchies and colonialism became a crucial one in Vietnam, far more so there than elsewhere in Indochina.

Vietnamese villages possessed hierarchical structures as complicated and as rigorous as any in Southeast Asia. In contrast, village life in Laos and Cambodia was amazingly egalitarian. Charles Robequain, in the famous study of Thanh Hoa province in north central Vietnam which he published in 1929, observed that in Thanh Hoa, as travellers moved west, the closer they approached the banks of the Mekong River and Laos, the simpler they discovered village "nobility" to be, the less heavily they found such elites weighing upon the population, and the less evident any local disproportions of wealth became. Such travellers were leaving the Vietnamese East Asian world of long vistas of irrigated ricefields where the local "nobility" based its power directly upon concentrations of landed wealth.[37] By the early 1940s, Vietnamese intellectuals themselves had stumbled upon this stimulating distinction between hierarchical Vietnamese villages and egalitarian Lao ones. Almost with the air of a Cortez discovering the Pacific Ocean, Nguyen Van To informed an important constituency of fellow-activist intellectuals in Hanoi in early 1943 that Vietnamese civil servants, returning from service in the colonial bureaucracy in Laos, had learned with surprise that in village meeting houses in Laos there were no class distinctions, either in seating arrangements or in the distribution of food. Unlike the Vietnamese, To commented, the Lao did not fight with each other at village meetings over who was to sit "in the highest place."[38] Possibly these egalitarian influences from Laos may have been absorbed in some way into the Vietnamese revolution. Nguyen Van To himself was to become the head of the ministry of social relief in Ho Chi Minh's first government in September 1945.

The contrast with Cambodia, while not as popular with Vietnamese intellectuals, was equally suggestive. In traditional Cambodia there were no large villages. The only real center of communal life was the Buddhist temple. The individualistic Cambodian peasant was not controlled by his membership in a specific lineage or village, socioeconomic inequities were minimal compared to those of Vietnam, and the French colonial government was actually forced to create artificial proto-villages known as *khum*, which lacked social or cultural or historical foundations, in order to master its own incomprehension of Khmer rural politics.[39] Colonialism, and the social changes it set in motion, confronted entrenched village hierarchies only in Vietnam.

Yet colonialism did not, most of the time, choose to confront the village hierarchies voluntarily. In the 1880s, the early colonialists mocked the mandarins, indulging in empty rodomontade about saving the peasants from "an aristocracy of scholars" and unleashing their kitchen boys in mandarins' clothes. This mood passed. The Indochina colonial regime soon began to hesitate over its answer to a crucial question. That question was:

would Vietnam's relatively self-contained villages, if their parochialism
were not threatened, turn out to be a force for resistance and revolution or
a force for docility and peace? In Tonkin especially, the villages' bamboo
hedges and relatively self-centered communal lives were a puzzle. On the
one hand, the fierce self-containment of every village made it more difficult
for the conquerors to manipulate and Gallicize the Vietnamese peasantry,
and permitted the village elites to decide for themselves the degree of their
villages' participation in national life and its institutions (like the examination system). On the other hand, such self-containment also seemed to
make it more difficult for the villagers to combine with peasants from
other villages against the colonial government, despite Vietnam's heritage
of peasant rebellions. The French ultimately decided—but never with total
conviction—that in a reduced form village "autonomy" was relatively
favorable to the perpetuation of colonialism, even though the first generation of colonizers in the 1800s had believed the opposite, having had to
fight village-centered resistance groups.

The rise of communism was the new imponderable. Whatever their
sentiments about the French, most oligarchical village notables of the
1930s and 1940s in Vietnam probably had very little fondness for the
prospect of a communist revolution. It threatened their privileges far too
much. Their preservation of their traditional position and power, therefore, guaranteed that such a revolution would find it difficult to penetrate
the villages. But between the 1920s and the 1940s a number of factors
weakened their position and sapped the strength of the bulwark they were
providing against a revolution.

Most obviously of all, informal status within the village became more
broadly differentiated culturally. This process threatened to outflank the
prestige of the notables. Teachers were crucial here, since they had always
been a key to the politics of opposition in the provinces in Vietnam, rural
revolution being by no means a matter of peasants alone. Indeed, the true
story of the Vietnamese revolution in this century probably cannot be
written until Vietnamese provincial and village teachers, as individuals and
as a group, are much more exhaustively studied. In Phi Van's book "The
People of the Countryside" (*Dan que*), written in the 1940s, the rich
village landlord was checkmated not by the peasants but by a small land-
holder schoolteacher, who was well enough educated to expose the landlord's land-appropriating machinations in a colonial court. The rich notable
who exploited villagers in Nguyen Cong Hoan's 1938 novel "The Dead
End" (*Buoc duong cung*) compelled the villagers to address him as if he
were a scholar-bureaucrat, but he was in fact uneducated, and he very
significantly considered books to be "his number one enemy."[40]

Especially in Cochin China, what commonly occurred was that young
French-speaking teachers, "understanding a smattering of French customs"
and armed with diplomas from Franco-Vietnamese primary schools, took
over the village schools and began to challenge the leadership styles of the

village notables, who for their part knew "a few" Chinese characters and belonged "a little bit" to the precolonial educational tradition of rote learning of the Chinese classics. Saigon newspapers, from the 1920s, became alarmed by the fact that village teachers and village notables "commonly disagreed with each other," competed against each other for "rank" among the villagers, and did not know "polite methods" for behaving toward each other. According to the newspapers, the two groups viewed each other according to the "narrow perceptions" of the "new studies" and "old studies" movements which each of them represented so imperfectly, and developed such resentments that they were unable to "pardon" each other.[41]

The fact that Sino-Vietnamese classicism had declined in southern villages, and that French culture had penetrated the villages only weakly, did not prevent a furious power struggle from breaking out between the tattered, self-appointed mini-champions of the two competing traditions. Indeed, it may well have been the very weakness of these two competing traditions in the villages which made the struggle so tense. Instead of a crystalline exchange between superbly educated, self-confident masters of Western and East Asian philosophies, this was a murky duel between the representatives of two diluted, partly homemade cultural immanences. Both the notables and the teachers were well aware that they fell short of really epitomizing the cultures they wanted to, and they were, consequently, psychologically insecure. Certainly the notables and their friends spared little invective in their public denunciations of the teachers. One of them asserted, in 1924, that the majority of village primary school teachers in Cochin China were "still young in years, and with dispositions that have not yet become complaisant; yet they pretentiously plume themselves on being men of rare talent and learning, comparable in status with mandarins, and they scorn the villagers . . . they flaunt natures that run wild, and free actions."[42]

Such an open conflict between what elitism stood for and what education stood for was unprecedented. But it was by no means the only source of the compromising of the notables' position in village society. What were the other sources? One factor was the misplaced faith of governing powers above the village, both Vietnamese and French, that they could depend forever upon the healthy existence of thousands of reasonably homogeneous village elites, and depend forever also upon the immutability of the ancient rituals that had supported such village elites for centuries, to keep the villages free of dissent and revolution. This faith was dangerous not just because it exceeded realities but because it caused these outside governing powers to place burdens upon the village elites which the latter could not always support. Another source of trouble lay with the reforms of village administration by the colonial government which heavily publicized the economic advantages village elites enjoyed and which also linked the village elites more closely to the provincial bureaucracy, reducing the symbolic separation between the two which had often saved the former during traditional peasant uprisings. And still another source of trouble could be located in the colonial government's attempts to freeze the size of the elites, and embalm the "customs" which underwrote their power, at a time when Vietnamese society was expanding. All these factors could be found, in varying degrees, in all three regions of Vietnam. Here, for reasons of space, they will be discussed only in connection with the regions where their manifestations were particularly marked. (The point of this exercise is to develop a greater appreciation of the peculiarities of Vietnamese village politics in a revolutionary age, not to suggest that French colonialism could have succeeded if it had tried other policies. Since so much Western-language literature on twentieth-century Vietnam has been a form of special pleading for alternative policies, I must emphasize this seemingly odd qualification, which would be unnecessary in a book dealing with European revolutionary history. Colonialism was doomed all over Southeast Asia, despite the variety of colonial administrations.)

The provinces of central Vietnam, and of the southern part of Tonkin, offered clear demonstrations of the colonial government's hope that it could count upon the magic of the old village elites and the traditional customs to maintain an inexpensive stability in the rural areas. Village administrations in Annam itself were not reorganized until 1942, thirty-eight years after the first reforms had been introduced into Cochin China villages and twenty-one years after Tonkin village administrations had been reshaped. Before 1942, there was little outside interference with the formation of village councils of notables in Annam; and only after 1942 were village chiefs in Annam villages "designated" by Vietnamese provincial governors and by French resident superiors.[43] Annam, however, was also the home of tax resistance movements and (in the late 1920s and early 1930s) of a vigorous communist movement. Why were its village hierarchies, and those of southern Tonkin (also a nursery of communism) not a perfect guarantee of political calm, assuming (and even this assumption requires more research and proof) that a majority of village notables, by the 1930s, preferred colonial order to revolutionary disorder?

First of all, the legitimate power of the village elites within the villages was much more limited than some foreign outsiders—and even Vietnamese bureaucrats—liked to believe. Village notables, for example, were expected to discuss the contents of the village expenditures account books at village meetings. A crisis erupted in a village in Thanh Hoa province in 1936 when the notables, who had stopped discussing village expenditures at village meetings after 1932, began privately disposing of the revenues from village communal lands and of the rice that was set aside, by custom, for the village's rice-field watchmen; the rest of the villagers protested. When these notables also announced plans for converting the rural market their village owned jointly with another village into a more elegant establishment with roof tiles, and began to spend small sums of money on this project even after their villagers had objected that a tiled market would be too expensive for the returns it would bring, the villagers denounced their notables' "corruption" to the provincial bureaucracy.[44]

The kind of despotic harmony that outsiders hoped the notables would provide, with or without a village consensus, was also marred by tensions and confrontations within the hierarchical elites themselves. For one thing, village chiefs who had served in their posts a long time and who had managed to accumulate some prestige—despite the fact that they were the agents of higher powers—could build a power base in the village that was equal to that of the notables, and by no means harmonious with the notables' ambitions. In one village in Ha Tinh province, a village which regarded itself as "more advanced" than neighboring villages because it had produced civil service examination degree-holders, the village chief, who had held his position "for many years," asked to be allowed to resign. The village held a meeting, in 1936, to elect a new village chief. It immediately split into two factions, one faction revolving around the former village chief and one faction revolving around the village elders. Villagers became "stealthily and secretly opposed to each other," and the village "lost its appearance of accord."[45] More local "elite confusion" could be created by changes in the government of the canton (*tong*)—the administrative unit which intervened between the village and the district government—in which village notables became rancorously involved. In one canton in Quang Tri province in 1935, some four or five marathon elections were held—without result—to choose a new canton chief. A three-cornered power struggle developed among the retiring canton chief, an intriguing assistant canton chief, and some village notables. When a notable from one of the villages in the canton publicly stated that the "master assistant canton chiefs of previous eras" were not "thick-headed" like those of the present, the assistant canton chief, stung by his attack, actually sued him.[46]

Lawsuits between village notables and assistant canton chiefs, as a result of acrimony generated by the public selection of canton chiefs, opened startling fissures in what was thought to be the normal serenity of rural life. These seemed of little consequence at the time to the Indochina governor-general or to the court at Hue. But over the decades they did make a contribution to the dissipation of the prescriptive prestige of the old hierarchies. Canton chief elections themselves, it is true, were probably contested much more bitterly in Cochin China than in Annam during the colonial period. A very famous example was that of the election of a new chief for Bao Thanh canton in Ben Tre province in the south in 1925, when two notables from the same village were among the candidates who ran against each other. Hundreds of villagers assembled before the provincial financial commissioner's office to cast their ballots, the results were not unanimously accepted, and rumors of "injustice" spread through the countryside like wildfire. Confucian intellectuals lamented such battles.

They provided damaging evidence of the extinction of a semimythological species: the "gentleman" who accepted competition only for the sake of principles, not for the sake of personal gain, and whose idealized decorum had been believed to be a kind of passive secret weapon against the European conquerors.[47] Revolutionaries, on the other hand, could exploit the increasing lack of that self-control which village elites had been presumed to have, and could introduce their own interests and causes into the competition.

Another factor in the degeneration of village elite persuasiveness in Annam was that the Vietnamese bureaucracy outside the villages often enforced an acceptance of hierarchy upon peasants who did not believe in it, *once meaningful economic issues preoccupied them.* To repeat, the bureaucracy above the villages clung to a stronger belief in the sanctity of hierarchy than the villagers did themselves. This was a particularly fertile situation for revolutionary groups. For example, the village of Trung An in Binh Son district of Quang Ngai province—a district which was wrested from colonial control with remarkable ease by the third company of the provincial Viet Minh revolutionary army in 1945—owned a piece of land which had been cleared but never taxed or divided into concessions. A former village chief quietly appropriated the entire parcel of land. The people of the village, reacting, filed a petition of complaint with the prefectural government, which resolved the issue by surveying the land and then awarding half the land to the aggressive former village chief and half the land to the rest of the villagers. But in 1935, the higher bureaucracy intervened. It rejected this more equitable decision by the prefecture, on the complacent grounds that the villagers who had sponsored the original petition of complaint were all "common people" who therefore did not have any "standing" for representing the villagers as a whole. This act—a declaration from Hue that only members of the village elite could represent a village—was significant because it no longer tallied with the political psychology of the villagers themselves, once a conspicuous socioeconomic controversy developed within the village. Petitions of protest were hung publicly all over Trung An village, with a number of peasants even signing their names and addresses.[48] In sum, the proposition was no longer automatically accepted in rural areas that in a legal confrontation between elite and commoners, members of the common people had no rights because they "lacked standing." Yet the upper bureaucracy was afraid to permit safety valves within the old hierarchical system.

Finally, there was the problem of village rituals. Rituals which, in the precolonial past, had helped to preserve the hierarchical ethos of the villages, now often created tension and conflict instead. This happened both because such rituals were being imposed from above in nervous, exaggerated ways, and because such rituals had become inextricably mixed up with society-wide ideological and religious schisms which overrode old village solidarities. Annam in 1936 provides a piquant illustration of this. A secretary in the Quang Ngai provincial government passed his district magistrate examinations. He immediately requested that his native village in Quang Nam province (in Dien Ban prefecture, a scene of tax resistance movements) give him the elaborate welcome-home parade, of homage and gifts, which in traditional Vietnam had been called the "glorious return" (*vinh qui*) and which had usually been extended to the graduates of the old Confucian civil service examinations. Since the "glorious return" was an ancient Vietnamese custom, his fellow villagers finally granted his request. But the actual performance of the ritual provoked a public uproar, and bitter public complaints by the villagers. The first reason for this was that when the new district magistrate arrived to begin the parade, the villagers offered to escort him into the village under a blue umbrella, and he angrily demurred, demanding that they escort him instead under a golden umbrella, of the kind once used to shade Vietnamese emperors. (They did not have a golden umbrella.) The second reason was that when the honored man did reach the center of the village, accompanied by flags and drums and under an improvised yellow canopy, he flatly refused to perform traditional rituals of thanks on the grounds that he was a Catholic; and he sought out the nearest Catholic church, leaving the villagers gaping with surprised anger.[49]

By the 1930s, of course, all over Southeast Asia, from Annam to Java, ancient rituals which had once reinforced social ties and the traditional social structures of local groups were now acquiring a strange latent explosiveness, beyond just failing to accommodate harmoniously the new faiths from outside Asia which were entering and commanding the villagers' consciousness. The fate of the Catholic provincial secretary who demanded a golden umbrella in a central Vietnamese village in 1936 showed how confused attempts to enforce the old rituals could result in mild public outrage—and in a reversal of the desired psychological and political effects. The governments which were sitting placidly on top of the villages remained unaware of these changes at their own risk.

Village politics in the south are worth discussing from a different angle. Before 1904, the council of notables in the average southern village comprehended roughly fourteen different positions, including those of the "village eldest" (*huong ca*), who usually stood at the top of the council; the "locality head" (*huong truong*), the "gentry councilor" (*huong than*), and others. (All these translations are very arbitrary and approximate, and give the impression of much more functional specialization than actually existed.) In French eyes, these councils lacked "standardization." They did not distribute responsibilities efficiently among their members. And they permitted notables the luxury of "indifference" to that sort of village business in which governments above the village had a keen interest. (This indifference had been, of course, the secret of their survival under foundering dynasties.)

In 1904, therefore, the Cochin China colonial government reorganized the village councils into "maintenance commissions" (*ban hoi te*), in which each notable who was a member of the council now received a specific duty or administrative task. The senior notable, the "village eldest," was placed in charge of the storage of documents; the "locality head," another notable, was made exclusively responsible for managing the village budget; the "gentry councilor" now had to serve as the formal intermediary between the colonial judicial apparatus and the village council; and a new post was created, the "chief recorder of registers" (*chanh-luc-bo*), whose incumbent was asked to keep the population registers and to guard against the spread of contagious diseases. In other words, the colonial regime made an effort to match prestige in the village not just with general qualities like age and scholarship, but with specific functions as well—ignoring the social force of the Confucian dictum that "the gentleman is not a tool." Apart from its attempt to connect prestige much more directly with specific functions, the Cochin China government, in 1904, also specified that village council members had to be elected from among the landowners in the village.

This meant that a crude economic determinism became embedded in southern village control policies. Such policies now conceded their explicit reliance upon landlords, whose preeminence depended, not upon the mastery of a cultural tradition which the French could not control, but upon an economy whose new legal and institutional framework the colonial government did control. In precolonial days, elite status in the Vietnamese village had depended nominally upon multiple noneconomic criteria (like age and examination system degrees), even if landownership had remained a primary qualification behind the facade of Confucian civic ideology. Now, with the disappearance of the examination system, and with the introduction in 1904 of this legal criterion that landowning by itself was sufficient to open the door to membership on the village councils, French administrative fiat performed a work of "terrible simplification" which made the economic inequities upon which the village political order rested, much more obvious. That political order's traditional Confucian disguises unravelled. Further village reforms in Cochin China in 1927 did change the 1904 "maintenance commissions" back to "councils of elders," increased the arbitrary power of the eldest notables, and made the lists of villagers who were eligible for election to the village councils slightly broader. The lists now included landowners, other men of wealth, retired civil servants from the middle ranks up, and ex-officers of the colonial militia. The new lists of 1927, however, were still more vulnerably precise than invulnerably diffuse. And their precision was increased by further reforms in 1944. The lists of that year spelled out the economic foundations of power holding in the villages in detailed, finite ways that would have been unheard of under the traditional dynasties, and lent themselves to the easy ideological caricatures of any revolutionary opposition which might develop.[50]

A classic analysis of village government in Long Hung village, My Tho province, written by its own ex-village chief and published in a Saigon newspaper in 1939, shows rather trenchantly that, without the examination system, political loyalties and performances in southern villages had indeed become much more directly commercialized than in the past. (The economic expansion of Cochin China under French rule must also be remembered.) As a symptom, village security managers and patrol superintendents resigned in great numbers from their positions. They no longer gained prestige from working for a culturally transcendent, semi-"autonomous" hierarchy of village notables, since these hierarchies no longer existed. On the other hand, there was little satisfaction in working as agents of the government above the village either, since it paid them too little to sustain them. Moreover, this government no longer permitted them exemption from certain trifling taxes, which meant that it was no longer publicly declaring to their fellow villagers that it "knew their merit." The result was that the prestige of their positions had vanished. The basis of village administration in Cochin China had become commercialized but underfinanced under colonial rule. And, as the Long Hung village chief suggested in 1939, the margin between relatively efficient and loyal village administrations, and those marked by absenteeism and simmering discontents, might be as little as twenty piasters per year per village (the additional salary which a village security manager needed) and greater selective tax exemptions.[51] By this time the village functionaries had indeed become incipient salaried agents of the government outside the village.

If central Vietnam presented a picture of regional bureaucracies which presumed that the traditional village elites were more homogeneous, more powerful, and more accepted by the people than they really were, and southern Vietnam presented a picture of commercialized village governments supported by an all too pedantically defined class structure, what special features characterized the ancient villages of the Red River delta? As late as 1943, the sensitive Nghiem Xuan Yem could refer to Tonkinese villages as self-sufficient beehives which had not been changed for centuries. Politically speaking, however, these beehives had been despoiled and then half-heartedly restored by three sets of village reforms, in 1921, 1927, and 1941.

By 1921, the generation of Vietnamese scholar-gentry which had fought the French invaders at the end of the 1800s had either died or had lost much of its vital force in northern villages. The village reforms which the colonial government introduced in that year were designed to weaken their power still further, although the justifications for the reforms that were given publicly naturally preached the need to rationalize village administration and to prevent abuses of power.

In these 1921 reforms, the colonial government created "councils of lineage representatives" to manage village affairs. The members of these councils were actually to be called "lineage representatives," and the villagers were to elect them every three years. Each lineage in the village had the power to elect one representative. The number of representatives on the councils varied with the size of the villages but could not exceed a maximum of twenty representatives per village. (There was a subtle difference involved in the French effort to rely upon landowners in Cochin China villages and lineages in Tonkin villages: while any practical distinction between the two categories was obviously limited, social strength in northern villages was still based upon less nakedly economic considerations.) Candidates for the councils had to be at least twenty-five years of age, had to be literate, and had to own some property; and they were to be chosen by adult males eighteen years of age and over. The "first officer" (*tien-chi*) and "second officer" (*thu-chi*) of the precolonial councils of notables in the north were replaced by chairmen and by vice-chairmen. The village reform laws of 1921 also required each village to keep a budget. Nominally, the creation of village budgets was intended to prevent "abuses" by the village elites; in fact, the budgets permitted the colonial government to gain a greater knowledge and control of village resources.[52] Just as de Tocqueville asserted repeatedly that the French Revolution was foreshadowed and fostered by all the centralizing activities of the eighteenth-century French monarchical regime, it would be possible to claim here that in Vietnam, the colonial government's greater interest in manipulating the villages—by such measures as the forced compilations of village budgets—paved the way for the bureaucratic penetration of local communities by later Vietnamese revolutionary organizations.

How did these reforms of 1921 look to elderly members of the Tonkin scholar-gentry? Their alienation and frustration were inevitable, and are worth describing essentially in their own terms.

The elders were accustomed to living in villages where "a few dozen well-off people," an oligarchy, chose the village chief and other village functionaries, taking care to select "experienced" men who were over thirty years of age and who were "feared" by people below them. In traditional Vietnam, this despotic oligarchy simply made its selections and presented them in the form of a signed petition to district officials, who rarely interfered. Troublemakers in the village who resented this oligarchy, or who had "dishonest reputations," could be curbed by being compelled to serve on village patrols, or even forced into a "category of slavery." Such an omnipotent oligarchy was tolerated because it was a defense against outside pressures, and the villagers understood this: the more omnipotent such an oligarchy was within the village, the more the oligarchs were respected rather than cajoled or bullied by court bureaucrats outside the village. (This important political myth of the village oligarchs as a defense against the world outside the village also permitted them, as noted, to survive peasant uprisings against the tax-collecting bureaucracy.)

In the eyes of the oligarchs, the 1921 laws "smashed" the village hierarchical order. For one thing, all adult males now had the right to choose village functionaries. This meant that the wise, experienced, "well-off" people now enjoyed no more than an equal status with other males. As a result, respect for them in the village declined. For another thing, there was a new, European-style specialization of tasks within village administration: the elected lineage representatives were being asked to accept the duties of a secretary, or a treasurer, or a registrar, once they were elected. As a result, any well-off people who overcame their distaste for democratic elections enough to seek and win council membership would have to "toil hard" at specific duties and obey the district bureaucracy, which would no longer respect them as it had in the past when they had played an aloof, autocratic, "supervisory" role. To ask them to toil directly in "the pursuit of government business" violated their "special nature"—whose qualities included "solemnity" and "magnanimity" and an avoidance of the petty man's menial labor.[53]

Had they lasted, indeed, the 1921 village reforms might well have made revolution easier in Tonkin. For they homogenized the village elites and the local administrations outside the village, from the standpoint of mass psychology, making it difficult for the former to withhold the support of their villages from revolutionaries' attacks upon the latter. The "smashing" of the village hierarchical order was in the interest of more direct colonial control, but it was also in the interest of revolutionaries advocating land reform who had to approach the villages from the outside too. Of course, qualifications could be added here: in 1945 it was not impossible to find some village elite property-owners who supported the Viet Minh, on patriotic grounds. Vietnamese history is far too rich to be constrained by the formulas of economic determinism. Still, in general, it was not surprising that as unrest sponsored by nationalist groups centered in the towns increased in Vietnam, the colonial government began to reconsider its antipathy to the old, conservative village elites, whose "aid the king" instincts had meanwhile waned.

In 1927, the French reestablished "councils of elders" in northern villages, side by side with the continuing councils of lineage representatives, in order to coopt all the ex-notables who had been resisting the 1921 reforms. The reestablished councils of elders were not restricted in numbers, and their members, as in the traditional period, served without limit of time, in contrast to the members of the councils of lineage representatives. Bureaucratic penetration of the villages continued, however—in 1927 a "household registrar" was added to the administrations of Tonkin villages, and made responsible for recording births, deaths, and marriages—and the French still failed to win the support of many village notables, despite their conciliatory revival of more traditionalistic village government.

In 1941, conciliation went a step farther. Both village councils were abolished in Tonkin. They were replaced by "councils of worthies," which sought to embrace only the tiny group of males in northern villages who owned diplomas in higher education, or bureaucratic rank. Elections were abandoned, as was the idea of status based upon village administrative function. The status of the new worthies was to depend entirely upon more general society-wide educational and bureaucratic attainments: primary school certificates, grades in the mandarinate, middle-level or high-level positions in the civil service, rank in the army or militias. What resulted was a kind of Indian summer for severely contracted versions of the traditional village elites—a terror-clouded Indian summer, filled with Japanese soldiers and Communist guerrillas. By "designating" village chiefs (since 1930) rather than allowing them to be chosen by village councils, the French hoped at least to hold their self-serving loyalties, even if the loyalties of the worthies who surrounded the chiefs were more problematic.

These 1941 reforms were molding the politics of northern villages at the time of the August Revolution in 1945. In effect, they concentrated power in the villages in the hands of a very few people. The pendulum had swung from an attempt to diffuse this power in 1921, back to an almost eery enthusiasm for a devout reconcentration of it two decades later. What was the nature of its reconcentration?

After 1941, the northern councils of notables or "worthies" seemed to enjoy complete power over village management, village laws, decisions about the amounts of village expenditures and receipts, the apportionment of tax levies, the organization of defense patrols, the control of peasant hygiene. By himself, the leading notable or "first officer" (the title of *tien-chi* had been revived as part of the return to traditionalism) had the power to manage the common lands, and to impose solutions when petty disagreements erupted among the peasants. He was almost beyond challenge: ways in which villagers could complain about notables' behavior were not at all broadened. During the two decades between 1921 and 1941, when village councils had been elected, "upstarts" had been able to buy enough votes, in the "shameful buying and selling" of support which occurred, to win access to what had been the oligarchs' domain; and many of the natural leaders of the village had withdrawn at least formally from village politics. After 1941, with elections at an end, the rigorous qualifications for council membership which had been introduced to please the old oligarchs were so conservative that formal village elites actually shrank in size. In one Tonkin village which possessed more than four hundred adult males, for example, after the 1941 reforms, only three men of the entire village satisfied the requirements for a place on the council of worthies; and one of them, a law court secretary serving in a distant province, was unavailable to preside over village business.[54] In some other villages, the effect of the 1941 reforms was to give certain lineages an almost unprecedented opportunity to dominate their neighbors, given the expansion of council powers and the weakness of complaint procedures. For the members of these villages' councils now suddenly all belonged to one lineage or even to one lineage branch.

In the short run, this reconcentration of power in Tonkin villages in 1941 may have made the work of the revolution more difficult. It consolidated the positions of the conservative upper class. The opposite could be argued—namely, that further diffusion of power, rather than its reconcentration, would have created enough political counterattractions to have made the mass recruitment of young revolutionaries from the villages less likely. But this argument is undone by the facts that the colonial regime would probably never have permitted enough diffusion of real power to blunt the coming revolution and consummation of Vietnamese nationalism, and that as the inequities and miseries of Tonkin rural society multiplied, the only remaining barrier to revolution, apart from foreign soldiers, was the autocratic power and prestige of village patriarchs hostile to communism.

On the whole, the reforms of 1941 gave such patriarchs a much freer hand in their villages. And the short-term results were fairly clear. In 1948, at the height of their nationalist war against France, the two Viet Minh youth federations had managed to mobilize, and organize, only 15 percent (800,000) of the youths of Vietnam, despite the fact that these federations were given the greatest latitude in recruitment and allowed to aim at "assembling all social classes of youth, without making any distinction among social classes, political tendencies, races, and religions." The communists themselves regarded this statistic as shocking and disappointing.[55] Communist mass youth organizations expanded dramatically in size in the north only after 1956—following the destruction of gentry power in the villages by a revolutionary government in power.

To let this conclusion stand by itself would be misleading. For if the power of the village notables was strengthened in 1941, it was strengthened by artificial decisions which came from outside the villages, and not by any village consensus. This had long since waned. And the colonialists' effort in the 1940s to maintain self-serving anachronisms in a context of social change certainly created some long-term vulnerabilities and confusions. Could the oligarchs of 1941 have survived through the 1950s, even without the interference of a Ho Chi Minh? The reforms of 1941 had sought to return power to the village's natural leaders. But by this time, despite the exodus of many educated people from the villages to the towns, as mentioned, the populations of some Tonkin villages had still changed enough to cause their precolonial status orders to begin to break down. The rise of overlapping educational systems, and the juxtaposition of modern professions with anachronistic Hue court sinecures, created an unusual confusion of status perceptions. The 1941 laws ignored the possibility of "new elements" in the villages. And there were just enough "new elements," resisting the trend toward urban living, to make the crust of custom volcanic in places.

Who deserved to be "first officer" of the village council of notables more—a Vietnamese with a Western-style bachelor of arts degree, or a degree-holder from the old Confucian examinations, a man with a grade in the Vietnamese mandarinate or a more modern law court clerk or medical officer? These choices are not imaginary: they were actually encountered by Tonkin villages after 1941.[56] The multiplication of hierarchies in Vietnamese society, as a result both of limited Westernization and of the colonial dyarchy, now made it impossible for villagers to agree as comfortably as in the past upon which men among them enjoyed the most "status." And the laws of 1941 were accompanied by no guidelines. It was merely decreed that they be applied according to the "customs" of the villages. Indeed, beginning in 1931 the colonial regime had compelled northern villages to compile written records of their customs so that these could be scrutinized. Tradition-bound village notables of the 1930s, in responding to this request, had exploited the vagueness of local customary laws and of knowledge about them to buttress their own positions. They had also used their own interpretations of village customary law as a weapon against the few modern diploma-holders who resided in the villages and who threatened them. They characteristically argued that such people did not deserve power in the villages, on the basis of customary laws, because they had not held the traditionally prescribed feasts and rituals of status celebration (*khao vong*) or because they lacked the seal of the emperor on their credentials.[57]

Hence the colonial regime both practiced a greater bureaucratic penetration of Tonkin village life (village budgets, household registrars) and, at the same time, insisted upon preserving the anachronistic, socially invidious customary codes of the relatively more isolated villages of the past—and imposing them upon an expanding society.

Village Structures and the Modernizing Impulse

To trace the influence of all these village-control policies upon the growth of the Vietnamese revolution is not easy. Any cyclopean theory-builder would be frustrated and baffled: there are so many exceptions, so many local idiosyncrasies, and even so many general phenomena which still must lack any solid, stereoscopic definition in the eyes of scholars with three decades' worth of hindsight. Possibly many of the changes in village elite politics which have just been described had little directly to do with the revolution, which, after all, sprang from nationalism and from social and economic grievances. Such changes did provide the rural political environment in which the revolution emerged. From the point of view of comparative history, the special significance of these colonial village reforms in Vietnam was something else: that they occurred without any corresponding increases in village organizational or associational life. As usual, the comparison between Vietnam and Japan is unfair, prejudiced, and illuminating. How did Vietnamese villages of the 1920s and 1930s compare with the modernizing villages of Japan, of the same or of a slightly earlier period?

Battles between policies of "assimilation" (of old East Asian customs and institutions by modern European ones) and "association" (of the old and the modern customs and institutions, side by side) were famous in French Indochina. But although they were critically exaggerated by colonialism, they were not peculiar to it. For after the Meiji Restoration of 1868, the Japanese government, which had managed to avoid any period of colonial captivity by the West, still had to decide whether to preserve the pre-modern laws of Japanese villages in association with a modern national government, or to assimilate the villages directly into a new, Western-style administrative system. Between 1890 and the 1920s, under the influence of Albert Mosse, a Berlin expert on constitutions and local government who had been brought to Japan, the Japanese government imposed a German-style "county system" upon the Japanese countryside which paid very little attention to the traditions of Japanese villages. Modeled upon the county assembly electoral system of Prussia, Japanese county assemblies of the 1890s conferred special privileges upon big landlords, who were defined very precisely as men who possessed taxable lands of a certain high value. While these privileges of "large landlords" were later eliminated in reforms of the county assemblies, Japanese village assemblies (which chose mayors) were also elected by restricted, Prussian-style electorates which gave two classes of taxpayers (rich and poor) an equal share of village political power, regardless of their numbers. Voting, in sum, was weighted in favor of the rich. The basis of political leadership in Japanese villages seemed to shift, or be about to shift, from family status regardless of wealth to wealth regardless of family status.[58]

Of course there was no group of landlords in the Japanese countryside who possessed the historical pedigree and ancient juridical rights of the landed nobility of Prussia. But the Japanese government's rapturous search for nonexistent Prussian landlords in the Japanese countryside was very much like the French search for French-style proprietors—or even for "indigenous notables" whose economic power could be defined with enough precision to satisfy Europeans—in Vietnam, especially in Cochin China. The Japanese inflicted the consequences of this infatuation with Western formulas upon themselves; the French inflicted them upon the Vietnamese.

The decline of village communal lands in Vietnam, a pronounced feature of the French colonial period there, also had a parallel in Meiji Japan, which was not a colony. Before 1868, Japanese hamlets had maintained their own lands and woodlands. The livelihoods of the poorer peasants in the villages, those who owned little or no lands, had depended upon the existence of such hamlet properties. In 1889, when the Tokyo government first began to apply its new, standardizing town and village administrative system, the hamlets all lost their identities as legal persons or collectivities. This meant, also, the loss of the hamlets' previously unequivocal right to possess land. Local government above the villages was now increasingly forced to serve the needs of centralization and economic development; village chiefs, who might be businessmen or landlords, increasingly submitted to the wishes of prefectural governors; the new administrative laws led to a decisive reduction in the acreage of hamlet lands; and Japanese peasant movements inevitably appeared demanding the revival of the original hamlet landholding customs.[59] Much of the economic and administrative disruption of peasant life in Vietnam could therefore be found, possibly to an even stronger degree, in another East Asian society which had not even been colonized.

But the crux of the matter, surely, was that as the powers of the traditional "natural village" shrank in Japan, they were replaced by vigorous new forms of associationism—by a host of new village organizations and institutions which prevented Japanese peasants from discovering fully what the loss of a sense of organized community meant. There was always a spectacularly high density of organizations in Japanese rural life. In the 1920s, after the inappropriate Prussian-style county system had been withdrawn, Japanese villages began to combine with each other to finance projects that were too expensive for single villages to undertake, such as the building of schools and hospitals or the creation of irrigation and water supply cooperatives. Multiple village associations of this kind would have been unheard of in colonial Vietnam. The colonial regime there permitted inroads to be made on village communal property, but it did not destroy the legal and customary separateness of Vietnamese villages, so that often the self-contained shells of rural life remained but without all their previous resources. In Japan, the central government strongly encouraged the proliferation of new village organizations. These ranged from associations which shaped the interests of specific age and sex groups—like village adolescent male groups (*seinendan*), mature male groups (*sōnendan*), and women's associations (*fujokai*)—to associations dedicated to economic progress, such as agriculture associations, forestry associations, fisheries associations, and animal husbandry associations. By 1912 the methods of modern farm life were being debated and promoted in Japan, and farming information was being exchanged and disseminated, by 46 prefectural agricultural associations, 557 county agricultural associations, and no less than 11,629 village agricultural associations.[60]

It would be disingenuous to pretend that all these associations were brimming with barefoot, propertyless peasants rather than with villagers who were educated and owned land. The very poor could very easily become victims of isolation as well as economic change in Japan too. Japanese villages, moreover, may well have begun the modern period with a higher density of organizations in them than could be found in Vietnamese—and Chinese—villages. Certainly their organizations covered all segments of the village population. For example, neither Chinese nor Vietnamese villages had traditionally placed much stress upon the training of youths, in village-wide groups, to serve the village. In Japanese villages, there had been the famous "young men's companies," organizations of unmarried male youths from fifteen to thirty years of age who were taught to build roads, fight fires, and carry out patrols. These youth groups had often been the mainstay of order in Japanese villages, whose young adult male populations practiced a conservative self-management that would have surprised their counterparts elsewhere in East Asia.[61]

But the general picture is that the oligarchs who governed Japan after 1868 did not hesitate to encourage the creation of rural organizations—especially more than twelve thousand agricultural associations—which communist revolutionaries were required to create much later in China and Vietnam. While the rulers of China and Vietnam in the 1920s and 1930s inherited the traditional dynasties' deep suspicion of organizations of any kind outside the imperial bureaucracies, the Meiji oligarchs in Japan appear to have worried only about a lack of sufficient organizations. And the reasons for this difference are not very difficult to appreciate. The Japanese government enjoyed such solid claims to political legitimacy in its own country that it had little to fear from most rural organizations it did not directly control: its legitimacy was based upon the support and existence both of an uninterrupted imperial line and of an effective parliament. Neither the French in Vietnam, nor the various warlords and political movements in China of this period, could enjoy equivalent claims. Hence they could not afford to encourage and permit all the crucial organizational life at the local level that modern economic prosperity depended upon; and the needs and demands of organizational entrepreneurship which confronted Chinese and Vietnamese communists, after they came to power, were to be formidable indeed. The legitimacy of the regime which ruled Vietnam in the 1920s and 1930s was most in question, this regime being fully colonial. Therefore the paucity of organizations for improving and consolidating rural communities was significantly worse in Vietnam than it was even in China, let alone Japan.

To understand this, it is only necessary to bear in mind the striking and complete absence of farm cooperatives in the villages of colonial Vietnam. Japanese peasants, reacting to the invasion of their villages by newfangled economic development programs, were allowed to create cooperatives as early as 1884, under the leadership of the new agricultural associations. Such cooperatives spread throughout the most backward Japanese hamlets. They comprehended groups of five or more families, and pooled resources and ideas about the use of better farm tools. By 1928 there were some 157,439 of these small farmers' cooperative societies in Japan, spanning more than 4.5 million members.[62] In China, the China International Famine Relief Commission sponsored the development of credit cooperatives among the peasants of Hopei province no later than 1923. And by 1936 the Kuomintang government at Nanking was claiming the existence, in China as a whole, of more than 37,000 farm cooperatives with more than 1.5 million members.[63] (Many of these Chinese cooperatives were gentry-controlled. The Nanking government was conscious that its writ did not run deeply in the countryside, or below the gentry class; but the point is that at least it accepted and advertised the idea of cooperatives.) Above all, various parts of rural China in the 1920s and 1930s became private theaters of social reform, in which intellectuals like James Y.C. Yen (educated at Yale University and closely associated with the Young Men's Christian Association) could make their own contributions to the salvation of China's villages. In 1923, Yen founded the Mass Education Promotion Society, his objectives being a war against rural illiteracy and the transmission of a knowledge of at least one thousand written characters to every Chinese peasant. In 1926, he received the opportunity to conduct a total reform experiment in one whole rural district, that of Ting-hsien, in Hopei province, not far from Peking. In this model district James Yen hoped to improve hygiene, inculcate proper organizational habits, and teach Chinese peasant children how to read and write and how to use an abacus.

No cooperatives or model districts of this kind were ever allowed in Vietnam. This did not go unnoticed, because the achievements and theories of Chinese rural reformers like James Yen were very well known to Vietnamese intellectuals. Hoang Dao, in fact, wrote in the late 1930s that when he first learned of James Yen's Ting-hsien experiment "I began to think in a dream-like way about our own country. . . . The people of our country are just like the people of China, degenerating by degrees. The words of this Chinese youth can be words capable of arousing us, we must begin to carry out social enterprises."[64] But the gap between knowledge of such reform movements in China and the real enactment of "social enterprises" in this Chinese image in Vietnam was never crossed.

Appeals were made by Vietnamese intellectuals at various times to visiting representatives of the French government, asking them to encourage or tolerate the growth of Vietnamese peasant cooperatives. A good example was the eloquent, pathetic, unanswered supplication of a writer in the "Journal of the Future" (*Tuong lai tap chi*) on April 8, 1937, aimed at Justin Godard, the emissary of the French Popular Front government who had been sent to Indochina to study social problems there. Certainly by 1937 it was common knowledge among many Vietnamese that the more new formal organizations their villages could spawn, the more likely it would be that their technology and marketing power would improve. Through their participation in such organizations, their peasants would become more widely acquainted with the existence and desirability of farm innovations, and would be less at the mercy of better organized urban businessmen. The "unorganized village," in effect, became the symbol both of the insufficient sense of community in Vietnam, which revolutionaries lamented, and of economic stagnation. Both evils could be noisily blamed upon colonialism. At the outbreak of World War II, a handful of Vietnamese consumers' cooperatives, none of them very successful, had been put together in cities like Saigon and Phnom Penh. Beyond the cities, the villages continued to wait—in vain.

Rural notables and landlords, not entirely convinced that the colonial government feared the growth of modern organizations in the countryside as compulsively as they did (when such organizations meant mobilizing the peasantry), created their own buffer institutions. Cochin China in the 1930s saw the rise of a number of provincial cooperative banks, which were controlled typically by mandarins (for example, ex-prefects or former councillors), and whose atmospheres were pseudofamilial (portraits of the elders who had founded or headed them hung in their meeting halls, in order to receive homage and even a kind of ancestor worship). These banks attempted to mediate the relations between more central colonial credit and agricultural science facilities and the Vietnamese peasantry, preventing these relations from becoming too intense and direct and thus preserving the power of the property-owning village elites. They also functioned as gentry credit cooperatives, lending money to landlords, auctioning their estates if they could not repay their debts, but in general seeking to help them with their chronic capital shortages. From a reading of some of the annual reports of these Cochin China gentry credit associations, it seems clear that although French province chiefs sometimes requested them to help restore the vanishing acreages of village communal land in the south, they were much more concerned with restoring bankrupt members of the landlord class to prosperity. In 1937, for example, the Tra Vinh agricultural bank, which lent more money by its own claim than all the other organizations of its kind in Cochin China, sold 926 acres of land in its possession on easy terms to individual landlords, and only 70 acres of the land in its possession to villages for communal ownership.[65]

As Vietnam entered the decisive decade of the 1940s, therefore, revolutionary members of the intelligentsia faced a countryside whose lack of peasant organization was not an accident. Despite all the village reforms and vicissitudes they had gone through, the most conservative village elites had managed to survive by blocking the formation of all new formal organizations and voluntary associations which they could not control; and their interests in doing so coincided exactly with those of a colonial power whose own security was increasingly in doubt. In retrospect, the situation could almost be described (especially in the 1940s, less so in the 1920s) as an unspoken power-sharing arrangement between the colonial government and the more conservative members of the village hierarchies. And the very success of this arrangement depended upon the conspicuous undermobilization (by Japanese and even by Chinese standards) of the Vietnamese peasantry's capacities for new social and economic activities.

At the end of 1941, the General Association of Students of the University of Hanoi created a Committee for the Dissemination of Hygiene and Medical Studies. They then asked the permission of the French resident superior of Tonkin to let them circulate pictures and diagrams demonstrating better hygiene in the villages. He granted them the immediate right to do so in precisely one village. After a year, and only when he had become assured that the purpose of the committee was not political, he belatedly authorized them (in January 1943) to hold exhibitions and discussions of modern medicine, and create "sickness inspection committees," in as many villages as they could manage.[66] On the other side of this invisible power-sharing arrangement, there were the troubles of the Society to Disseminate the Romanized National Language, another reform instrument of the urban intellectuals of the early 1940s. Its ambition was to teach reading and writing to the peasantry. But it discovered that its capacity to expand into the villages was being limited by the "excessive class consciousness" there and by primeval time-consuming village rituals sponsored by the village elders. The society wished to develop village-wide literacy classes, and then to offer its newly literate peasants competitions in the writing of fifty-line epic poems, ten-page short stories, and "scouting songs," as proof that literacy could be immediately rewarding to them. The village oligarchs responded with garish renewals and elaborations of traditional sacrifices and feast days, especially those of the kind where "the father eats and his children fast" and where the virtues of a highly stratified tyranny of old men were headily celebrated.[67] The society, without any chance to oppose the gentry politically, could only mourn its own inorganic patriotic dignity.

Synthetic and Real Village Patriotism: The Tam Dao Youth Farm and the Binh Da Firecrackers

The more conservative gentry and the colonial government could prevent either the growth of village cooperatives or the extension of urban intellectuals' organizations into the villages. But they could not suppress the tremendous need which the countryside felt for new means of social integration. By the 1940s, most of what unequivocal social and moral standards there were, were disappearing from the villages, as has been emphasized. Society was becoming more heterogeneous; it was producing a greater variety of conflict-ridden personality types. The result was that both conservatives and revolutionaries were driven to invent what could be appropriately called synthetic environments, model communities with their own kinds of psychodynamics which might in time replace the morally collapsing old communities.

Especially in Tonkin in the 1940s, there was an intensification of moral indoctrination on all sides and from many quarters. Revolutionaries of the left were not confronted just by colonial administrators and village oligarchs with a shared dislike of popular organizations even for nonpolitical purposes. They also had to grapple with conservatives who were building their own synthetic communities, communities complete with their own psychological conversion processes, whose purpose was to salvage as much of the old Confucian culture as possible. To some extent the whole revolution in the rural north in the 1940s involved a subtle competition between the synthetic environments of the political left and of the political right or center, rather than a relatively more simple conflict between the unimpeachably new and unimpeachably old. Whose version of a synthetic environment would be the most effective?

The world scouting movement, like labor unions and urban consumers' cooperatives, came to colonial Vietnam (or was permitted to come there) much later than in other East Asian societies. The Boy Scouts Association of China, for example, was founded in April 1913 in Shanghai; similar associations did not begin to flourish in Vietnam (and then only on a regional, not on a national, basis) until the early 1930s. When the scouting movement did come, it pleasantly surprised the colonial regime by serving as a potent, if temporary, antidote to communism. In 1935, at the time of the first congress of the Indochina Communist Party, party leaders admitted that an inability to crush "the scouting ideology" was the reason for what they regarded as the party's curious inability to recruit youths under the age of twenty-three years and for the general ineffectiveness of its youth corps.[68] During World War II, the Tonkin Scouting Association organized student youth farms, in cool, mountainous areas of northern Vietnam. Their object was to reconstruct the traditional moral order in the countryside and to combine it with the now inescapable Western virtues. A famous example of a student youth farm organized by the Tonkin Scouting Association was the Tam Dao student youth farm, more popularly known as the "Tran Quoc Toan village."

In this farm, Vietnamese youths were assembled in the early 1940s to be taught the ideals of family life and to be indoctrinated in the proper ways of maintaining "accord and harmony in organized communities"—organized communities again being the central obsession. The cardinal formula in the farm's indoctrination process was a richly classical one, "the study of eating, the study of speaking, the study of wrapping things up, and the study of opening things" (*hoc an, hoc noi, hoc goi, hoc mo*). (The study of eating meant the proper moral behavior at meal time, like allowing the aged to eat first, or older brothers saving some food for younger brothers; the study of speaking meant speaking coherently but courteously, according to one's position; the study of wrapping things up and opening them meant learning how to express feelings indirectly and cryptically if necessary, and learning how to understand the indirect words of others. In short, the opposite kind of behavior from that associated with, say, French—and later, American—soldiers.) The youths were taught the importance of their "status" and their "destiny" or "fate" within the family. They were also taught household chores (like keeping their sleeping quarters clean) and useful economic pastimes that would help reinforce the self-sufficiency of families, like raising animals, repairing bicycles, or rebinding old books.

As part of their indoctrination, the youths were encouraged to regard their camp as a mythical village. The different sections of the camp to which they were assigned were referred to as "hamlets." Indeed, in defense of its classical utopia the Tonkin Scouting Association pushed its fantasy-laden psychodrama much farther: the youths were further subdivided into "lineages," with seven or eight boys being assigned to each one. Each scouting lineage was then given the name of a traditional moral virtue, like Benevolence, Right Conduct, Politeness, Knowledgeability, Loyalty, Filial Piety, or Respect for Elders. No inconsistencies were permitted to mar this atmosphere of indoctrination. Each lineage had a "lineage head," and the "village" had its own "council of elders," along with a dispensary, a granary, and a meeting house whose hall prominently displayed the Chinese characters for "loyalty" and "filial piety." While communist guerrillas plotted a general uprising only a few miles away, in a very different kind of mountain retreat, this stifling Confucian dream-kingdom was faithfully sustained by the Tonkin Youth and Sports Office in Hanoi, which transported food for more than two hundred youths, and their teachers, up into the mountains to the camp.

However, for all their admiration of traditional ethics and culture, the leaders of the Tam Dao youth farm were practicing the same arts as their communist rivals. They were attempting to create "new men" in the rural areas of Tonkin, and to encourage at least moderate personality transformations among their disciples. While their youths were taught to "bow their heads" respectfully to strangers, in the best classical manner, they were also taught Western-style physical training, and exhorted to compete with each other in running, jumping, and climbing. The work rhythms and time consciousness of Western industrial societies were inculcated: the youths were forced to observe precise time schedules, and, when they were allotted work assignments, the farm leaders blew whistles to give them work signals. Most important, the farm made a frontal attack upon the ancient Confucian disdain for the physical labor of "petty men." The youths were ordered to keep all the kitchens and the public toilets on the farm "as clean as those of Westerners," even though many of the farm's members, in the first days of its organization, complained that being assigned to toilet or kitchen cleaning duties was a "dishonor." Even the Tonkin Scouting Association recognized that the traditional moral order of the villages could not be completely retrieved or rebuilt. The crucial question now was what social and political forces were going to control the inevitable cultural changes, and upon what basis.

But because the Tonkin Scouting Association and its youth farms were sanctioned by the colonial government, they worked within sharply defined limits in their efforts to create new, viable organized communities. What were these limits?

First, the association and its farms had to accept, and idealize, the old village hierarchies. They did this by installing a make-believe village hierarchy on the Tam Dao youth farm itself: the director of the farm had to be officially addressed on the farm not as "mister director" but as "mister first notable." Second, they could not promote village cooperatives or multi-village economic associations or newfangled rural organizations of any kind, but had to stress the ideals of "self-sufficiency" of individual households and single villages instead. The very foundation of the Tam Dao youth farm was not, as it might have been, a vision of economic transformation and material progress through better rural organization, but rather— as the director of the farm himself put it—a "psychological trick." In order to get the youths on the farm to "play" at being members of a new, special village, the director assembled them and told them that he had just experienced a dream. In this dream Tran Quoc Toan (a famous Vietnamese general who had helped to defeat Mongol invaders of Vietnam back in the thirteenth century A.D.) had appeared to him and had informed him that he was going to communicate magical methods of training to him that would enable him to convert his "crowds of youths" into "vigorous men of power"—and that Tran Quoc Toan himself agreed to serve as the "tutelary deity" of their "village." To reinforce this rather ornate crowd hypnosis, the director assembled the youths in the meeting house of the village every morning, where they sang indoctrination songs, prayed for the "assistance" of the "Lord Tran Quoc Toan" in helping them to fulfill their fate and strengthen their families, and listened to small talks on ethics. Afterwards, in the courtyard, before beginning their sports or work, the youths gathered around a flagpole and shouted the greeting "Tran Quoc Toan! We obey your words!"[69]

In this atmosphere of obsequious athleticism and spasmodic pieties, therefore, the battered ghost of a thirteenth-century general was used to provide all the reinforcing symbolism for the conversions to new forms of social behavior that the Tonkin Scouting Association hoped would occur. And such a shared fantasy, or such a shared dream, was not by any means an inept instrument for molding a new group and giving its members a sense of mutual identification. This was true even though Westerners, who generally live in societies where fervent personality transformations are not well liked or approved, might have difficulty appreciating the technique. What was important was that this shared dream did not provide real solutions for the poverty of rural Tonkin.

On the other hand, the Tonkin Scouting Association's calculated invocation of the memory of a thirteenth-century Vietnamese military hero, in the countryside of north Vietnam in the summer of 1944, did imply a response to a growing nationalist spirit in the villages. How deeply did nationalism affect Tonkin village life, as opposed to the life of the educated elite in the cities? Was the revolution, when it entered the villages, entering a context where social and economic issues alone monopolized everyone's attention, or a context where social and economic issues were linked to nationalism? The answers to these tremendous questions cannot be offered definitively, no doubt, without much further research. But it will be argued here that nationalism did affect village life, and that its presence had to be recognized by the community syntheses which scouting associations and revolutionary movements were inventing. The famous story of one village, indeed, shows that nationalism in this period could both sharpen the economic (especially the marketing) expectations and orientations of some Red River delta peasants and weaken, very slightly, the hold upon them of nonproductive religious habits. This was the story of what Vietnamese referred to ruefully in the 1940s as "the rise and fall of the Binh Da firecrackers."

For centuries, the Tonkinese village of Binh Da, instead of setting fire to the firecrackers it manufactured, had worshiped them. The formulas for the village's firecracker powder were transmitted from one generation of villagers to the next, in circumstances of secrecy. But the practice of this handicraft industry was dedicated to a curious religious cult, not to the sale of firecrackers for profit. For holidays and celebrations, Vietnamese peasants actually burned Chinese firecrackers: in 1908 Tonkin alone imported 540,625 kilograms of firecrackers from China. In 1919, however, a nationalist movement to boycott the purchase of Chinese goods in favor of domestic ones sprang up in Vietnamese cities and towns, as part of the Vietnamese intelligentsia's concern over the inferiority of Vietnamese commerce. Significantly, this "local goods" crusade spread from the cities to the villages. The villagers of Binh Da decided to convert their firecracker-making handicraft to economic purposes, under the pressure of such nationalism, and to attempt to capture the regional revenues of Chinese firecracker manufacturers.

The circumstances seemed ideal: an obvious market existed, the amount of capital investment required was small, the villagers possessed an ancient firecracker powder formula, and little machinery was needed. Furthermore, the expansion of such a handicraft did not threaten to drain labor away from the village's harvests, which remained its primary economic concern. The light work of rolling the firecracker paper, making the fuses, cramming the powder, and binding the fuses, could all be performed by old people and by children. And since the process of making firecrackers did not require prolonged periods of work, villagers could make them in their spare time from agricultural chores, at daytime or at night, in the sunlight or in the rain. The firecrackers were, in fact, most commonly manufactured in the seventh and eighth lunar months (after the fifth-month harvest had been brought in) and in the twelfth and first lunar months (after the tenth-month harvest.)

By the middle of the 1920s (especially 1926–1928, the peak years of the "local goods" movement in Vietnam) the purchase of Binh Da firecrackers had become something of a nationalistic fad among the people of the north. By this time, the village was producing two kinds of firecrackers, a cardboard firecracker wrapped in red paper and the famous "all red" firecracker that was made entirely of red paper. More than one hundred households in the village made the firecrackers. Their paper and powder were stored in the village schools (which also designed and printed the fire-cracker labels), and the Vietnamese governor-general of Ha Dong province even went so far as to authorize the decorative official name of "Southern Seas Imperial Flowers" for the village's products. At first, Binh Da fire-crackers were sold by peddlers with little capital, who displayed them in flat winnowing baskets at country markets. By the late 1920s, however, shops in Hanoi and in the provincial capital of Ha Dong had begun to specialize in marketing them, and many of the firecrackers were made to order for Vietnamese bureaucrats celebrating promotions in other provinces. In 1930, after the Yen Bai affair, the sky fell. The French Colonial Office suddenly reserved the manufacture of explosives of any kind exclusively for French citizens. This was a death sentence for the Binh Da handicraft. Its prosperity and suppression were encompassed in a single decade, 1920–1930.[70]

It is fashionable to describe the colonial economies of Southeast Asia as "dual economies" in which the stimulation of foreign-controlled export production for world markets coexisted with a discouragement of indige-nous commercial institutions and indigenous markets for manufactured goods. The French tolerance—for a while—of neotraditional handicrafts in Vietnam which catered to Vietnamese consumers, yet depended upon Western suppliers of raw materials (French pharmacies, in the case of the Binh Da firecrackers) was perhaps a mild if not very important departure from any "dual economy" in its classical form. (But it was a departure which victimized Chinese businessmen, not French ones.) The more important point is that the distillation of a new industry from a traditional religious cult by one Tonkin village, under the influence of nationalism, shows that northern rural communities were far from being perfectly insu-lated against the penetration of modern creeds and emotions. And of course, the Binh Da firecracker handicraft affected a number of villages, not just one: it included the village from whose market the people of Binh Da bought carbon and the villages from which they bought firecracker paper and colored dyes. The Binh Da firecrackers are a fascinating, and famous, parable of the effect of economic nationalism upon rural Tonkin. But the general representativeness of this parable is a problem, not to be solved until many colonial village studies are undertaken.

However, it can hardly be denied that nationalism potently associated with local economic issues had germinated in at least a few northern vil-lages long before communist guerrillas had appeared upon their thresholds.

The Decline and Fall of the Tonkin Village Economy

By the middle of the 1940s, the rural economy of northern Vietnam may well have deteriorated to a point where it was almost beyond rescue by anything but a political cataclysm. The August Revolution of 1945 took place against the background of this deterioration.

While the colonial government itself had not entered that competition to create new community ideals which the Tonkin Scouting Association and the Vietnamese communists (among others) were engaged in, it had seen the need—suggested by its own desire to survive—to create one or two primitive safety valves for the growing population pressures in the Red River delta. In 1925 it launched a campaign to induce impoverished Red River delta peasants to migrate to the Tonkin highlands, which were still underpopulated. The centerpiece of its campaign to broaden the geographical base of peasant smallholder agriculture in the north was its policy of offering "small concessions." Peasants who were willing to go to the highlands were allowed to claim small parcels of unowned land, of no more than five and one-half hectares, simply by submitting a petition and a map to the French province chief; by clearing at least 25 percent of the lands within the first eighteen months of their settlement upon them; and by clearing and planting all these lands within a three-year deadline.

Before 1925, very few lowland peasants had migrated on a permanent basis to the highlands. Most of those who had gone to the highland provinces had done so to stay only for a few months or no more than a year, in order to work as tenant farmers or coolies on big plantations in which they had no property stakes. Then they had returned to the delta. In a period of four decades (1896–1935) the highland province of Yen Bai had welcomed the arrival of precisely 337 adult males from the lowlands. Yet the small concessions policy now aimed at flooding highland provinces like Yen Bai, Phu Tho, and Thai Nguyen with a tide of energetic peasant families who could clear their previously uncultivated hills and valleys. After all, the policy's rules of application were simple; it gave the peasants the right to landownership and therefore incentives for remaining in the highlands which wage workers on the plantations lacked; and the parcels of land it awarded were small enough for single peasant families to cultivate without difficulty. But the flood of migrants never materialized, and the failure of this colonial small concessions policy in the Tonkin highlands was one of the most telling tragedies in the agricultural history of colonial Southeast Asia.

For the small concessions were founded upon a European hallucination, that Tonkin was filled with individualistic peasants with reasonable amounts of household capital. Since the Red River delta was filled instead with communalistic peasants without any capital, the colonial government's grandiose dream of an epic migration into the unfarmed hills cruelly exposed its own complete separation from countryside realities.

As Nghiem Xuan Yem pointed out in 1944, the policy suited the needs of "middle category peasants," those with "developmental minds" who had enough capital to finance their own resettlement in the highlands— that is, enough money to build a house, to purchase tools and cattle, and to buy food for a month or for half a year. The vast majority of northern peasants lacked even this much money, and therefore dared not petition for small concessions. In fact, the penury of the Vietnamese peasants who had migrated to the highlands to work as tenant farmers was so notorious that plantation owners there actually preferred to recruit members of the highland Tho people to work on their estates. For even the Tho people were more likely to have cattle, tools, food, and capital than Vietnamese refugees from the delta. Furthermore, the small concessions, by seeking to attract applications and migration on an individual family basis, ignored the psychology of Vietnamese villagers. Unlike Canadian and American homesteading families of the nineteenth century, few Vietnamese peasant families wished to abandon their ancestral villages all by themselves to move to the lonely, malarial highlands. Between 1925 and 1939 only about one thousand people came to clear land in Yen Bai province; and even families which had acquired permanent rights to small concessions tried to sell them, take the capital, and return to their lowland villages, where they no longer felt like "vagrants" cut off from a vital supporting milieu, from the graves of grandparents, and from traditional mutual-help organizations. Individual migration was encouraged when only communal migration, and the reconstitution of delta village "atmospheres" and frameworks in the highlands, might have worked. For these reasons, permanent lowland migration to the highlands, which might have relieved some of the grievous effects of population pressure, never occurred on a large scale. Yet by the early 1940s there were as many as 1.5 million poor people in the Red River delta who lacked any farm land to cultivate.[71] The ancient villages in which they lived enclosed increasing misery. But their structures and customs had not completely broken down. The lack of migration to the highlands, an alternative of desperation, did indicate this—or at least it indicated that middle-peasant society, that part of the peasant world with enough capital to migrate if it had to, had not broken down.

The competition for increasingly scarce resources of lowland land, however, was only one of the keynotes of Tonkinese poverty. It is possible to gain another kind of perspective on the state of the society of the north, on the eve of the August Revolution, simply by considering the great Tonkin cattle shortage. In 1944, it was estimated, some 500,000 cattle were needed to farm the lands of the Tonkin delta adequately, given the complete absence of farm machinery. Yet Tonkin possessed only 450,000 cattle (far more water buffaloes than oxen); and it had informal pasture resources (mainly burial grounds, paths at the edges of rice fields, grassy strips along the dikes) that were capable of supporting only 15,000 cattle by Western standards of pasturing and nutrition. In other words, the great animal husbandry revolution which had begun in western Europe in the eighteenth century, involving the rotational planting of fields and the scientific production of fodder crops, had not been imported. Even the cattle herds on European plantations in Vietnam were poorly fed and their breeding was ignored: their sole reason for existence was to supply fertilizer for tea and coffee crops.

Because the available pasturelands were forced to sustain some thirty times the number of cattle they were really capable of sustaining, Tonkinese cattle remained undernourished, emaciated, and vulnerable to disease. And because there was, in addition, a cattle shortage, peasants themselves had to be used as substitutes for implement-pulling cattle in the fields. There was also a drearily repetitive circulation of aging livestock throughout the north, engineered by cattle dealers who, for example, might purchase emaciated discards cheaply in the highlands and bring them to the delta to be resold. Here, then, was an economy blighted by much more than a land maldistribution problem. The entire northern farm economy was a nightmare of bizarre imbalances and shortages, and its whole configuration appeared to reinforce poverty. What was awaited was a government powerful enough to break this centuries-old configuration and transform an unfeatured, technology-poor, subsistence agriculture so unspecialized that it could not even produce well-fed cattle. But such a government would have to risk upsetting traditional village oligarchies, and risk ending as well that isolation of individual villages which had been so convenient to dynastic and colonial states with limited economic aims.[72]

The highland plantations, rather than the delta villages, were the places where decomposition of political or managerial controls had accompanied economic deterioration most remarkably in Tonkin in the 1940s. Not surprisingly, it was out of the highlands that Viet Minh guerrillas were to emerge in strength in the spring of 1945.

Up in the cinnamon forests and limestone hills of the province of Thai Nguyen, for example, there existed large coffee plantations whose ownership was unstable and whose transient peasant tenant farmers and sharecroppers were not dominated in the traditional manner by any councils of notables. One of these plantations, with more than ten thousand coffee trees and tea bushes, was carefully studied by Vietnamese researchers from Hanoi in the summer of 1944. It was located about one kilometer from the Thai Nguyen provincial capital, which no more than 450 Viet Minh soldiers, armed with a few bazookas and American automatic rifles, were to seize with relative ease on August 19, 1945.[73] What the researchers discovered, less than a year before the Viet Minh victory, was a plantation about thirty years old which had already passed through the hands of some six French owners and which was now in the possession of its seventh absentee owner, a Vietnamese businessman who lived in Haiphong. The managers of this plantation, an unpredictable collection of lightweights, had been shuffled even more rapidly than the owners: the first manager who worked for the seventh owner had been a youth who specialized in Western boxing; and the second manager (in residence at the time of the researchers' visit) was an aged, retired civil servant. The fifteen hundred agricultural workers and their families who planted and harvested crops, weeded, and roasted coffee beans for an owner they had never seen, were divided into twenty-seven different "villages." But these villages were administered by an appointed, paid "settlement master." They lacked the elaborate, long-descended hierarchies of villages in the lowlands.[74]

Another northern highland coffee plantation, this time in Son Tay province, was also observed by Vietnamese researchers less than a year before the August Revolution. It also had a new absentee owner (a European who owned a large meat store in Hanoi), an inexperienced manager (a Vietnamese youth), European foremen, and worker villages run by artificial, appointed settlement masters rather than by notables. Like other Tonkin highlands coffee plantations, its decay at the end of 1944 was clearly apparent. Only two of its twenty electric coffee grinding machines were still in use, and weeds could be seen growing among its coffee trees. By this time the price of coffee had fallen so low that coffee sales no longer paid for the plantation's manpower costs. (The Pacific war had destroyed Vietnam's coffee export trade, and the consumption of coffee in Vietnam itself was small.) The plantation's annual production had dropped from 160 tons of coffee buds to 10 tons, much of its produce was rotting in storehouses, and cultivation of the more fragile types of coffee tree, which required large amounts of manpower, had been suspended, leaving only the toughest kinds of coffee tree—known in Tonkin as "jack-fruit coffee"—still in cultivation.[75]

The political implications of this desolate highland economic landscape would hardly be difficult to suggest. Many of them were even proposed by the plantation researchers of 1944, who could not have foreseen the coming revolution. The fact that Haiphong merchants and Hanoi beef firm owners possessed plantations in the Tonkin highalnds—even manifestly unprofitable ones—demonstrated the tenacity of the traditional elite investment patterns in Vietnamese society. Land was still regarded as the best insurance against economic and political instabilities. Yet, by 1944, this insurance was wearing very thin. For one thing, the constant ownership and management turnovers on these highland plantations meant that, throughout the colonial period, there was little accumulation of managerial (or political) knowledge about the region. On the eve of the revolution, as the Hanoi researchers of 1944 found repeatedly, the managers of these plantations knew nothing about their past history. For another thing, these plantations were very inefficient despotisms, or inefficient authoritarian systems. The managers and foremen enjoyed great power over the welfare and daily life of their agricultural workers. There were few reliable public institutions to check the power of the owner and the manager, which meant that the grievances of the plantation coolies were rarely mitigated, or even properly ventilated outside the plantations. But at the same time, these inefficient despotisms were very poorly defended in Tonkin by the 1940s. They lacked the private police forces of, for example, modern Brazilian sugar plantations; they lacked the control apparatus of even their more affluent southern counterparts in Vietnam itself; and they lacked the ritualistic reflexes of control which were still being exercised by the oligarchs of Red River delta villages. They were not even very compact, socially (and politically) speaking. The researchers who visited the Son Tay coffee plantation in 1944 found that its manager could not assemble its tenant farmers for interviews because they lived in too "scattered" a fashion, far from the plantation's center. The reason for this was to prevent the plantation cattle herds, located at the center, from devouring the crops (maize, sweet potatoes, rice) which the tenant farmers privately grew for their own food.

Into this environment of decadent highland plantations and overcrowded lowland villages, the colonial government began to introduce unprecedentedly draconian tax pressures at the outset of the Pacific War. After 1940, it began to create "emergency granaries," under the control of the state and of its local agents. To these emergency granaries all Vietnamese farmers had to sell even their unhusked paddy, at prices the French resident superior of Tonkin decreed. Both small landowners and big landowners had to comply with these forced sales. But the amounts of paddy which they had to contribute were not assessed on a progressive or sliding basis. Smallholders, in some instances, might have to contribute as much as big landlords. All this meant two things: first, that the colonial government was now practicing a massive, dictatorial intervention in the Tonkin rural economy in the 1940s, because of the abnormal exigencies of a world war; and second, that it was, at the same time, attempting to preserve rather than to change the inequitable distribution of property and resources which characterized this economy. The regime was not a superficial, laissez-faire government which left the villages essentially undisturbed, but it was also not a government which used its permeative power to carry out reforms.

On May 21, 1943, the French resident superior of Tonkin declared that the price of the paddy which was to be transferred to the emergency granaries by these forced sales would be 14.5 piasters per one picul of paddy (one hundred kilograms). At first sight, this fixed price seemed fair enough: the average market price of one picul of paddy in 1940, three years before, had been 11.5 piasters. Subsequent research by Vietnamese investigators soon showed that, because these state-determined prices of paddy were too low, farm households all over Tonkin were losing what little capital they possessed. In Hoai Duc prefecture in Ha Dong province, for example, whose rice fields were renowned for their high productivity, by 1943 it cost a big landowner who hired agricultural laborers to work his lands about 10.4 piasters to produce one picul of paddy (counting the costs of taxes, fertilizer, irrigation, rice seeds, and wages); it cost a small landowner, who worked about one-half of his own lands himself, only 8.82 piasters to produce one picul of paddy; but it cost a tenant farmer, who had to rent his land and his water buffaloes from his landlord, 15.62 piasters to produce one picul of paddy. And it was the tenant farmers rather than their landlords who had to sell their paddy to the state, which meant that the landlords, insulated from state intervention, could charge the same rents regardless of what emergency price measures the government introduced. Tenant farmers, therefore, who were the predominating rural group, were being bankrupted by this state intervention in the rice market. Statistics for areas of Tonkin other than Hoai Duc prefecture were even more ominous.[76]

Furthermore, by 1943 Tonkin had become a jigsaw puzzle of multiple inflationary patterns. The state manipulation of rice prices from 1943 onward paid insufficient attention to the inflation of the prices of other goods and services. While the state-determined price for one picul of unhusked paddy had risen only 26 percent between 1940 and 1943, the price of a catty of soap had more than tripled, the price of beef had quadrupled, the price of fish sauce had almost tripled, the price of conical hats had doubled, the price of earthen pots had quadrupled, and the price of a box of matches had nearly tripled. (These prices, moreover, were the legal public prices fixed by the state, not black market prices.) General inflation was to be as much a harbinger of revolution in Tonkin as it was to be the harbinger of revolution in China in the late 1940s. It was accompanied by a grim disequilibrium among all the rising prices.

All these new state demands for rice continued to coexist with the privileges of the old Tonkin village hierarchies, whose members had been tendered their final lease on political life by the reforms of 1941. With the vacant, abstracted self-indulgence of a sleepwalker, the colonial government made ever-increasing demands for rice and revenue between 1940 and 1945 upon an environment whose inequitable distribution of economic resources it could not, or did not wish to, disturb. And up until the end of 1944 this government succeeded in slowly brutalizing the life in this environment without really greatly disrupting it, precipitating only the spread of an anguished confusion among northern peasants, rather like the confusion of the society which Michelangelo depicted in his painting, *The Last Judgment.* At the end of 1944, the requisitioning and hoarding of rice, by both the French and the Japanese occupiers of Tonkin, had reached its inevitable crisis point. Vietnamese rice was being burned for fuel in factories, or transported to Japan; the wartime breakdown of rail and sea transportation prevented the importation of Cochin China rice into Tonkin; and in the winter of 1944–1945, between 400,000 and 2 million Tonkinese peasants died in a great famine. The impact of the famine temporarily blasted and withered the northern social order. It loosened family obligations. It even caused people who were "absent-minded from hunger" to try to sell their ancestral altars, at horror-filled New Year's markets in the early spring of 1945.[77] Out of this rural famine and dislocation, a communist coalition led by Ho Chi Minh seized power in the north in August 1945.

5

The Origins and Expansion of Communist Power

Ho Chi Minh and the Vietnamese Political Tradition

Despite the enormous number of outlooks and programs which they share, the Chinese and Vietnamese revolutions are not the same. Some of the factors which have distinguished the Vietnamese revolutionary process from its counterpart and sometime model in China have already been alluded to: the greater importance of demystifying colonialism in Vietnam; the absence of influences from any powerful traditional utopianism in Vietnam; the more intense Vietnamese search for new forms of *doan the* or organized communities; the greater inability of Vietnamese opponents of revolution to convert Confucianism into a satisfyingly national ideology of conservatism; and the inheritance of a more critical deficiency of new organizations in the Vietnamese countryside between 1900 and 1950 than could be found in China, let alone Japan. A sense of the different emphases in the two revolutions could also be gained merely by glancing at the early, pre-Marxist careers of the most important progenitors of Chinese and Vietnamese Communism, Mao Tse-tung and Ho Chi Minh.

Mao Tse-tung, as is well known, formally entered Chinese public life in April 1917, when he published an article in the journal "New Youth"—the central organ of the Peking and Shanghai intellectuals who wished to change China's culture—on the subject of "The Study of Physical Training." (This historic article appeared, incongruously enough, beside a Chinese translation of Edmund Waller's poem "On The Rose.") Not yet a Marxist but very much a nationalist, Mao declared that China's "national strength" was feeble, partly because the physical qualities of the Chinese people themselves were daily becoming more enervated. Of the civilized countries, Germany was the most prosperous (Mao was writing in early 1917), and a great cause of Germany's prosperity was the diffusion of the German elite custom of dueling among the German people. In Japan, the upper classes at least still remembered "the way of the warrior" (*bushidō*) and (Mao's cultural nationalism was obvious) had fabricated the art of judo from the remnants of Chinese culture which existed in Japan. In Chinese education, on the other hand, there was a tragic bias toward intellectual training rather than physical training, and Chinese primary schools were accordingly filled with sickly, scrawny children reading books aloud. The young Mao wrote angrily: "The curricula of our country's educational system are as dense as the hairs of an ox, but no one is able to raise the question of strong bodies."

Mao's target was Chinese schoolteachers rather than their schools. In his picture, Chinese schools as institutions had adopted the methods of Western countries, but Chinese schoolteachers had not changed their inner value systems, which relegated people who performed physical work or activity of any kind to a lower social order. Mao concluded his article by outlining his own six-part physical training program. A kind of 1917 Chinese Taoist anticipation of the RCAF physical fitness booklet, it recommended such "movements" as doing leaping dances ten times in a row, then breathing deeply three times.[1] Was Mao ultimately converted to communism by his personal search for a generalized political form of *bushidō*? What is important is that he strode onto the Chinese stage in 1917 talking about educational reforms, excessive intellectuality, and the need to combine booklearning with physical activity—and he was still talking about these things, in very different political surroundings, fifty years later.

In the 1960s, of course, Mao Tse-tung's educational philosophy was occasionally regarded as an East Asian attack upon Western technocratic civilization and values (especially his argument that human willpower was more potent than the atomic bomb), as an attack upon the supposedly neutral, all-conquering world of the Western scientific order and of the machine. Historically speaking, it had not originated as such. It had begun instead as an attack against the cultural and social residues in modern China of the Sung Neo-Confucian philosophers' deprecation of athletics and of physical aggressiveness. The twelfth-century philosopher Chu Hsi, moving beyond the traditional Confucian distinction between intellectual labor and physical labor, had condemned even the practice of such pastimes as archery and swordsmanship by the educated elite, in his effort to duplicate, within the Confucian sphere, the ascetic control of the body and of the emotions taught by certain strands of Buddhism. To Mao, this Sung Neo-Confucian legacy was dooming the Chinese nation, through the spell it cast over Chinese educators, to a position of international weakness. He told his readers that they should imitate, as antidotes, the lives of anti-Sung philosophy intellectuals of the 1600s, like Yen Yüan (1635–1704), a philosopher who had walked more than one thousand miles and had studied fencing with swords.

In 1917, Ho Chi Minh was also still in his pre-Marxist phase. But he was already a hardy Vietnamese nationalist, with very different patterns in his immediate background from those of Mao. Ho was the youngest son of a poor but indelibly upper-class Confucian intelligentsia family. He was born (as Nguyen Sinh Cung, later changed to Nguyen Tat Thanh; his most famous pseudonym will be used throughout this book) in the north central province of Nghe An about 1890. His father became a regional degree holder in the civil service examinations of 1894, and eventually (1909) reached the status of district magistrate. Few communist revolutionaries have ever made less effort to claim lower class antecedents, for the ideal of the scholar-bureaucrat pervaded the atmosphere of Ho's natal village: a recent Hanoi study has proudly advertised the fact that the village itself, in 96 regional and metropolitan examinations from 1635 to the 1900s, had produced 193 winning degree holders, of which 53, the most, came from Ho's own hamlet.[2] By no coincidence, this village was also a hotbed of "aid the king" activity in 1885. The illustrious village schoolteacher, Vuong Thuc Mau, created a village volunteer company to fight the French. It was defeated in 1886, four years before Ho was born. But the scholar-gentry who had served in it survived its dissolution and could still be found plotting resistance, at nightly meetings in the village temple which masqueraded as Buddhist sutra-chanting sessions, as late as 1910. Ho received his nationalism from his father, from these village traditions, and from such local spectacles as the massive (and murderous) colonial conscription of Vietnamese peasants, in his village and others, to build the Cua Rao highway into Laos. At the end of 1911, as yet another young, unknown representative of Vietnam's pillaged, humiliated "aristocracy of scholars," he enrolled as a ship's boy on a French ship, and left Vietnam for the West. He was not to set foot on his native soil again until 1941—under rather different circumstances.

If the young Mao Tse-tung was concerned with the malignant effects the survival of Sung Neo-Confucian attitudes in Chinese education would have upon the health and power of the new China, the young Ho Chi Minh—and other members of his generation in Vietnam—were almost certainly more concerned with the curious problem of loyalty which was the cardinal legacy of *their* past. How could men born into the social and intellectual milieu of Vietnamese scholar-gentry families gracefully make the transition from Confucianism to revolution, given the facts that "loyalty" to the prince was a basic Confucian virtue, that Vietnamese emperors were still sitting upon the national throne at Hue, and that the Vietnamese throne had been, for centuries, the symbol of a people's pride? The dilemma was much greater in Vietnam than in China. The Chinese monarchy, which had come to an end in 1911, had never symbolized Chinese ethnic pride and had in fact been frequently and easily captured by non-Chinese dynastic houses.

The answer which Vietnamese interpreters sympathetic to Ho Chi Minh give to this complicated question is that Ho and his family deliberately linked themselves to a rebel tradition of Confucian loyalism, or to a semi-indigenized tradition of Confucian loyalism, which was not part of the orthodox, fully imported philosophical system of the Nguyen court. In this semi-indigenized tradition, the concept of "loyalty" to the prince became much more conditional than it ever was in Chinese philosophical texts. The Chinese philosopher Mencius had emphasized that in the event of an external crisis, it was better for a ruler to cede territory than to lose the hearts of his people because of a lack of personal rectitude. But in Vietnam, although Mencius was widely read, this dictum had been (historically) far less acceptable or applicable. Loyalty to the monarch remained unconditional only as long as the monarch did *not* cede national territory; and the ruler's personal rectitude was much more intimately associated with his successful defense of his political patrimony than it was in China.

The great difference between traditional Vietnam and traditional Japan, as has been mentioned, was that Vietnamese resistance to Chinese invasions and influences over the centuries had never found mature philosophical expression in any separate, national Confucian intellectual system. During the eighteenth-century Japanese enlightenment, Japanese Confucian thinkers like Miura Baien and Kaiho Seiryō and the Osaka merchant intellectual Yamagata Bantō had converted Confucianism into a kind of "national studies" which focused upon the Japanese classical past rather than upon the Chinese classical past and which used Confucian teachings as tools of inquiry rather than as revered objects from China.[3] Eighteenth-century Vietnam had known no equivalent "enlightenment" in which formal Confucian philosophies had been, in effect, nationalized. On the other hand, the Vietnamese Confucian intelligentsia had undergone a profound practical crisis of conscience over the issue of loyalty in the late 1700s. And the thought and behavior of their twentieth-century descendants has almost certainly borne the imprint of this crisis.

The eighteenth-century intellectual with whom Ho Chi Minh's own name is most often associated by Hanoi biographers is Ngo Thi Nham (1746–1803). Ngo Thi Nham had withdrawn his loyalty from the Le dynasty emperors in the 1780s, when it had become apparent that they could no longer hold Vietnam together, and had offered it to the revolutionary Tay-son movement. In effect, he had linked loyalty to a concern for the survival of the Vietnamese kingdom, in a way that might have shocked more universalistic Confucian philosophers in China. And even his historian brothers, who did not shift their loyalties with him, were appalled enough by the ineptness of the Le rulers to describe the last emperor of the Le lineage rather sacrilegiously as "a piece of meat in a bag of skin."[4] It has been pleaded that Ho Chi Minh married Marxism to the rebel Confucian tradition in Vietnam represented most notably by eighteenth-century politicians like Ngo Thi Nham, and that, under Marxist influence, he expanded the content of traditional Confucian values—filial piety, loyalty, industriousness—in ways that would not have wholly outraged the more indigenous side of Vietnamese Confucianism.[5] Ho's great concern with the issue of loyalty may be indicated by the fact that when he read Tolstoy's short story "Father Sergius" during his Paris years, he was most impressed by the relatively unimportant beginnings of the story, which he was to remember vividly for decades, in which the St. Petersburg nobleman who becomes "Father Sergius" removes himself from contact with the tsar who has betrayed him.[6]

The intellectual odysseys of Ho Chi Minh are more difficult to expound than his geographical ones, but both have their mysteries. His very decision to go to the West, in 1911, was extremely unconventional. It revealed a highly original internationalism. At that time—not in 1921, or 1931, but certainly in 1911—most anticolonial members of the Vietnamese intelligentsia, in the afterglow of the "Eastern travel" movement, still chose to spend their time in Japan or China or Siam but not yet in Europe. The Vietnamese who visited France before World War I were, with obvious and rather forced exceptions like Phan Chu Trinh, mainly interpreters or pro-French civil servants or businessmen attached to French firms in Indochina. Even in 1911, however, Ho Chi Minh did not want to limit his perspective to Asian countries. The crucial fact is that his internationalism preceded his Marxism-Leninism, which he did not adopt until 1920.

After 1911, Ho spent long periods in such countries as England and France, working in such menial occupations as ship's boy, sweeper of snow, stoker of furnaces, cook, draftsman, and photography worker. The cycle of social revolution had reached a strange completion: instead of the kitchen boy wearing the clothes of the mandarin, as in the 1880s in Saigon, the mandarin was now wearing the garb of the kitchen boy, but for a different purpose. He remained in Paris from the early stages of World War I until the end of 1923, ensconced in a cheap hotel (No. 9, Impasse Compoint) in the seventeenth *arrondissement.* He studied industriously, especially foreign languages: he made it a point to write ten foreign words a day or more on the backs of his hands and memorize them before falling asleep at night. Under the pseudonym of Nguyen Ai Quoc (discarded some time in the 1930s) he earned about 120 francs a month by working at a small photography shop (from 1919 to 1922). Friends secured him a reading permit at the Bibliothèque Nationale, and it was at the French national library that he apparently first read the Marxist classics. Once he had learned to speak and write French fluently, he edited and published a newspaper (*Le Paria*) in French—beginning in 1922—and wrote essays and even a play ("The Bamboo Dragon") in the language of the conqueror.

Ho's internationalism differentiates him powerfully from Mao Tse-tung, if not nearly so much from other early Chinese communists. It was to lead him to function as a Comintern agent for other Asian countries than his own, and to write dialogues in a European language addressed directly to European workers—two things that it would be impossible to imagine Mao doing. But it could also be argued that his perceptions of social class memberships, and their traumas, at least originated in very different circumstances from Mao Tse-tung's, even if Ho eventually used the same Marxist jargon to describe them. Mao became an inflamed observer of the decaying village power structures of inland China. But Ho, perhaps, was far more directly concerned with the connections between the colonial hierarchy of races and the colonial hierarchy of occupations which were all too visible in the Franco-Vietnamese colonial world. Social class symbolism, in this world, was accentuated by the manner in which jobs as ship stewards were reserved for Frenchmen and jobs as cabin boys were reserved for Vietnamese. Once Western theories of social classes were accepted intellectually—and this was not easy in East Asia—it did not require great leaps of the imagination to believe that certain class arrangements, and colonialism, were intertwined. Vietnamese revolutionaries almost certainly experienced these realizations more vividly than their Chinese counterparts. Making periodic visits to the International Settlement in Shanghai was not the same thing as toiling as a humble, underpaid photography shop worker in Paris.

Ho Chi Minh as a Young Communist Revolutionary

In June 1919 Ho signed a famous petition, which was presented in vain to the Versailles peace conference, demanding democracy and self-determination for the Vietnamese people. He read Lenin for the first time in the fall of 1920. His starting point—and the work of Lenin which influenced him more than any other—was the "Preliminary Draft Theses on the National and Colonial Questions." These, Lenin had prepared for the second congress of the Communist International. At the congress of Tours in December 1920, Ho participated in the creation of the French Communist Party. Here he denounced the crimes of imperialism in his own homeland, and made it clear that his conversion to communism was inspired essentially by nationalism. He spent a year in Russia (January–December 1924) studying Marxism-Leninism and sharing enthusiasms with the motley crowd of Asian and European revolutionaries who had foregathered in Moscow. Yet despite the fact that he was a lover of Tolstoy and an ardent student of languages he never fully entered the Russian world, and in 1941, when he returned to Vietnam, he carried with him, significantly, a history of Russian communism written in Chinese.[7]

The fifth congress of the Communist International, meeting in Moscow in the summer of 1924, created an "eastern bureau" of which Ho became an important member. It sent him to China in December 1924 with a mandate to guide revolutionary movements, not just in Vietnam but in the other countries of Southeast Asia as well. Before 1924, the Comintern had paid no attention to Vietnam. Its first Vietnamese-language appeal was issued on February 27, 1924. This tract summarized the history of the Comintern and explained that it was designed to represent and bring together all "people who worked for a living" (*nguoi lam an*). The Comintern's second Vietnamese-language appeal, issued on August 1, 1924, stated that Lenin was a Russian who had seen the profit motives behind World War I and had persuaded the Russian people to overthrow their monarchy.[8] These two rather shallow documents, together with back copies of *Le Paria,* found their way to Vietnam and became the basis of the first circulation of communist ideas there in the mid-1920s.

Making contact with veteran Vietnamese revolutionaries who were living in such Chinese cities as Hangchow, Shanghai, and Canton, and exploiting every regional and kinship tie he possessed, Ho emphasized the need for a better organization of the nationalist cause. On February 19, 1925, he sent a letter to the Comintern in Moscow jubilantly proclaiming that he had formed the first secret communist organization in Vietnamese history. This was a group based in Canton, and led by himself, which had a total of nine members, two of whom had been elected to return to Vietnam, three of whom were members of a local Chinese army, and one of whom was engaged in military work for the Chinese Kuomintang.[9] Beyond this secret organization, he established a bigger, more public one, whose title is conventionally translated into English as the "Vietnam Revolutionary Youth League" (*Viet Nam thanh nien cach mang dong chi hoi*). Its membership came from a reshuffling of several previously existing Vietnamese nationalist groups in south China, and its purpose was to train young cadres for revolutionary evangelism (and direct action) in Indochina. At the headquarters of the Youth League, on Wen-ming street in Canton, between 1925 and April 1927, Ho personally taught the Leninist creed and formulas of organization to Vietnamese youths who had come from places as far away as Siam. The members of his training classes then returned to all three regions of Vietnam to create fresh Youth League cells.

Ho's full-fledged Leninist revolutionary party itself did not emerge until February 1930. It was the product then of some formidable cross-fertilization, of a little discreet plastic surgery, and of the techniques of "waiting for the right moment." It was born at a Hong Kong conference of Vietnamese communist associations' representatives, managed by Ho Chi Minh as the representative of the Comintern. In addition to the old Youth League and the several regional parties the Youth League had sponsored, this conference embraced the leading elements of "The New Vietnam Revolutionary Party" (*Tan Viet cach mang dang*), a central Vietnamese movement (with one cell in the northern province of Hung Hoa) which had cooperated and quarrelled with Ho Chi Minh's Youth League for some four years. The "New Vietnam" party had been even more obsessed by the need for secrecy of style than the Youth League. In addition to giving its members secret names, it had given secret names to geographic places, referring to Tonkin, for example, as the "region of benevolence," Cochin China as the "region of bravery." But it had been far less receptive to the claims of Marxist class analysis. Unlike the Youth League, it had not provided different kinds of "preparatory periods" for prospective members purely on the basis of their presumed class memberships.[10]

The intellectuals and students of the "New Vietnam" party had flirted with some Marxist-Leninist ideas, however, and enough of them were willing to acknowledge the more experienced Ho Chi Minh as their political mentor to collaborate in the emergence of the coalition-like Vietnam Communist Party at the February 1930 Hong Kong meeting. The name of the new party was subsequently changed in October 1930 to the Indochina Communist Party (ICP). Tran Phu, a former member of the "New Vietnam" party, became its first secretary-general. The first blueprint for revolution which he composed, "based upon collective opinions," specified a two-stage revolutionary process for Vietnam. Stage one, that of the "bourgeois democratic revolution," meant the winning of national independence, the overthrow of imperialism and feudalism, and land reform. Stage two meant Vietnam's journey into socialism, a journey which could bypass any development of capitalism.

Ho Chi Minh had accomplished the transition from ship's boy to architect of the Indochina Communist Party in less than twenty years. To some extent, his achievement was a stunning mixture of the old with the new. Much of his political prestige, in the eyes of other Vietnamese revolutionaries in 1930, rested upon his international Comintern accreditation, and it is irresistible, if not entirely fair, to compare this accreditation with the seals of investiture traditional Vietnamese emperors had received from China. Moreover, the analogy—and the suggestion that Ho exploited traditional Vietnamese patterns and expectations of leadership—could be pushed much further. For one of his cadre training classes in Canton in August 1926, Ho translated the anthem "The International" into Vietnamese six-eight poetry, and taught it to his students, in a paternalistic way that was at least mildly reminiscent of the Tu-duc emperor's translation of the Confucian Analects into Vietnamese word songs less than a century before at the Hue court. Had Ho merely modernized the role of the emperor-translator, of the ideal leader as culture hero who domesticates treasures from other countries?

Even the order of his cultural borrowing was, in part, a reflection of the set of priorities which Vietnamese emperors had used in the past. Many of the symbols, and the rituals of participation, preceded many of the statutes and institutions of substance. The Gia-long emperor, in the early 1800s, had built a "Hall of Supreme Harmony" in Hue to match the building of the same name in Peking before he had begun to import many vital Chinese bureaucratic institutions, which work in fact he left to his succes-

sors. For their part, the early Vietnamese communists acquired a translation of the "International" (August 1926) before they acquired their first
newspaper inside Vietnam ("Hammer and Sickle," *Bua liem,* appearing in
the fall of 1929); their first domestic newspaper appeared before their first
biography of Lenin was written (January 1930); and their first biography
of Lenin was published before their first serious revolutionary plan for
Vietnamese society was devised (October 1930).

Unfortunately for classicists, the analogy has its limits. The work of
domesticating the theories, programs, and symbols of world communism
engaged the attention of many Asian revolutionaries in this decade—
revolutionaries who did not come from countries whose rulers had been
consistent and conspicuous cultural borrowers. In China, for example, the
"International" was translated into Chinese by Ch'ü Ch'iu-pai, who became
the Chinese Communist Party's secretary-general in 1927. Ho Chi Minh,
moreover, was supposed to be the progenitor of revolutions across Southeast Asia, and his far-reaching public identity as the servant of the Comintern might (in some eyes) have diminished his lustre as a purely Vietnamese
cultural broker. However, the evidence suggests that he actually saw Southeast Asian countries other than Vietnam purely from the "metropolitan"
point of view, evaluating their struggles not on the basis of their own
national histories but on the basis of the relative importance of their Western colonial oppressors. An important index to the mind of Ho Chi Minh
in the 1920s is the small book "The Road of Revolution" (*Duong kach
menh*) which he wrote and had printed in Canton in 1926. Written in an
experimental, nonstandard form of romanized Vietnamese which must
have puzzled its readers, and on its cover a small drawing of a circle with a
shackled man inside it, this book was intended to serve as a primer for the
Youth League cadre classes. The "national peoples" in whose revolutions
it took an interest were the Vietnamese, the Indians, the Koreans, the
Filipinos, and the Chinese. By this book's standards British imperialism in
India and China was much more significant than British imperialism in
Burma or Malaya, Dutch imperialism attracted little interest at all, and the
Filipinos were apparently important chiefly because they were oppressed
by the Americans.[11]

"The Road of Revolution" did present an explicit, and eloquent, argument for cultural borrowing which seems very Vietnamese, and which
could probably be found much less readily in Chinese communist texts of
the period. Ho informed his readers that the revolution in Vietnam required
four things: an educational crusade, an understandable ideology, "concentrated" organizational strength, and a capacity to make "world movements" understood to the Vietnamese people, who were ignorant of the
situation outside their own country, so that the people would "know how
to make comparisons." Here Ho broke down the elitism of traditional
Vietnamese cultural borrowing, implying some degree of popular participation in the selection of new political forms and slogans. Citadel-bound

Vietnamese emperors of the 1800s had preferred "to make comparisons" between Vietnam and the outside world entirely by themselves.

Equally significantly, however, the Ho Chi Minh of the 1920s ascribed very little importance to the mediating, transforming effects which Vietnamese popular culture might have upon borrowed foreign ideas and movements. Lenin, of course, was famous for arguing in the years before the Russian Revolution that the concept of "national culture" was a bourgeois deception. In his view, the proletariats of the world would systematically create a single "international culture" whose potpourri of themes would include the best democratic and socialist elements that could be found in each country. Behind this approach lay some general communist assumptions: that economic motivations governed human nature; that there were therefore few if any really significant variations in human nature throughout the world; and that it was frivolous to stress or accept seriously the great variety of ideal personalities and of culturally sanctioned solutions to social problems which might exist in different civilizations. In "The Road of Revolution," Ho Chi Minh made almost no mention of culture, except to refer to it as a weapon of the capitalists and imperialists—along with religion—which these exploiters used to keep the Vietnamese people "stupid." The Vietnamese communists did not discover the favorable political potentialities of traditional Vietnamese popular culture until they launched their soviet movement in 1930. Indeed, they did not produce any basic, important theoretical statements on culture until 1943. Ultimately, the Vietnamese party came to believe passionately in the bright pageantry of heroic Vietnamese folk traditions and of virtuous Vietnamese cultural and historical idiosyncrasies—such as the specially creative roles of Vietnamese "feudal" women, or the special Vietnamese talent for social cohesiveness in times of need. But hindsight must not put this belief into the minds of party leaders during the period of the party's gestation, in the 1920s and 1930s.

Could the Vietnamese peasantry be found at the center of the "road of revolution," or must it be confined to the edges? It has been argued by some that Ho Chi Minh preceded Mao Tse-tung in calling attention to the vital role peasants could play in African and Asian revolutions. The chief justification for this assertion is little more than Ho's speech to the fifth congress of the Comintern, in Moscow in 1924. Here he pointed out that peasant revolt in the colonial world was ripening, and that if such revolt failed it would be solely because of lack of the leadership which the Comintern could supply.[12]

Ho as a clairvoyant, pre-Maoist prophet of peasant politics: it would be difficult to find much solid evidence for this picture elsewhere. In "The Road of Revolution," Ho defined the workers and peasants as the "roots" of any revolution, because they were the most oppressed people in society. He stipulated that three other social groups—the students, the small businessmen, and the small landowners—might play the part of "revolutionary friends" of the workers and peasants, because they were oppressed too, but not to the same degree. He declared that there were two kinds of revolutions, "revolutions of national peoples," which were not class revolutions, and "world revolutions." At one point he explained that world revolutions were led by the "propertyless class," whom he defined as "plowers and workers." At another point he explained that world revolution would mean simply the combination of "workers" all over the world, "like older and younger brothers of one family," for the sake of ushering in "the great unity of everything under Heaven" (*thien ha dai dong*)—an idea straight from the Chinese classics. The terseness of these statements only reinforced their ambiguity—and their malleability in the interests of a cool empiricism.

What is clear, however, is that the Ho Chi Minh of the 1920s publicly conceded very little to the peasants, except the fact that they were brutally and unjustly oppressed. Nowhere in his writings of this decade did he supply Vietnamese peasants with that hard armor of practical intuition and honesty and intolerance of cant with which Mao Tse-tung romantically invested his Hunanese peasants in his famous 1927 report of his investigation of the Hunan peasant movement. (This is not to say that Ho Chi Minh was not profoundly aware of the culture and folklore and psychology of Vietnamese peasants; the argument is simply that he did not stress these things as positive revolutionary factors in his writings of the 1920s.) In an article on "Chinese Peasant Conditions," published in *La Vie Ouvrière* on January 4, 1924, Ho concluded that Chinese peasants would become fully aware of their strength *only* when they had benefited from an intensive campaign of education "by our Chinese comrades"; they could not, apparently, do so spontaneously.[13] What was particularly remarkable, both in this and in other writings of the time, was Ho's avoidance of any mention of traditional Chinese and Vietnamese peasant uprisings, his avoidance of any discussions of historical traditions of peasant activism in East Asia. The Vietnamese communist movement's development of its remarkable populist historical vision, brimming with the feats of centuries-old mass movements, did not really begin until after 1940. Before 1940, according to one Hanoi theoretician, the party failed to solve the problem of how to deviate successfully from Russian revolutionary precedents.[14] The principal Vietnamese custodian of these precedents was Ho Chi Minh himself.

If the Vietnamese communists found themselves in a Russian straitjacket until 1940, it is appropriate to ask how much of the early Marxist tradition—of Marxism before it received its Leninist extensions—Ho had deeply examined. In "The Road of Revolution" he pays homage to Leninism alone, rather than to Marxism-Leninism, as the most "genuine, stable, revolutionary" ideology the Vietnamese people can exploit. What Western philosophy he read and absorbed between 1911 and 1920 remains a mystery;[15] he did, of course, carry a copy of "The Communist Manifesto" in his small rattan suitcase when he reentered Vietnam in 1941.

Lenin's ideal of a secret, professional, revolutionary party—a concept which Marx presumably had never envisaged—had certainly captured Ho's imagination. But in his mind such a party transcended its normal Leninist purposes and became an antidote to Vietnamese regional fragmentation. He wrote in "The Road of Revolution" that Vietnam was blighted by the fact that southerners were "suspicious" of men from central Vietnam, that people from the center were "disdainful" of Tonkinese (no mention here of class memberships or of class struggle), that Vietnamese political movements were dissipated by regional thinking, and that only a Leninist party could "concentrate" the strength of the Vietnamese revolution. In other words, a prime virtue of Leninism, even to this most devout, apostolic precisian of Leninist doctrines, was that it provided remedies for the weakness of "organized communities" in Vietnamese life.

Lenin was concerned both by imperialism and by the "class nature" of non-revolutionary states. Ho Chi Minh gave much greater weight to the malignancies of foreign imperialism as a force in modern history. He suggested, indeed, in a 1924 article in *La Vie Ouvrière*, that "modern feudalism" (the Vietnamese court and bureaucracy under French colonial rule) was worse than the precolonial variety: precolonial Vietnamese courts had at least based their taxes upon land classifications which reflected differences in productive capacity, but "modern feudalism" ignored such differences in levying its taxes.[16] He did not, however, supply any cogent Marxist explanation for this theme of the deterioration of tax-collecting rationality, which is perhaps the closest that the young Ho Chi Minh ever came to the "golden age in the past" reflex of so many other Vietnamese nationalists. Ho Chi Minh's views of imperialism, moreover, contained interesting biases and anachronisms, beyond those biases contributed by Leninism. To regard the Vietnamese revolution, or any revolution, as a confrontation between (on the one hand) an *ancien régime* whose ideas are all out-of-date and detached from reality, having outlived the conditions which gave them rise, and (on the other hand) new revolutionary groups which monopolize prescience, and which are attuned to only the most contemporary historical developments, would be a gross oversimplification. Both entrenched governments and their revolutionary oppositions may harbor intellectual divergences from the facts of the world in which they operate. Both may be afflicted by excessive ideological continuity, the creeds of both may tend to reflect the exposure of past generations of believers to the environments of earlier eras, and the crucial differences between the anachronistic postures of the *ancien régime* and the revolutionaries who are seeking to overthrow it may be only a matter of degree.

In 1930 Ho Chi Minh saw France not as a declining world power but as an expanding one. He had no appreciation whatsoever (it would seem) of the gravity of its political and military decline after World War I. In the words of appeal which he wrote on February 18, 1930, on the occasion of the creation of the communist party, he seriously argued that France was increasing its military forces, not just to destroy the Vietnamese revolution, but to prepare a "new imperialist war in the Pacific," with the object of seizing and occupying even more territories. When France's new Pacific war broke out, he predicted, colonialist terror would increase in Vietnam. France, however, was not the only imperialist power. In the minds of the early Vietnamese communists, imperialism and the West—or at least all Western countries except the Soviet Union—were one and the same. Tran Phu, the first party secretary-general, wrote in 1930 that in the period after 1928 the proletariats in "the imperialist countries" were "struggling violently." He gave as his evidence for this claim the "big work stoppages in Germany, in France, in Poland, etcetera"—although he did stop short of naming any nearby Polish colonies.[17]

In no small measure, the story of the intellectual genesis of Vietnamese communism, before 1925, remains the story of Ho Chi Minh's response to a single potent text—Lenin's 1920 "Theses on the National and Colonial Questions"—rather than the story of any momentous, comprehensive immersion by Ho, or any other young Vietnamese, in Hegelian philosophy or the writings of the young Marx or even Lenin's detailed writings on the nature of the bourgeois state. The "Theses" alone were the pivot of early Vietnamese communist nationalism. The "Theses," of course, did not mention Vietnam directly: Lenin referred in them rather confusedly to "Eastern peoples"; to China, Korea, and Japan; to Negroes in America; and to Ireland; but not to Indochina. Nevertheless, they did accuse the Treaty of Versailles of being an "act of violence" against weak nations, and they did propose the establishment of a close alliance between the "West European Communist proletariat and the revolutionary peasant movement in the East." No revolutionary in East Asia ever believed in the desirability and the feasibility of such an alliance more vividly than Ho Chi Minh. It was the inspiration for one of his most remarkable works, "French Colonization on Trial," which was published in Paris in 1925.

"French Colonization on Trial" was written in French. A Vietnamese language translation of this book did not appear in Hanoi until 1960, long after the communist movement had come to power. For the book was aimed, not at a Vietnamese audience, but at French workers, and was designed to persuade them to enroll in that alliance Lenin had called for five years earlier. The author tried to cast himself in the role of a prosecutor in a Western-style courtroom, summarizing the crimes of the colonial system, and making asides to his readers: he discussed the martyrdom of Vietnamese women, he explained, in order to enlighten their "sisters in the metropolitan country." Ho's purpose was to write an original essay in applied Leninism for French readers, with the hope that they could abandon what he regarded as their racial prejudices by understanding the iniquities of the colonial system as a whole. (The book used such techniques as carefully identifying cruel local functionaries in Vietnam as "colleagues of governor-general Merlin," in order to show how all the parts of colonialism were connected.) But Ho was also struggling to demolish the influence of such French writers as Pierre Loti and Emile Nolly, popular authors who had produced vaporing romances about "Tonkinese customs" and who usually took a sentimental, "Madame Chrysanthemum" approach to East Asian civilizations.[18] Much of his work was really a mixture of Leninism and of the contents of old-style Vietnamese gentry placards. Ho's descriptions of Catholic priests as land-hungry pillagers of Vietnamese villages tapped a century or more of anti-Christian gentry propaganda in Vietnam and China, but his recurrent presentation of statistical information in the book—as part of his countroom-like indictment of colonialism—was a relatively new device in Vietnamese polemical writing.

It is difficult to imagine any Chinese communist leader of the 1920s specifically addressing himself to the better nature of English or American or Japanese workers in their own language. Yet it would be wrong to regard "French Colonization on Trial" merely as further testimony to Ho Chi Minh's remarkable internationalism, but without having any significance for Vietnamese cultural borrowing. For one thing, Ho was attempting to master the peculiarly Western styles of irony and satire of one of his favorite writers, Anatole France. Parts of "French Colonization on Trial," incongruously or not, have the flavor of "Penguin Island." (Another example of the young Ho Chi Minh's simulation of Anotole France could be found in his article "Menagerie," published in *Le Paria* in 1923, in which he jokes about the wickedness of the monkey (Belgium), the cock (France), the tiger (Clemenceau), furry cats (French judges), and the exotic beasts imported to Marseilles for the colonial exhibition of 1922. Here, however, one can also detect a characteristic Vietnamese love of animal allegories which goes back centuries.)[19] For another thing, his determination to put French colonialism "on trial" sprang from his desire to absorb and domesticate Western logic. He was especially interested in that kind of universalistic logic, relatively new to Vietnamese intellectuals, which was used in presenting arguments in Western law courts, and which assumed that reactions to crimes, or public assessments of their harm, would not be conditioned by the importance of the immediate kinship or personal relationships involved or not involved. This kind of logic was, of course, serviceable to the causes of both nationalism and internationalism.

The High Tide and Ebb Tide of the Rural Soviets

The Indochina Communist Party (ICP) was born in the year the world depression came to Vietnam and caused foreign trade, the price of rice, and living standards all to decline.

The sixth congress of the Comintern, meeting in Moscow in 1928, had decreed that a "high tide" of revolutionary struggle was about to wash over eastern Asia, especially China. This presumption had become linked in China to a drive (since 1927) to create local "soviets." In Leninist theory, soviets were new types of national organs. They took the forms of councils with both legislative and administrative powers, councils that were neither mass congresses on the one hand nor small organizations of leaders on the other, but organizations "directed" by the masses and in harmony with them. They were a "first step toward socialism," the antidotes to "bourgeois" parliaments which the lower classes could not control, the agencies of mass struggle which were required to embrace all workers, soldiers, and rural poor.

What the creation of "soviets" really meant in China, after the defeat of the Canton commune at the end of 1927, was the Chinese Communist Party's creation of armed bases in the Chinese countryside, the construction of many levels and types of revolutionary institutions within those bases, and experimentation with party blueprints for social and economic change. The climax of the Chinese communists' "soviet" movement was, of course, the proclamation of the Chinese Soviet republic at Juichin, Kiangsi, in November 1931. The Kiangsi soviet republic was nothing less than an independent country within a country in the mountain fastnesses of southern China. It lasted from November 1931 to October 1934 and controlled the fortunes of up to thirty million Chinese peasants.[20] The 1931–1934 soviet republic of the Chinese Communist Party had its own legal system, its own budgetary process, its own Ministry of People's Committees for education, and its own complex land inspection operations. Nearly all the major figures in the communist movement who were to become the rulers of China after 1949 were deeply involved in the development of the Kiangsi republic, and were able to draw upon the lavish fund of experiences they acquired during its three years of existence when they attempted to revolutionize all of China in the 1950s and 1960s.

Perhaps one of the major keys to a comparative study of the Chinese and Vietnamese communist revolutions is the striking fact that the Vietnamese party had no soviet republic in its background when it finally came to power in 1945 or, more effectively, in 1954. Its own soviet movement, thanks to French repression and to Vietnam's relative smallness, had not been able to produce a complete experimental republic, despite the industry with which Vietnamese communist promoters of the movement borrowed extensively, in terminology if not in ideas, from promoters of the bigger soviets in China.

The leaders of the Indochina Communist Party, anxiously attempting to interpret the wishes of the Comintern, accepted the idea that a "high tide" (*cao trao*) of struggle would prevail in Vietnam in 1930. But they were frankly uncertain whether Indochina was one of the places where the world revolution should actually try to seize political power. The very first Vietnamese "soviets"—revolutionary village councils created to replace councils of notables—probably made their appearance in five districts of the two north central provinces of Nghe An and Ha Tinh at the beginning of September 1930.[21] The whole soviet movement was to be confined to these two provinces, and is known accordingly as the Nghe-Tinh soviet movement. But the ICP Central Committee's General Affairs commission, located in Saigon, decided upon the prosecution of a policy of armed violence in Vietnam only a month later, in October 1930. The soviets, in other words, were the product of regional ambitions and impulses within the party, ambitions and impulses which had not been exorcised by the emergence of a single national party in Hong Kong in February 1930. The Annam regional committee of the party, and the Nghe An provincial committee, had simply carved out the "soviets" within their own bailiwick, without waiting for any orders from national leaders living a harassed underground life in Saigon.

While Mao Tse-tung was closely associated with the work of the Chinese soviet republic, Ho Chi Minh had little to do with the Vietnamese soviets. He may or may not have approved of their policies. He continued to live outside Vietnam, sometimes in prison. In 1958 Tran Huy Lieu, a senior scholar of the history of the Vietnamese communist movement in Hanoi, made the astonishing confession that in going through the party archives he had not been able to find a single party directive outlining guidelines and formulas for the struggles of the soviet period—what their objectives should be and what methods should be used to achieve them. Rather lamely, he categorized the soviets not as a "general uprising" but as an "isolated high tide" in one region.[22]

What was this curious "isolated high tide"? It began in the Ben Thuy match factory just south of the city of Vinh. Its workers, organized by the Nghe An provincial committee of the ICP, staged a series of strikes in the spring and summer of 1930, demanding a reduction of taxes and of working hours, a resistance to "white terror," and the payment of damages to "families slaughtered in the Yen Bai violence." The match-factory workers were supported by sawmill workers, porters, and coolies in the city of Vinh, who distributed leaflets and practiced labor slowdowns. Then the spirit of rebellion, again well organized, spread to the countryside. Peasant demonstrators, accompanied by the beating of drums, the waving of flags, and the burning of firecrackers, attacked the headquarters of district magistrates, burned documents, released prisoners from jail, and smashed the rural offices of the Indochina wine monopoly. Local structures of colonial rule collapsed with breathtaking suddenness, exposing their superficiality. Some Vietnamese district magistrates and their armed guards, confronted by crowds of peasants, simply ran away. Others were captured and forced to don their blue ceremonial gowns and publicly state their approval of the demonstrators' slogans (the abolition of special taxes, the distribution of public lands to the poor, and the overthrow of imperialism and the Hue court). To compensate for the collapse of these local structures of authority, the colonial government had to bring in air power and hastily deployed squads of the French Foreign Legion. From this point forward, indeed, the colonial regime and its spiritual successors were to rely upon increasingly destructive doses of air power for almost half a century in a desperate attempt to stop revolution.

That the soviet movement of 1930–1931 began and ended in north central Vietnam was hardly any accident. From the perspective of Vietnamese classical history, the provinces of Nghe An and Ha Tinh had a number of special characteristics. For one thing, of all the regions of the early medieval Vietnamese kingdom, they were the farthest from China. Until the middle of the fifteenth century, therefore, Vietnamese patriots habitually assembled in their mountainous terrain and recruited armies from their villages in order to "drive north" against Chinese threats or actual Chinese invading armies. Second, among all the regions of that kingdom, they were the closest to the non-Vietnamese polities of central and southern Indochina. This meant that the Vietnamese people's "southward advance" to the Mekong delta had been launched from their soil. Even in the 1930s, shrewd Vietnamese observers thought they could detect a "mystique of migration" in these two provinces, a restless acceptance of the need to move (into the south or into Laos) which stemmed from more than just poverty and which gave the inhabitants of Nghe An and Ha Tinh an inherited psychology more inclined to tolerate and even welcome instability than that of many of the peasants of the Red River delta.[23]

In the nineteenth century, these two provinces, which were also the stronghold of more independently minded Confucian intellectuals, had been a powerhouse of resistance to French military pressures. And in 1930, the soviet movement was to reach its peak (meaning peasant demonstrations every day) in some ten districts of Nghe An and Ha Tinh. At least four of these districts (Dien Chau, Anh Son, Huong Son, and Duc Tho) had been the bases of a famous scholar-gentry uprising against the French presence in Vietnam in 1874. The district where the first village soviet appeared in 1930 (Thanh Chuong district) had been the home of the two most prominent leaders of the 1874 uprising, Tran Tan and Dang Nhu Mai.[24] Five at least of the most famous leaders of the Indochina communist movement of the 1930s, no matter how far removed they were from the planning of the soviet movement, had come from sovietized areas in these two provinces—Ho Chi Minh, Phan Dang Luu, Le Hong Phong, Tran Phu, and Minh Khai.

As traditional local government vanished in large tracts of the countryside of Nghe An and Ha Tinh, ICP cells and "mass organizations" claimed power in dozens of villages and began to reorganize them. The "mass organizations" had appeared as early as June 1930, with forms and titles that were to become suffocatingly familiar to their opponents in Vietnam in the next forty years: "workers' associations" (*cong hoi*), "peasants' associations" (*nong hoi*), "students' associations" (*sinh hoi*), "anti-imperialist youth" (*thanh nien phan de*), women's liberation units, and self-defense companies. The new "soviet" village governments, whose authority depended upon the self-defense companies, annulled French colonial taxes, reduced land rents, forced village notables to repay public funds which they had borrowed, and distributed to the poor public lands which had been under the notables' stewardship. But they did stop short of confiscating the private estates of landlords. Unlike the Chinese soviet movement, the Vietnamese one lacked the means or the time to devise a major land-reform enterprise. Even the reduction of land rents lacked coherent rules.

The Vietnamese soviet movement, in fact, produced an explosion of confused rural energies, with contradictory tendencies: virtually everything that was tried was called "socialist." On the one hand, some Vietnamese peasants attempted to organize agricultural cooperatives, to provide communal ownership of their villages' economies. This move horrified more "scientific" party theoreticians when they learned about it, since, according to the most magisterial European texts, cooperatives did not belong to this stage of "socialist development" and the circumstances of Vietnamese peasant life did not yet permit them. On the other hand, the soviet movement also accidentally revived the inter-village wars which had been endemic in central and north central Vietnam for at least a century. In 1931, with the fortunes of the movement declining and with bad harvests and storms creating a threat of famine, ICP cadres called for "rice struggles" to seize the rice of rich peasants (there were few rich landlords in the region) in order to redistribute it to the poor. But this simply precipitated the expansion of traditional patterns of conflict, under the exotic new slogan of the "soviets": the people of one village would unhesitatingly steal the rice of the people in another village.[25]

By the spring of 1931, French repression and the soviets' own internal weaknesses had brought them to an end. In March 1931 the colonial regime broke up the General Affairs commission of the ICP Central Committee in Saigon. Pockets of resistance lingered, of course. In Anh Son district in Nghe An province the ICP district newspaper, "The Proletarian Mirror" (*Guong vo san*) was published as late as August 5, 1931. Moreover, some of the reapportionments of public lands which had occurred during the brief 1930 climax of the soviets, in a number of north central villages, survived for two decades, despite landlords' protests. They were rescinded, ironically, only when the Hanoi communist government pressed its formal land-reform campaign upon the peasantry in the 1950s. That a serious psychological and economic mortification of the traditional village elites, as well as of district governments, had not taken place could not be pretended, even in the most airless inner precincts of the Hue court.

Nevertheless, from the standpoint of the comparative development of East Asian communism, the different degrees of success of the Chinese and Vietnamese soviets were something of a turning point. Up until 1930 the Chinese and Vietnamese communist movements were almost equal in terms of experience and political sophistication. After the "soviet" period, the Vietnamese communists were at a profound disadvantage with regard to their Chinese counterparts. During the life of the Kiangsi soviet republic, for example, the Chinese red army became a mature political and military force in China. In just the last year of the Kiangsi soviet, from August 1933 to July 1934, the red army claimed to have recruited some 112,105 new soldiers from its shrinking base area.[26] The ICP for its part lacked any army; its first real guerrilla units were not to appear until 1940; and at the height of the Nghe-Tinh soviets it could muster only a few village self-defense companies. The Chinese soviet republic had its own banks, issued its own paper currency, and developed a hierarchy of village, district, provincial, and national institutions. The Vietnamese soviets, on the other hand, seem to have lived off the land, almost like a traditional bandit movement, rather than operating through a more permanent tax-collecting and budgeting and banking apparatus. While the Chinese soviet "national bank" was issuing tens of millions of its own paper dollars, many Vietnamese communists were arguing in the same period that "revolutionaries do not need money."

Even the mass organizations which the ICP created in villages under its control were "mass" in name only. In addition, they did not belong to any hierarchical system of administration running up to the provincial level. The "peasant associations," which were the strongest, had a total membership of 8,718 peasants at their peak, despite the fact that any Vietnamese villagers who mutely raised their hands during a public reading of the associations' rules were instantly allowed to join them.[27] The nucleus of actual party members in the Nghe An–Ha Tinh region in 1931 was more formidable, in a way: 1,332 members, or already more than one-quarter of the number of members (roughly 5,000) the ICP was to possess in the entire country in 1945 when it seized power in Hanoi.

For all these reasons, there was a certain tortured wistfulness in the letter the ICP sent to the Chinese Communist Party in June 1934; the letter declared that the ICP was bringing all its resources to bear "to lead the Indochina masses to battle in defence of the Chinese soviets," that "the influence of the Chinese soviets had even spread out into all Indochina," and that "such circumstances . . . must raise high the level of the Vietnamese revolution, so that it catches up with the level of the Chinese revolution."[28] By this time the Vietnamese soviets themselves had been dead for three years, and the leadership of the ICP had been almost decimated by repression.

Yet to say that Vietnamese communism after 1934 lagged behind Chinese communism in certain crucial realms—an army, experience with the building of revolutionary institutions—is not to say that it lagged behind other political movements in Vietnam. For even in the early 1930s the ICP had begun to come closer to solving the central problems of the relationship between national revolution and community sentiments than any of its rivals. Even in the 1920s, in fact, it was possible to observe an important difference in the structures of Ho Chi Minh's Youth League and of the Vietnamese Nationalist Party (VNQDD). The structures of both were based upon a Leninist hierarchy, which meant that they began with organizations at the village and street zone level and then formed higher organizations at the levels of districts, provinces, regions, and the nation. But the criteria which were used to determine the composition of the cell units in the Youth League and in the Nationalist Party were not at all the same. Nationalist Party cells embraced all the members of the VNQDD of a given territorial unit, even if their occupational backgrounds were diverse. One Nationalist Party street zone cell, for example, might include students, civil servants, merchants, and workers. Youth League cells, in contrast, tended to be more fastidiously chosen single-occupation cells, or cells which held people with a similar style of life: workers at a yarn factory would have their own cell, as would the students at a particular school.

Communist organizers, as early as the 1920s, engaged in a pertinacious search for existing personal ties, primordial social attachments, and existing corporate bodies in Vietnam which they could exploit and expand in the interests of their world revolution. Ironically, they appear to have perceived more profoundly than any other Vietnamese revolutionaries the rather simple sociological truth that a large movement could derive cohesion and even dynamism from multitudes of small-group attachments which fell short, in practice, of attachments to the movement's most complex central ideologies and philosophical doctrines—provided that these small-group attachments were associated with concrete local issues which harmonized with the general purposes of those ideologies and doctrines.

Obviously, it is difficult to measure the distribution of attachment to the central symbols of any movement. Sometimes such attachment, even if it exists, must be reinforced by the personal ties and ambitions which are found in social primary groups: comradely solidarity, loyalties based upon common experiences, the private grievances of the members of a given group. The Vietnamese Nationalists, during their brief crescendo of activities between 1927 and 1930, had lavished far more attention upon the making of bombs than upon the dissemination of written propaganda. The Communist party—partly, perhaps, because it attracted a higher percentage of intellectuals to its membership, although this point must be studied more exhaustively—was different. It stressed the production and circulation of newspapers. But, significantly, the ICP saw to it that separate occupational groups and corporate bodies in Vietnam received their own private newspapers. During the soviet period, for instance, a special newspaper (*Boi bep,* "Kitchen Boy") was created for the cooks and waiters and kitchen boys of Haiphong; another newspaper (*Thung dau,* "Oil Barrel") was created for the workers of one specific oil company; and yet another newspaper (*Xi-moong,* "Cement") was created for the Haiphong cement-company workers. Generally, these newspapers were printed on wax paper by secret printing houses which could assemble their printing equipment in a single suitcase. They were distributed free. Workers were encouraged to write articles for them.[29]

With all the advantages of hindsight, it is not too difficult to see how these studied techniques of revolutionary parochialism, when joined to a universal ideology (or religion), could methodically transform the potentialities of community politics. The French colonial government in Vietnam, in the 1930s, found itself in the position of being an agency of moderate administrative and economic change. At the same time that it was introducing some new court procedures, some new tax formulas, and some new (if limited) influences of capitalism, however, it hoped not to disturb or change unduly the attitudes and relationships of the traditional Vietnamese family or village or other primary groups. In the long run this was, of course, a contradiction. Yet the ICP was the first Vietnamese political movement vigorously to exploit these fundamental colonial incongruities. It did so by creating organizational arrangements and psychological associations which bridged the two sectors and laid the groundwork for revolution within the accepted atmospheres of those very primary groups and occupational groups whose communal concerns and political instincts the colonial government had hoped would remain magically embalmed. The introduction of occupational-group newspapers was particularly important. As innovations, these newspapers were capable of arousing all kinds of new desires within the previously sluggish atmospheres of such groups, in much the same way that the invention of the automobile created a host of new consumer wants in the modern West. Specifically, these group newspapers stimulated desires for a more efficient literacy, for a more effective associationism, or for improved wages to match those of workers whom group members could now read about in other companies or in other cities. From this point, revolution in Vietnam would no longer have to depend so heavily upon the relatively narrow experiences and formulaic entreaties of traditional secret societies. The reflexes of political demand had suddenly lost their old rigidity.

In the villages themselves during the soviet period, the ICP also used traditional communications techniques to spread new ideas. These techniques did not necessarily revolutionize demands, like the group newspapers, or force the changing and unchanging sectors of Vietnamese society into an unexpected confrontation with each other. But they did diminish (or the ICP hoped they would diminish) the alien nature of communist rhetoric and symbolism.

Rhythmic talking to the accompaniment of a musical instrument (*noi ve*) had been one of the prime entertainments—and one of the means by which information had been circulated—in many provinces of Vietnam. The performers of these talking songs traveled extensively, employing word tones and rhymes that would make their *ve* easy to recite and easy to remember. Like modern newspapers, these traditional talking songs paid

attention not only to recent news but to the exploits of important personages and to customs and morals. (There were, for example, a number of
talking songs which dealt with gambling.) Talking-song performers also
disseminated information about economic facilities, and might be
responsible at times even for helping to integrate entire regional economies.
In the south central province of Binh Dinh in the traditional period, there
were some 120 markets. And peasants might learn about all of them from
a famous talking song which wove together all their names and characteristics and employed a comfortable four-word verse form as a memory device:
"Clouds drift and duckweed floats, that is where the Phu Ly market is.
Digging pits for casting lead objects, that is where the Ca Dao market
is . . ."[30] In 1930–1931, the cadres of the Nghe-Tinh soviet movement
attempted to rally peasant adherents with a talking song which bore the
impressive title of "A Wife's Advice to Her Husband to Make Revolution."
The lyrics of this talking song explained that:

> . . . from the time when mister Marx made his appeal in London, it
> was only at that time that the propertyless felt their souls awaken. In
> just a few full years, they conquered Paris as easily as if it were play,
> they captured political power as easily as if it were play. Although
> they were defeated, their influences were limitless. The invincible
> strength of the workers and peasants was such that the five conti-
> nents all felt chills at the backs of their necks, the powers all felt
> chills at the backs of their necks. Oh husband, husband, from that
> point the propertyless of France and Germany and Russia became
> completely forgetful of themselves and of their families. They
> resolved to struggle within society, they resolved to build socialism.[31]

This breathless, muddled summary of the rise and fall of the Paris commune, written for Vietnamese peasant audiences, did not just exploit the
ancient form of the traditional rural talking song. It also appears to have
been a deliberate echo of a famous section from the early fifteenth-century
work the "Songs of Family Exhortation," supposedly written by Nguyen
Trai, which has already been mentioned (see page 98). The section of this
medieval poem which the communist song imitated had born the more
modest title of "A Wife's Advice to Her Husband," instead of "A Wife's
Advice to Her Husband to Make Revolution." And it had, assuredly, conveyed a very different kind of moral advice from that which the ICP was
now espousing. The earlier wife, addressing her husband, had been made to
say:

> I obey the teachings of tradition, I vow to watch over the lock and
> the bolt of our household and to keep your tunic and turban in
> order. First of all comes the duty of worshiping the ancestors, and of
> helping you with great solicitude every moment of the day. For your
> part, husband, be sure to manage your business affairs everywhere.

> Toil assiduously at the classics and the histories and practice your
> archery. A name with merit will receive favors from above. . . . I beg
> you not to pay rapt attention to gambling dens. . . . The tender
> peach, the weak willow, entrusts herself to a hero.[32]

There were many ironies here. Despite the nimble transition from fifteenth-century Confucian messages to twentieth-century communist ones,
the styles of poetry which expressed the messages remained little altered,
as did the conspicuous use of women to anchor men to certain codes of
action. What happened in north central Vietnam in 1930, moreover—if the
literature produced by the soviet movement is a true index—is that international political themes and symbols were not only being insinuated into
art forms supplied by medieval poets but were also being married to a
traditionalistic provincial culture. The poetry of the Nghe-Tinh soviets was
shot through with localisms and parochial linguistic usages which Vietnamese living in other regions would have found awkward and clumsy.[33]
By the early 1930s, the Vietnamese communist movement was making
strong efforts to associate itself with national cultural and literary traditions and discovering at the same time that even the invocation of a framework of traditional symbols and linguistic conventions at the national level
was not enough to reach the mass constituencies it sought. Beyond the
struggle to nationalize the Paris commune and Lenin and Rosa Luxemburg,
culturally speaking, the party also had to "provincialize" them. After all,
no Vietnamese cultural borrowers in the premodern period, with the
possible exception of the early Buddhists, had ever required a large rural
following steeped in regional vagaries actively and quickly to ratify their
imported inspirations from other civilizations. All these experiments raised
the question of just how smoothly communism could be adapted to the
general interests and tensions which Vietnamese culture—national and
regional—harbored in the 1930s.

The Conflict between Religious Sectarianism
and Communism

No matter how populist or "proletarian" they might pretend to be, the
first generation of Chinese and Vietnamese communist leaders came for
the most part from the ranks of the new, Westernized intelligentsias. And
one of the things which the early Chinese and Vietnamese communist
movements had in common was that both were confronted and opposed
by a revival and renovation of traditional folk religions.

These religions managed to recruit thousands of members in social
circles outside those of the new intelligentsia—the social circles occupied
by peasants, rural peddlers, the petty merchants of provincial towns, district and prefectural officials in decaying provincial administrations, and
(in China) by the officers in warlord armies. On the whole, such religious

revival groups tended to flourish most in those regions of China and Vietnam where the classical high culture of the scholar-gentry, as institutionalized by the examination system and by the periodic production of degree-holders, had been relatively weak. This meant, in China, the northern provinces of Shantung, Hopei, Honan, and Shansi more than the scholar-rich provinces of the Yangtze River delta, and, in Vietnam, Cochin China rather than Tonkin or Annam. Degrees of commercialization or of Western penetration seemed less significant in determining the popularity of these groups. (But the subject deserves further study.) Temple-filled north China was more exclusively agricultural and less exposed to Western contact than the south; but the same could not be said of Cochin China, the home of the new religions in Vietnam.

Adherents of these new religions very obviously did not believe that communism had found adequate solutions for the traumas of social disintegration which afflicted so much of East Asia. When the Chinese communist Eighth Route Army sought to expand its north China base in 1944 against the Japanese, it was blocked by a "counter-revolutionary organization" full of "landlords," "rich peasants," "vagabonds," and "rowdies."[34] Its enemy was in fact a quite coherent religious sect known as the "Great Way of Former Heaven" (*Hsien-t'ien tao*), which believed that history was a matter of three major cycles, those of the "former heaven" (when truth had come into existence), the "middle heaven" (the present) and the "later heaven" (when the messiah Buddha would appear). In 1945, and later, when a Vietnamese communist coalition attempted to gain control of southern Vietnam, it was blocked by religious sects which also cherished, in part, the ancient hopes of messianic Buddhism. A quarter of a century later, these sects still offered formidable obstacles to communist proselytization in the south. What was the nature of this great East Asian duel between communist cadres and religious revival groups?

Many of these tradition-oriented religious societies which sprang up like mushrooms in the 1910s, 1920s, and 1930s stressed spirit worship and divination. They created local altars, to which professional mediums came, and these mediums, claiming to be animated by the spirits of the gods of the altars, transmitted messages from these gods to the clienteles whom the altars attracted. The instruments of divination which the mediums commonly used were winnowing forks, although in Vietnam many of the early members of the Cao Dai movement had made a transition, by 1925, to European ouija boards.[35] Sand-writing divination in China, employing winnowing forks, can be traced back as far as the fifth century A.D. By the twelfth century the spirits which were believed to inhabit these spirit altars, and to express themselves in cryptic poetry and songs through the mediums, had begun to include those of dead literary men, emperors, and military heroes.[36] Divination had, in sum, become a well-entrenched "false science" whose mediums usually occupied lowly positions in life but who could use their state of "spirit possession" to throw off ordinary restraints, behave in ways not sanctioned by social convention, and make predictions about the future.

Partly for this reason, the Confucian upper class in both China and Vietnam regarded mediums as dangerous upsetters of the social order. In his "Songs of Family Exhortation" Nguyen Trai teaches his model fifteenth-century Vietnamese woman to say that "I must concern myself with rice and with medicines and not become infatuated by spirit mediums. There is the house that is unswept, but also the house that, when swept, produces [previously undetected] litter. Once the medium has issued her prophecies, how are you able to ignore them?"[37] The harmonious environment was like an "unswept" house—spirits and ghosts were everywhere, and it was better not to stir them up. Yet many medium cults were essentially conservative. They merely attempted to endow with spiritual meanings unwanted social and economic changes (which were often regarded as having emanated from the world of spirits) in order to permit more poorly educated people to accommodate and understand them, while keeping traditional values intact.

A second important feature of the religious revival groups was their syncretism—their effort to reconcile invading Western belief systems with traditional East Asian religions, as an antidote to the chaos of cultural change and as a means of facilitating East Asian adjustment to Western contact. The Chinese "New Religion To Save The World" (*Chiu-shih hsin-chiao*), which originated among a group of Buddhist acolytes in Peking about 1919, stressed the existence of six historical sages whom its members were to worship: Confucius, the Buddha, Lao-tzu, the Lord of Heaven, Jesus Christ, and Muhammad. Armed with this evangelistic message it spread through China faster than any political party, acquiring branches in such places as Tientsin, Harbin, Tsinan, Nanking, Shanghai, Foochow, Yünnan, Kansu, and Kweichow by 1925. The "Fellowship of Goodness" society (*T'ung-shan-she*), which began about 1915, had spread through north China by 1921. It struggled to adopt deities from the Western religions which had come to China and then combine such adoptions with the popular belief in mediums and divination and spirits descending to spirit altars. In the 1920s, mediums of the "Fellowship of Goodness" regularly claimed to be possessed by the spirits of Confucius, Lao-tzu, the Buddha, Muhammad, Christ, Napoleon, George Washington, and Tolstoy.[38] All this, of course, represented an attempt by the less Westernized sectors of Chinese society to bring under control the stormy mental phantasmagoria of China's cultural revolution. Threatened by the popularity of the "Fellowship of Goodness" in inland China, Ch'en Tu-hsiu, one of the founders of the Chinese Communist Party, was driven to propose in 1921 that punitive laws be invoked to curb its startling growth.[39]

But the furious battle between communist intellectuals and neotraditional East Asian religious sects never achieved the dogmatic grandeur in north China that it was to achieve in the Mekong delta. Of the two major religious sects there that were to prove antipathetic to communism, the earlier one, Cao Dai, was formally created in 1926. In the autumn of that year the governor of Cochin China received a letter from the leading activists of the movement announcing its intentions—the harmonization and unification of Vietnamese religions. The signers of the letter included Vietnamese clerks and secretaries and interpreters in Saigon government offices, elementary schoolteachers, canton and village officials, prefects and district magistrates, and Buddhist monks.[40] But although the leadership of Cao Dai originated as a town-based social body of clerks, teachers, property owners, and monks, the movement soon won mass peasant support. By 1928 it may have had anywhere from 200,000 to 1 million members, mainly (at first) in eastern Cochin China.[41] It acquired a territorial base in Tay Ninh province northwest of Saigon, and this base evolved into the famous "holy see" of the Cao Dai religion, an obvious Vietnamese imitation of Roman Catholicism's Vatican City.

Like most of the new religions in China, Cao Dai attempted to defend and revive the influences of Confucianism in Vietnamese daily life: it urged its members to practice ancestor worship and to maximize the family relationships. And like many of the new religions in China, it sought to give the old moralities a new prestige, in the eyes of peasants buffeted by sudden change, by enclosing them within a Western-style, self-advertised universal religion. The "Hall of the Way" (*Tao Yüan*) religion in China, which had spread like wildfire from Shantung province in the northeast after 1921, had claimed to be the sixth and final religion of mankind, transcending the previous five universal religions of Confucianism, Taoism, Buddhism, Islam, and Christianity. In Vietnam, Cao Dai for its part claimed to represent the third and ultimate period of "universal passage" (salvation of souls) in human history, the first period of universal passage having been the work of Moses and of Fu Hsi and the second period the work of the Buddha, Confucius, Lao-tzu, Jesus, and Muhammad. (The founder of Cao Dai, Ngo Minh Chieu, may in fact have been connected to Chinese folk religions through the Chinese uncle by marriage with whom he lived when he was a boy, a seller of Chinese medicines in My Tho.[42] Cao Dai literature compares the small hut in Gia Dinh where Ngo Minh Chieu was born, in 1878, to the manger where Christ was born in Bethlehem.)

Like the Chinese religious sects, moreover, Cao Dai relied heavily upon divination and spirit mediums: the psychological medicine of twelfth-century China remained as potent as ever in twentieth-century Saigon. Cao Dai, indeed, began to develop its own literature, the poetry sung by its own mediums as they danced upon rural spirit altars throughout southern Vietnam. The "Heavenly Emperor Appears," an early Cao Dai medium song which was first written down in 1919, was reasonably typical in being cryptic in meaning but conveying great verbal force to Vietnamese listeners:

> The Heavenly Emperor appears with a halo. Everywhere there is calmness and acceptance of the three lights. In the circulating movement of Heaven and Earth the Heavenly Emperor hides his face. . . .

On the altar of the homeland, mediums sing "y, y, y, y, y." What a demonstration of compassion, that fate is caused to be good fortune, and desires heroes to catch the winds and make their sails fly. Truly that is good fortune, truly that is good fortune! There are years, months, days, and hours of praying by the mouth next to the hands, but the sound of the pear-shaped guitar is hidden before it rises. . . . Heaven and Earth usually rescue righteous people from suffering. . . .[43]

While this song may have lacked the unchastened precision of Lenin's theses on the national and colonial questions, it and others like it had earned Cao Dai a much more dependable mass consituency in the Vietnamese countryside in the 1920s and 1930s than any following the communists could claim. Why was Cao Dai so popular? To be a Cao Dai leader was not to invite the same violent martyrdom at the hands of the secret police, yet Cao Dai did not enjoy a completely unmolested freedom: the Hue court, for example, prohibited its dissemination in Annam until 1938.[44]

First of all, the Cao Dai movement was in the van of the Vietnamese search for equivalence with the West. (The communists, with their more alien educations and ideologies, took longer to establish themselves in this obligatory position.) Cao Dai created its own holy see in Tay Ninh to compete with the Vatican, its own universal symbol of a "heavenly eye" to compete with the Christian cross, and its own complex hierarchy of officials—who were roughly similar to pope, cardinals, archbishops, bishops, priests, and deacons—in order to compete with the colonial Catholic hierarchy. Here, once again, there were Chinese parallels. The "Hall of the Way" movement in Shantung had developed an elaborate hierarchical structure in the 1920s, of a kind more elaborate than any found in traditional hierarchical Chinese White Lotus sects, and had also produced a philanthropic organization, the "Red Swastikas Society," which was a mixture of traditional Chinese charitable concerns and a Chinese imitation of the Red Cross in the West.[45]

More important, Cao Dai made its own contribution to the Vietnamese search for new forms of organized communities. Responding directly to the colonial fragmentation of Vietnamese society, it not only rehabilitated the ancient Confucian virtues but cast into artificial institutional forms the religious syncretism which had always existed implicitly in Vietnamese peasant religion, but which now needed to be defined explicitly against the pressures of an alien culture. Like traditional White Lotus sects, the Cao Dai movement divided its power between a religious leader (or *ho phap*, "defender of the faith," referred to as "pope" by Westerners) and a leader who was concerned more with material affairs and with political organization. Under this second leader, however, Cao Dai deployed an unprecedentedly symbol-heavy hierarchy of assistant officials. These were divided into three categories, meant to reflect the satisfied presence in Cao Dai of the traditional "three religions"—Buddhism, Confucianism, and Taoism. In an atmosphere of almost voluptuous nostalgia and strict liturgical discipline, the assistants who symbolized Confucianism's role in the Cao Dai hierarchy were required to wear red tunics which also stood for "prestige"; the assistants who symbolized Buddhism's role in the hierarchy wore yellow tunics which stood for "virtue"; and the assistants who symbolized Taoism's role wore blue tunics which also stood for "tolerance." In this way, the very Cao Dai hierarchy itself was supposed to define and celebrate the traditional coexistence of "three religions" in Vietnam, in so vivid a manner that peasants confused by Western missionaries would not forget it. The three categories of assistants had parallel duties. The Confucian assistants were concerned with rituals, the Taoist assistants were responsible for charitable works and the education of Cao Dai members, and the Buddhist assistants were in charge of finances, public works, and the rural markets which Cao Dai had organized to protect peasants from Saigon-Cholon price manipulators.

The rise of Cao Dai and communism in the same decade implied two polar reactions or types of reaction in Vietnam to French colonialism and the decay of the old society. One reaction, represented by Cao Dai, expressed itself in a search for, and attempted recovery of, a lost social equilibrium, by means of spiritualism and a reform of personal habits in such matters as sex, business practices, methods of worship, and personal relations. The second reaction, the communist one, expressed itself in the belief that social equilibrium itself was mythical, undesirable, exploitative, and "feudal," and that the more violations of social harmony there were— like labor disturbances or peasant uprisings—the more the Vietnamese people could claim to have matured and progressed in the cause of expanding their political and class consciousness. While both Cao Dai and communism were hostile in varying degrees to the colonial regime, the former considered social stability to be a great good, and claimed the colonialists had destroyed it, while the communists considered it to be a selfish fiction of first the dynasties and then colonialism, designed to obscure the circumstances and issues of the class war. Apart from antipathy to the French, the leaders of Cao Dai and communism shared another significant attribute: the claim to be the prophets of a universal faith.

In their competition with the folk religions, the communists enjoyed one advantage and two serious disadvantages. Their advantage was that all communists were activists. They had managed to escape the classic dilemma of choices at the heart of the Confucian tradition which forced more traditionalistic Vietnamese to waver between working for "world salvation" and concentrating upon personal self-cultivation and even "non-action." (As proof that the folk religions had not escaped, Ngo Minh Chieu, the very founder of Cao Dai, separated himself from the formal movement in order to pursue unmistakably personal religious interests.) Their two disadvantages were, first, their inability to describe any very tangible paradise at the end of communism (apart from the vague, unlit beatitudes of the stateless society) and, second, the fact that the classical culture had been more discredited at the upper levels of society than at the lower and that the eighth-century Chinese poet Li Po (whose spirit regularly entered Cao Dai mediums in the 1920s and 1930s) still touched the hearts of more Vietnamese peasants than did the Paris commune. The ripening popularity of Hoa Hao Buddhism in western Cochin China in 1939 and afterwards exposed these disadvantages particularly clearly.

Huynh Phu So, who founded the Hoa Hao sect, began his career as a rural faith healer in Chau Doc province. He preached his doctrines at the same time that he cured illnesses—in a manner reminiscent of Christ, his followers claimed. Like the founders of Cao Dai, he was anticolonial but culturally conservative: he deliberately grew his hair long in order to prove that he was not under European influences. The Hoa Hao movement itself demanded an end to idol worship in Buddhist temples. It urged a simplification of sacrifices to the Buddha (in which only water, flowers, and incense should be used, not food or money) and stressed the need for inexpensive marriage and burial ceremonies, its puritanism appealing to poor peasants who were exhausted by traditional funeral, wedding, and religious expenses. Like Cao Dai it offered salvation to its believers, and like Cao Dai it sheltered influences from the centuries-old Chinese White Lotus religion.

Many Hoa Hao members themselves claim descent from a thirteenth-century Vietnamese Zen Buddhist sect, the "Bamboo Grove of Yen Tu Mountain" (*Truc Lam Yen Tu*) sect which took its name from a mountain in Quang Yen province east of Hanoi. More specifically (and more credibly), however, Hoa Hao traced its roots to the "Precious Mountain Miraculous Fragrance" (*Buu Son Ky Huong*) sect, a messianic Buddhist movement which had been created in Sa Dec province in the south in 1849, during a violent cholera epidemic. The traveling salvationist who had masterminded the "Precious Mountain Miraculous Fragrance" sect, Doan Minh Huyen, had recommended the compassion of the Buddha and a return to the old moralities to thousands of peasants as the only antidote to cholera and death. He encouraged the belief that he was a reincarnated Buddha himself, and consequently became known among his followers as the "Buddha of the Western Peace" (*Phat Thay Tay An*). Huyen preached the coming of the great "dragon flower assembly" when the messiah Buddha would descend to earth and dispense immortality from the mountains of western Cochin China, under the mythical dragon flower tree; and he wrote poems which could be read either horizontally or vertically, poems whose deliberately concealed meanings compelled their listeners to "bend words and turn sentences upside down" in order to understand them. These poems still circulated in western Cochin China in the 1930s. For although the "Precious Mountain Miraculous Fragrance" sect was banned by the

French in 1867—it had participated in anti-French resistance movements—it kept reappearing under other names, such as that of the "Way of Goodness" (*Dao Lanh;* the Vietnamese term for "goodness" here has an anti-Catholic flavor.) Not surprisingly, Huynh Phu So declared that he was a reincarnation of the "Buddha of the Western Peace"; when a large number of secret followers of the old "Precious Mountain Miraculous Fragrance" movement accepted his claim, the success of his political ambitions was assured.[46]

But the political career of the Hoa Hao movement was a stormy one. In the early 1940s the anxious French colonial regime deposited Huynh Phu So first in a hospital and then in Laos, only to be forced by Japanese invaders of Indochina to release him and permit him to return to Saigon. So declined to become a submissive Japanese puppet. But he did exploit his opportunities between 1942 and 1945 to make himself, by the end of the Pacific War, the master of much of Cochin China south and west of Saigon. In 1946, he claimed to have admitted more than one million believers to his religion. Between 1945 and early 1947 he made some 107 tours "recommending agriculture and explaining the laws" through the provinces of the south, swelling the ranks of his adherents. More than two decades later, even in 1968 the Hoa Hao movement could claim the loyalty of 18 percent of the population of the south, by its own reckoning, including the loyalty of 39 percent of the population of the western "back river" region.[47]

Being a peasant himself, Huynh Phu So was so successful at building a rural constituency that he earned the flattering informal title of "general of the common people." Urban communist orators, impressed and annoyed by his power and his ability to hypnotize peasant audiences by "speaking volubly without end," at first made shameless pilgrimages to the Hoa Hao "lord teacher" to ask him for his secrets. On such occasions, So smiled seraphically and informed them that he was hostile to ideas of social classes and of warfare among social classes. Unable to conquer Cochin China politically as long as such a formidable adversary stood in their path, in 1947 the communists apparently murdered Huynh Phu So, who disappeared without a trace. According to spokesmen of the Hoa Hao movement, the communists also murdered three of So's closest disciples and two hundred and thirty-three Hoa Hao cadres between 1945 and 1947.[48]

These crimes represented the climax of the bitter clash between a communist movement which was slowly domesticating itself and the vast cultural hinterland of East Asian folk religions. The Vietnamese version of the clash was more serious than the war between Mao Tse-tung and the "Great Way of Former Heaven" in north China, or Ch'en Tu-hsiu's rancorous demand two decades earlier for legal suppression of the Chinese "Fellowship of Goodness." With the Hoa Hao vision of the future the communists sometimes found it difficult to compete. Beyond their nationalist crusade against colonialism, which was certainly potent enough, they had no convincing picture of "un-alienated man" to accompany their vivid dramatizations of what being an "alienated man" meant in a repressive colonial environment. They had few perspectives which fitted comfortably with Vietnamese tradition which depicted what the virtues of a completed communism would be like or of what the virtues of primitive communism had been. The Hoa Hao vision of the future was, to some extent, stereotyped Taoist utopianism: it even reiterated the ancient dream of a sacred mountain in the sea inhabited by immortals who possessed immortality drugs (the island of Bong-lai, P'eng-lai in Chinese.) Intense "merit making," the performance of good deeds for oneself and for others, would bring this dream within reach. Huynh Phu So, speaking poetically through a medium, had enveloped paradise in an intoxicating mysticism which may have seemed like nonsense to Westernized intellectuals but which penetrated peasant life and peasant ears very forcefully:

> Those who are profiteers and who covet wealth are those who bring misfortunes flying to them, causing additional sufferings to their families. They had better listen to the sacred teachings, and their worldliness will be lighter. They will soar like angels through the country of the mind and the hills of benevolence. For months and days they will have no cares, and their bodies will be worth enormous sums of gold. If one considers the four sufferings of this world, life, death, sickness, and old age, they are the cyclical way of this lower, misfortune-immersed world. One sits and meditates and ponders. . . . Why should so much hardship be spawned? If one follows and clings to the fate of worldly people, one is fettered to sorrows and shoulders worldly cares, endlessly traveling in circles the vast seas and the long mountain ranges. . . . When it escapes beyond the circle of life and death, the soul witnesses the peace and the leisure of Bong-lai. You evade the this-worldly circle of sickness and physical defects. You gain the appearance of an angel and . . . roam the universe in grass shoes. Happily you watch the heron croaking and the phoenix flying. In the spring, you examine the different shrubberies, in the summer you become drunk on red wine. In the autumn the state of your heart is calm and peaceful. If the wind shakes and the rains spray, your mind-spirit will become all the clearer. In the winter, when the cold wind shakes your body, will a body that is never old be disturbed by the winds of this world?[49]

This extravagant outpouring was filled with classical clichés: the "shrubberies and red wine" section was a paraphrasing of the medieval poet Nguyen Binh Khiem, for example, and the heron and phoenix were very commonplace symbols of the supernatural world in Vietnam. But this fact only improved, rather than diminished, its acceptability. The closest young Ho Chi Minh came to countering such religious oratory on its own homespun terms was to refer, in his 1926 "Road of Revolution," to the "world revolution" as a prelude to the global "great unity." The concept of the "great unity" (*dai dong*) came, of course, from the second century B.C. Chinese classic "The Record of Rituals" (*Li-chi*) and described a utopian world without kinship distinctions or private property or banditry and stealing. It had been a stock rallying cry in Chinese rebellions, had been invoked by K'ang Yu-wei, was used by some of the new religious sects, and now was borrowed by East Asian Marxists. Mao Tse-tung also employed it to cast an encouraging classical sheen over the goals of communism for Chinese audiences.[50]

But the Hoa Hao movement combined its vision of a utopian future with exploitations of popular traditional Vietnamese mythologies which, no matter how popular they were, the supposedly more "scientific" communist party was in no position to exploit itself. According to the traditional Vietnamese founding myth, the first Vietnamese people were the offspring of a male dragon, which came from the water, and of a female immortal, who belonged to the land. The implication of this legend, as it was expounded in such medieval Vietnamese texts as the *Linh Nam Chich Quai* ("A Collection of Strange Tales of Linh Nam") of A.D. 1492, was that the primordial Vietnamese nationhood was founded upon a mixture of military strength and prowess (the gift of the dragon) and of uncommon spiritual arts (the gift of the immortal) and that the Vietnamese people had therefore possessed a special "subconscious" for thousands of years. Under Huynh Phu So's inspiration, Hoa Hao partisans suggested that all the secular, "modern" political and military power of France would eventually be circumvented and undone by the subterranean magic of this legend. Huynh Phu So himself wrote, with his usual cunning ambiguity, that "a mad person like myself possesses the madness of the race of the Immortal and the Dragon. Mad, and yet able to extricate myself from the yoke and the chains of mortal life"[51]—and of conventional politics.

By the 1970s, the Hanoi communist government was willing to tolerate the survival of this indomitable legend of the dragon and the immortal: it was evidence of a healthy patriotism among the Vietnamese people whose continuation was desirable during a war with the United States.[52] But in the 1940s, when the legend was monopolized by Hoa Hao propagandists, it added even more fuel to the conflict between the communists and the religious sects. For one thing, it was an offense to the more rationalistic, Westernized nationalism of the less sophisticated early communists. For another thing, there was the risk that it could become an effective dissolvent of the theories of class war which the communists were busily importing. For the legend linked the formation of the Vietnamese national character to an event, the intercourse of the dragon and the immortal, which necessarily occurred before the formation of social classes. It thereby negated the influence of the latter upon the emergence of the former and supplied more traditionalistic Vietnamese nationalists with a mythically homogenized picture of a Vietnamese national unity—or potential national unity—which could or should transcend temporary social and economic inequalities.

The central Hoa Hao political doctrine, of the repayment of the "four favors"—the benefactions one received from one's ancestors and parents, from one's national homeland, from Buddhism, and from one's compatriots—was a creative, highly significant Vietnamese reinterpretation of the doctrine of the repayment of the "four favors" of Chinese folk Buddhist sects, which had typically emphasized repayment of the *ruler* rather than repayment of the *nation*. (Moreover, this Vietnamese reinterpretation appears to have originated with the "Precious Mountain Miraculous Fragrance" movement in the nineteenth century.) Obviously, the Vietnamese version of the doctrine emphasized nationalism and the need to fight foreign aggressors (repaying the second favor). But it omitted making any connection between colonialism and inequitable distributions of property. Depending upon the circumstances, this could be either a strength or a weakness politically.

The Buddhist Revival and the Communist Revolution

While they were engaged in a struggle with the new religious sects for identification and control of those political thunderbolts that might arouse the Vietnamese countryside to action, the communists faced the possibility of their position being outflanked among the Vietnamese intelligentsia, by the Buddhist revival movement in the cities and towns. For the "Buddhist restoration" raised many of the basic issues of Vietnam's intellectual modernization in a way that no political party, not even the ICP, was managing to do.

After its formal inauguration in Saigon in 1926, Cao Dai had proclaimed that the traditional religions, East and West, were bankrupt. And it had wrested both followers and temples from Vietnam's mainstream Buddhists. Groups of Buddhist monks were goaded into a competitive reaction. In stimulating this reaction, influences from China were crucial. The modernization of Chinese Buddhism had begun after the revolution of 1911. It had been marked by the appearance of Buddhist studies groups and institutes in such cities as Nanking, Peking, Shanghai, and Hangchow. The Chinese Buddhist thinker who actually won the greatest admiration and support among educated Vietnamese monks in the 1920s and 1930s was T'ai-hsü. Although he is far too poorly known even among students of modern Chinese history, T'ai-hsü deserves a place with Liang Ch'i-ch'ao, Sun Yat-sen, and Mao Tse-tung as one of the more influential Chinese figures in the evolution of twentieth-century Vietnam. T'ai-hsü was in fact a revolutionary monk who had read Bakunin, Proudhon, Kropotkin, and Marx in addition to the Buddhist sutras. He had organized an Association for the Advancement of Buddhism in Nanking in 1912. In 1928, he made a world tour to popularize Chinese Buddhism, lecturing in such diverse places as Yale University and the Musée Guimet in Paris. Basically, T'ai-hsü was celebrated for asserting that Buddhism and Western science were quite compatible: Western astronomy, for example, had merely confirmed the statement in Buddhist scriptures that space was endless and the number of worlds infinite.[53]

Vietnamese monks, engaged in the same kind of search for equivalence with the West, fastened upon these ideas. Many of them regularly read a Chinese Buddhist monthly periodical which T'ai-hsü had begun publishing in 1920, a journal entitled "The Voice of the Tide" (*Hai-ch'ao yin*). The leading radical Buddhist of this period in Vietnam, a monk named Thien Chieu who taught at the Linh Son temple in Cochin China, declared that Buddhist doctrines of compassion and of salvation from misery compelled Buddhists to participate in patriotic activities like the Phan Chu Trinh funeral in Saigon in 1926. In the 1930s Thien Chieu and his associates commenced the publication of a newspaper, the "Buddhist New Youth," whose title imitated that of a Buddhist New Youth Society which had previously flourished in Peking. The French quickly suppressed it.[54]

The leaders of the "Buddhist restoration" in Vietnam had a number of purposes. For one thing, they wished to disseminate the sutras and Buddhist thought and history in books and newspapers written in romanized Vietnamese. In this way they could remove them from their dangerously obscure, threadbare classical Chinese swaddling clothes, which had permitted only a small minority of monks to understand them at a time when Catholic missionaries were shrewdly popularizing Christian Bible stories among the peasants. For another thing, the leaders of the "restoration" wished to develop effective modern schools for training monks and nuns, so that monks and nuns would have sufficient command of doctrine to be able to hold their own intellectually in a changing society. For a third thing, they wanted to give Buddhism a greater organizational coherence—the *doan the* theme once again—in order to permit it to match its Catholic rival. Between 1932 and 1934, Cochin China, Annam, and Tonkin all acquired regional Buddhist studies societies. But the colonial government, inheriting the fears and instincts of traditional dynasties, refused to allow the formation of a national Buddhist organization. Nevertheless, the regional societies that did exist managed to publish their own journals. The more radical and more nationalistic of these Buddhist periodicals made their appearance in the south.

In numbers and in organization, the Buddhist revival was no match for the Cao Dai and Hoa Hao movements; in organizational potency, it was no match for the communists. In 1935, for example, the Tonkin Buddhism Society could claim no more than two thousand monks and nuns and ten thousand lay people as its members. Furthermore, its membership lacked even a modicum of ideological discipline and participatory zeal. Despite the fact that provincial branch societies of the Tonkin Buddhist movement in the 1930s kept registers of the names of their members, and created their own flags and meeting halls and lectures and schools, their adherents were never fully captured by their religious ceremonies and rituals, but spent their time in the temples instead merely gossiping, smoking, or chewing betel. In 1939, indeed, a disgruntled member of the Bac Ninh provincial Buddhist society in the north angrily denounced this religiously indifferent behavior as "night markets Buddhism," suggesting that no really significant Buddhist religious revival was genuinely transforming the minds of the Tonkinese peasantry.[55] If the Buddhist revival was incapable of mobilizing the villages, how could it possibly threaten the Indochina Communist Party?

Reformed Buddhism had the opportunity to win the allegiance of many leftist or potentially leftist intellectuals in Vietnam in the 1930s for two reasons. First, it could offer them a context in which to demonstrate altruism and asceticism; and second, it could supply them with a scheme of history which certainly emphasized change. For with regard to this last point, all schools of Buddhism, no matter what their disagreements, believed that everything in the universe changed unceasingly. In the 1930s, moreover, Vietnamese Buddhist journals like "The Voice of Exposition" (*Vien am*), a Hue monthly, began to combine Buddhism with the approach of the eighteenth-century English philosopher Bishop Berkeley in order to give Buddhism what they hoped would be a more "modern" flavor. They proposed now that everything was a dream with only a "nature of being visible," and that the very existence of the Perfume River at Hue (a favorite example) depended upon someone observing it; if no one observed the river, it did not exist. The founder of the Chinese Communist Party, Li Ta-chao, had been heavily influenced by Buddhist metaphysics. His inclinations were repeated in Vietnam by notable leftist intellectuals like Nguyen An Ninh, the self-conscious upper-class architect of Cochin China secret societies. After the suppression of his secret society, Ninh became an ardent spokesman for Buddhism. He shaved his head and went barefoot, but he also took pains to make a rigorous study of Buddhism, and of various analyses of it, in French, English, and German as well as in Vietnamese.

Eventually, what diminished Buddhism's appeal for intellectuals like Ninh was its lack of activism. Once again, communism's long-term advantage over both Buddhism and the new religious sects was the intensity and the consistency of its activist style. In 1937, in another agonized reversal of positions, Ninh published a book ("Criticizing Buddhism," *Phe binh Phat giao*) in which he suddenly condemned his former subject of enthusiasm. He stated now that Buddhism's weaknesses were that it sought to save only individuals from suffering; that it sought to save them only by force of imagination; that desire was at the root of social reforms of a practical kind, yet Buddhism sought to eliminate desire, and worldly ambitions; and that knowledge, and evolution, were the products of restless striving, not of the peaceful contemplation of Buddhism.[56] The path of

Buddhism, in sum, led away from that of the Faustian man—and of triumphant revolutionaries.

Yet not all Vietnamese intellectuals perceived these supposed vulnerabilities of Buddhism quite so clearly, even in 1937. The early communists boasted that they possessed a powerful if sometimes seductively arcane formula for restoring Vietnamese pride and independence. They advanced this claim in a society which was still not entirely able to decide whether true "power" reposed in Western political and economic doctrines or in a transcendental East Asian mysticism. For the strength of the Vietnamese Buddhist revival was that it fed upon many vital, poorly translatable East Asian inspirations. Vietnamese Buddhists visited Japan in the 1930s. There they were influenced to some extent by Japanese religious trends; as an example, some of them attempted to reinvigorate Buddhism in Vietnam by invoking the relatively unfamiliar model of Japanese Shingon Buddhism, known as "esoteric Buddhism" in Vietnamese. In Shingon Buddhism, the mysteries of the body and the mind (ranging from various ways of holding hands to methods of understanding truth) were passed on orally from master to disciple, rather than being written down in books; and this required an extremely close relationship between master and student. While Shingon sects had emerged in Japan as early as the ninth century A.D., no independent Shingon sects had ever really flourished in traditional China—or in Vietnam. In 1937, however, one enthusiastic Vietnamese Buddhist writer announced to Hanoi intellectuals that it was only after he had been to Japan and had studied with Japanese Shingon teachers that he had learned the real meaning of spiritual "power." In his view, esoteric Buddhism, if it were transplanted from Japan, might carry Vietnamese society closer to the "truth" and to a useful future.[57] Oracles like these, stressing the expansion of power *via* esoteric techniques, competed with the oracles of the ICP, which sometimes advanced the same themes, albeit in a very different guise and on a different plane of action.

Apart from the question of new kinds of power, there was the question of egalitarianism..This was another vital realm where Buddhist theorists could attempt to compete with communist ones, deliberately or accidentally. Nguyen Trong Thuat, a prewar Confucian scholar with a passionate interest in the Buddhist revival, made characteristic claims for Buddhist egalitarianism: he argued that it was more profound and more generous than the European Enlightenment variety, which of course had informed the ancestry of Marxism. As Thuat saw it, the "French concept of equality" paid constrained, exclusive attention to "the human race," and proposed that only when people regarded other people as being similar to themselves would they "love each other" and attain the state of "love without distinction." Superficially, he admitted, these theories now seemed more appropriate than ancient Buddhist ones. Using French thought was like using "electric fans" and "ice" to alleviate the heats of summer, whereas using Buddhist thought seemed to be like wearing "a quilted blanket." But in fact the "scope" of the egalitarian meanings of Buddhism was much broader than the scope of the meanings of egalitarianism of the "current age." Buddhist equality embraced all living things, not just mankind. For the Buddha had taught that all living things had, in common, a "Buddha nature": people and nonhuman living things alike knew happiness and sorrow, and had an equal chance to become Buddhas. Western egalitarianism, being too narrow, did not escape completely from discrimination, and could be used only as a "means," not as an "end." Buddhism offered total egalitarianism. It did not distinguish even relative degrees of property rights, or differentiate ownership of material possessions in any way. It led infallibly to salvation and to "universal love."[58]

The egalitarianism which communist intellectuals advocated was, of course, far from total, even in the purely human sphere. Works like the *Critique of the Gotha Program* (1875) had specified that even when the communist millennium was finally entered, society would inscribe upon its banner merely "from each according to his capacity, to each according to his need"—a slogan which hardly suggests an absolute equality of wealth. Were communist propagandists in Vietnam at all disadvantaged by the fact that even the most idyllic pictures of the future which they could paint seemed anticlimactic beside "the law of equality of the Great Vehicle"?

They were, it appeared, outflanked by time as well as by metaphysics. Polemicists like Nguyen Trong Thuat also asserted in the late 1930s that during the golden age of Buddhism in Vietnam (the Ly dynasty, A.D. 1010–1225) Vietnamese emperors had married peasant girls, and marriages had been free therefore of class distinctions. Buddhism, in other words, had actually tested its egalitarian spirit during the early period of Vietnamese history. And practical Buddhist egalitarianism in Vietnamese life had supposedly endured right down to the present in Vietnamese villages. This was shown by the fact (Thuat argued) that whereas the village meeting houses, the symbols of the "spirit" of Confucianism in rural Vietnam, were battlegrounds in which there was a constant competition for hierarchical prestige, worshippers lacked any conspicuous status order whatsoever in the village temples, which were the symbols of the "spirit" of Buddhism. Nguyen Trong Thuat attempted to give the coup-de-grace to all the pretensions of Western-influenced political egalitarians in Vietnam by pointing out that the Buddha had said that politics was limited but religion was limitless: politics amounted merely to deductions from the results of religion, which "educated and changed" people.[59]

At first sight, the "absolute" nature of the spirit of "religious" Buddhist egalitarianism dimmed the prestige and prospects of its "political" rival from the West. As David Thomson has shown, the ideal of equality of modern Western democratic radicalism is tragically devoid of spiritual content, if only because the eighteenth-century democrats and secular rationalists who created it were acutely conscious of their peculiar need to fight an entrenched Catholic church.[60] Translated into Vietnamese terms, it still retains its obsession with material welfare and pleasure, and continues its neglect of men's spiritual needs. In a society that was less "secular" than most in the West, this might have added to the difficulties of domesticating an appreciation of the virtues of modern Western egalitarianism in its communist form—although peasants vulnerable to famine were far from disinterested in questions of material welfare.

Yet Buddhist approaches to the ideal of equality had their own fatal weakness. Huynh Phu So, the leader of the Hoa Hao, found such Buddhist approaches useful enough to absorb them and popularize them from the more learned formulations of writers like Nguyen Trong Thuat. But he nonetheless exposed their fatal weakness when he explained, in a 1946 Saigon newspaper article produced shortly before his death, that Shakyamuni had not actually *applied* any of his "radical ideas" in this field, because the "social environment" of the India in which he had lived had not been favorable to them.[61]

In brief, Buddhist egalitarianism as Thuat and as Huynh Phu So defined it was far too broad and too nebulous to be practically institutionalized. It had nothing specific to say about law or the uses of law to protect more modest concepts of equal political and economic rights. It avoided the whole burning question of property redistribution, regarding discussions of property matters as an unworthy abbreviation of its cyclopean field of interest. In supposing, furthermore, that religion transcended politics, the former being a process of education and change and the latter being merely deductions from the process, it deprecated the acquisition of purely political skills. Like their communist rivals, the Buddhist revivalists were not especially interested in searching for legally guaranteed forms of socially dispersed power, or for legal systems which defined the rights and duties of groups and individuals. Unlike their communist rivals, however, they shunned questions of economics, and of the distribution of economic resources.

This last tendency was dangerous, because even the Buddhist monkhood itself experienced directly or indirectly the tensions of the colonial society, and was more of a barometer of social discontents than might be thought. For example, in Cochin China in 1916 the colonial regime had exempted Buddhist monks from paying the notorious body tax, and had issued to all monks certificates proving their eligibility for exemption. But in practice, these ecclesiastical tax exemptions never worked as smoothly in Cochin China as they did in neighboring Cambodia, leaving Vietnamese monks with the impression that they were receiving poorer treatment than their Cambodian counterparts. In Cochin China the French were not willing to exempt more than one monk per temple (or about twelve hundred monks), whereas many southern temples had twenty or thirty monks attached to them. Nevertheless, in the 1930s unemployed Vietnamese were habitually disguising themselves as monks, in order to escape from colonial taxation, by shaving their heads and dyeing their tunics.[62] Their grievances and frustrations then filtered into the lives of the real monks, who were stimulated by increasing contact with such "proletarian" false monks.

Indeed, to turn the argument completely around, some of the intellectual debates within the Vietnamese Buddhist revival movement probably facilitated rather than hindered the domestication of at least the less complex kinds of communist rhetoric. One of these debates, for instance, centered upon the question of whether or not the Buddhist religion possessed gods. The radical monk Thien Chieu, reflecting the ideas of the Chinese monk T'ai-hsü, published a book in 1929 ("A General Summary of Buddhism," *Phat hoc tong yeu*) which he called a "letter of blood." His book was designed to prove to Vietnamese intellectuals that Buddhism was a religion without any gods and that it did not accept the principle of the existence of a supreme diety with vast powers of reward and punishment. In a later work ("A Disquisition on the Absence of Gods," *Vo than luan*) the fiery Thien Chieu pushed even farther, claiming that bumptious priests were the real moral arbiters, the real managers of rewards and punishments, and that the concept of a supreme god was merely a device which ambitious priests could exploit. Another southern monk, Le Khanh Hoa, influenced by Montaigne and by Bayle, proposed a world view in 1936 based upon a prayer associated with the Manjusri Bodhisattva, according to which "emptiness" had produced the four elements (earth, water, fire, wind) which were the foundations of Nature. These ideas of Thien Chieu and others did not circulate in Vietnamese temples unopposed. But they were greeted with eloquent approval by many of the educated physicians and teachers and other lay Buddhists in the cities who were participating in the Buddhist revival; and the debate, and the outlooks it reflected, had a definite connection with the Vietnamese acceptance of the propriety of revolution. For if a supernatural power which rewarded and punished human beings for their good and bad deeds in this life did not exist, then the way was clear for small groups of men to try to set the world in order by themselves.

Another intellectual crisis in the Buddhist revival which was also linked to the acceptance or the rejection of revolutionary acts assessed the problem of whether or not the paradise known as the "Pure Land" really existed. The battle over the existence of the "Pure Land" could be regarded as a battle over the existence of religious emollients which contributed indirectly to the lack of a revolutionary temper in Vietnam. A denial of the existence of the "Pure Land" might be instrumental in turning men's minds to the construction of utopias on earth.

Thien Chieu, predictably, maintained that paradise was merely a state of mind; he advanced his position in a number of pungent articles in major Saigon newspapers. But defenders of the "Pure Land," attempting to compete both with communist propagandists' revisions of the "great unity" and with Catholic soteriology, began to publish unusually vivid descriptions of the "Pure Land," even in intellectual journals. These descriptions exploited modern, this-worldly political terminology to astonishing degrees in an effort to endow the old idea of paradise with newfangled ideological enchantment. A Buddhist schools examiner in Tonkin published an essay upon the "Pure Land" in 1940 which particularly scandalized communist intellectuals then and has continued to do so ever since. He portrayed it as the "ultimate point civilization," full of gold and silver and precious gems, access to which was guaranteed by chanting the name of Amida Buddha. Every man could have a "lotus throne" in the "Pure Land," because such a throne was like a place in the village meeting house, reserved for its owner even when he was absent from his village. Perfect equality existed in the "Pure Land" because its "root of goodness" nourished egalitarian norms. (Inequality on earth, presumably, was merely a function of language—people did not speak "cruel words" in the "Pure Land"—and of admonishable personal behavior.) Above all, the inhabitants of this "ultimate point civilization" were in complete accord with each other. What was the secret of this accord? None of them "spoke with two tongues."[63] In other words, discord in real-life society did not reflect disagreement over different but equally legitimate vested interests, to be solved through compromise; it reflected a personal failure of ritual and morality, "speaking with two tongues," which had to be solved by religious cultivation. This attitude was still a basically favored one in many sectors of Vietnamese society. Indeed, for all their idiosyncrasies and underestimation of social and economic issues, "Pure Land" utopia builders did have interesting points of agreement even with communist ones: their emphases upon personal cultivation and upon the possibility of an "ultimate point civilization" were perhaps two.

To a surprising extent, the religious sectarians, the Buddhist intellectuals, and the early communists in Vietnam drew from a common medley of elixers and shared a variety of common impulses. These impulses included a search for equivalence with the West, a desire to be part of a movement with universal claims, an interest in expanding power through new techniques, a tendency to celebrate the virtues of egalitarianism, and a determination to be "scientific," whether this last aspiration led to Cao Dai divinations of the future, or Buddhist intellectuals' advocacies of "godlessness," or Marxist determinism.

But two unique features of the early communist movement were crucial. First, while the religious sects acquired a mass following much more rapidly, by accepting the existence of an only semiliterate peasantry and building their appeal upon those traditional symbols and themes which had been stabilized and conserved by Vietnam's extraordinarily rich traditional oral culture, the communists planned and promoted an era of expanding literacy, in part by developing their small group newspapers, which also in time created new wants among their readers and began to "unfreeze" traditional political reflexes. Second, the communists focused upon specific social and economic grievances which their rivals ignored. In the long run, Nguyen Trong Thuat to the contrary, politics was to be more important than religion in the Vietnamese revolution—at least in enough important areas of the country to make a difference.

The communist determination to be "scientific," however pretentious, meant a truly unprecedented determination to analyze social problems, to overcome a Confucian tradition which, for centuries, had subsumed many pressing social questions under the inflexible headings of orthodox morality and its violations. The importance of the discovery, by a number of Vietnamese intellectuals after World War I, that a host of what they had been taught to regard as *moral* concerns were actually *social* concerns which could be objectively studied and remedied in new ways, cannot be exaggerated. Languishing in a Saigon prison in the late 1920s, the revolutionary Phan Van Hum—who was, significantly, later to become a Trotskyite communist—wrote with a strange ecstasy:

> I have been reading a book, "The Chinese Labor Question," and see that the Chinese have investigated the problem of prostitution in a way that is very clear and scientific, showing us that the "prostitution question" is one which people can pay attention to and investigate. When you just hear of this it sounds obscene, but you don't doubt that this is a very urgent problem for society just like any other problem related to . . . the people's livelihood. Because prostitutes have a relationship to moral customs and to the race, and also have a relationship to the survival of a society. Therefore . . . is it not obvious that we should pay attention to investigating the roots and searching for the substance, in order to know of ways to eliminate crimes in society at their very sources?[64]

6

The Mandarin Proletarians and the Redemption of the Past

United Front Politics and the Vietnamese Labor Movement

Two events outside Vietnam shaped the evolution of the Indochina Communist Party in the late 1930s. The first was the seventh congress of the Comintern, which met in Moscow in July 1935. It decided that because of recent developments in Italy, Japan, and Germany the task of world communist parties was not to overthrow capitalism but to fight against fascism: such parties must therefore now create broad popular fronts which could embrace as many "patriotic" and "democratic" political parties as possible, as well as miscellaneous social groups opposed to fascism. The second event was the rise to power of a popular front government in France itself in the spring of 1936, led by the socialist Leon Blum. This government relaxed many of the existing political restrictions in Indochina.

The executive commission of the ICP Party Central, assembling in the summer of 1936, and basing itself upon the line proclaimed at the seventh Comintern congress, as well as upon the unprecedented liberalism of the Blum regime, resolved that a "democratic front" must be the appropriate party policy. The slogans of "overthrow the French" and "confiscate landlords' lands and divide them among the tillers" were temporarily abandoned. The first united front organization that the ICP experimented with in 1935, the "Indochina Anti-Imperialist People's Front" (*Mat tran nhan dan phan de Dong Duong*), was quickly dissolved because it was not sufficiently discriminating. It failed to isolate "bellicose French Fascists" and "colonial reactionaries." But it adroitly changed itself into the "Indochina Democratic Front" (*Mat tran dan chu Dong Duong*) which survived until the autumn of 1939, when the French government ended its brief tolerance of "legal" activities by Vietnamese reformers and revolutionaries and attempted to return Indochina to its pre-1936 political straitjacket. During this "Democratic Front" period of 1936–1939, the ICP operated in Vietnam both legally and illegally. In Hanoi, for example, a group led by Truong Chinh which published the journal *Tin tuc* ("News")—a "public" communist group—directed the activities of the "Front," while other party apparatus remained concealed. What Vietnamese urban dwellers actually saw in this period were orthodox Marxist revolutionaries who made little public mention of a communist program, but who published books and journals (banned before 1936) which called for the introduction into Vietnam of such modern European political and cultural heirlooms as freedom of assembly, freedom of organization, freedom of travel, labor laws, and an eight-hour working day.

In sum, the ICP made an unusual, short-lived search in the late 1930s for a peaceful, graduated political method that would produce what armed uprisings had so far failed to produce: a mature revolutionary consciousness among the Vietnamese people. As it did so, it was subject to three sets of influences. Comintern decisions in Moscow were no doubt the dominating set. But changes in Chinese politics across the border gave these decisions a special reality among the Vietnamese communists. One party historian has claimed that the agreement between Chiang Kai-shek and the Chinese communists at the end of 1936 to fight China's Japanese invaders rather than each other, an agreement achieved after Chiang's abrupt, sensational kidnapping at Sian, helped Vietnamese communists to see the "accuracy" of the new Comintern line.[1] Apart from Comintern instructions, and the Sian affair in China, the ICP also took an acute interest in this period in trends elsewhere in the French colonial empire. The *cahiers algériens,* the collected requests of Algerian popular councils of the 1930s—documents which had a moderate nature, requesting more schools and less taxes—were carefully studied in Indochina.[2]

Was Ho Chi Minh in eclipse in this period? At least he remained abroad, and did not lead the "Democratic Front" movement directly. Yet he supported the concept behind it to the bitter end, informing the Comintern as late as July 1939 that the "Front" must embrace all "progressive Frenchmen" and the "national bourgeoisie," and must not demand Vietnam's national independence.[3] The paladin of the "Front" in Vietnam was Le Hong Phong (1902–1942). Phong was another Nghe An firebrand who had studied both at the Chinese Whampoa Academy and at the Russian airforce school, who had created the "Overseas Leadership Committee" of the ICP at Macao in the early 1930s after the collapse of the soviets, and who had led the ICP delegation to the 1935 Comintern congress.[4]

From its formation, the ICP stressed the idea of a "worker-peasant" alliance in a much more tenaciously orthodox Leninist manner than the Chinese Communist Party was to do under Mao Tse-tung. The "Democratic Front," seeking to strengthen the movement's associational foundations, welcomed the participation of the "indigenous capitalist class" and of "reformist nationalists." But it still concentrated in theory and practice upon workers and peasants, disdaining the counsels of "rightists" infatuated by "legalism" who wished to neglect both the party's secret, illegal organizations after 1936 and the recruitment programs of these organizations among the lower classes.

To further their Western dream of being the revolutionary vanguard of hosts of industrial workers, the Vietnamese communist elite strove in 1936 to create "action committees" among the workers of factories, shops, offices, and plantations. These action committees were to serve as the "underside" of the united front, to function as substitutes for illegal labor unions, and to justify a groping party's almost phosphorescent sense of its own mission among proletarians. The action committee movement also spread to the villages, where the action committees became organs of opposition to village councils. To some extent, the campaign was a success, especially in Cochin China. Here some six hundred action committees appeared within one month in 1936. In the cities, it was true, the action committees may have been little more than renovated guilds. Typically, an action committee was composed of the workers of a single handicraft, such as the barbershop workers of the province of Can Tho, the Saigon shoemakers, or the tailors of the province of My Tho.[5] The real question which hovered over the action committee campaign was far too sensitive to be commonly discussed or routinely acknowledged by party members. It was obvious enough: how much value did the central Marxist-Leninist idea of a "proletarian revolution" have in a preindustrial agricultural society like Vietnam?

At first glance the idea possessed no value at all. Critics of Marxism would argue, of course, that it is a fallacy (or at least has never been proved conclusively) that the most heavily oppressed people in a society are the ones most likely to revolt, since they have nothing to lose but a bitter life. (Ho emphasized this theory in his "Road of Revolution.") Such critics, indeed, would place this theory on the same level with the equally dubious belief that a given social class could ever have a single dominant conception of what its interests are and of how these interests should be defended; or with the equally debatable notion that industrialization leads to simplifying social polarizations rather than to a vastly more differentiated social structure with more intermediate positions. But even in a purely East Asian context, the obsession of the

Vietnamese communists with a "worker-peasant" alliance seemed to be an unusually inappropriate example of uncreative submission to a foreign ideology. In all of Indochina at the end of 1929, there were only 221,000 "workers." Not all of them were Vietnamese, and more than one-third of them were located on agricultural plantations.[6] In China, the city of Shanghai alone could boast of having 170,000 factory workers in 1919; and this was a rigorously refined statistic which did not take into account people outside Shanghai factories such as railway workers and dock workers.[7]

What this meant was that there were fewer genuine factory workers in all of Indochina than there were in one Chinese city. Therefore the Vietnamese communist leaders' emphasis upon the revolutionary potentialities of urban workers—an emphasis more consistent than Mao Tse-tung's—reflected a desire to be orthodox much more than it mirrored the actual social facts of Indochina. Their own personal experiences were also a factor in this attitude. As exiled intellectuals in Europe, many of them had been forced into extremely menial work in the cities or merchant marine of metropolitan France. The acculturation ordeal of a Ton Duc Thang, for example, may well have transcended in importance the unpromising weakness of the meager working class back in Vietnam itself. (Ton Duc Thang, who became president of northern Vietnam upon Ho Chi Minh's death in 1969, learned his revolutionary politics as a young man through service as a mechanic in the French navy and then in the French Renault factory, between 1912 and 1920; he returned to Vietnam to organize secret communist labor unions there in the early 1920s.) In England at the end of the 1600s, according to Gregory King's famous estimate, there were 240,000 artisans—including their wives and children—in a population of 5.6 million.[8] It is not too unfair to conclude that Vietnam in the 1930s could barely match the size of the labor force of preindustrial England. And despite the fact that the Vietnamese labor world erupted with four hundred different strikes in 1937—the highest total number of strikes in any one year before 1945[9]—between September 1939 and June 1940 the colonial regime found it relatively easy to ship some twenty thousand Indochina workers and soldiers, mostly Vietnamese, to France to serve in the lackluster French war effort.[10] This represented a coolie traffic on virtually the same scale as that of the four years of World War I. Communist agitation among Vietnamese workers in the 1930s, therefore, had not been nearly significant enough to loosen the colonial power's grip upon Vietnamese manpower.

Vietnamese communist theoreticians themselves would of course concede that because France was opposed to Indochina's industrialization and in any case lacked the capital to create many heavy industries there, the number of Vietnamese workers was tiny compared to the population as a whole. They nonetheless argue that members of the

Vietnamese working class—miners, or contract laborers on colonial railways, or workers in wine distilleries, textile mills, and cement factories—developed "class consciousness" remarkably early, for a variety of reasons. First, the lack of any general industrialization process evenly spread throughout the countryside meant that what workers did exist, were "concentrated" in a few places—Tonkinese mines, or the cities of Saigon, Hanoi, Haiphong, and Nam Dinh. Second, virtually all Vietnamese workers came from peasant villages. This insured that they had already been infected by the spirit of revolt of fathers and uncles and grandfathers who had participated in rural insurrections like the "aid the king" movement, long before they were formally "proletarianized." Furthermore, there were many instabilities and a high turnover among Vietnamese workers like the northern miners: these men kept returning to their villages, especially at lunar New Year's, forcing many mine owners to have to recruit their labor forces entirely anew after every New Year's celebration. But this fact only illustrated the "close bonds" between the world of the workers and the world of the peasants, bonds which could facilitate a revolutionary alliance. Third, since the French introduced very little machine technology into Vietnam—steam hammers were not introduced into Tonkinese mines until the 1930s, and in northern open-air coal mines, workers were more likely to dig for coal with their hands than with pickaxes—Vietnamese workers never developed that naive tradition of machine breaking which the workers of early industrializing Western countries had made so famous. From the beginning, they were able to recognize very clearly the human enemies behind their privations and unemployment, rather than fruitlessly blaming machines, like the English Luddites.[11] These factors, it is postulated, gave the Vietnamese proletariat impeccable revolutionary credentials.

It is not a complete waste of time to observe that within the framework of such an analysis, the features of classical Marxism have faded to the point where they become unrecognizable. The claim is made that Vietnamese workers were revolutionary precisely because they were peasants, wholly unconfused by any regime of machines, whose "class consciousness" came originally from the old Vietnamese village tradition of resistance to foreign invaders, rather than from the economic relationships of a capitalist society which were alienating them.

The irrelevance of classical Marxist theories, moreover, had a practical side. At least in the early 1930s, the degree of alienation and rootlessness which did prevail among workers in Vietnamese cities was an obstacle to the growth of communist organizations rather than an encouragement. For the revolution depended upon the development of new "organized communities" and the revitalization of old ones, and the most rootless urban workers were far removed from any practicable *doan the* ideal, new or old. In the villages, once the oligarchies were circumvented, it was relatively easy to organize secret groups: the peasants had known each other for years, were acquainted with the political leanings of their neighbors, and had a firm sense of whom to include and whom to exclude. Developing illegal worker organizations in the cities was often more difficult, despite the absence of watchful village elites. For the potential recruits of such organizations had come from "all four directions," lived apart from each other, and knew each other only at work. In the soviet period of 1930–1931, hardly any communist labor unions in any urban factory in Vietnam lasted more than one year.[12] Ironically, rural revolution may well have succeeded more spectacularly in Vietnam (and in China) not just because peasants were more numerous, or because their economic conditions were worse, but because, under the noses of the oligarchs, there were more layers of stable communal self-knowledge and communal interaction in the countryside than in the cities that a secret revolutionary movement could quietly exploit. Poverty and misery existed in both the cities and the villages. But exploitative rural landlords and notables were more familiar enemies, about whom hostile village consensuses had long ago developed; urban labor bosses were less familiar, less long-descended demons. Rootless urban anomie, in other words, was not the most promising key to a secret revolution in a colonial country.

But the history of the Vietnamese revolution is so complex that it is easier to demonstrate the gap between the revolution and classical Marxism than it is to suggest that Vietnamese workers were unconscious of being oppressed. Strikes were prohibited by colonial law. Yet there was a work stoppage in the Haiphong cement factory as early as 1912. On an East Asian basis, it is not entirely unreasonable to compare the prewar Vietnamese labor movement to the prewar Japanese labor movement. The comparison is not entirely unfair because although colonialism was absent in Japan, the scope of labor unions there still remained extremely narrow until the end of World War II: in 1931, when the percentage of the prewar Japanese work force that was unionized was at its highest, only 7.9 percent (368,975) of all Japanese workers (4,670,275) belonged to unions.[13] And if the comparison is made, it can be shown that the Vietnamese situation did actually possess potentialities for greater worker radicalism.

Unions were weak in Japan for much the same reason they were weak in Vietnam. Apart from government repression, there were several explanations for their plight. An abundance of the prewar Japanese labor force consisted of temporary workers who still remained based in their rural villages and who therefore found it difficult to form anything like a "class identity" as workers. Higher up in the labor world, government workers were still inspired by the lingering Confucian elitist ethic of the Tokugawa warrior class, refused to consider themselves as workers, and regarded it as virtually immoral to make an issue of material concerns. The union movement itself was split by factionalism and paralyzed by excessively radical, impractical theoreticians. On the other hand, Japan did differ from China and Vietnam in one important respect: while the Chinese and Vietnamese intelligentsias, stung by their military defeats of the late 1800s, became obsessed by the need for political and military self-strengthening, Japanese intellectuals, living in an environment of military success and economic expansion, were able to turn their attention relatively early to Western-style studies of domestic labor conditions and to the application of practical sociology to labor questions. Yokoyama Gennosuke published an incisive report on "Japan's Lower Class Society" (*Nihon no kasō shakai*)—a book which was something of an East Asian imitation of Engels's study of the English working class—as early as 1898. Serious analyses, statistical and otherwise, of Vietnamese workers were not to be produced by European observers and Vietnamese intellectuals for another three decades.

In what ways did the Vietnamese labor scene harbor greater potentialities for revolt than the Japanese one? First of all, while modern entrepreneurship in different industrial branches—military-related industries and textiles—developed rapidly in Japan, its development coexisted with the survival of other industrial branches where much more traditional management and entrepreneurial styles were preserved by ubiquitous "small enterprises." These traditional "small enterprises," linked to the big wholesalers and export businesses, often subcontracted part of the work of large industrial factories, thus enabling Japan to produce cheap commercial goods. Linked to modern industries but preserving traditionalistic labor relations, this profusion of "small enterprises" prevented industrialization in Japan from creating the enormous concentrations of workers that it might otherwise have done. A properly scaled comparison might well show (but much more research is needed) that there *were* greater concentrations of workers (relatively speaking) in Vietnam, since the colonial regime there could hardly produce comfortable symbiotic connections between, for example, the new-style rubber plantations or the mines, and traditional Vietnamese handicrafts. Secondly, by the 1930s the Japanese economy had experienced a tranquilizing rationalization of labor recruitment and management which never occurred in Vietnam. In the early 1900s, Japanese industries like the cotton-spinning industry had relied upon a confusion of labor recruitment techniques, including the wanton commissioning of confidence men and swindlers as recruiters. Gradually, however, the Japanese textile companies began to create their own permanent recruitment and personnel offices, and to provide welfare facilities for their employees, whom they regarded now as their "eternal factory workers" rather than as mere part-time flotsam and jetsam.

This crucial change in labor management which the Japanese textile industry pioneered spread to other industries. It meant the conversion of workers into permanent company loyalists who could count upon lifelong employment with benefits. And it was accompanied by a new industrial ideology, probably unique to Japan. Literally this ideology was described as "the ideology of warm sentiments" (*onjōshugi*): it required the kind treatment of employees, and their reciprocation of this treatment with loyalty to the enterprise which had hired them.[14] In contrast, labor recruitment in Vietnam in the colonial period never got beyond the "confidence man recruiter" stage; and the confidence men who recruited Vietnamese peasants for plantations or mines were notorious for their arbitrary dishonesty and cruelty.

Even more important, "progressive employers" in Japan financed the creation of substitutes for autonomous labor unions, with which the unions themselves then had to compete. Such substitutes included company unions, "moral culture groups" in the factories, and above all workers' cooperative organizations, subsidized by employers, which provided such benefits as accident compensation. The impact of this deliberate cultivation of counter-attractions soon became clear: a Japanese government report indicated that in 1923 there were 2,050 workers' cooperative organizations with 434,596 members, but only 432 labor unions in Japan with 125,551 members.[15] Japanese industrialists also promoted factory committees that would "combine" capital and labor, in order to increase factory solidarity. And if all these labor union substitutes failed, at the end of a strike by an independent labor union many Japanese employers would go so far as to make donations of money and valuables to the union which had just been fighting them, in order, presumably, to reestablish harmonious relations: obedience to the hierarchical obligations code ingrained by Tokugawa feudalism could not be neglected.[16] The contrast with Vietnam could not have been more stark. As with village cooperatives, an organized society of any kind, no matter who organized it, was considered a threat to the status quo; until the 1930s, therefore, the colonial government in Vietnam obstinately forbade even the creation of "yellow unions" or company unions. This simply ensured that the communists would, at the outset, have a free hand to organize Vietnamese workers secretly. Legal competitors or counterattractions would not be permitted to trouble them.

Despite the Confucian background it shared with Japan, then, there were reasons why Vietnam was not likely to enjoy Japan's relatively greater industrial peace. It would be disingenuous not to point out that many of these reasons could be traced to colonialism. For colonialism destroyed all chances of any real survival in Vietnam of an equally potent traditional solidarity ethic between workers and employers. In such a tense bicultural, biracial situation, French owners and Vietnamese laborers were under no shared traditional cultural imperative to "harmonize" relations with each other. Not that the French owners always maintained intimate contact with their workers: to a surprising extent, the fate of Vietnam's colonial industrial hierarchy was determined by the behavior of the foremen, usually Vietnamese, who functioned as intermediaries between French businessmen and Vietnamese peasants and were quite capable of exploiting both.

In fact, a special feature of Vietnamese labor history in the 1930s was strikes and demonstrations which demanded the dismissal of tyrannical foremen, whose limitlessly arbitrary power might even extend as far as beating workers to death. In the second half of the year 1936 alone, ferment at camps on the Dau Tieng rubber plantations, at the Haiphong cement factory, at the Bien Hoa sawyers' mill, and in the port of Saigon, all focused upon the excesses of foremen.[17] The Saigon newspaper *La Lutte,* which served as a famous beacon of radicalism and particularly of Trotskyite communism during the "Democratic Front" period, published a detailed analysis of the world of the Cholon rice-mill labor contractors in 1936. The thirteen thousand rice-mill workers of Cholon, it was revealed, were not directly hired or managed by the rice-mill owners themselves. The owners delegated these jobs to contractor foremen, who often enjoyed a corrupt relationship with the colonial police, were supported by their own small armies of riverfront bullies, and completely dominated the porters whom they hired, by violence and by money-lending.[18] Instead of Japanese-style institutionalized company recruitment, the boom-or-bust Cochin China rice industry, as well as the Tonkinese mines, continued to depend upon what *La Lutte* aptly called "merchants of men"; and between these "merchants" and their prey it was idle to look for any comparable vestige of the traditionalistic, congenial "boss-follower" (*oyabun-kobun*) relationship which had prevented labor unions from developing among Japanese mine workers for such a long time.

The Rubber Plantations and Colonial Social Totalitarianism

To say that the Vietnamese labor world possessed greater potentialities for revolt is not to say that these potentialities were ever realized in action. What was really important here was that the inadequacy of all forms of communalism, new or old, in the lives of Vietnamese workers, when combined with the widening gulf between Vietnamese social ideals and the realities of labor employment under the European colonial regime, gave Vietnamese revolutionaries still another powerful incentive to concentrate upon the search for "organized communities" that could resist the West and recast Vietnamese society. Nothing gave this incentive a greater impetus, or falsified Vietnamese social ideals more grimly, than the Cochin China rubber plantations. The story of these plantations has no parallel in the modern labor history of either China or Japan.

Rubber came to Vietnam as early as the year 1887, when the first rubber tree was imported and planted experimentally in the Saigon Botanical Gardens. Rubber plantations themselves did not become prominent features of the Cochin China landscape until after World War I. "Rubber country" was to be found especially in eastern Cochin China, in such provinces as Gia Dinh, Bien Hoa, Ba Ria, and Thu Dau Mot, and also in Tay

Ninh. At the peak of the Indochina rubber boom, when Vietnam ranked third in Southeast Asia behind Malaya and the Netherlands Indies (Indonesia) in terms of amounts of acreage planted with rubber, about 500 rubber companies, large and small, controlled more than 130,000 hectares of land in this region. Unlike the rice plantations, native Vietnamese entrepreneurs could find only a small role to play in the crevices of this foreign-dominated rubber plantation system. Even in 1962, nearly a decade after the official end of French colonialism, resident Vietnamese rubber planters owned only about fifteen thousand hectares of rubber acreage. The big French rubber companies, like Michelin, were given labor-recruiting monopolies over whole localities.

Hundreds of thousands of Vietnamese peasants were brought from northern and central Vietnam to work as contract coolies on the southern rubber plantations. The majority of them came from the five provinces of Thai Binh, Nam Dinh, Hai Duong, Quang Binh, and Quang Tri. Attempting to flee a situation of overpopulation, scarce land, and conservative councils of notables in the north, such peasants soon found that labor service in the new "rubber cities" often carried with it greater oppression. Sometimes it carried with it a death sentence. For of the more than 45,000 Vietnamese peasants recruited to work on the Michelin rubber company's big Dau Tieng rubber plantation (8,847 hectares) in Thu Dau Mot between 1917 and 1951, company registers indicate some 11,376 workers died on the plantation, usually either of disease or maltreatment; and the plantation registers for the colonial period which survive in south Vietnam present "official" figures, which refer only to contracted "enlistment laborers" rather than to more irregularly recruited coolies who did not sign contracts.[19]

The French referred to the profitable streams of white latex which oozed from the rubber trees as "white gold." Vietnamese coolies working on the plantations matched this expression by calling the latex "white blood" (*mau trang*). The difference in points of view was not an incomprehensible one. Indeed the tragic death of one rubber coolie, known to his fellow workers as "Brother Seventy," on the Courtenay plantation at Xuan Loc in Bien Hoa province, became a kind of emotional storm center in the Vietnamese labor underground, and was still remembered vividly decades later by pioneers of the Vietnamese labor movement living in Saigon in the 1960s. Suffering from heavy malaria, "Brother Seventy" was nonetheless beaten and forced to tap rubber trees, by a cruel Vietnamese plantation superintendent, until he collapsed and died. Other coolies on the plantation, as a protest, gave him an anguished funeral: thousands of them followed his body as it was transported in an old oxcart in the rain to the primitive, disheveled rubber plantation cemetery. When the same workers then began to maintain a cult of remembrance at his grave, after his burial, the rubber company leveled the grave on a stormy night in the summer of 1941. It did no good. By this time, children on the plantation had learned

to sing a certain anti-French song, built around the episode of the martyrdom of "Brother Seventy." The song soon spread throughout the provinces
of eastern Cochin China. Despite the belated attempts of the rubber
companies to ban the singing of the song, "Brother Seventy" successfully
became a legend in lower-class social history. My translation of this song,
based upon the only written text of it I have seen, unfortunately falls far
short of doing justice to its emotional force or imaginative integrity:

> Attention, oh brothers and sisters! Attention, oh brothers and sis-
> ters! What is the cause of our sadness and anxiety? Brother Seventy
> died, not because superintendent Lu beat him, and not because of
> the heavenly god. Brothers, we need to examine carefully the circum-
> stances of life, the circumstances of life. Superintendent Lu indeed
> listens only to the words of this crowd, this crowd of French own-
> ers. Oh brothers and sisters! Attention, oh brothers and sisters! Let's
> keep still and listen to these words: superintendent Lu is dim-witted,
> it's just the crowd of Frenchmen that is merciless. So if we brothers
> and sisters want to end our miseries, let's stand up and unite in
> breaking our cangues and fetters once and for all, try it once and for
> all, once and for all let's see![20]

While this song is a suitable introduction to the strange world of "white
gold" and "white blood," it does not describe all the sociological tendencies on the rubber plantations which most concerned Vietnamese revolutionaries. The big rubber companies habitually hired Vietnamese
confidence men to travel through poverty-stricken villages in Tonkin in
pursuit of more coolies. These agents would enter hamlets, erect cotton
tents, and show the villagers photographic exhibits of the almost encyclo-
pedically idyllic life which supposedly awaited them if they journeyed to
southern plantations—rent-free houses, gardens, schools, temples, kinder-
gartens. But when the peasants arrived at the southern plantations, they
were given numbers to replace their lineage and personal names—as in the
case of "Brother Seventy." The numbers the plantations so abruptly
assigned to the coolies followed a series of numbers that had begun from
the day that a plantation was first opened. The coolies themselves seem to
have assimilated this drastic scheme completely. They even made their
own informal modifications in it: they customarily abbreviated their own
numbers, addressing each other by the last two numbers in each man's
"number name."

On occasions when the two tail numbers in each man's "number name"
coincided with those of other men, however, additional numbers—or nick-
names describing physical appearances—would be added. For example, if
the last two numbers in the "number names" of two men on the same
plantation shift were both "31," one man might be called "31-4000"
(indicating that his full number was 4031) and the other man might be
addressed, incredibly enough, as "31-4000-100" (indicating that his full

number was 4,131). Or the clash might be resolved more simply by calling one "31 thin" (*31 om*) and the other one " 31 plump" (*31 map*). Children who were born on the rubber plantations sometimes knew their parents only as numbers, and were not clearly acquainted with their lineage names. Workers were listed by numbers rather than by names in plantation account books and registers, at times when their labor was being graded or when they were being issued rice and wages.[21] From the French plantation managers' point of view, one advantage of this system was the avoidance of confusion. Vietnamese peasants' names were difficult for European minds to remember.

In this context, it was the Western colonialists, not the communist revolutionaries, who first flirted experimentally with social totalitarianism in Vietnam. For the colonial rubber plantations had introduced a degree of structural amnesia into the complex kinship-dominated Vietnamese social system. Moreover, the obliteration of private family memories—which might be construed as a kind of negative communism imposed upon Asian peasants in the interests of colonial entrepreneurship—was accompanied by the important fact that no rational legal framework of any kind covered the fate of the thousands of rubber coolies. Plantation owners could beat or imprison their workers without owing explanations to anyone. If it is unsurprising that Western colonialism did not bring a reign of law, or guarantees of individual and familial rights, to Vietnam, the behavior of the rubber plantation elite does seem surprising in another respect: it appeared to contradict the general colonial policy of the 1930s of trying to preserve what remained of the traditional Vietnamese social order, as a barrier against revolution. Would not this forced atomization of the rubber plantation workers have made them more susceptible to mobilization by revolutionaries?

In fact, the social atomization of the rubber coolies was limited. Despite the stunning disappearance of the symbols and the bonds of many historic patrilineages on the plantations, hierarchy itself was scarcely abolished: the plantation work forces were rigorously stratified. The first category of rubber workers, aptly known as the "master" (*thay*) category, included the superintendents, sergeants, foremen, and records keepers; it accounted for about 10 percent of the Vietnamese employed by French plantation owners, from whom its members, like a privileged caste, received special favors. The second category of workers included those with special skills—such as chauffeurs, or men who could process latex—and accounted for about 5 percent of the plantation employees. The nameless, numbered contract and noncontract coolies made up the remainder. Apart from this stratification, the plantation owners, as ambitious social engineers as their enemies the revolutionaries, carefully channeled their coolies into new (if inferior) settlement units—artificial villages and village-like clusters, each of which, like the coolies themselves, had a number. Such plantation-sponsored forms of mobilization usually worked. The residents of these spurious rubber plantation "villages," starved for effective points of reference in their lives, might develop such intense group feelings that lethal quarrels would break out between "villages" at theatrical performances, or over women.[22]

The uprooting totalitarianism which the rubber plantations practiced enabled Vietnamese revolutionaries who opposed colonialism to cast themselves in the roles of social rehabilitators. In fact, they hardly had any alternative. Revolution, for many Vietnamese, now came to mean both the modernization of the Confucian patriarchy and (sometimes paradoxically) the restoration of a sense of society and of communal ties and memories at the same time. Jeffrey Race, among others, has shown how crucial the theme of "communalism" was in permitting communist guerrillas to seize large parts of the countryside in southern Vietnam in the 1960s at the expense of the Saigon government. But the efforts of the southern National Liberation Front guerrillas to develop "forces assimilated into rural areas," and to strengthen communal loyalties to their cause by an emphasis upon the solution of local problems,[23] were the application of a tradition some three or four decades old which had originated, in part, as a reaction to colonial demolition of a variety of old group values.

In a series of articles which he had written for his Canton journal "Youth" (*Thanh nien*), the organ of the Revolutionary Youth League, in October and November 1926, Ho Chi Minh had explained that the formation of labor unions in Vietnam must begin with the formation of smaller mutual aid and "friendship" societies, so that the Vietnamese people could learn the advantages of intermediate social organizations which extended, but did not threaten, traditional communal patterns.[24] During the later stages of the "Democratic Front" period (in 1938 and 1939) the ICP translated these prescriptions into practice. It vigorously encouraged the proliferation of "friendship societies" either among the workers of a single factory or among the handicraft workers of a given locality (such as the chauffeurs of the province of Bac Lieu, or the haircutting workers of a single town.) When many of the new societies found it difficult to remain solvent, ICP cadres were compelled to rescue them by stipulating that they give their members "spiritual" assistance rather than financial aid, the latter being reserved purely for members who were unemployed or incapacitated. Such "friendship societies," which were normally run by elected committees, did widen the organizational experiences of a considerable number of lower class Vietnamese urban dwellers. On the eve of World War II, they were the brightest hope of the communist-led labor movement in Indochina. They were also one of the chief targets of the Vietnamese Trotskyite movement, whose stronghold was the city of Saigon.

The Trotskyites, like some of the more orthodox Saigon communists (Nguyen Van Tao, for example) were French-educated radicals whose triumphs were won in the 1930s mainly in newspaper wars and in Saigon municipal council elections. Cochin China politics were more free of colonial repression than the politics of Tonkin and Annam; they were particularly free in the city of Saigon, where the municipal council was elected by a relatively general franchise[25] and where circumstances were more likely to favor the use of "legal methods" in stirring up popular discontents. A communist was publicly elected to the Saigon municipal council as early as 1933. The Trotskyites, however, gradually became more successful in these Cochin China electoral battles than regular ICP members. By the middle of 1937 they had also captured possession of the potent Saigon newspaper La Lutte. The Trotskyites attacked the ICP for subservience to the Soviet Communist Party, which they claimed was presiding over a "Thermidorean reaction" in the Soviet Union; they accused the Chinese Communist Party of surrendering to the Kuomintang; they denounced the French Communist Party for having become a collection of reformist strike-breakers; and they criticized the ICP for its efforts to develop a multi-class united front in Vietnam.

On the theoretical level, the advantages in this confrontation belonged entirely to the Trotskyites. For one thing, most of them had an edge in theoretical sophistication over their ICP rivals. In 1938 the secretary-general of the ICP, and the man who bore the brunt of this conflict on its behalf, was a 26-year-old youth from Bac Ninh, Nguyen Van Cu (1912–1941). Cu had read the works of Marx, Engels, and Lenin, in French, *after* he had become a communist: the books had been unceremoniously smuggled to him only four or five years before, while he had been serving a prison sentence on Poulo Condore. The book which he published in 1939 in an attempt to demolish the position of the Trotskyites, "Self Reproofs" (*Tu chi trich*), was a hurried, unoriginal digest of Lenin (especially of "Left Wing Communism: An Infantile Disorder," and of "The Proletarian Revolution and the Renegade Kautsky") which rested upon remarkably fragile intellectual foundations.[26] In addition, the Trotskyites were better able to tap Vietnamese urban nationalism directly: they did not have to offer even a liturgical loyalty to the pronouncements of a foreign power. At first, despite the strangeness of their name, they were better able to exploit the general assumption in Saigon—an assumption suggested by the ageless tradition of Vietnamese cultural borrowing from other societies—that any patriotic Vietnamese who indulged in such borrowing would make independent modifications in what he had borrowed. One ICP historian has even revealed that some orthodox party members themselves in the late 1930s went so far as to differentiate improperly the Vietnamese Trotskyites from world Trotskyites. They obediently accepted the ICP leaders' dictum that "world Trotskyism" was "counterrevolutionary," but continued to believe that Vietnamese Trotskyites themselves were sincerely antiimperialist.[27] In this setting, the Trotskyites built a considerable following among the Cochin China intelligentsia.

Advantages on the dialectical level, however, were far from everything.

To the Trotskyites, ICP "friendship societies" were reactionary symbols of the orthodox communists' abandonment of the fight for labor union freedom in Vietnam. The "friendship societies," Trotskyite newspapers declared, would kill the idea of labor unions in Vietnam rather than stimulate it. ICP newspapers responded by arguing that the "friendship societies" were the "ladder" to real labor unions. Once again, a classic issue of the Vietnamese revolution was being ventilated. Was the ICP's "small-group" approach or communalist approach to social organization capable of leading the way to mass movements that could save the country? In retrospect, it might be concluded that the Trotskyites were poor at the mechanics of building organized communities—a fatal weakness, considering the problems of modern Vietnam. Their skepticism that small, modest "friendship societies" could develop an awareness of mutual needs and interests among workers, or that the old Vietnamese mutual-help ethic could be expanded to socially significant dimensions, was a mistake: these things did in fact happen. Better at journalism, and at building urban audiences for their journalism which they never tightly controlled, the Trotskyites saw their power wane when Indochina, tied to France, was suddenly hurtled into World War II.

The Japanese Occupation of Indochina and the Creation of the Viet Minh

The "democratic front" and "legal" revolutionary activities ended abruptly in September 1939. ICP "friendship societies" were dissolved and left-wing journals in the cities were suppressed. (It is a measure of how vigorous such journalism had been in the late 1930s that the colonial regime closed some fourteen journals in Saigon in September 1939, including four sponsored by the orthodox communists.)[28] The colonial government's control of the economy intensified. Civil servants were forced to contribute parts of their monthly salaries to a special Franco-Vietnamese war fund. Legal and semilegal ICP organs and cadres scurried for secrecy. In so doing, they rediscovered the Vietnamese countryside. From this point until 1945, when the August Revolution brought Ho Chi Minh to power, peasant villages were to function as the bases of the Vietnamese revolution. The era of rural guerrillas and of a much more extravagantly nationalistic communism was at hand.

The August Revolution was to develop unevenly, achieving greater successes in Tonkin than in the south. Because of this, it is attractive to search for what has loosely been called an "ecology" of revolution, or at least for an explanatory scheme which emphasizes the differences among the economic and geographical factors in the regions where the revolutionaries triumphed and failed. But the fact is that some of the geographical unevenness of the revolution—not all—could be attributed merely to the unevenness of ICP planning, as much as to the sociology and the economic geography of various localities. Party planning was remarkably decentralized. At least in part, this was an effect of French repression.

The Tonkin Regional Committee of the ICP, alarmed by the implications of the Munich crisis of September 1938, withdrew many of its cadres from public to secret activity a whole year before war broke out in Europe, and began stressing the creation of firm positions in the villages even in 1938, in order to insure itself against a revival of repression in the cities. This superior caution of the Tonkin Regional Committee undoubtedly gave the revolutionaries a distinct head start in the north. And although the Annam Regional Committee ordered its cadres to withdraw into secrecy only in late 1939, the Quang Tri provincial committee—Quang Tri was another area where the revolution was to become relatively well established—had "anticipated" this decision and had moved its apparatus into the mountains and rural hinterlands long before colonial repression resumed.

Southern communists, on the other hand, still vainly tried to operate semilegally into the early 1940s. They continued diligently to pin their hopes upon the creation of public associations for roofing houses, or guilds for plowing and transplanting rice, or sickness-curing groups, in such places as Gia Dinh, My Tho, and Tra Vinh. The very concept and purposes of the Viet Minh were not communicated to southerners until 1942, long after Viet Minh "national salvation associations" had been spawned in northern provinces. The Party Central was located in the north, and it took time for its directives to be clandestinely passed to Saigon.[29]

The Japanese imperial armed forces conquered Southeast Asia between 1940 and 1942. The whole area from the Philippines to Burma was brought under the direct or indirect control of the Japanese Greater East Asia Co-Prosperity Sphere. By the end of 1940, Japanese forces had occupied northern Vietnam as far south as Hanoi. By the summer of 1941, the Japanese army had arrived in Saigon. During the next four years, while wars in China and in the south Pacific reached their climaxes, Indochina became a tense backwater. The Japanese permitted the forms of French colonial rule to continue undisturbed until March 1945. They had no taste for carrying out a major administrative upheaval in Indochina that would drain resources from their military efforts against the British and the Americans. But the decision-making capacities of the French governor-general in Hanoi were now subject to the wishes of the Japanese military command.

The result was that two foreign powers sought to manipulate Vietnamese society instead of just one. Indirectly, at least, the Japanese army worked to undermine the French hegemony, through competition for the allegiance of the Vietnamese elite. Japanese army leaders circulated the slogan that the Japanese and Vietnamese peoples "had the same literature and were of the same race." General Iwane Matsui, the bloody-handed conqueror of Nanking back in 1938, confidently assured Vietnamese journalists, in a speech which he gave in Saigon in July 1943, that Japan would liberate Asia from the Americans, the British, *and* the French.[30] The invaders opened schools to teach the Japanese language to Vietnamese children; showed Japanese movies; promoted Vietnamese-language journals which celebrated the rise of the "new Asia"; and encouraged more numerous exchanges of Japanese and Vietnamese Buddhist groups.

Reacting to the fact that the Japanese occupation had transformed its colonial monopoly into an unstable, volatile Franco-Japanese duopoly, the French colonial regime made eleventh-hour alterations in its own strategy and tactics. More schools were built, and the number of Vietnamese occupying middle- or high-level positions in the Indochina colonial administration doubled between 1940 and 1944.[31] To checkmate the Japanese cultural campaign in Vietnam, the regime quickly permitted a host of Vietnamese youth organizations to germinate with almost magical timeliness: the Association of Catholic Youth, the Association of Catholic Student Youth, the Association of Catholic Civil Service Youth, and the General Association of Indochina Students. In other words, at the very moment that the Japanese were making overtures to Buddhists, the French attempted a new sectarian mobilization of Vietnamese Catholics: the period of the Japanese occupation was to do little to interrupt the consolidation of feelings of religious separateness in Vietnam. Few of the youth organizations which the colonial regime suddenly authorized after 1940 successfully extended themselves to the organization-hungry countryside, it should also be observed.

Nonetheless, a forced spirit of innovation hung in the air: the French governor-general, Admiral Decoux, actually sponsored a youth-oriented physical training and sports movement. Up until the 1930s, the colonial power had had a horror of almost any form of aggressiveness or organization among young Vietnamese. Now, in the 1940s, it encouraged bicycle races, swimming competitions, boxing contests, boy scout groups, torchlight parades, and physical training schools like the one at Phan Thiet. This policy did of course reflect similar trends back in Vichy France. But in the Vietnamese context it had a significance of its own. For the first time in its history, the French colonial regime in the early 1940s permitted controlled expressions of Vietnamese nationalism. The Vietnamese "people," recently claimed to be "descendants of the Gauls" in their own schools, were now allowed to celebrate the anniversaries of such national heroes as the Trung Sisters or Le Loi or Quang-trung. This decision represented the shadowy origins of what might be called a homeopathic cure policy directed against Vietnamese communist nationalists. With such a policy, efforts were made to borrow and use enough of the communist programs and ideological symbols (fellowship organizations, national heroes) to weaken what was dangerously becoming the uniqueness of the communist appeal. The precedent which the Decoux government set was to be invoked more comprehensively by future anticommunist governments in succeeding decades, from the 1940s to the 1970s.

Ending thirty years of exile, Ho Chi Minh crossed the Sino-Vietnamese frontier into his homeland on February 8, 1941. At Pac Bo, in the northwestern part of the borderlands province of Cao Bang, he convened the ICP Central Committee for the eighth time in its history in May 1941. This meeting formally produced the Viet Minh or "Vietnamese Independence Brotherhood League" (*Viet Nam Doc Lap Dong Minh Hoi*). In brief, the Viet Minh was designed to be a heterogeneous coalition of nationalists, drawn from a variety of social classes and sponsored by the Indochina Communist Party, which could fight to achieve Vietnam's national independence. Communist doctrines of class war were to be muted (but not forgotten) by the new movement, in the interests of fostering a more effective, integrative nationalism. The party's crusade for a landholding revolution had already been temporarily abandoned, a year and a half earlier, at the November 1939 sixth meeting of the Party Central at Ba Diem, Gia Dinh, which Ho had not attended. By postponing their plans for social and economic revolution in this way, the leaders of the Viet Minh hoped that they could attract the support of Vietnamese who hated colonialism but who had previously shown no liking for communism. They also hoped that the Viet Minh could more conveniently attract assistance from foreign powers for the purpose of fighting the Japanese, including assistance from those foreign powers which had found a more blatantly communist movement offensive. Among these foreign powers, the Chinese Kuomintang government of Chiang Kai-shek seemed both the most important and the most problematic to the new Viet Minh organization in 1941. It was the most problematic because it still possessed, or seemed to possess, an alarming capacity to intervene in Vietnamese politics against the interests of the communists.

In a sense, Vietnamese communist foreign policy was born in 1941. The forces behind its parturition assumed the long-term weakness of Vietnamese national movements and were prepared for vigilant, limited accommodations with the West. On December 21, 1941, the General Affairs commission of the ICP Party Central, in a circular entitled "The Pacific War and the Essential Responsibility of the Party," carefully calculated what communist policy would be in the event of Allied military penetration of Indochina. This December 1941 circular baldly declared that if English and American armies came to Indochina to reestablish French colonialism, they would be met by uprisings and resistance. If, however, the English and Americans arrived to "help the Indochina revolution," the party was willing to cede them an unspecified share of economic privileges in Indochina as a reward. This 1941 policy decision—which is poorly known in the West—remains one of the most controversial developments in the long history of Vietnamese communism, at least among members of the movement itself. In 1970 the Hanoi government found it necessary publicly to defend it, arguing that it was not an "illusion" to believe in 1941 that English and American armies might bring freedom to Vietnam, and that the ICP had to have allies, no matter how "provisional, unstable, conditional" their support might be.[32] Ho Chi Minh's cultivation of the American Office of Strategic Services in 1944, which is much better known, was not therefore a quixotic personal game. It had been arranged and accepted as a formal party policy almost three years earlier.

The need for international contacts, moreover, influenced the ICP in other ways in 1941. Ho Chi Minh is reported to have personally chosen the northern borderlands province of Cao Bang as a base area for the Viet Minh for three reasons: its party organs were relatively strong and stable; it was well located from the point of view of spreading revolution into the lowlands; and yet as a border province it permitted the preservation of links with Yenan (the wartime north China domain of the Chinese Communist Party) and even with Moscow.[33] Cao Bang, of course, had other significant features. Its population (perhaps 200,000 people in 1973, less in 1941) was distributed among seven different ethnic groups. The Vietnamese ethnic group itself was a marked minority, since the Tay and the Nung highland peoples together constituted 80 percent of the people of the province. In such an ethnic farrago, there were few solid stretches of imperturbably hierarchical Vietnamese villages, dominated by Confucian notables, that were capable of impeding the early momentum of a revolutionary insurrection. What made the situation even better was that Cao Bang was a province with a history of revolt against lowland power holders.

The Nong brothers' peasant rebellion of the early 1830s, which had spread through Tuyen Quang, Thai Nguyen, and Lang Son provinces as well as Cao Bang, appears (geographically speaking) to have been almost a dress rehearsal of at least some patterns of Viet Minh expansion. The province's history of revolt may well have been tied to the fact that for a long time it had straddled important border trade routes, which made it anything but a picture of backward, undercommercialized stability. Even in 1812, for example, before the French conquest, Nguyen court records had shown that Cao Bang had more primary customs-tax collection areas than any other northern province.[34] Communists themselves had been active in Cao Bang since the 1920s. The first party cell in the province appeared in April 1930. The Tay highland people of Cao Bang and of nearby Lang Son province produced a number of early ICP leaders, including Hoang Tu Huu (who represented the Indochina minority peoples at the 1935 Moscow Comintern congress) and Hoang Van Thu, who rose to the crucial position of secretary of the Tonkin Regional Committee of the ICP in the fall of 1939. Thu, indeed, had even organized communist political training classes for borderlands recruits at Lungchow, across the Chinese border in Kwangsi province, as early as 1932. He had also led the Bac Son armed uprising in a mountainous subprefecture of Lang Son province in September 1940, an uprising which failed but which produced the first guerrilla companies in Vietnamese communist history. For all these reasons, the Viet Minh base in this region in the 1940s was not entirely an artificial transplanting of political activities which had long flourished more luxuriantly elsewhere. The obvious comparison with Yenan has its limits.

On the other hand, the Yenan style of revolutionary politics certainly did have its echoes here. The Ho Chi Minh of Paris had been a cosmopolitan ideologue who had specialized in influencing literate public opinion in the colonial metropolis and in writing French-language analyses of global imperialist patterns. This man now disappeared. The man who replaced him, the Ho Chi Minh of Cao Bang, was a backwoods insurrectionist who stressed the mystique of the Vietnamese national tradition, and who encouraged the spread of popular literacy classes for both cadres and peasants. Without the emergence of this second Ho Chi Minh, there would have been no August Revolution.

Ho Chi Minh's teaching and indoctrination program at Pac Bo therefore deserves to be considered. To begin with, Ho wrote a profusion of poems with historical and national themes in order to incite a revolutionary spirit. For peasant audiences, he formulated a 236-line "six-eight" poem entitled "The History of Our Country from 2879 B.C. to 1942" (it was first published in 1942) which magnified the theme of Vietnamese resistance to foreign aggression. Virtually for the first time, Ho linked the communist cause to glorious Vietnamese historical memories like the Tay-son victory over the Chinese at Dong Da in 1789. His poem was also designed to counter the influence of histories of Vietnam written by noncommunist intellectuals, of which the most famous was the short history of Vietnam which had been published by Tran Trong Kim in 1920. A parade of symbolism from the past governed the new Viet Minh-sponsored flowering of nationalism in other ways. At the beginning of 1942, Ho ordered guerrillas at his Pac Bo base to scatter in nearby villages in order to prepare a secret armed force for a "Southward Advance" (*Nam tien*): the term "Southward Advance" described the communist insurrection that was to come, but also artfully recalled the heroic medieval migrations of the Vietnamese people into central Vietnam and later into the Mekong delta. By early 1943 the Cao Bang base itself had been renamed the Le Loi war zone, while other Viet Minh bailiwicks inevitably bore the names of Hoang Hoa Tham and Quang-trung.

The Vietnamese communists' optimistic belief in the stimulation of local pride as a step toward a more stable nationalism, rather than as an obstacle to the growth of nationalism, also appears to date from the early 1940s. Ho inaugurated it by writing a poem, "The Geography of Cao Bang," whose purpose was to give local guerrillas a sense of their own province—as opposed to just their villages—and to heighten their local self-respect. This was accomplished by many references in the poem to the "thriftiness" and "intelligence" of the "more than ninety thousand compatriots" of Cao Bang. As a parallel to this modernized provincialism, however (which was regarded as a means to an end), Ho wrote another poem, "The Geography of Our Country," which consisted of simple five-word lines, a little like a traditional Vietnamese schoolboy's primer. Memorization of a sample passage from this poem meant memorization of such exact visions as "Vietnam is shaped like the letter S, / A very elegant peninsula, / On the shores of the Pacific Ocean, / In the southeast of the continent of Asia."[35] The ambition behind this literature was, of course, the diffusion of Western-style nationalism—"topographic" nationalism, with more impersonal, scientific symbolism—among cadres and peasants, so that they would think of the Vietnamese nation-state *not only* in terms of loyalty to cult-honored heroes of bygone centuries (the staple content of Vietnam's humanistic premodern patriotism) *but also* in terms of fixed territorial and economic proprietorship.

By this time, the Vietnamese communists had made the momentous discovery that the peasantry were characterized by more than a state of oppression. Now it was deemed proper to argue that they possessed latent qualities of courage and resourcefulness as well. It was a sign of the times that when Dang Thai Mai, a notable spokesman and warden of the cause of left-wing culture in Vietnam, translated into Vietnamese in the early 1940s "The Story of Ah Q" by the great Chinese left-wing writer Lu Hsün, he notified his Hanoi audience that Lu Hsün's feckless, self-deceiving hero was "an especially Chinese peasant personage."[36] Ah Q was too much of a failure to be Vietnamized even as a role caricature the way Chinese literary paragons of filial piety had been Vietnamized or borrowed as role models in the past.

But the practical side of the new Viet Minh approach to the peasantry was contained in the "culture-teaching movement." Everywhere that Viet Minh organizations appeared, noontime or evening reading classes were held for illiterate adult peasants, as well as daytime classes for children. The text used in these literacy classes was a new "Five Character Classic" especially written for them by Ho Chi Minh. Like classical primers, it was an instrument of indoctrination. It expounded such things as the communist organizational ethic ("The minority follows the majority, In all tasks unity is needed, Our associations are very secret, They must be preserved with all our strength") but in a way which excluded elitist nuances and alien-sounding doctrinal subtleties. "Culture tests" (meaning reading tests) were given at the end of every series of classes. The early high point of the Viet Minh "culture movement" in Cao Bang was the "congress of students" held in Ha Quang district in January 1943, which attracted more than one thousand people.[37]

It could be argued that this borderlands "culture movement," together with the Viet Minh stress upon popular education, represented only a very partial revelation of communism to the Vietnamese people, a deliberately partial revelation, the "exoteric" side rather than the "esoteric." In the summer of 1941, Ho Chi Minh, wearing the clothing of Nung highlanders, was inclined to explain to his young recruits among the Nung people that communism meant nothing more than food and clothing for everyone, no exploitation, and villages filled with electric lights, public health services, and movie-showing facilities like those of the cities.[38] Limited revelation was an essential part of the strategy of the Viet Minh, which was not, in any case, formally concerned with the second stage of the revolution—the "socialist" stage—but only with the first stage, the "bourgeois democratic" one.

Yet to an important extent the members of the second and third ranks of the Vietnamese communist movement themselves, if not some of the members of the first rank, probably had only the most marginal understanding of the complexities inherent in the long European philosophical tradition upon which Marxism-Leninism drew. Possibly no national communist movement has ever paid less attention, for example, in the period before it has come to power, to Marxist (or Hegelian) metaphysics. Even in 1926, the Revolutionary Youth League school in Canton, the earliest formal nursery of Vietnamese Marxism, had offered no lectures whatsoever on dialectical materialism, although Ho had made a point of using a few "dialectical methods" to explain the rise of revolution.[39] If Bertrand Russell is right in suggesting that Marxist metaphysics served the purpose merely of giving Marx a certainty about the future which was not scientifically warranted,[40] it is appropriate to observe the even greater irrelevance of such metaphysics to Vietnamese revolutionaries. Nationalism, rather than the cloudy influences of Hegel, supplied the Vietnamese communists with their hopeful faith in their own prevision. But if they had not fully mastered the "esoteric" side of their own doctrines themselves, could they appeal without confusion to the Vietnamese intelligentsia?

By the early 1940s, the Chinese Communist Party had already won the allegiance of many of China's most distinguished writers. It could afford to discipline them at Yenan with "thought reform" campaigns. In contrast, the ICP had remained much more of a tightly knit oligarchy, even with respect to writers, throughout its formative years from 1930 to 1941. In fact, the most prestigious group of writers in Vietnam in the 1930s—the writers of the "Self-Reliance Literary Group"—were almost as hostile to communism as they were to colonialism. Only in 1943 did the ICP belatedly turn its attention to the question of systematically recruiting the Vietnamese intelligentsia as a "class," and of considering the desirability of a Vietnamese cultural revolution. The inspiration for this change plainly came from the Chinese Communist regime at Yenan. In 1943 the ICP issued a document entitled "General Propositions about Vietnamese Culture" (*De cuong van hoa Viet-Nam*) which argued, first, that the cultural front must be one of three fronts (economic, political, and cultural) upon which communists must be active; second, that a cultural revolution must accompany the political revolution in Vietnam; and third, that the party must acquire a leading position in cultural movements in Indochina if it wished its propaganda to enjoy a sufficiently effective impact. According to the "Propositions," the party's cultural goal was to be the building of a "new democratic Indochina culture," which meant, in turn, a "national, scientific, mass-oriented" culture.[41]

The ICP was now transposing to Vietnam the approach to culture which Mao Tse-tung had first enunciated in China in January 1940, in his famous formulation "On The New Democracy." This had urged (among other things) the "absorption of the democratic essence" of China's "glorious ancient culture" by the communist movement, as part of any "national, scientific, popular" cultural posture. The Vietnamese communists' own importation of Mao's nationalistic theories of a "new democracy" in the cultural sphere was, of course, designed to interrupt any possible gravitation of Vietnamese intellectuals toward either the French or Japanese camps which were so urgently beckoning them. The promulgation of the "Propositions" was quickly followed by the creation, with party cadres' assistance, of a "Vietnamese National Salvation Culture Association," which was intended to facilitate the absorption of Vietnamese intellectuals into the Viet Minh, and of a "Democratic Party of Vietnam" (June 1944) whose mission was to keep "national bourgeois and petty bourgeois patriotic intellectuals" from supporting the Japanese. There is no doubt that these two timely extensions of the Viet Minh's "united national front" bolstered the communist position, in the unprecedented three-cornered political battle for the loyalties of the Vietnamese elite which raged in Indochina between 1941 and 1945.

"New democracy" theories sanctioned cultural nationalism. This had consequences for the Vietnamese communists' relations both with China and with the other peoples of Indochina. The memorable new theme of a national, scientific, mass-oriented culture survived the era of suddenly created fronts, associations, and subsidiary political parties of the early 1940s and became the Viet Minh's sustaining creed in the guerrilla war against the French from 1946 to 1954. But although it was an idea borrowed from China, it became capable in the late 1940s of being converted into a weapon against excessive borrowing from China—a truly ancient Vietnamese pattern. In a notable exposition of the mass nature of Vietnam's "new democratic" culture in 1947, Truong Chinh, the secretary general of the party since 1940, was to say:

The current struggle is a great turning upside down of things . . . . The cities and towns, formerly the centers of culture, are now undergoing enemy occupation and changing into a barbarian darkness brimming with degenerate culture. On the other hand, the rural villages, formerly dilapidated and backward-looking places, now can become regions of advanced civilization . . . . In such a situation

various writers and artists acknowledge quickly their own slaves'
diseases of being half Westerners and being half Chinese, and are
making themselves of the people.[42]

This did not mean that diagnoses of the "slaves' disease" could not be
narrow or expedient ones. For a subordinate but important element in
Mao's "new democratic culture" was a new respect for the "glorious
ancient culture" of the Chinese classical period, and the Vietnamese could
regard parts of this heritage as belonging equally to them. A definite
revival of classical scholarship helped to shape the Viet Minh sense of
strategy and of community. In the early 1940s, Ho Chi Minh translated
into colloquial Vietnamese from classical Chinese the source book of all
Chinese military thought, the *Sun-tzu.* His borderlands cadres were also
required to read another one of his translations, a Vietnamese version of a
Chinese book which outlined the leadership doctrines of the classical
philosophers Confucius and Mencius. To his translation of this book Ho
appended the significant Vietnamese title "Methods of Training Military
Cadres." At the very moment that mass-oriented nationalism was to reach
its zenith, in other words, the classical heritage of the mandarins who led
the Viet Minh was also deliberately renewed, and extended into new fields
of interest. Operating as a transmitter of the most recent military techniques from Yenan, Ho wrote two other training manuals for his Cao Bang
cadres, "Methods of Guerrilla Fighting" and "Experiences of Chinese
Guerrillas."[43]

The accentuated nationalism of the Viet Minh coalition raised in a new
form the question of Vietnamese communist leaders' approaches to the
thorny issue of what "Indochina" stood for. In October 1930, the name of
their fledgling party had been dramatically changed from "Vietnam Communist Party" to "Indochina Communist Party": even to party insiders, it
is still not clear who took the initiative in introducing this change. Justifications had to be found for it quickly. In February 1931, therefore, an
ephemeral communist journal anxiously attempted to supply some. It
argued that the three countries of Indochina were intimately interrelated
economically and that, politically, all three countries had been occupied
by French imperialism, which had placed them under one law and one
policy of exploitation. (In fact, there was far less French interference in
Cambodia.) The "proletarian class" and "toiling masses" in all three
countries, as a result, wished to overthrow French rule. They further
wished to overthrow their monarchies in order to escape from slavery
(there was, in fact, little antimonarchical sentiment in Cambodia and Laos
in the early 1930s); and they wished to overthrow their landlords in order
to reclaim their lands (there was relatively little landlordism in Cambodia
and Laos, compared to Vietnam.)[44]

Such an extraordinary vision of the existence of a single "proletarian
class" in all parts of Indochina might well be regarded as a disingenuous
mixture of the thought of Marx and of the Vietnamese emperor Minh-

mang. It combined an adaptation of Marx's view that "proletarians" were homogenized into one relatively undifferentiated class by their working conditions (in the early industrial revolution, which had hardly come to Cambodia and Laos) with Minh-mang's aggressive early nineteenth-century belief in the Vietnamese mission to dominate and enlighten the other two Indochina countries. No facts supported this expansive myth. And no ICP apparatus even existed in Laos and Cambodia in the early 1930s.

But in 1941, the Viet Minh transformation of at least the surface of the communist movement brought with it a striking new awareness of the distinctive cultural roots of national politics, and a moderation of the ruthless Leninist cosmopolitanism of the past. This, plus practical necessity, led the eighth Party Central meeting of the ICP in 1941—the meeting which created the Viet Minh—to decide to grant each one of the three nations of Indochina its own "framework" for revolution.[45] At this point the ICP also belatedly recognized the legitimacy of the various literatures of the Indochina highland peoples, guaranteeing "free development" to the culture of every Indochina ethnic group. (Here it lagged some four years behind the Chinese communists, who had announced self-determination and self-government for Moslems and other minority peoples of China as one of the "ten great policies" of their united front against Japan in August 1937.) As a concrete demonstration of their official abandonment of any ambition to impose Vietnamese influences upon the rest of Indochina, on August 29, 1945, a delegation of the Viet Minh central committee staged a moving if carefully arranged ceremony in Savannakhet, Laos. At this ceremony Vietnamese civil servants partial to the Viet Minh who had been staffing government offices in Laos, under the French, now publicly transferred their functions to Lao representatives who had been invited to the meeting.

The Enactment of the August Revolution

To the Vietnamese communists, the August Revolution of 1945 is unique. They regard it as an imitation neither of Russian nor of Chinese revolutionary examples. Their party's Historical Research Committee declared in 1967 that the October Revolution of 1917 in Russia had depended entirely upon a general military uprising, featured by concentrated military violence in Petrograd, Moscow, and other important places. The Chinese revolution of the 1940s, for its part, had combined political struggle with military struggle, but the role of armed force and of military struggle had had a "decisive nature from beginning to end." In Vietnam, in contrast, political struggle and military struggle had again been combined; but the revolutionary victory had basically been won by the "political force" of the people taking advantage of the most favorable opportunities.[46] The two differences between the Vietnamese revolution and the Chinese one were the Vietnamese revolutionaries' lesser use of military force and—the

Vietnamese movement's more faithful Leninism coming to the fore again—the Vietnamese revolutionaries' more painstaking devotion to the preservation of a balance between urban and rural mobilization and agitation.[47]

The validity of these occasionally self-serving generalizations cannot be assessed in a moment. It is certainly true that between 1941 and 1945 the Viet Minh were concerned with transcending the gap between the towns, with their students and civil servants and book publishers, and the rural hinterlands, with their tenant farmers and political communications networks dominated by oral poetry. By early 1943 the Viet Minh had entrenched themselves in their Cao Bang base and had opened "security zones" or "preparatory security zones" in the rural areas of at least five provinces beyond the borderlands—Phuc Yen, Ha Dong, Bac Ninh, Bac Giang, and Thai Nguyen. As an aspect of the quest for "balance," however, part of the ICP Party Central struggled to retain its urban connections by remaining hidden on the outskirts of Hanoi throughout the Pacific War. (This decision did allow the party to respond relatively rapidly to the Japanese coup on March 9, 1945.) In spite of this, the General Affairs Committee of the Party Central, meeting at Vong La (Phuc Yen) in February 1943, expressed the fear that the movement lacked sufficient clienteles in the cities, especially among workers and students. The Vong La conference concluded, with real pessimism, that in early 1943 there were no prospects for a successful revolutionary uprising in the "pulse areas" of the enemy army (cities, mines, plantations, major transportation routes). Because of this, any uprising which did occur could have only a narrow regional nature and would almost certainly be repressed. Ho Chi Minh did not attend the Vong La conference. He spent two years in China (1942-1944) developing ties with, and intrigues among, Vietnamese exiles there and Chinese militarists and politicians who he thought might provide assistance to the Viet Minh.[48] His first year in China (August 1942-September 1943) was spent ignobly enough in a Kwangsi jail.

Despite the pessimism of the Vong La conference and Ho Chi Minh's absence, the Viet Minh issued its first directive ordering its followers to begin preparing an armed uprising as early as May 7, 1944. By the end of the summer of 1944, the Viet Minh was releasing its own letters of credit to finance these preparations. It derived other revenues from the members of its "national salvation associations" and "self-defense companies," who contributed money to special gun-buying funds. By August 1943, the movement's pioneering guerrilla forces—called at this point the "National Salvation Army," with divisions commanded by Vo Nguyen Giap and by the Tho highlander general Chu Van Tan—had managed to open a "corridor" between the two most important Viet Minh borderland havens. The Viet Minh also turned its attention to the seduction of Vietnamese soldiers and servants in French pay, some fifteen years after the Vietnamese Nationalists had made the first venture into this realm of anticolonial politics. In Hanoi alone, in 1943, clandestine "national salvation service-men's groups" were organized within the First Indochina Infantry Regiment and the Fourth Colonial Artillery Regiment. At the beginning of 1944, the Viet Minh even established weak contacts with German communists and Austrian socialists employed by the French Foreign Legion in Indochina.[49] The official organ of the ICP, the "Flag of Liberation," predicted in a famous issue on September 27, 1944, that the "covered boil" of Indochina politics—the festering rivalry between the French and the Japanese—would soon inevitably erupt. In December 1944 the first platoons of Vo Nguyen Giap's "Liberation Army" were formally created in Cao Bang.

The Japanese army's overthrow of French rule in Indochina on March 9, 1945, was of course prompted both by the tensions of the "covered boil" and by Japan's increasingly desperate position in the Pacific War. The coup was only feebly resisted by French forces in Hanoi and Hue, while other French soldiers surrendered, scattered, or fled into south China. Tran Trong Kim, the gentle, elderly intellectual who had retired as director of Hanoi primary schools in 1942, was installed as the chief of an "independent" Vietnamese government, under the last Nguyen emperor, Bao Dai, at Hue. Kim had spent much of the year 1944 in a Singapore hotel translating Chinese T'ang dynasty poetry into Vietnamese, and waiting for a Japanese decision on Vietnam's future. Summoned to Hue after the coup, he told Bao Dai that he was too old and too nonpolitical to establish a government, and that the Catholic mandarin Ngo Dinh Diem, a reformer and provincial governor of the 1930s, would be a much better choice than himself. But Diem evaded Bao Dai's summons. Kim unwillingly formed a government as quickly as he could, in order to forestall the nightmare of a direct Japanese military administration of Vietnam.[50]

Most of the Kim government's energies were spent attempting to persuade the Japanese army to make Vietnamese independence real instead of a convenient fraud. The Japanese did return the French "protectorate" of Tonkin to the Hue court. But they refused to give up Cochin China, or the French concessions in the cities of Hanoi, Haiphong, and Da Nang, or control over the basic fiscal, judicial, educational, and public security agencies (or even the postal service) which had previously sheltered under the centralizing aegis of the French governor-general. Faced with such Japanese hypocrisy, the Kim government lacked an army of its own to challenge it. And it feared to create even a defense ministry, because this act might permit its Japanese patrons to conscript Vietnamese men and force Vietnam to join their losing war against the Western allies.[51] Defenseless and inept, the Kim regime was not even extensively favored by the Japanese, who hoped for better things from the Cao Dai and Hoa Hao religious movements in the south, and from such pro-Japanese organizations as the "New Vietnam Nationalist Party" and Cochin China's "Japanese-Vietnamese Defense League." As for the Viet Minh, Tran Trong

Kim was largely unfamiliar with it. Even in his memoirs, he refers to its creation as having been "around 1936–1937."[52]

In Viet Minh eyes, the Japanese coup portended, at last, the "favorable objective circumstance" for a general uprising. Truong Chinh, the party secretary-general, summoned the General Affairs Committee of the Party Central to a meeting in a Bac Ninh village some sixteen kilometers from Hanoi (March 9–12, 1945). This conference initiated what it called the "uprising preliminary period" on the strength of three factors: one, the political crisis which prevented either the French or the Japanese armies from having a free hand to deal with Communist revolutionaries; two, the devastating famine in Tonkin, which caused the peasantry to hate the occupying armies which were appropriating rice paddy for their own use; and three, the military climax of the Pacific War, which meant that Allied armies might soon be landing in Indochina.

The March 1945 party conference, in brief, explicitly recognized the famine—which was peculiar to the north—as constituting one of the "three opportunities" for the making of the revolution. Japan was identified as the primary enemy. The peasants were now to be mobilized to destroy the paddy granaries of the "imperialists" in order to "solve" the famine and to foster an anti-Japanese "high tide." The general uprising itself, it was decided, would be precipitated by one of two possible events: an Allied troop landing in Indochina, or a communist revolution in Japan which caused Japanese expeditionary forces in Indochina to "lose their spirit." All the decisions and prescriptions of the March 1945 conference were embodied in an historic text ("The Warfare Between The Japanese And The French And Our Own Actions") which was to guide the ICP and the Viet Minh in the next six months. The role of party secretary Truong Chinh at this conference appears to have been crucial.[53]

Vo Nguyen Giap's liberation army—augmented by defecting militia commanders, one of whom surrendered four platoons—now began to move through the villages of Tonkin. On its sweeps it systematically collected the certificates, diplomas, and seals of office of existing canton and village chiefs, and set up "revolutionary political power" in the place of the disestablished village elites. To protect the new pro-Viet Minh village governments, the army inspired the formation of village "self-defense" companies. United front tactics were used where possible: in Bac Can province, the Viet Minh created a short-lived "Franco-Vietnamese Anti-Japanese Committee" whose purpose was to sell scarce rural foodstuffs to the five platoons of French and Vietnamese colonial soldiers still in the province, in return for their neutralization and recognition of Viet Minh control. In Bac Ninh province, within one month of the Japanese coup, village meetings organized by the Viet Minh had confiscated the "syndicate rice paddy" which Japanese soldiers were hoarding in local granaries, had redistributed the rice among hungry peasants, and had organized "self-defense" companies which promptly seized the credentials of village notables. In

Bac Giang province also, the Viet Minh mobilized groups of "hundreds of people" to attack paddy granaries. The "National Salvation Prison Youth," a separate and highly significant Viet Minh association in Bac Giang, organized jail prisoners to attack the few colonial militiamen who had remained to guard them, seize their weapons, and destroy the prisons; this group then merged with other youth groups to form Bac Giang province's first guerrilla military company. By the summer of 1945, the Viet Minh in Bac Giang had become strong enough to confiscate the lands of French landlords, and to give them to tenant farmers and to families who had "shown support for the revolution." The destruction of the prisons and the redistribution of land became the twin symbols of the breathtaking transformation of the structure of power in this province.[54]

Ho Chi Minh appears to have exercised his authority selectively. He did not participate prominently in any of these activities. And it was Truong Chinh, once again, who presided over the important ICP military affairs conference in April 1945 (at Hiep Hoa, Bac Giang) which formally christened the Vietnam Liberation Army; decided to divide all of Vietnam into seven different military zones (four in Tonkin, two in Annam, one for all of Cochin China); and elected a revolutionary military affairs committee. Ho, however, decided upon the formal creation of the "liberated zone" which appeared on June 4, 1945. Within this zone (which ran across the mountainous northern borderlands, and which included almost all, or part of, some ten Tonkinese provinces) revolutionary people's committees were to be elected immediately to carry out the Viet Minh program: the confiscation and redistribution of the property of "Vietnamese traitors," the reduction of land rents, the abolition of miscellaneous French and Japanese taxes and their replacement by a single progressive tax, the introduction of compulsory primary education and an attack upon illiteracy, and the promulgation of labor laws which would cover minimum wages, social insurance, and an eight-hour working day.[55]

This program was still being developed when the Japanese surrendered unconditionally to the Allies in the second week of August, 1945. The communist response, decided at a party conference at Tan Trao, Tuyen Quang (August 13–15, 1945) and ratified by a Viet Minh "national congress" in the same village a day later, was a resolution to seize power by means of a general uprising *before* Anglo-American armies entered Vietnam. The conference concluded that the party should exploit "contradictions" among the French, English, Americans, and Chiang Kai-shek, and should avoid having to deal with many enemies at once. The congress in turn chose a national flag (red, with a five-pointed yellow star) and elected a provisional government, of which Ho Chi Minh was chairman.

Was a balance between urban and rural revolutionary actions really preserved in August 1945? The question remains close to the hearts of Vietnamese theorists. In the heat of the battle, however, theory not unnaturally retreated before expediency. Party analyses at Tan Trao were, significantly, sensitive to this issue, but finally concluded that "places where victory was certain should be occupied immediately, without calculating whether they were urban or rural."[56] And this was certainly the real pattern of the August Revolution. The two big cities which were conclusively seized in late August by the Viet Minh—Hanoi and Hue—do not seem to have been captured because of overwhelmingly strong pro-Viet Minh forces and sympathies among the normal residents of the cities. In both instances, these city revolutions depended upon the mobilization of the peasants who lived on their outskirts. In Hue, for example, as a result of Viet Minh arrangements, more than 150,000 people are claimed to have marched into a city whose own normal population was not more than 50,000, in order to seize its public buildings and overpower the Kim government. (The Kim government had been naively planning a rally of its own to celebrate Japan's far too belated "return of Cochin China to Vietnam.") In Hanoi, after the Japanese surrender, Vietnamese civil servants supported the Kim regime, not the Viet Minh. The Viet Minh city "uprising committee" managed to usurp control of a pro-Kim rally by the General Association of Civil Servants in a Hanoi theater, only after police assigned to protect the rally had defected. And the Viet Minh gained control of all of Hanoi itself only after thousands of peasants from villages in Ha Dong and Bac Ninh provinces had marched into Hanoi to attend demonstrations and attack police stations there, armed with sticks, scythes, knives, reaping hooks, and even a few rifles.[57]

Yet the fact that this was, at bottom, a peasant revolution, hardly qualifies the magnitude of the Viet Minh achievement, even if it does undermine the "balance" theory which Hanoi historians so deeply cherish. Once Hanoi and Hue had fallen, province chiefs and mayors elsewhere began to capitulate, and the Bao-dai emperor agreed to the demand of the Viet Minh provisional government that he abdicate. The final overthrow of both the Nguyen monarchy and the surviving remnants of colonial power was accomplished by the Viet Minh in a mere twelve days (August 14–25, 1945). The Japanese army was too demoralized to fight. Its one gesture of defiance was to defend the headquarters of the Bank of Indochina in Hanoi, since it evidently feared punishment from the Allied powers if it surrendered the bank; and Hanoi analysts of the August Revolution, with their intense sectarian consciousness of history, compare the way the Bank of Indochina eluded their grasp in 1945 to the Paris Commune's failure to occupy French banks in 1871. The ICP Central Committee gave Le Duc Tho (later famous as chief negotiator of a peace treaty with the Americans, in Paris in 1971–1972, and for scholarly studies of Dimitrov, the Bulgarian communist) the honor of escorting Ho Chi Minh in triumph from Tan Trao back to Hanoi. The two men arrived on foot on August 26. Ho retired to a small apartment on Hang Ngang street to draft a Vietnamese "declaration of independence." The servants in the building where he was writing had the impression that he was merely "an old man who lived in the countryside" who had come to town for pleasure:[58] the events of August 1945 were much more "charismatic" than any one man.

The "Democratic Republic of Vietnam" was proclaimed in Hanoi on September 2, 1945. Ho Chi Minh was both its chairman and its minister in charge of foreign relations. It had to face, in its immediate future, the aftermath of the famine, the depredations of a Chinese occupying army (1945–1946), a cutthroat competition with noncommunist Vietnamese political parties (in which the communists apparently cut the most throats), and, ultimately, a long but victorious war with France (1946–1954).

Even though the Bao-dai emperor himself had been little more than a political cipher before 1945, his abdication was a sacramental climax of the revolution. It meant the end of a thousand year-old monarchy which had often been linked with moments of Vietnamese heroism and military glory in the past. The poet Huy Can, one of the members of the Viet Minh delegation which Ho Chi Minh sent to Hue to receive the abdication, has told of how he and his colleagues drove from Hanoi to Hue in a black-painted automobile, and of how they were repeatedly stopped by crowds waving Viet Minh flags. On such occasions, Tran Huy Lieu, another member of the delegation, would stand upon the roof of the car and explain that after a century, Vietnam had regained its independence and had washed away "the grievance of having lost the country" to French colonialism. During the abdication ceremonies themselves, the Viet Minh flag was raised above the Zenith Gate of the Hue imperial city, where only a century earlier Vietnamese emperors had stood to review parades of captured political rebels. Bao-dai, wearing imperial robes, a golden turban, and glass bead shoes, transferred to the Viet Minh delegates the emperor's sword and the dynastic seal (which had been cast in the Minh-mang reign, 1820–1841). The delegates responded by asking the crowd below the gate to cheer "Citizen Vinh Thuy," Bao-dai's postrevolutionary incarnation.

But even communist revolutionaries could retain some awe of the monarchy—either for reasons of strategy or for reasons of personal psychology. Before they met Bao-dai for the abdication spectacle, Ho Chi Minh's emissaries had heatedly discussed among themselves the question of how to address the retiring emperor. As a concession to the revolutionary political mood, they decided not to address him as "your imperial highness" (*Hoang thuong*) or as "your imperial majesty" (*Ngai ngu*) or as "Sire" (*Be ha*). Even with the city of Hue in their hands, however, they could not muster enough iconoclasm to address him as "mister" (*ong*). With a lingering sense of hierarchy still floating in the air, the delegates agreed to use the compromise term "majesty" or "excellency" (*Ngai*).[59] At the peak of the French revolution, a timber merchant was subject to arrest by the Parisian *sansculottes* for insisting that the word "sir" still be used in his house; such a fever of superficial egalitarianism was plainly missing from the August Revolution, if only because it was forced to look outward as well as inward. The fragility of its legitimacy in the eyes of the international superpowers, of which it was well aware, forced upon it an equivocal vocabulary even when it was dealing with Vietnamese "feudal" opponents.

One imaginative French historian, Roland Mousnier, has speculated that famines helped to produce revolt in countries as far removed as France and China in the early seventeenth century: he proposes, indeed, that the staggering mortality rates from such famines, and the political instabilities which they caused, even coincided in nature in French and Chinese societies in the 1620s and 1630s.[60] Should the Vietnamese revolution be added to this list, for the twentieth century? Is it one of the best examples in all history of an explosion ignited by a food crisis? To advance such an argument unconditionally would be to deny the importance of all the other themes discussed in this book. Yet the pestilential northern famine of 1944–1945 was far from trivial politically. That there was broad support for the Viet Minh in northern and north central villages, and less support in southern ones, could be explained in a number of ways: the greater political clairvoyance of the Tonkin Regional Committee in 1938, the excessive and self-deluded "urbanization" of the anticolonial movement in the south after 1936, the Hoa Hao phenomenon. But it is also true that there was no comparable famine in Cochin China.

As early as 1943, Viet Minh campaigns in the Red River delta had focused upon the food supply issue. They had revolved around such propaganda appeals as "oppose the uprooting of rice and the planting of jute." (The Japanese army's interest in 1943 in substituting jute crops for rice had already provoked bloody confrontations with Vietnamese peasants, such as the Dong Son village incident in Bac Ninh on June 14, 1943.) Vo Nguyen Giap's Liberation Army was specially organized to direct into revolutionary channels the trenchant but leaderless iconoclasm of Tonkin's starving peasants. The ICP military affairs conference of April 1945 stated quite candidly that "the art of agitative movements is to cling to the difficulties of the famine, the policy of collecting paddy."[61] The committee which ran the Liberation Army created "Liberation Army paddy granaries," and undertook to plan the emergency opening of harvest roads and the transportation of salt. The colonial government's requisitioning of the Tonkinese peasants' rice crops from 1943, at prices which ignored the wartime inflation of agricultural costs, has been described in an earlier chapter (see pages 158–159); this policy coincided with the strengthening of the political privileges of the Tonkin village notables from 1941, also described earlier (see pages 139–142). A bizarre result of this conjunction was that northern canton and village chiefs continued obediently to collect paddy—for the French *and* for the Japanese behind the French—despite the starvation of the peasants around them, in the spring of 1945. But under the relentless magnifying and focalizing power of the famine and its rising death toll, the inequities of the local Tonkinese political and social structure became a commonly understood outrage whose elimination was now a matter of survival. Politically and socially apocalyptic, the disaster created unprecedented desperation—and hatreds.

The Viet Minh, indeed, rode to power upon two slogans—"national independence" and "destroy the paddy granaries and solve the famine." A campaign to destroy elite-controlled or foreign-controlled granaries became the centerpiece of revolutionary mobilization. In some villages the Liberation Army tore down granaries belonging to Vietnamese landlords, or to Japanese and French interests (like the Fontaine wine factories) and distributed their rice to the peasants. In other places, the peasants themselves did so. Hundreds of canton and village chiefs who were collecting paddy for the Japanese were "detained" by the Viet Minh, preventing the Japanese army from using this local government infrastructure. In Vinh Yen province on the north bank of the Red River, between March and May 1945, some fifty granaries controlled by the Japanese or by Vietnamese landlords—including one with nearly six thousand tons of paddy in it—were demolished, and their contents distributed.[62]

Although fighting did break out around a few urban granaries, this rice-supply war was essentially a rural affair. For this reason it is not difficult to understand why the revolution had matured before urban elites really began to taste its ethos: the first provincial capital seized by Viet Minh guerrillas, that of the province of Quang Yen, did not fall until July 20, 1945. In southern Vietnam, where the Viet Minh gained control of Saigon only briefly at the end of August, before it was taken back by the British and the French, the revolution was a very different proposition. For the Viet Minh "general uprising" in the south mainly began much more artificially and less spontaneously in the provincial capitals; efforts were then made to export it to the districts and villages. One important fact expresses the regional contradictions of the Viet Minh crusade: only five provinces outside the north really shared the northern pattern of a "general uprising" which moved from the villages to the district capitals to the provincial capitals to the big cities. These provinces were Thua Thien, Khanh Hoa, My Tho, Sa Dec, and Quang Ngai.[63]

Of course it would be false to attribute geographical discrepancies in the conduct of the revolution entirely to the prepotent effects of a regional crisis like the Tonkin famine. Competing ideas about revolutionary strategies were certainly a factor, although their precise influence is unknown. Far from being a monolithic political machine, the Indochina Communist Party (to say nothing of the Viet Minh) was a tiny, clique-riddled movement with many unpredictably inflamed recesses. In 1941 the Party Central was opposed by an "anti-Bolshevik group" (*bon AB*) which was attempting to recruit dissatisfied members of the Tonkin Regional Committee; in central Vietnam Dinh Van Di led another clique which opposed the party leadership. In 1944 Ho Chi Minh, the iron-willed impresario of the revolution, was compelled to block an obstinate effort by the provincial committees of three borderlands provinces to launch a local armed uprising in their area which would have ignored the unfavorable "concrete situation" prevailing throughout Vietnam as a whole.[64] After the Japanese coup in March 1945, two Cochin China ICP newspapers, "Vanguard" (*Tien phong*) and "Liberation" (*Giai phong*) conducted a bitter polemical dispute with each other in which both newspapers rejected the policy of the party leaders in shrill tones: "Vanguard" wished communists to cooperate with the Japanese army in order to gain power, while "Liberation" scorned the united front tactic, endorsed by the Party Central, of working with selected Frenchmen against the Japanese. In Binh Dinh province, two separate Viet Minh groups existed; they insisted upon working independently of each other. At this time, indeed, the romantic idea of an "uprising" floated in the air all over Vietnam: ICP members in Quang Ngai province boldly formed their famous Ba To guerrilla company on March 14, 1945, without even waiting for any decision from a Party Central meeting. Communications were difficult and tensions ran high.

Moreover, unlike the Chinese Communist Party in this period, the ICP could not claim to have a mass following which was content to receive orders from a stable leadership hierarchy. In 1945 the Chinese communists enjoyed a party membership of more than 1.2 million people.[65] The ICP, in contrast, had slightly less than five thousand members at the time of the August Revolution. What this meant was that as of 1945 China, which had 20 or 30 times the population of Vietnam, had more than 240 times the number of communist revolutionaries. In the smaller Vietnamese movement, it appears, a much higher percentage of members regarded themselves as "leaders," and had many moments of isolation from the Party Central when they could play such roles. To some extent, Vietnam's situation as a total colony had kept the ICP from mass recruitment of new, callow, but obedient followers: it lacked such facilities for expanding its ranks of cadres as the Chinese communists had in their "Resist Japan Military University" in northwest China. In fact, until 1944, when the ICP admitted the new Hoang Van Thu class of cadres to the party, it sought to strengthen its forces mainly by the nostalgic device of recovering old cadres from colonial prisons. The expansive Chinese communist style in the early 1940s stressed cohesion through the control, indoctrination, and thought reform of a large, growing membership bloc. The more conservative Vietnamese communist style relied much more heavily upon painstaking selectivity during the initial recruitment of members. Only after 1945 did this distinction between the two movements begin to fade.

The Triumph of the Mandarin Proletarians

The August Revolution represented the culmination of work over many decades by men who spoke of a "worker-peasant" alliance. Yet most of these men themselves came from unmistakably mandarin backgrounds—

backgrounds darkened by recent ancestral memories both of the "loss of the nation" and of the specific humiliation of the nineteenth-century Vietnamese scholar class. The early years of Tran Phu, the first secretary-general of the ICP, reveal a great deal about the roots of Vietnamese communism. Tran Phu's father was a district magistrate in Quang Ngai province in the early 1900s. He had appeared first on the list of degree winners at the regional civil service examinations. In 1908, when his son was only four, this distinguished scholar-official committed suicide in his district magistrate's yamen [headquarters]. The reason was simple: representatives of the French colonial government had been harassing him continually with demands that he draft thousands of local Vietnamese militiamen and coolies for cheap, menial labor. Such a suicide—of a district magistrate who had been shamed by cynical French magnifications of the exploitative side of the traditional Vietnamese bureaucracy—could send shock waves through an entire province. Its effects upon Tran Phu himself were incalculable.

The early years of Nguyen Thi Minh Khai, the most celebrated female pioneer (and martyr) in Vietnamese communist history, are also worth considering. Her paternal grandfather was a provincial governor. Her father was a classical scholar who refused to wear Western clothes. As an impoverished eccentric, he was compelled to work as a clerk in the Vinh railway station. Both Tran Phu and Minh Khai, moreover, came from the same region and received their baptism into revolutionary politics at the Cao Xuan Duc primary school in the city of Vinh, where Tran Phu was a teacher and Minh Khai was a pupil. Much of the early revolution in central Vietnam was, indeed, spread by schoolboy networks, in schools in such cities as Hue and Vinh. Here the families of the traditional scholar class were concentrated; and here early political interaction was very much a product of neotraditional social ties like school memberships.[66] The mandarin nature of the communist leadership in Vietnam could be demonstrated by many other examples, ranging from that of the second secretary-general of the ICP, Nguyen Van Cu (whose family publicly claimed to belong to the lineage of the fifteenth-century scholar-patriot Nguyen Trai) to that of Pham Van Dong (whose father was cabinet chief to the Duy-tan emperor.)

Paradoxes and contradictions raise important questions. How could these Marxist mandarins reconcile, in practical terms, the ideologically high status which dogma compelled them to give to peasants and workers, with the low positions peasants and workers necessarily held in the hierarchy of knowledgeable men required to plot a revolution and to industrialize a backward society? Or, more simply, how could such a socially exalted elite claim to lead a "proletarian" revolution? Such questions run irrepressibly through the twentieth-century histories of both China and Vietnam. And the very obvious response that might be made to them—that such questions could only be resolved, or camouflaged, by a drastic self-induced reorganization of the values of members of the upper class, rather than by an instant reorganization of all actual social classes—deserves amplification (if not qualification) by historians.

The sociologist Karl Mannheim once proposed that modern intellectuals could undertake "voluntary affiliations" with social classes to which they did not originally belong. They could do this because they were no longer a priesthood, but were being recruited from an increasingly wide area of social life and were therefore essentially "unattached" to any one sharply recognizable social class themselves. Such "assimilability" of intellectuals into an outside class was, Mannheim admitted, colored by their need for psychic compensations: the fanaticism of radicalized intellectuals of the left, for example, was a compensation for their lack of a more basic integration into the class with which they most wished to identify themselves.[67] Whatever its merits, Mannheim's scheme cannot explain very much of either the Chinese or the Vietnamese revolution. These revolutions occurred after all in societies whose intellectuals, while not members of any priesthood, did belong to a relatively self-contained social stratum. This social stratum may have harbored extensive poverty, but it did not harbor very many peasants' or laborers' sons.

To escape from the consequences of such social self-containment, early Vietnamese communist intellectuals practiced a ritual known as "proletarianization" (*vo san hoa*). Many of them, like Nguyen Van Cu, actually volunteered to dig coal in Tonkinese mines. (In China, of course, the young Liu Shao-ch'i was a famous example of a communist intellectual who sought "proletarianization" in the coal mines.) By itself, however, this ritual did not dissolve mandarin elitism. In the period between 1929 and 1931, many Vietnamese leftist students volunteered to labor with their hands. They became so inordinately proud of their own "proletarianization," the moment they had grasped a hammer or the handle of a plow, that, as members of communist committees, they felt they no longer needed to carry out party directives ordering them to increase the percentages of the *real* workers who were serving in such committees.[68] In other words, for such students "proletarianization" could become simply a way of looking for new forms of ethically sanctioned elitist identities comparable in power to the old forms they wished to abandon. Yet the ritual did symbolize the determination of a part of the old elite to change its own "class" postures in order to salvage its leadership mission.

Some of the secrets of East Asian revolutionaries' capacity, such as it was, to convert themselves into leaders of the lower classes, lay deep in their own history rather than in the modernity of which Mannheim spoke. In modern Western thought, many theorists have tended to view socially depressed outcasts as being the people most likely to become eloquent universalists on behalf of human betterment, including their own. Beside Marx's alienated proletariat, the most famous example, one could place such other examples as, say, the disillusioned bum who denied the worth of fighting for his native land in *Rameau's Nephew* by Denis Diderot. But in East Asia, the Confucian gentleman was the universalist concerned with other people's troubles and with the troubles of the universe, the free spirit least bound by the particular concerns of the "petty man." If memories of the self-serving "feudal" bureaucrat were anathema to the "proletarianized" intellectuals of the 1930s and 1940s, recollections of the classical "gentleman" whose universal humanitarianism recognized no social class boundaries, in its reactions to human misery, were probably far less repellent.

More particularly, there was the rich tradition, in both China and Vietnam, of the romantic "knight errants" (*yu-hsia* in Chinese, *du hiep* in Vietnamese) who robbed the rich and helped the poor, and who formed group compacts based upon mutual trust, while adopting a rather anarchistic attitude toward governments and laws imposed upon them from above. Such knights were supermoral beings who, in one popular novel after another, "practiced the Way on behalf of Heaven." Unlike the real knights of medieval Europe, what distinguished the "knight errants" of popular fiction in China and Vietnam was their complete lack of class consciousness and social snobbery: they owed loyalty to sworn comrades no matter what their social status, and they made something of a fetish of breaking down overly smug social barriers.[69] The leaders of early Chinese labor unions were deeply inspired by this class-free "knightly right conduct" ethic. In twentieth-century Vietnam it has also been invoked repeatedly, and was especially useful to the organizers of the well known Phnom Penh Vietnamese consumers' cooperative in 1937.[70] Such a relatively classless organizational model from the traditional culture was certainly available to communist intellectuals who wished to transcend the circumscriptions of a precise social class background—even if such intellectuals were reluctant publicly to sing its rather old-fashioned praises.

One difficulty with the "wandering knight" ethic, however, was that while it provided inspiration for common action by men of different social backgrounds, its celebration of the antics of a small coterie of comrades-in-arms working to improve an unjust world did not look forward to the growth of real mass movements. And perhaps it was more than a coincidence that the labor movement which the early Vietnamese communists led was bedeviled by its cadres' inability to distinguish between elitist "vanguard" organizations and non-elitist mass organizations. A small tract entitled "The Worker Movement" (*Cong nhan van dong*), which the ICP printed in 1931 and circulated privately inside party circles, complained that far too many party members "erroneously" believed that labor unions should only mobilize workers who already had an enthusiasm for struggle before they joined—like knight errants, perhaps, although the tract did not say so. This, the tract concluded, had led to union members being chosen as carefully and as fastidiously as party members, which meant that there were not many of them.[71]

For many Vietnamese radical intellectuals, residence abroad provided the most convenient opportunities for first discarding deeply rooted upper class personalities. Ho Chi Minh's life as a photography shop worker in Paris was the most famous example, but it was not the only one. In fact the whole Vietnamese community in Siam became something of an experimental laboratory of revolution—almost the way New England served as a laboratory for Puritan preachers like Hugh Peter during the English revolution. Siam became a laboratory, not just of acculturation, but of the suspension of class or status formalisms, in a locale where the effects of such suspensions could be coolly and comfortably observed for the first time by practicing revolutionaries.

In general, Siam's Vietnamese colony could be divided into three categories, reflecting three small waves of immigration. Category one embraced Vietnamese living in the environs of Bangkok, many of them partly assimilated at least, whose ancestors had come there in the 1700s, as part of the future Gia-long emperor's mission to Siam to seek Thai assistance in claiming the Vietnamese throne. Category two included Vietnamese whose Catholic ancestors had fled to Siam in the middle of the 1800s to escape from the Vietnamese court's religious persecutions. And category three covered the Vietnamese who had come to Siam at the end of the 1800s during the violent French repression of the "aid the king" and literati revolts. The last group, known as the "new compatriots" to distinguish them from the "old compatriots" of category one, lived scattered in places like Nong Khai and Udorn in northeastern Siam. There they became carpenters, sawyers, brickmakers, or perhaps farmers.

Phan Boi Chau, subsidized at first by King Chulalongkorn, began political work among Vietnamese exiles in Siam as early as 1910. The "Association of Fraternal Vietnamese Residents of Siam" (*Hoi Viet kieu than ai*), an organization with links to Ho Chi Minh's Canton-based Revolutionary Youth League, emerged at Udorn in 1926. It sponsored Vietnamese language newspapers, Vietnamese language schools, and participation in the coming revolution. But of all the early Vietnamese political agitators in Siam, perhaps the most artful was Dang Thuc Hua (1870–1931), like Ho and Chau the son of a Nghe An degree-holder. In a lecture which he gave to younger Vietnamese revolutionaries who had come to live in Siam in 1930, he delivered as concise an exposition of the technique of abandoning mandarin styles for the sake of slipping inconspicuously into peasant society, as it would be possible to cite for the first years of the communist movement's development. Life in Siam was ideal for experimentation with identity changes, Hua found:

> If you want to be able to learn the many details of a given locality, the only way is to work patiently and look for an appropriate occupation that will allow you to visit many places without arousing anyone's attention. On occasion I myself went to investigate a very large area. I worked at an occupation of obtaining cakes from Chi-

nese stores in order to go out and peddle them. This occupation is very easy to perform and in the beginning only needs a small amount of capital. If you gain the confidence of the Chinese shopkeepers, afterwards you only have to take the cakes out and sell them, and pay the Chinese when you return in the evening. Such an occupation only requires you to go out frequently and be careful keeping the cakes fresh so that you can sell them easily and return them easily. We must regard these commodities [the cakes] as the instruments of our work . . . . Becoming a cake peddler doesn't have any value in a capitalist society, but to us in our political activities it has many advantages. . . . Not only did I gain an understanding of the methods of livelihood of the people, what the professions of each family and each person were like, but I also knew everything about the eccentric behavior of rural bandits. Now as I tell this to you surely some of you will say, "O! I didn't know you were that talented." But . . . the only talent is a pair of blue trousers, a pair of legs that work industriously, and a pair of eyes for examining things. . . .[72]

Tradition and Revolutionary Military Doctrines

To the Western world, this strange diaspora of scholars turned photography shop workers and cake peddlers became truly formidable only when it returned to Vietnam and supplied part of the command structure of a revolutionary peasant army. It was in the crucible of the "people's war" that East Asian traditions and Western political theories finally did complete their joint production of a new kind of populist egalitarianism. Theories of guerrilla warfare itself had had many apostles in premodern China and Vietnam. Probably there had been more apostles of it in these two countries than in medieval Europe, at least before the long era of the heavily armored knight and the fortified castle came to an end there. In seventeenth-century China, for example, the Szechwan philosopher T'ang Chen (1630–1704) had brilliantly attacked the concept of set, specialized, overly hierarchical armies, proposing instead the deployment of "wandering soldiers" to harass the enemy, "connecting soldiers" to "drag" the enemy, "form soldiers" to "deceive their eyes," and "noise soldiers" to "deceive their ears": in such a fluid, unconventional theater of war, T'ang wrote, "the small can conquer large masses, the weak can defeat the strong."[73] It was, however, the Taiping revolution in China (1851–1864) and the earlier Tay-son revolution in Vietnam (1771–1802) which supplied many of the prototypes of military populism upon which the Chinese and Vietnamese revolutions of this century have drawn. Some of the differences between the Taipings and the Tay-sons, ironically, also foreshadow modern differences between Chinese and Vietnamese communists.

The Chinese example might be demonstrated first. It is of course true that Mao Tse-tung, in a text written for a Fourth Red Army conference in

December 1927, referred to the Taipings, and to Hung Hsiu-ch'üan their "heavenly king," as historical personages who reflected "bandit thought" rather than the thought of "scientific" revolutionaries. However, by this time Taiping history had become a folk tradition among Chinese peasants; an inspiration (along with the "wandering knight" ideal) to early labor union leaders like Ma Ch'ao-chün; an object of admiration to Sun Yat-sen; and an epic which even Mao himself knew intimately. Similarities between Mao's movement and the Taipings can hardly have been accidental.

They appear first of all in the realm of battle tactics, especially those of mobile raiding warfare. One famous Taiping battle tactic, for example, called "the battle formation of the crab" (p'ang-hsieh-chen) required the deployment of an army with a numerically small center and two numerically strong wings: the task of the center units was to feign defeat, lure the enemy into chasing them, and provide the two wings, lying in ambush, with an opportunity to envelop the foe. What Mao was to call the "warfare of surrounding" (pao-wei-chan), less than a century later, was the twentieth-century equivalent. Another Taiping battle tactic, known as the "battle formation of the hundred birds" (pai-niao-chen), came into play when a small number of units, scattered in the wilderness, feinted continually at the enemy, trying to exhaust him by forcing him to make inconclusive forays. Mao Tse-tung adopted this raiding tactic and made little more than a name change ("the war of the house sparrows," ma-ch'iao-chan) before adding it to his own repertoire.[74] Both the Taipings and Mao were devout students of the military arguments presented in such traditional Chinese sources as the Sun-tzu and popular novels. Mao, of course, was also in a position to exploit, as he did, the military theories and experiences of Napoleon and Clausewitz and Lenin.

Had the similarities and continuities ended here, there would be little point in mentioning them. But uncanny similarities also existed between the methods of military mobilization and of education employed by the Taiping and communist movements in China. The Chinese red army, from the early 1930s, heavily stressed the formation of "soldiers' committees," and of conferences of soldiers' representatives: at meetings of these groups, especially before battles, problems would be discussed on a face-to-face basis. The further development of conferences of representatives of workers and peasants and soldiers, linked the army to the people, encouraging the soldiers to feel that they were not fighting merely for a selfish elite. The Taipings, however, had pioneered a less efficient version of this sort of political education in the nineteenth century. They called it "preaching moral doctrines"; but to them "preaching moral doctrines" did not just mean expounding Taiping Christianity at services of worship, it meant instructing Chinese peasants in every aspect of the Taiping movement, and haranguing crowds of peasants before and after every battle. Both movements assumed that there were important political energies among the peasants which could be unleashed. Both the Taipings and Mao emphasized child education, the Taiping army's child "apprentices" (*t'u-ti*) serving as the forerunners of the red army's "young demons" (*shao-kuei*) youth corps of the 1940s.

Above all, both movements produced astonishingly similar canons of ascetic military discipline. Such canons of discipline, as instruments for fighting a peasant society war, typically forbade actions by soldiers that would harm, or increase the miseries of, peasants, or actions that would scandalize countryside morality. For example, the sixth command of the Taiping "Rules of Behavior for Military Camps When On The March" (*Hsing-ying kuei-chü*) forbade Taiping soldiers to seize peasants who sold tea or rice gruel and convert them into army porters and coolies, or to take tea or gruel from them without paying. Items two to five of Mao Tse-tung's "Three Great Disciplines and Eight Items to Pay Attention To" (*San ta chi-lü, ba hsiang chu-i*), apparently first written in 1928, stressed that red soldiers must buy goods and services fairly, that anything that was borrowed from rural people must be returned, that compensation must be made for anything destroyed, and that soldiers should not beat or scold people. The fifth command of the Taiping "Rules of Behavior for Stationary Military Camps" (*Ting-ying kuei-t'iao*) ordered the separation of male and female battalions, and stipulated that the men and women in them were not to visit each other; Mao's "Eight Items" forbade red army soldiers to flirt or to dally with women, and also ordered soldiers to avoid the presence of women when they wished to bathe. By following the analysis of the Japanese political scientist Yamaguchi Ichirō,[75] this list of virtual point-by-point correspondences could be extended considerably. It would not be much of an exaggeration to claim that the Taiping revolution was the prime historical harbinger of puritanical, egalitarian, military populism in modern China.

The connection between the eighteenth-century Tay-son uprising in Vietnam and the Vietnamese communists was, if anything, far more explicit. General Van Tien Dung, a member of the ICP Tonkin military affairs committee before the August Revolution and an alternate member of the politburo in Hanoi a quarter of a century later, has publicly paid tribute to the Tay-son Quang-trung emperor's magnificent uses of speed and of tactical suppleness in his great victory over a much larger invading Chinese army in 1789, and to the importance of this victory as a model for twentieth-century resistance movements. Dung's written discussions of the Tay-son "military genius" are notable for displaying familiarity with some of the most obscure classical historiography on the subject.[76] (To find an American parallel for this, which would be difficult, one would have to imagine someone like General Eisenhower discussing modern military and political issues on the basis of his own detailed personal research into eighteenth-century American colonial archives.)

Vo Nguyen Giap himself, the chief military architect of Vietnamese communism, identified five major elements in the military thought of the

Vietnamese revolution. The first one was the total involvement of the entire population in military operations: the earliest full exemplification of this came in December 1946, when hostilities broke out between France and the Viet Minh government, and Ho Chi Minh appealed for women with hoes and children with pickaxes to fight alongside adult males. Such a form of war meant combining war with politics, and the development of three different types of armies (Giap called these three types the "creative organizational specialty" of the Vietnamese revolution), namely, a "main force" regular army, local militias, and armed guerrillas. The second major element was a positive, constant philosophy of attack, continuous and on all fronts, using every kind of weapon and every type of formation. Attack was particularly important because it developed political consciousness and solidarity (*doan ket*) among the people much more powerfully than a stagnating defensive posture ever could. The third element was the art of using small resources to defeat large resources: this, Giap suggested, was perhaps the most traditionalistic and least Western of all the five. The fourth element was the determination to destroy the enemy behind his lines as well as on the battlefield, with special emphasis upon the destruction of the enemy government at its various levels and upon the destruction of the enemy's armed "civil organizations." The final element was the defeat of the enemy by secrecy and surprise—with regard to direction, objectives, timing, methods of using forces, and methods of fighting.[77]

Not all these elements had taken their final place in modern Vietnamese military theory at the time of the August Revolution in 1945, of course. On the whole, the military doctrines of the Vietnamese communists developed later than those of the Chinese communists. Their principal period of germination was the five years between the August Revolution and the victorious borderlands campaign against the French in 1950, during which time Viet Minh military forces expanded from "several thousand" soldiers to more than 200,000 regulars, supported by hundreds of thousands of guerrillas and a million armed civilians.[78] And the most noteworthy elements which Giap borrowed from the Tay-son peasant leaders of the 1700s were the second and third of the five he listed. Notice that the second element, the principle of rapid and continuous attack, was also the element most firmly linked in Giap's mind with the "solidarity" obsession of the Vietnamese revolution—with the expansion of organized communities among the people whose collective enthusiasms could sustain the war. Rapid shock offensives had been at the core of the Tay-son military art. The Tay-son army at the peak of its development is claimed to have been able to travel at an average of twelve to fifteen kilometers a day, an extraordinary statistic for eighteenth-century Asia.[79] Moreover, the Tay-son army, as a social force at war with many of the norms and rituals of "feudal" society, had a tendency to ignore conventions—especially the conventions of holding astrological consultations and sacrifices before battle. Part of the secret behind its shattering victory over the

Chinese invaders of Vietnam, in 1789, had been its deliberate suspension of the celebration of lunar New Year's, in order to take the more conventional and more complacent Chinese generals by surprise.[80] There is no doubt whatsoever that the famous modern lunar New Year's offensive (the "Tet offensive") of 1968 by communist armies in southern Vietnam, which astonished the West and perhaps led to the retirement of an American president, was a fiery reproduction of 1789, a practical application of Giap's visionary historicism. People pay a price for their ignorance of history.

The link between the Vietnamese communists and the Tay-sons should not be exaggerated. Communist military triumphs in Indochina have amounted to more than the unwearied exploitation of a prophetic eighteenth-century ghost-world. Giap's own attitude to the past is ambivalent. In the premodern period, in his view, Vietnam's "progressive feudal leaders" implemented "definite democratic forms" in their mobilization of the Vietnamese people against foreign (Chinese) aggressors, but they never completely transcended the "antagonism" between the "feudal state" and the "masses" which more modern Marxist-Leninist revolutionaries have supposedly learned to transcend.[81] Nor was Ming or Ch'ing China as disproportionately formidable an adversary, on the technological level, as either France or the United States. In addition, even the most romantic Vietnamese nationalists would admit that there was a less magical (and less useful) side to the Tay-son revolution, which at the end displayed many of the politically sterile characteristics of normal traditional Chinese and Vietnamese peasant rebellions: a tendency to degenerate into a bandit movement which victimized other peasants, an inability to manage urban life and urban needs, and a fanatical attachment to the concept of the chastisement of tyrannical rulers and bureaucrats which nonetheless failed to produce significant alternatives to such objects of hatred.

At least by the time of the second Indochina war in the 1960s, if not long before, Giap had become a master of Marxist military doctrines; and this fact must be remembered by historians, who are naturally overly fond of searching for the modern consequences of more traditional historical influences. To some extent, Marx and Engels are the real fathers of modern total war. Giap's knowledge of Marxist military thought embraces all its remarkably scattered sources, ranging from the insights found in the large, poorly explored Marx-Engels correspondence (which he has read thoroughly) to the discussions of war in Friedrich Engels's *Anti-Dühring*. But the Marxist work which is probably as indispensable as any to the mature Vietnamese communist military philosophy is *The Civil War in France* (1871) by Karl Marx, with a preface by Engels. According to Giap, who is not a parochialist, the Paris commune taught the "world proletariat" a "life and death lesson": the first necessity of revolutionaries is the "smashing into disintegration" (*dap tan*) of the "permanent army" of the "bourgeois" (i.e. enemy) government, and the replacement of this army by a much more broadly recruited and indoctrinated one—that of the "armed people."[82] Even by Marxist standards, Giap's belief that wars are constant and inevitable features of human evolution, short of the attainment of the communist utopia, is an extraordinary one. To prove the magisterial normality of wars in human history, Giap publicly calculated in 1972 that there had been at least ten thousand "relatively large scale" wars in the past five thousand years of the world's existence.[83] This calculation was made in a "scientific" tone, without any sense of sick-room awe or horror. Such a vision certainly places a large distance between Giap and the more modest Tay-son revolutionaries—who admittedly faced more modest enemies.

But if this is so, what did the Tay-sons really offer twentieth-century revolutionaries, apart from military lore? The answer perhaps is that both the Tay-sons in Vietnam and the Taipings in China provided examples of organized communities which had begun to break down the customary barriers prevailing in their two societies which separated elite from peasantry. There was a remarkable parallel between the two movements, for example, in their work of struggling to popularize the remote upper class language of politics. The Taiping "heavenly king" issued an edict in 1861 warning against the employment in documents of "frivolous literature and artful language" which the masses could not understand; and the ambitious Taiping alterations of Chinese written characters, which constituted a dramatic change in the Chinese writing script, sometimes (but not always) were occasioned by a desire to use colloquialisms familiar to peasants. The Tay-son Quang-trung emperor, for his part, ordered his followers to translate all the Chinese classics into *nom,* the more idiomatic and colloquial Vietnamese writing script, and established special facilities for this purpose.

But the difference between the Taipings and the Tay-sons was significant too. The Taipings were religious utopians. Their king, influenced by Christianity, claimed to be Christ's younger brother; and their government organization was based upon ideal blueprints, never humanly achieved before, which had reposed for centuries in a Chinese classic known as the "Rites of Chou" (*Chou-li*). The Tay-sons may have been populists but they certainly were not utopians: they lacked a religious ideology, and their government, with its famous "identity cards" system, rested essentially upon principles of draconian but pragmatic military control. It would be tempting to argue that this difference is alive today in the Chinese and Vietnamese communist movements, most notably, perhaps, in the fact that the frenzies of almost utopian populism which the Chinese Cultural Revolution unleashed in the late 1960s awakened no sympathetic echoes in wartime northern Vietnam. No doubt the evidence so far is rather inconclusive.

Yet at least where the question of military politics is concerned, the Chinese communist movement did develop spectacular schisms in the 1950s and 1960s between party members who idolized mass guerrilla warfare almost as an end in itself, and opponents of this untrammeled nostalgic dream, such as P'eng Te-huai, who were accused by the movement's Maoist leadership of wishing to move away from revolutionary guerrilla politics toward the ideal of a less politicized "regular" and "contemporary" army with the most modern technology. In terms of the Cultural Revolution, this was the "capitalist military line" as opposed to the Maoist "proletarian military line." No such schism has ever appeared among the Vietnamese communists. Their chief advocate of guerrilla warfare, Vo Nguyen Giap, has also been their most tireless advocate of the P'eng Te-huai position: the need for an army that could and would "advance" from being a "guerrilla army" to being a "regular and contemporary army," fed not by volunteers but by compulsory military service and using the most up-to-date weapons.[84] In sum, guerrilla populism has never been allowed to become the symbol of a new political millennium to Vietnamese communists. It has been perceived consistently as a necessary, temporary means to a far from unconventional goal: a decolonized, highly organized Vietnamese nation-state, capable of competing on even terms with the West.

7

Revolution and the New Organizational Ethic

The American Intervention in Vietnam and the
Frustration of Vietnamese Nationalism

The world has become almost too familiar with the main outlines of the
history of Vietnam since 1945, if not with many of the decisive subtleties
behind them. The beginnings of what were to become an almost demoni-
cally repetitive tragedy may be traced to the French colonial reoccupation
of parts of Cochin China and the western highlands in late September
1945. In 1946 the French erected a puppet government in Saigon (under
Nguyen Van Thinh) and reoccupied cities in the north. Here they could
take advantage of Viet Minh unwillingness to fight both the French and
the Chinese army which was temporarily plundering and exercising influence in Tonkin. But the Chinese army withdrew; France refused to give
genuine independence to any part of Vietnam outside the north; and hostilities between the two governments—that of the "Democratic Republic
of Vietnam" (DRV), now ruthlessly purged of "reactionaries" or members
of the old noncommunist parties, and that of France and of French spon-
sorship—erupted in December 1946. The Viet Minh did not win a significant victory in this war until the border campaign of 1950. Nor was the
Viet Minh government publicly accepted as a stepchild of the Russian and
Chinese revolutions until relatively late: the Soviet Union and China
recognized the DRV only in January 1950. But the distorting spirit of
cold-war conformism spread quickly, on both sides. By August 1953, on
the eighth anniversary of the August Revolution, Pham Van Dong was
paying tribute to the victory of the Russian armies alone over Germany,
Italy, and Japan.[1] And by this time, of course, the ex-emperor Bao-dai

had returned to politics as a hollow, shop-soiled pro-French "chief of state" (July 1949), surrounded by illusory independence and by increasing American interest and assistance.

When the Viet Minh victory over French armies at Dien Bien Phu finally sealed the fate of French Indochina (1954), the Bao-dai-Buu-loc government yielded to a new regime at Saigon under the Catholic mandarin Ngo Dinh Diem. The Geneva Agreements of 1954, to which neither the United States nor its Saigon protégés were formal parties, gave further legitimacy to the DRV government north of the seventeenth parallel and provided for general Vietnamese elections to be held in 1956, as a step toward the reunification of the country. Diem's American sponsors promised in 1954 that they would not attempt to modify the Geneva settlement. Nevertheless the 1956 elections, which would have endangered Diem, were successfully avoided by Saigon and its foreign friends. And when Ngo Dinh Diem's regime, and the military elites which replaced it at Saigon after a triumphant November 1963 coup against Diem, began to lose heavily to the soldiers of the communist-organized "National Liberation Front" (*Mat tran dan toc giai phong mien Nam*), which had made its formal appearance in the south in December 1960, American military intervention in Vietnam became massive. Its public justification changed over time. Support for Diem in 1954 was defended by the thesis that the Russian and Chinese communists were jointly bent upon the creation of a worldwide satellite empire. Support for Diem in 1961 sprang primarily from the assumption (in public) that a worldwide Russian threat existed, and that Vietnamese communists were its submissive local agents. The importance of escalating the war in 1964–1965 was attributed to the need to defend Southeast Asia against China. Throughout this period Vietnam was viewed through a screen of sympathetic, devouring ignorance as if it were another Hungary or Czechoslovakia, not as if it were a Southeast Asian society just emerging from Western colonialism.

From early 1965, American warplanes regularly bombed northern Vietnam. American bombing of the north never really matched the less publicized bombing in the south. But the north felt more than enough of the fury of an American war effort which—it has been estimated—exploded more bombs, artillery shells, and grenades, and scattered more destructive chemicals, than had been exploded and scattered in all the other wars fought in mankind's history. Local atrocities were committed on both sides. But what accompanied this implacable modernization of Western gunboat diplomacy in Asia was equally significant. Between 1954 and 1974 American policy makers, basing themselves upon the 1954 Geneva Agreement's temporary division of Vietnam into two parts, publicly elaborated and sanctioned the fiction that there were and ought eternally to be "two Vietnams," culturally and otherwise. They did so with a superstitious self-righteousness that would have been worthy of the ancient Egyptian sun worshipers. Regional differences in Vietnamese society, ranging from local dialects to minority group psychologies, were all noisily advertised as proof of the fiction. Far more important regional differences in other, more friendly countries—such as India, with its separate regional languages—were ignored, so long as it seemed politically convenient to the United States government to regard such countries as unities. The presence of northern Vietnamese soldiers on southern Vietnamese soil was described in Washington as "aggression." The ghost of Jefferson Davis, at least, might have enjoyed the irony.

The whimsy that there were permanent "two Vietnams" obviously mocked many of the basic Vietnamese drives to search for a new community spirit—on the national level, as elsewhere—which had animated so much Vietnamese history since the French conquest. Yet the American government plainly regarded the survival of this fiction, as part of the peace settlement of 1973, as a guarantee of stability in Indochina. Since the fiction contradicted the long-term ambitions of virtually every nationalist, north and south, in what Henry Cabot Lodge once airily dismissed, in 1963, as a "medieval country," it could safely be predicted at the end of the Paris peace negotiations (January 1973) that nothing but instabilities would result, as long as American policy continued its predatory belief in the necessary existence of two Vietnams.

The American assault provided the most violent forcing house imaginable for the Vietnamese communist movement's continued search for the secrets of an organized national community. This book, despite its interest in comparative history, cannot try to do justice to the interaction between the Vietnamese and Chinese communist movements which occurred after 1954. Another book would be required to begin to treat such a subject adequately. The discussion which follows is, for reasons of space, little more than a provisional, impressionistic epilogue to the story—of the traumatic decline of traditional Vietnam, and of the germination of the revolution and its purposes—which has preceded it.

The Village and Revolution in the North

Most Vietnamese communists might well have agreed with the noncommunist intellectual Hoang Dao's famous, extremely harsh analysis of Vietnamese organizational deficiencies, first published in the late 1930s. They might well have agreed, too, that the phenomenon it described was a central problem for the revolution in Vietnam. Hoang Dao had written:

> Our organizations are created from a temporary burst of enthusiasm, and all gradually decline and degenerate. There's no reason for such failure other than a lack of careful organizational methods. Suppose that a mistake appears, everybody clicks their tongues and comforts themselves, "Well! Any way we do it just so long as it's finished." The chairman of an organization does the work of the

treasurer, the treasurer does the work of the secretary, and all say to themselves, "Any way we do it just so long as it's finished." ... In the countries of America and Europe, nothing like that ever happens. ... The task of reforming village government in any given year is just one among hundreds and thousands of examples I could cite. Our carelessness, our ideology of "any way we do it just so long as it's finished" causes the reform project to have only one dividend: and that is the creation of more new titles and offices in the villages. Apart from that, work in the villages is still confused and awkward as in the past.[2]

There were, of course, powerful historical reasons for the continued existence in Vietnam of what Hoang Dao called "the ideology of any way we do it just so long as it's done" (*chu nghia the nao xong thoi*). His lament, as I have shown elsewhere,[3] was part of a general East Asian belief that the West was strong because it had "organization" and East Asia was weak because it did not. During their war with France between 1946 and 1954, the old questions of how to build rural organizations returned to dominate the consciousness of the Viet Minh. And by 1948 the Viet Minh had discovered that village-control structures organized purely on the basis of lower-class radicalism—or what was presumed to be lower-class radicalism—would not be strong enough to defeat French colonialism. The social apocalypse of the great Tonkin famine had ended. (It should be added, however, that food production throughout the 1946–1954 war could never be taken for granted: the French attempted to destroy the crops of communist-occupied areas, and these were often mountainous lands without a long tradition of agricultural cultivation.)

In the spring of 1945, the "national salvation peasant associations" (*nong dan cuu quoc hoi*) of the August Revolution had swept up peasant demonstrators against colonial and landlord-owned rice granaries. After 1945, these units were changed into simple "peasant associations" (*nong hoi*). Their purpose now was to mobilize all peasants for participation in the war of resistance. But a report delivered by Hoang Quoc Viet to the fifth central conference of Viet Minh "popular agitation" cadres made it clear that in August 1948, nearly two years after the war with the French had begun, these peasant associations were startlingly weak: they had managed to recruit only 820,000 members in the entire country.

To expand the peasant associations, therefore, their leaders were ordered to absorb "rich peasants" (*phu nong*, those who owned more than enough land to support their families) in order to exploit their "anti-imperialistic capacities," in addition to "middle peasants" (who usually owned enough land to sustain their families), "poor peasants," and "hirelings" (completely landless agricultural workers.) In the same fashion, by 1949 communist labor unions were going so far as to admit "small owners" of shops and factories who were only minimal "exploiters." The party, which itself was officially extinct between 1945 and 1951, nevertheless issued a

"Summary Program for the Construction of Village Political Power" in June 1948. This document stipulated that at least 50 percent of the memberships of the people's councils elected in Viet Minh villages had to be composed of middle peasants, poor peasants, and hirelings. But the tensions between theories and social facts continued unabated. Of some 2,470 people's council members elected in the province of Phu Tho in 1948, for example, only 333 were poor peasants. In Ho Chi Minh's own province of Nghe An, the people's council elections of the year 1951 produced councils 3 percent of whose members were landlords, 6 percent of whom were "small capitalists," 10 percent of whom were rich peasants, and 50 percent of whom were middle peasants,[4] all owners of property.

What all this meant was that after 1948, when the Viet Minh began to gain momentum, organized power in many Viet Minh villages was controlled by landowners from middle peasants up. The discontents of the landless villagers themselves were far too narrow a foundation for victory. Only in October 1953, a few months before Dien Bien Phu, when the war was almost won, did the party issue an edict that poor peasants and hirelings, the two categories of villagers without land, constitute a majority by themselves of the members of village people's councils. Real agrarian radicalism—and significant redistribution of rural resources—came after military victory, in effect, rather than before.

On the other hand, the Viet Minh undoubtedly gained strength between 1948 and 1953 from a skilfully engineered climate of rising expectations which dramatized the movement's essential bias toward the poor. This psychological climate was more important than any real transfers of wealth. Moreover, on the organizational level, the Viet Minh showed a fondness for the construction of multiple hierarchies in the rural areas it controlled: its people's councils, peasant associations, and administrative committees represented in the villages the terminal points of a variety of hierarchical structures. And these multiple hierarchies allowed the Viet Minh and the party to confer what Western sociologists might call "status consistencies" or "status inconsistencies," abruptly and authoritatively, upon selected rural groups. As a major instance of this, the party announced a resistance-war land policy in 1948 whose important aspects were the reduction of land rents, the confiscation of land belonging to "reactionaries" and to French plantation owners, and the more equitable management of village communal lands. Once the rent reduction policy was truly under way (after 1949), rich peasants continued to be allowed to serve as members of the people's councils but were suddenly forbidden to enter the peasant associations which had sought to recruit them only a year or so earlier. Such an artificial manipulation of their social and political acceptability, depending upon the organizational context, obviously created psychological uncertainties and anxieties for rich peasants and indeed for everyone but party members and the very poor—the two groups whose political standing remained consistently high in every organization.

The prestige of organizational principles based upon ephemeral social coalitions faded out of the air completely after the Geneva conference. The Hanoi regime embarked upon its controversial land reform program in the middle of the 1950s. What this program did was to overthrow forever the economic power of the old Tonkinese landlords. Some 810,000 hectares of land possessed by the big landowners of the colonial period were seized and redistributed among 2,104,000 peasant families which had previously been landless or which had owned only a little land. In the aftermath of these land reforms, however, virtually all landowners, including poor ones, lost most of their lands, at least on paper. For the reign of cooperative agriculture, designed to end the traditional inefficiencies of the "small producer," was now announced in northern villages. By the end of 1960, more than 68 percent of all farm land in the north and 85 percent of all peasant families had entered the new cooperatives, a small minority of which were considered to be "high category" ones (and therefore fully socialistic) rather than "low." By the end of 1968, nearly 80 percent of the 22,360 farm cooperatives in northern Vietnam were considered to be high category, with an average size of 136 families per cooperative. And nearly 95 percent of all farm families in the north had become members of cooperatives by this time.[5]

Now at first sight this program appeared to be relatively conservative, compared to the changes which were convulsing the Chinese rural world at the same time. (The reader should of course bear in mind that some of the Chinese large-scale experiments of this period were subsequently modified.) By the end of 1958, and before the Vietnamese cooperatives movement had really even begun, nearly all Chinese peasants had become members of agricultural communes—units much more vast than cooperatives. Whereas the Chinese communes were multifunctional—they not only grew crops but operated factories, schools, and banks—the Vietnamese cooperatives were much less all-embracing, being more concerned with one or two given socioeconomic tasks and no more. Whereas Chinese communes, with average memberships ranging from two thousand to five thousand households at different times, were so large that they transcended traditional village boundaries, Vietnamese cooperatives were usually no larger than a single village; indeed one village might sometimes harbor several cooperatives. As of 1973, the Vietnamese communists had shown much more deference to the territorial and social integrity of the traditional village in their society than the Chinese communists had shown to village integrity in theirs. Supporters of the more extreme Chinese example of agricultural change existed within the Vietnamese movement, but they were rebuked by the December 1963 meeting of the executive committee of the Vietnamese Party Central, for lacking a "spirit of independence" and for not daring to "wash away the mentality of servitude to foreign countries produced by the residue of influences of having been ruled for a thousand years" (by China).[6]

But however conservative Vietnamese land reform schemes and cooperatives seemed when compared to those of China, the absence of a deep
reservoir of peaceful organizational experiences within the Vietnamese
movement helped to produce a land reform campaign of occasional chaos,
bloodshed, and indiscriminate assassinations—some of the "grave errors"
(*sai lam nghiem trong*) which are conceded in most party histories of the
campaign. In 1957 Pham Van Dong indicated particular concern over the
fact that the cadres who had implemented the land redistribution scheme
had seriously violated state policies toward religions and toward ethnic
groups.[7] Presumably he meant by this that Catholics and non-Vietnamese
minority groups had been victimized under cover of the grandiose land
reform slogans. In 1953, before they had come to power, the communists
had organized people's tribunals to "punish adequately" those "reactionaries" who had adopted "religious disguises."[8] Since false priests were by
no means an impossible occurrence in the stormy Vietnamese countryside
of the 1950s, exact measurement of the excesses and injustices of the DRV
land reform campaign, even by its own leaders, is difficult. Many of the
suspiciously precise statistics which have flooded the West on this subject
are simply propaganda; but it is clear that the campaign caused extensive
suffering and upheavals.

It is also clear that Hanoi paid prices in other spheres for the sake of
switching Vietnamese agriculture to its new cooperative mode. With the
onset of the cooperatives, the total number of cattle in the north declined
after 1960, and not because of biological or soil conditions. Many cooperative families in the Red River delta who received oxen or water
buffaloes to breed, on a contractual basis, from the cooperatives which
now owned them, failed to look after such cattle responsibly, since they
no longer owned them themselves. A compensating spread of scientific
animal-breeding techniques to Vietnamese villages was just beginning at
the end of the second Indochina war. Thus its endemic cattle shortage
continued to undermine the Tonkin economy: even in 1958–1960, when
its herds were at their peak, northern Vietnam possessed about 13 cattle
per 100 people—as opposed to Cambodia, for example, with 23.5 cattle
per 100 people.[9]

Of more direct interest was the curious way in which the reputations of
village-level political institutions rose and fell as the mobilization styles of
the communist revolution oscillated between a relatively greater emphasis
on social coalitions (1948–1953) and a relatively greater emphasis upon
class war (after 1953). The checkered history of the "people's councils"
(*hoi dong nhan dan*) in the north, institutions which have already been
mentioned, is extremely instructive. For the composition of the people's
councils was supposed to satisfy both the needs of "class conflict" and the
needs of the "national conflict" over reunification—the latter meaning
that the councils, which were the crucial state organs in the localities, were
the "forms" by which the movement assembled all those "progressive

classes of people" with whom it had long worked. What really happened, however, was that remnants of the traditional village elites—"ugly elements" such as big landlords, "bullies," and conservative notables—soon captured control of the people's councils at the village level.

Their "monopoly" of the councils forced the regime to dissolve and suspend the people's councils for four years, between October 1953 and July 1957, providing startling evidence of the breakdown of local political power in the villages during land reform.[10] In 1959, the people's councils were hopefully revived: in elections of that year, some 5,016 villages elected 121,430 people's council members. The importance of the people's councils was confirmed in the 1959 DRV constitution, moreover, but to make the councils more resistant to counterrevolutionary diseases, their memberships were dramatically expanded. (The members of each village council were increased from twenty to thirty-five representatives. Provincial and city people's councils were, of course, larger, but small in comparison to the inflated village councils: the people's council of Hanoi, or of a complex province like Thanh Hoa, had one hundred representatives, that of the city of Haiphong had seventy-eight.)[11] But even these 1959 elections failed to bring the councils into the van of the revolution. Further embarrassing, homiletic autopsies had to be performed upon many of them. Laws of 1962 anxiously reconfirmed the role of the councils as the state organs "with power" in the villages, and gave assurances that every community which had an administrative committee would indeed have a people's council.

To summarize, the consequence of the bad reputation the councils had earned in the mid-1950s was that party cadres in the villages apparently feared to emphasize them or to take them seriously, necessitating the promulgation of new laws in 1962 to rectify such an attitude—even after the constitution of 1959. In the 1950s and 1960s, institutions themselves tended to acquire moral personalities which they had difficulty changing, in contrast to the prerevolutionary centuries when dynasties had declined without pulling the permanent legitimacy of bureaucratic institutions down with them. And the relationship between the national revolutionary government and local power holders was a critical one, as it is in every revolution. The problem, of course, was that the revolutionary ideology, which had to be preserved at all costs, assumed that the villages subscribed to the goal of a national social transformation more energetically than they did. The discrepancy here could be caused, not so much by village conservatism, perhaps, as by what is commonly called "goal displacement": genuine village councils, embracing heterogeneous social elements, were inclined to become much more involved and interested in internal village concerns than in the blueprints of party cells or of national cadre revolutionaries. In addition, interorganizational power disputes probably lurked behind the troubled reputations of the people's councils. Their widely discussed susceptibility to the influence of the old social order in the 1950s permitted cadres and village administrators to seize power at their expense for a decade afterward. Laws of 1962, seeking to end this strange erosion, stipulated that village administrative committees *must* report their work before the councils, and that the councils must encompass all "committees" and "cells" which ensured public order and prepared community budgets.

The war with the Americans from 1965, which made national solidarity more important than experimental social engineering, accelerated the rehabilitation of the people's councils, if it did not rescue them entirely. Another law of 1967 gave them a more elaborate role and greater prestige. By the late 1960s, about 50 percent of the village people's councils were composed of women—as opposed to 13.3 percent of their membership in 1959. (The war, however, produced a more massive political elevation of women in the villages than it did at higher plateaus of the northern political system. The corresponding percentages of women members for provincial people's councils were 30 percent in the late 1960s as opposed to 19.2 percent in 1959.)[12]

In a strange upside-down way, the people's councils were reminiscent of the past. In the traditional village, organizational positions had not been separated from social prestige, and the gentry had been regarded as the natural rulers. The link was still there, but now it was inverted: peasants and workers, being regarded as the natural revolutionaries, deserved and received a majority of positions on the people's councils, and the structure and norms of such village organizations were still being designed to reflect a desired social order as much as to serve specific functions. But this meant that the councils, whose functional differentiation was limited, were sometimes cast into a position of deeper inferiority vis-à-vis a modernizing national party and bureaucracy than premodern village notables had ever been, face to face with a static imperial court. Even in the early 1970s, the resurrected people's councils remained the focus of an inveterate conflict in the villages between executive and participatory authority styles. "Commandist" party cadres ("commandism" is an official epithet in both China and Vietnam) continued to bypass such elected agencies, pointing to the "urgent" nature of their work as grounds for making decisions privately, without public reports. Because of such "commandism," at the end of the war with the Americans official views had it that the councils were still developing "more slowly" than the revolution itself. First, the prestige of the party, which the cadres represented, remained higher than that of state electoral organs whose disgrace in the 1950s still floated in the air as a warning. Second, Vietnamese villages now knew a tension between two kinds of organizations, those of a small group of professional revolutionaries and economic specialists, and those of larger, less select bodies of people who were not elite specialists but who did have continuing, permanent ties with historic subcommunities.[13]

Organizations with such diverse styles were multiplying, it might be noted, in a countryside whose social and economic and ethnic features were anything but uniform. For example, there was the province of Hung Yen, east of Hanoi, whose ancient motto was the pessimistic lament "drought nine years of every ten, where the fifth month rice is burned and the harvest putrefies" (unless saved by extensive irrigation.) Then there was the mountainous multi-ethnic province of Hoa Binh on the borders of Laos, where even in 1971, hundreds of party cadres engaged in a fifteen-year-old "mass culture movement" (whose concern was the recording of ethnic oral literature) could muster among their own ranks representatives of no more than five of the seven ethnic groups in the province. There was the central province of Quang Binh, north of Hue, with the lowest rice productivity of any province in the DRV (even before American bombing began in 1965), where field acreages were still computed in "central acres" in the 1960s, preserving the burdensome distinction between Tonkinese and Annamese measuring systems of the colonial period. And apart from the natural variability of the Vietnamese rural world, there was the fact that farm cooperatives in northern Vietnam were virtually unknown before the communist victory there, in contrast—as has been shown—to the situation in China.

Speaking very generally, the purposes of the agricultural cooperatives movement have been to increase the north's food supply through large-scale rather than individualistic agricultural planning; to help finance industrialization; and to bring "democratic management" to the villages, a phrase which refers to the expansion of political participation. Above all, there has been an effort to encourage the cooperatives themselves to draw up their own internal regulations or bylaws (*noi quy*) in order to renounce forever what Hoang Dao called "the ideology of any way we do it just so long as it's done." These internal regulations are supposed to define clearly the privileges and duties of cooperative members—in brief, to increase powers of social and economic mobilization in the villages by overcoming the lack of sufficient written laws in a rural society where written laws had not, traditionally, received active, unqualified respect.

In theory, the cooperatives' bylaws are discussed and amended by cooperative members' congresses (*dai hoi*), which are supposed to be more powerful than either the cooperative director (*chu nhiem*) or the coopera-tive administration board (*ban quan tri*). On paper the congresses have the rights to arrange production orientations, planning, the distribution of cooperatives' income, and the election or dismissal of cooperative cadres. The congresses also have the power to elect "control boards" (*ban kiem soat*) to inspect the management of cooperative projects during those periods when the congresses themselves are not convened. In fact, of course, such congresses are often convened very irregularly, for perfunc-tory, cadre-manipulated meetings; and this has blocked the emergence of a potent sense of collective ownership among cooperative members. The executive paramountcy of the cadres is reflected by their exclusive access to theoretical literature as well as to more common practical reading materials. The members of an ideal production brigade in a northern village, as of 1973, might regularly read four different journals: a provincial newspaper, the Hanoi daily newspaper *Nhan dan,* the journal "General Scientific Knowledge" (*Khoa hoc thuong thuc*), and the journal "Agricultural Technology Sciences" (*Khoa hoc ky thuat nong nghiep*). The party cadres alone read two other journals, "Study and Practice" (*Hoc tap*) and "Building the Party" (*Xay dung Dang*), both of which deal with problems which include the political management of the cooperatives.[14]

Despite these gradations in authority and in access to political knowledge, the cooperatives have been the fundamental test of the Vietnamese communist movement's resolution to build rural organized communities substantially superior to those relatively more isolated nineteenth-century Vietnamese villages which failed to act together strongly enough either to prevent French conquest or to improve their own livelihood. The diffusion of both political ideology and farm information is much greater in Tonkinese villages of the 1970s than in those of the 1940s. Diffusion of the latter, bringing with it an awareness of the achievements in other villages and provinces and thus stimulating a new, knowledgeable competitiveness among Vietnamese villagers, is obviously crucial from the economic development point of view. On the other hand, in line with the communists' "small group" approach to revolutionary politics, the 22,000 or more northern cooperatives are more dedicated to the principle of the modernization of parochialism than to its abolition. Radical increases in the geographical mobility of Vietnamese peasants are discouraged by the cooperatives system. When a peasant enters a cooperative (at the age of sixteen) he contributes farm tools, animals, "share money," and land to it, withholding only a small percentage of whatever land he still may possess— the "five percent soil," for growing fodder and for residing on—for private use. If he transfers to a different cooperative he is not obligated to withdraw his share money from the first one and contribute it to the second. Yet it is easy to see that casual migrations are awkward. The circumstances of cooperative organization call for progress through economic investments by communities with fixed, lifelong members.

As another example of conservatism at the heart of the revolution, the cooperatives much of the time call for the application of a revolutionary "mass line" primarily to areas of agriculture which *traditionalists* regard as central. This means that the transformation of work styles in northern farming may lag behind the worldwide expansion of agricultural sciences. For as one Hanoi analyst observed in 1971, all too often such vital, new, untraditional concerns as plant genetics—the choosing and mating of better strains of rice—are regarded in the north as the private pastime of a few "geniuses," and are not incorporated into collective programs.[15] The revolutionaries, it seems, have a frozen, conventional view of the privileged intellectual enterprises whose aristocratic complexions they wish to remove.

The enormous expansion and intensification of organizational planning in the north since 1954 is a fact. Given this fact, the preservation of a balance between centralized and decentralized planning, in the capital and in the villages, harbors its own influences from the past. It is not very much of an exaggeration to suggest that whole states may have risen and fallen in Indochina, and the political history of the entire region may have been irrevocably altered, merely by degrees of centralization of irrigation management. The medieval Cambodians filled their empire with a system of huge reservoirs (*baray*); as vast artificial lakes, these reservoirs stored the rainwater which fell in the rainy season for the purpose of irrigating fields (by canals) during the dry season. But the *baray* system required a strong central political power to maintain it and improve it, being made vulnerable by the very fact of its interlocking technical complexities. When the Cambodian central authority decayed, so did the apparatus of hydraulic surveillance and maintenance; and a failure or rupture anywhere in this system could devastate the entire economy. On the whole, premodern Vietnamese civilization seems to have discovered the secret of keeping a more artful equilibrium between village irrigation activities and society-wide flood control and irrigation needs. Such an equilibrium partly insulated Vietnamese village economic life from the consequences of dynastic political disasters.[16] And in line with this ancient Vietnamese reflex, in northern Vietnam even in the 1970s, the rural revolution allows localities rather than the Hanoi government to calculate their water needs by themselves, on the basis of their own "concrete situations." Risks of a new kind are involved here. In 1970 many villages, driven by new production quotas, attempted to increase their agricultural output by extending their cultivated acreages—without carefully assessing whether they had enough water resources to irrigate their newly created fields.[17] The result was a water-supply crisis in some regions.

With the introduction of the cooperatives, the DRV sought to eliminate two kinds of poverty which had overshadowed Vietnamese villages in the past. Material poverty, of course, was the first kind. In 1969, at the end of almost half a decade of the American "war of destruction" against the north, a member of the Hanoi State Planning Committee could still claim that "a few thousand" cooperatives in more than thirty districts had achieved the almost miraculous objective of producing rice at a rate of five tons of paddy per hectare.[18] Were such a rate to be truly generalized throughout the society, it might reduce to a dark memory the famine-ridden *via dolorosa* of Tonkinese peasants under the French colonial regime. Besides material poverty, however, the rural revolution in the north has also stood for the elimination of a very different type of poverty among the majority of the peasantry—a type that could only be described as "status poverty," much more rarely considered by Western economic development textbooks. Specifically, efforts have been made to banish the symbolically infantile positions of peasants as receivers of work (and, occasionally, largesse) from paternalistic landlords. The economic value of these positions fluctuated with the prosperity of rural harvests, but their social value had always been permanently, monotonously degraded. Now the peasant is required to view himself as an adult contributor to his own society. The war against this less obvious kind of poverty—as well as a desire to control the population by networks of community regulations, and to make its economic performance more predictable—has been the reason behind the regime's emphasis upon the cooperatives' private creation of their own internal bylaws, at congresses of all their members. The idea is to facilitate the spread of a consciousness of "collective ownership" with regular group discussions of technology, divisions of labor, and the sometimes troubled issue of the awarding of labor points.

Such discussion, of course, also ventilates grievances at an early stage. This is important: it is the peasantry who have paid for the north's war effort and for the strengthening of stagnating industries. In 1960 the state launched a mobilization of private savings campaign: its aims were to encourage the Vietnamese people to economize on immediate expenditures in favor of long-term ones, and to supply the Hanoi government with additional fixed sums of capital. Every Vietnamese household in the north was asked to pledge in writing that it would deposit its savings regularly in a public investment fund or "thrift fund" (*quy tiet kiem*). Significantly, in 1970 the director of the Hanoi state bank of Vietnam proposed that peasant families pledge a minimum remission of 36 piasters a year per family. Cadres, urban workers, government officials, and military men, on the other hand, were asked to remit only 24 piasters per year.[19]

Quite apart from the tension between executive and participatory organizational styles in northern villages, already mentioned, rural politics under the DRV are also affected by the fact that residual social ideologies cannot be changed as rapidly as local institutions. Hence the real quality of the recent evolution of Tonkinese villages, whose bamboo hedges have enclosed a distinctive way of life for centuries, is a most subtle, difficult matter to gauge. As an example, in many northern villages before 1954 the ritual of "becoming an elder" (*len lao*) was a very important one for high status males, including scholars, notables, and village chiefs. When such men reached a certain age (sixty, seventy, or eighty years of age) they had special flags sewn and flown in their honor, conducted lavish sacrifices in the village temple, and invited other villagers to a public feast, in return for which their neighbors now saluted them with an especially prestigious pronoun of address (*cu,* "elder.") To the communist government after 1954, such village celebrations for newly emerged elders were "superstitious," economically "wasteful" (of the village resources consumed by the banquets and the sacrifices) and undemocratic (because they ignored lower-class males, known as "dark people," and women). Yet after more than two decades of rule, and after a record of having fought French and American military might to a standstill or better, the DRV government has still been unable to end such rural customs. They have survived land reform and "cooperativization." In some northern villages in the early 1970s village elders were even found to be restoring the old ritual processions to the *dinh*, the village communal house, whose mystique—and the politics associated with it—had supposedly been transformed and transposed with the downfall of colonialism.

Not having the power to suppress such habits completely, Hanoi has decided to accept them but to "reconstruct" them. Old village communal houses have been replaced by (or renamed as) village "conference halls" (*hoi truong*). In some villages, villagers who reach the age of sixty or seventy are dissuaded from holding banquets and sacrifices, but they are now awarded paper certificates at special ceremonies: the documents they receive certify that they have attained a "silver age" or a "golden age." The village "conference halls" are sumptuously decorated by village militiamen; the newly christened elders are greeted by students wearing red turbans who beat drums of celebration; the secretary of the local party committee burns firecrackers in honor of the elders' achievements and longevity; and the elders receive their actual certificates from a representative of the provincial committee of the "Ancestral Land Front" (*Mat tran To quoc*), a united front mass organization and instrument of social mobilization created in 1955. Women are allowed to become formal certificate-carrying elders: the traditional ritual monopoly of the male gentry has at least been shattered.

Hanoi's "reconstruction" of the old village eldership rites naturally serves a variety of purposes. It is a way of controlling the remnants of the pre-revolutionary village elites, by insuring that the regime controls the distribution of all the symbols of status in village society, including traditional ones which have informally or surreptitiously survived. It is a way of reinforcing the revolution: at the time they receive their certificates, the elders are invited to express their "impressions" about having lived under "two systems" and having known the "backward" past. And it is a mark of the regime's acceptance of yet another characteristic of the old Vietnamese communalism: respect for old age as an ingredient of the traditional village's cohesion. According to the rules of some northern provinces, the elders' certificates are given only to those old people who have carried out state policies well and who have positively participated in agricultural work.[20] But even this can be regarded as a new piece of an old tradition. The Le dynasty's forty-seven regulations for village government, issued in 1663 and in 1760, specified that all village males who reached an advanced age had to receive "imperial orders" and "government tallies" before they could preside over "incense and fire" cults at their local temples.[21] The truth is that the moral certification of the privileges of old age has always been a political issue in the Vietnamese countryside.

Does this suggest that all the old traditions of Tonkinese villages are ripe for exploitation by a communist elite, once the debris of the old class structure has been swept aside? If so, nothing could be farther from the truth. These traditions are far too complex, and "revolutionary tradition-alism" has its limits. In Quynh Hong village in Nghe An province, for example, agricultural cooperatives were introduced in 1959 and 1960, but for years failed to work. In 1967 party cadres in the village launched a movement to revitalize its cooperatives, and decided that their "best method" would be to remind the peasants of the fighting traditions of Quynh Hong village during the soviet period of 1930–1931, in order to rekindle the villagers' pride at having fought the French. That such a theme from the past should be chosen even at the height of the American bomb-ing was significant enough. But what was more important was that the traditions of 1930–1931 evidently failed to arouse the entire village: of its six hamlets, two were devoutly Catholic, while the other four were not.[22] In such a society—where even the hamlets of a single village may march to different political and religious memories—the invocation of tradition is far from being a casual art.

In addition, some of the spirit of the old class structure, and the premises about the development of local power upon which it was based, may return circuitously from time to time in new forms. The most blatant demonstration of such a return would of course be the evolution of party cadres into a *de facto* private landholding class. It was revealed in July 1971 that in "many places," especially in the mountains and the midlands, cadres had violated the ban upon private ownership of anything more than residential land and "five per cent soil," and that such cadres, relying upon "illegitimate reasons," had encroached upon collectively owned lands in order to dig ponds, establish private gardens, and exceed their legal property allotments.[23] Of more interest, perhaps, is that the ancient localized cult of land ownership has shown a tendency to migrate from the extinct colonial landlord class to the cooperatives themselves, which may or may not reflect surviving lineage political blocs. The cooperatives have sometimes sold or traded land with other cooperatives without informing state planning agencies in Hanoi. In the summer of 1971, the government was forced to issue a ten-article resolution on land use which forbade cooperatives to trade or cede lands without the permission of the district administrative committee; and if the lands involved belonged to the juris-diction of more than one district, provincial administrative committees would also have to ratify the transaction.[24]

Industrialization and Problems in the Definition of New Communities

Changes in the organization of communities in the north must naturally be studied against the background of what the Hanoi regime calls the "three revolutions"—those of the mode of production, of technology, and of culture and thought. A desire to achieve all three revolutions lay behind the implementation of Hanoi's first five-year plan, which made its appearance in 1961. It spawned, like similar plans in China, a number of officially sanctioned models for nationwide emulation: Dai Phong (a model agricultural cooperative in Quang Binh province), Duyen Hai (a model Haiphong machinery factory), Thanh Cong (a model Thanh Hoa province handicraft cooperative), and Bac Ly (a model school in Nam Ha province) were among them. Nothing distinguishes northern Vietnam more from its neighboring Southeast Asian states than its intense dedication to the goal of industrialization, a goal which is inspired in part by ideology and in part by the fact that the territory Hanoi rules can claim considerable mineral resources and a long-descended foundation of handicraft industries.

When it inaugurated its industrialization drive in 1955, Hanoi faced the fact that the members of its new industrial labor force—its factory workers—would have to be recruited from swarms of young, inexperienced peasants. In the decade between 1955 and 1965, indeed, an estimated 650,000 peasants were transferred from their villages to nonagricultural assignments in industry, construction, and transportation. Such an occupational shift of 650,000 peasants in just ten years may have amounted to a profound social revolution, unequalled elsewhere in Southeast Asia. But it raised the question of just how rapidly an untutored army of factory workers whose origins were predominantly rural could absorb modern industrial technology.

These workers were young and unskilled. Northern sociologists calculated that by 1965 about 70 percent of the entire industrial labor force in the north was no more than thirty years of age. Older workers tended to be found in centers where there had been some industrial development under colonialism, so that in the city of Hanoi itself the number of young workers dropped to only 30 percent of the total in some enterprises, and in the Quang Ninh mining region, fewer than half the 14,886 workers there in 1964 were "labor youths." The factor of inexperience was equally prominent. In one enterprise belonging to the Thai Nguyen iron and steel company, it was found by the mid-1960s that more than half the workers were recently mobilized peasants and that only 4 percent of them had authentic "proletarian" backgrounds, which included the marginal but important political capacity to remember what factory life had been like under the French.[25]

How were peasant workers to be converted from traditionalistic village backgrounds into industrial technologists? Fresh from growing rice and other crops in the countryside, such workers were accustomed to an economic environment in which the possibilities of production were influenced not by machines but by nature—by amounts of rainfall and sunlight. Many times peasants who had suddenly been moved into factories elsewhere in Asia had difficulty recognizing that they now enjoyed greater power over the production process, that they had entered a world where the cycle of events might take only moments rather than a season and where causes and effects were much more completely under human control. In turning 650,000 peasants into machinery workers, chemical-products workers, coal miners, or electricity workers, a formula had to be found to dissolve their presumed conservatism, to encourage them to think technologically rather than fatalistically about economic advancement. (It would, however, be easy to overestimate the "fatalism" of premodern Vietnamese peasants.)

Hanoi's answer to this question—an answer upon which much of the future of Indochina will turn—has been, to begin with, the answer of more and better "organized communities." The regime has attached its 650,000 raw peasant workers to labor unions, industrial labor fronts, youth organizations, factory social clubs, and other overlapping units of social mobilization. Then, through these organizations, it has involved these 650,000 new workers in campaigns within the factories which will, it is hoped, give them industrial outlooks. The number of labor unions themselves more than quadrupled in the north between 1955 and 1965. From 1,099 labor unions and related agencies in 1955 (with 140,000 members) it rose to 4,534 in 1965 (with 766,493 members). In the orthodox communist manner of making a chameleon-like change from an anti-industrial posture to industrial entrepreneurship, the new labor union law which the DRV issued in 1957 made it clear that the unions were no longer "struggle" organizations but had changed into "economic management schools."

Through these unions and other organizations, factory workers were encouraged to produce "opinions" (*y kien*) and "initiatives" (*sang kien*) in which they made complaints, or in which they recommended the reform of work rules, or the improvement of tools, or remedies for technical difficulties. In line with the small-group communalism of the early revolution, it is worth noting that the resolution of discontents seems to be contained within the walls of each factory, in much the same way also that Vietnamese village notables in the 1800s orally decided disputes with which district magistrates above the village were not to be bothered. Of the more than two thousand worker "opinions" generated in discussions among workers and staff members at the Hanoi machinery factory in 1959, for example, only ten were forwarded to authorities above the factory administration, the remainder being "solved" or "studied" by representatives' conferences inside the factory.[26]

But the production of worker initiatives was the heart of the matter. One "socialist competition movement" within northern factories whose rationale was to fight for the "three highs" (of productivity, quality, and thriftiness) claimed to have won from Vietnamese workers more than 150,000 initiatives. These ranged from subjects like the cutting of metals (among machinery-branch workers) to ways of evading the need to import as many foreign raw materials in order to produce chemical goods. The apotheosis of this specialized concept of initiatives, so alien to Vietnamese industrial workers before 1955, was designed to arouse an interest in the promotion of industrialization among peasants who might have been transplanting rice seedlings out in the countryside a few months before. It was designed to induce them to think empirically about industrial concerns. It also appeared to reflect a belief in technical advances through industrial populism. And to stimulate such populist technological thinking, ceremonies of public adulation were held in which symbols from the past, even monarchical symbols, were revived and used in a new context. One lowly worker in the Hanoi machinery factory who was particularly fertile in constructive initiatives was actually honored with the fascinating title of "emperor of initiatives" (*vua sang kien*) in the 1960s.[27]

At the time the American air attacks began in 1965, about half of the north's total labor force was still engaged in relatively small-scale handicraft industries, rather than in Western-style factories. But the nearly four years of air attacks themselves (1965–1968) may have caused the acceleration of Hanoi's previously conceived program of industrialization as much as they distorted it, at least from the point of view of social management. This program, as it was enacted during the war, involved both the subdivision of existing factories and the dispersion of industrial labor into non-industrialized provinces, with the twin ambitions of protecting production from American destruction and, at the same time, breaking down the social and cultural taboos against industrial organization which existed in rural areas remote from the major cities and towns. Even during its subjection to heavy aerial bombardment, the Hanoi government appears to have adhered to its carefully calculated vision of the future nature of Vietnamese society.

What did this mean in practice? Between 1965 and 1968 virtually all factories and industrial enterprises in the north which employed more than one hundred workers were divided into numerous small-production agencies and scattered in different regions. In the city of Hanoi alone, 440 industrial handicraft cooperatives with 20,000 workers were "dispersed." The Thang-long cigarette factory transformed itself into four smaller factories. Big factories, indeed, adopted the slogan "the mother factory gives birth to many child factories" (*nha may me de nhieu nha may con*) which meant that they changed themselves into a litter of tiny enterprises and then reassembled these enterprises in many inconspicuous villages.[28] The organic metaphor was not an accidental one. Factories were now regarded as subdividing organisms as much as they were regarded as centers for an increasingly bloated concentration of workers, knowledge, and techniques. Once again, an external threat had called up the venerable theme of small-group communal solidarity which runs through the Vietnamese revolution.

If it is true that the industrial decentralization and dispersion campaign of 1965–1968 came into being not only as a temporary defense against American attack but as a long-term form of social expansion, both its advantages and disadvantages are easily perceived and stated. Small-scale, decentralized industries can be justified as a good way to make the transition to industrialization, in a society like Vietnam, because they avoid the disadvantages of urban concentration of the kind found in Europe and America; they make it easier to recruit labor (since decentralized industries are closer to the villages from which peasant manpower will have to be drawn); and they constitute a smaller threat than big, more impersonal city factories to the traditional patterns of social togetherness and integration. Such industries, however, may be much better able to solve the problem of the social diffusion of existing scientific and industrial cultural capital than they are at increasing the amount of that capital. Mother factories may successfully give birth to child factories. But if the mother factory itself is an outmoded industrial structure, a relic from the colonial period, the subdivision and rural dispersion of such a factory simply represents a self-diluting expansion of an archaic industrial organization, gratuitously maximizing the bad effects of its archaic nature.

The decades-old need for a stable, cohesive, national community, as much as any strategy for economic development, insures that the north's new organizational ethic will be a hybridized one, a mixture of old and new impulses. For the new impulses, by themselves, will generate tensions. Cohesion is needed not just to resist the West, as in the past (although that need had not disappeared in 1973). It is also needed to transcend even the moderate pressures of a moderate form of industrialization, such as the frustrations caused by longer periods of a more heavily technical schooling for Vietnamese youth, or those caused by a greater emphasis upon the adoption of competitive work roles. Unlike guerrilla warfare, factory work may be a realm where revolutionary romanticism and memories of the Tay-sons are not sufficiently inspiring to guarantee brilliant performances. The regimen of fixed norms upon which factory work depends may become as psychologically alienating, in a different way, as the destruction or increased unpredictability of traditional norms became in the colonial period. Nguyen Van Phung, a member of the Haiphong city committee, revealed in 1971 that during the American bombing of 1965–1968 the situation emerged in Haiphong factories and workshops "in a number of places" of:

> . . . free work stoppages, of coming to work late and going home early, of disorderly and negligent performances, of profitlessly prolonged meetings, of rules and regulations of production not being respected, and of internal discipline rules being violated. Because of this the number of days and hours of useful work was very low, productivity declined, and output gradually diminished. In addition, a number of social evils developed, such as dishonest trading, smuggling, the stealing of state property, lives of immoral obsessions, the loss of hygiene, odd and ridiculous hair styles and styles of dress, marauding and pestering, the singing of yellow songs, and the reading of indecent books. . . . The foundations of labor and of work and of life of before the war came close to being turned upside down."[29]

Properly to appreciate this statement, which was made long before the squalid B-52 carpet-bombing raids against Haiphong ordered by President Nixon at the end of 1972, it is necessary to remember the puritanism of political elites in the north and their tendency to underline past evils as a means of dramatizing present progress.) Then there is the question of peasants invested with a new empirical spirit, as a result of being encouraged to submit "initiatives" in factories, applying that spirit to the remaining sanctities of the Vietnamese family relationships.

Yet many features of the traditional Confucian family have survived in the north, in ideology if not in economics. This has been so for at least two reasons: first, it is too expensive to reject all the old sources of community spirit; and second, the family, like the ubiquitous "clubs" of the mass culture movement, offers a more "relaxed" secondary basis for popular mobilization for state tasks when the effects of more intense formal mobilization drives, with "heavy meetings," wear off or lose their potency. Within the family, two main changes have occurred since 1954. One has been the equalization of relations between husbands and wives. As one writer anxiously reminded his male audience in a 1971 journal article, "it follows from that that males will not . . . behave coarsely and crudely with women, and will not be inquisitive with regard to their private possessions, letters, notebooks, diaries, and private boxes."[30] The other has been the abolition of family property ownership. This second change is regarded as being particularly decisive. In the traditional period, a "firmly binding private ownership system" governed the relations between parents and children, with the children inheriting their parents' fields and possessions. But what children are supposed to inherit from their parents now are the national virtues of the Vietnamese people, which include a selfless sense of community, and the "glorious traditions of the family" itself, minus their old, laocoon entrenchments of wealth.

With the removal of the inflammatory property inheritance issue, the solidarity between older and younger brothers is supposed to improve, but remain hierarchical. Younger brothers must display "attitudes of respect" toward their older brothers and must avoid causing them annoyance. Adolescents must work away from home and must even eat meals away from the presence of their relatives. Indeed the number of communal dining halls in the cities of the north increased in the 1960s (in Haiphong, from 434 in 1964 to 996 in 1970),[31] not because of any real worship of a millennium of urban communes, as in China during the Great Leap Forward, but in order to save time and labor during the war. Yet, at the same time, such youths must also be prepared to slip back at any moment into an environment where all the teeming relatives of the traditional Vietnamese lineage must still be recognized, and where grandparents, for instance, must receive special respect because they can claim the "merit and grace" (*cong on*) of having taught the youths' parents. In sum, the Hanoi regime apparently believes in the preservation of a kind of purified, demonetized Confucian tradition; it does not believe in an expanding monetized society which throws up thousands of evanescent, impersonal relationships. The ultimate practicability of this belief is still, no doubt, an open question.

To stop the analysis here, moreover, would be to minimize absurdly the role and the interests of the revolutionary state. For this state, simply by its construction of a people's army, by its methods of manipulation, and by its attempting even the very decentralized patterns of industrialization it has attempted, has introduced dramatic increases in the scale of human communication and relationships. On the part of the people who experience these increases, normal reactions to sudden, unexpected expansions in the scale of human relationships may include efforts to reduce them again, in self-defense, or to avoid their traumas—such as by self-isolation, or by quiet resistance to government interference. Hanoi seems determined to stay ahead of this phenomenon. To preserve all the new forms of organization in Vietnamese life that it cherishes, the DRV government seeks not merely to control the expansion in scales of human relationships made necessary by its economic development dreams, but to manage and control their periodic contraction, as a necessary counterpoint.

At factories, Vietnamese workers are enrolled in "clubs" (*cau lac bo,* a Vietnamese version, via Chinese, of the Japanese term *kurabu,* itself a reproduction of the English word "club.") The clubs are organs of adult education and of the north's "mass culture movement." They are intended to inculcate the proper political attitudes but also to provide recreation, such as film sessions and theatrical performances. More important, the clubs are intended to replace the increasingly stale mobilization styles of the mass "meeting" (*mit-tinh*), whose successes have all too often been evaluated in recent years merely by computing the percentages of people in a cooperative or factory who attended them. Fresh styles are to be supplied by these more informal, smaller assemblages. One DRV analyst, the assistant director of the Hanoi province culture bureau, suggested in 1973 that the clubs needed to organize the daily "currents of sentiment" among people who worked in the same branches of production or occupations or among people who belonged to the same age group. In other words, the transition from "meetings" to "clubs" practically means a state-sponsored revival of traditional Vietnamese guild and age group solidarities, even if on a purely sentimental basis rather than on an economic one. The same analyst happily cited the work of "many comrades," directors of women's clubs in Hanoi province, who had organized their club assemblies in the traditional Vietnamese manner, with the various members being called upon to speak in strictly hierarchical sequence of age, in order to avoid the chaos of all the women "shouting their wares" indiscriminately on every subject.[32] Perhaps nothing illustrates better than this revival of the age hierarchy in such women's clubs the regime's appreciation of the psychological comforts and social controls that it can tap in small groups with limited scale relationships.

Culture and Education and the Creation of New Social Behavior

Much more evidence could be presented to show the DRV's fear of too great an imbalance between new, expanding relationships and ancient small group reflexes. Peasant cooperatives are encouraged to establish "literature and arts companies," financed in part by provincial culture bureaus. These companies must not become specialized units: they must not become the germs of a stratified entertainment world whose interests will diverge from, or suggest alternatives to, peasants engaged in agricultural labor.[33] Of course, in local theatrical companies at the village level, actors and their plays are often used to teach peasants the proper performance of new roles. Plays are produced which depict how modern army officers should conduct themselves, or how the chairmen of agricultural cooperatives should spend their time, in the hope that the village audiences watching such plays will absorb appropriate new behavioral models and styles.

Even here, however, cultural traditionalism exercises a controlling and leavening influence upon the public dramatization of new occupations and the behaviors associated with them—all of which are part of the inevitable "role proliferation" of an industrializing state. About 1968, Hanoi decided to turn its back upon many Western theatrical techniques, and to revive "courageously" the "basic trademarks" of symbolism of the premodern Vietnamese theater, which had called upon actors to express such acts as looking at themselves in mirrors, or building a house, or riding in a sampan, by means of "empty" or abstract movements. Drums and gongs, popular in the traditional theater, were used to replace Western musical instruments. Hanoi newspapers openly stated that these injections of traditionalism and neotraditionalism into the theater of an industrializing society were a "daring experiment." The danger, plainly, was that so much paraphernalia and so many conventions from the past, used on stage to reinforce the depictions of entirely new types of people (industrial workers, cooperative officials, secretaries), would submerge the "modern" content of these plays and prevent peasants from creating their own new hypothetical frameworks, puzzling them by the contradictory symbolism rather than encouraging them to make any effort to absorb the new.[34]

The decision to make the Vietnamese theater turn back to the past was perhaps a landmark in more ways than one. First, it represented one of many attempts by the DRV to minimize the economic costs of creating a "modern" society in an uncritically pure Western fashion. (The lavish promotion of "Eastern medicine"—of traditional medicine and traditional drugs, in place of expensive imported drugs from the West—would be another example.) Traditional stage techniques, which did not require furniture or intricate orchestras, could be applied widely but inexpensively in thousands of villages. Second, the decision represented a consummation of romantic traditionalism in Vietnamese nationalism, a strain evident in the communist movement itself since the 1940s. In the early twentieth century, uncompromisingly Western heroes and heroines, only thinly disguised, had been imported with great abandon into East Asian and Southeast Asian literature and plays. Almost every Southeast Asian society, for instance, suddenly seemed to demand its own fictitious, poetically individualistic Count of Monte Cristo. A Burman equivalent of Dumas's hero, a ship captain named Maung Yin Maung, had appeared in a Burman novel as early as 1904,[35] and the Vietnamese imitation of the Count, the hero of a novel entitled "The Ship Master of Kim Qui Island" (*Chua tau Kim Qui*) by Ho Bieu Chanh, had made its debut by 1923. Robinson Crusoes were also popular, as were Sherlock Holmeses (as has been shown). Now the pendulum has swung back, to introducing desired new forms of behavior through more traditional artistic forms.

No doubt the decision also represented efforts to give the revolution more durable foundations in the world of popular culture. In the first years after the Hanoi regime came to power, its imaginative exploitation of traditional communications methods, especially village theater and oral literature, may well have languished. An important segment of the northern intelligentsia, led by the prestigious Phan Khoi, rebelled against the regime in 1957. Demanding a broadening of democracy in the north, the termination of political interference in literature, neutrality in world affairs, and the acceptance of aid from both the American and Russian political blocs, these writers published their views in three famous Hanoi periodicals during a period when the government and party were still reeling from acknowledgment of the "errors" of the land reform campaign.[36] With the intolerance of broad intellectual and political deviations that is all too characteristic of communist states, the DRV ultimately suppressed the major sources of dissent. But the written work of this opposition group of 1957 was only the tip of the iceberg. They also attacked the regime's policies with quantities of oral literature, and even in 1970 a Hanoi literary journal admitted that the national heritage of oral literature in the north unfortunately included the still circulating oral formulations of "enemies of the revolution."[37] Under these circumstances, the "daring experiment" may have meant a new struggle to insinuate the revolution into unpredictable cultural underworlds.

At all events the decision to return to traditionalism in the theater was an aspect of the policy of controlled change of social roles. A crucial problem for the Hanoi government after 1954, apart from its own self-defense, was the problem of the reconciliation of the needs of industrial specialization (in order to achieve real equality with the former colonial metropolis and its allies) with the needs of community leadership. Such a reconciliation demanded ingenuity. For most Southeast Asian and East Asian countries, the cost of an avowedly Western-style specialized education and training, for a minority of the sons of the upper classes, had been the pronounced decline of this minority's ability to communicate with wider social circles, especially peasants, which had not undergone similar training or cultural change. The Chinese novelist Lu Hsün's rural ignoramus Ah Q, encountering a fellow villager who had returned to China from receiving a Western education in Japan, was badly flustered. He could only address this awesome returned student as an "imitation foreign devil": he seemed no longer Chinese. Durkheim was famous for assuming that increased professional specialization and division of labor would breed, in the long run, greater social solidarity; but this assumption became far from infallible in colonized Asian societies where such specialization was stimulated principally by alien cultural standards accessible, and comprehensible, only to a few.

The DRV educational system, like the one in China, searches for social solidarity in a different way: through the interchangeability of intellectual and physical tasks and functions, through the renowned "study and work" formula. Productive labor was introduced into the general educational curriculum in northern Vietnam in 1958—significantly, the same year in which Khrushchev's advocacy of more "polytechnical education," with a greater emphasis upon the combination of knowledge with experience, became implemented in Soviet Russia. In the disquisition upon education which he published in 1962, seven years before his death, Ho Chi Minh wrote with characteristic pungency that if people who performed mental labor did not also perform manual labor and people who performed manual labor did not also perform mental labor, the result would be "hemiplegia" (paralysis of one part of the body) for the entire working population.[38] While one ultimate goal of Hanoi's educational plans is the abolition of all basic invidious distinctions between manual workers and mental workers, the Vietnamese communists, unlike their Chinese counterparts, have never conceded the existence of any fundamental tension between "redness" and "expertness." In China, this tension provided a theme for much polemical (and political) ferment during the Cultural Revolution of the late 1960s. The battle could even rage around men's career habits. Should a Chinese agricultural engineer, for example, spend most of his time reading deeply in Mao Tse-tung's revolutionary philosophy and working in the fields with the peasants, learning at first hand the agricultural problems of a given village ("redness"), or should he spend less time reading Mao and planting rice and more time sitting in specialized libraries in Peking reading about the worldwide innovations in agronomy reported in foreign scientific journals ("expertness")?

Now almost any historian would notice immediately that the contrived but not infertile opposition of these two principles of "redness" and "expertness" in Mao's China echoed, in a strange way, some parts of a famous debate in China in the twelfth century A.D. between the philosophers Chu Hsi and Lu Hsiang-shan. The debate centered upon the issue of whether man, as Chu Hsi believed, should perfect himself by acquiring knowledge—by the "investigation of things" in the external world and in the Chinese classics—or whether he should perfect himself, as Lu preferred, by the relatively more intuitive exploration of the moral principles within him, shunning bookish research. And just as fiercely competing traditions or strenuously phrased dichotomies of this kind over the proper nature of self-cultivation were much more rare in Vietnamese Confucianism, which was a nervously preserved borrowed ideology, they are also much more rare, in public, in modern Vietnamese communism, at least since it has come to power. In a speech to the fourth congress of the representatives of Vietnamese university students' unions in 1970, Pham Van Dong, the prime minister, explained that there should be nothing but unity between "redness" and "expertness," and that the climax of such a unity was "absorption" (*say sua*) in work. The scientist Albert Einstein was a paragon of such absorption because, when he was making a great discovery, he imprisoned himself in a room in Switzerland for several weeks (according to Pham Van Dong), separating himself from his material environment in order to indulge in pure mental labor.[39] Einstein, of course, would not have been so lavishly admired for the same idiosyncrasy in the China of the Cultural Revolution.

In general, DRV schools do not appear to have gone much farther than the "half study half labor" Chinese schools of the late 1950s. In an effort to "pursue the tendency of being both red and expert," for example, by 1970 cadres at the northern Agriculture College had perfected a three-stage "study and work" (*hoc va lam*) program. In stage one, such cadres studied elementary farm science and trained for vocational manual labor at their college; in stage two they were made heads of production brigades, not ordinary farmers, in cooperatives in the countryside; and in stage three they were given more practical training by being made assistant directors of cooperatives for a period of one harvest, with special responsibility for technology and planning.[40]

The very idea of combining education with productive labor was hardly an innovation of Marxism-Leninism, or even of nineteenth-century European socialism. If anything, it was a routine cliché in Western utopian thought. It could be found, for instance, in such a book as the French utopia-builder Vairasse's *Histoire des Sévarambes* (published in the 1670s), in which "Sevarambian" children were deliberately moved to the countryside to spend four hours a day working the soil, in addition to the four hours they were to spend practicing their school skills. However the motives of a Ho Chi Minh in extolling such a cliché were perhaps very different from those of a Karl Marx. Ho was concerned, not with the bad effects of the alienation of a large industrial class, which of course did not exist in Vietnam, but with the bad effects of the old Vietnamese mandarin psychology, the mandarin belief that men who worked with their minds must rule those who labored with their hands while remaining socially remote from them. Medieval Europe had known a weaker equivalent of this tradition: its own distinction between "liberal arts" and "servile arts," which, among other things, gave a high status to physicians and a low status to surgeons (because the latter touched the bodies of their patients, and were therefore engaged in the manipulation of matter rather than in pure thought.) But in Europe this tradition faded; in Vietnam, as in China, the civil service examination system kept the world of the long-nailed scholar-bureaucrat alive well into the twentieth century. And when such scholars became immersed in Western culture without abandoning their psychology of superiority to, and separation from, the other members of their society who had to work with their hands, the problems of creating a cohesive national community became enormous.

In effect, Hanoi uses Marxism-Leninism as a state orthodoxy, installed by controlled acculturation, part of whose usefulness lies in its capacity to bring to Vietnam with synoptic efficiency many basic, necessary themes and qualities of European civilization which took centuries to develop. This is the context of modern revolutionary "study and work" education. The entire European Puritan work ethic, which Marxism happens to have absorbed, is being transported to Vietnam in Marxist baggage. In Hanoi's declaration that it will abolish the distinction between mental workers and manual workers one can hear echoing not just Marx, but (for example) John Locke's attack upon idle ruling classes, and Locke's stress upon industriousness as the index of social worth. Justification for Marxism's role as a synthesis of useful Western philosophies can, of course, be found in Lenin. In his essay on "proletarian culture," published in 1926, Lenin went so far as to claim that Marxism's significance as a revolutionary ideology was based upon its "assimilating and refashioning everything of value" in the "more than two thousand years" of development of (Western) human thought. Nevertheless, to the historian of East Asia, there is an almost irresistible temptation to draw a parallel between state Marxism-Leninism (which, because of its comprehensive Europeanness, encourages and facilitates manageable cultural borrowing from the West) and state Sung Neo-Confucianism in Vietnam (which, for centuries, permitted the importation into Vietnam of many useful things from China, under cover of Vietnam's international claim to embody the correct philosophical orthodoxy.)

Succumbing to this temptation may or may not be fair. But it is true to say that education in northern Vietnam has enjoyed an uneven career. First came the difficulties of "decolonizing" education. This meant substituting Vietnamese language textbooks for French language ones; expanding education to reach the society at large (the more than three million students in the north's primary school and middle school "general education" program in 1966 represented a sixfold multiplication of the number of students which could have been found in all of Indochina in 1939);[41] attacking illiteracy; and introducing a society-wide cult of practical science. The number of primary school teachers rose from 20,000 to 180,000 between 1956 and 1971; and the numbers of cadres in economic management and in the technological sciences with university or specialized middle school educational backgrounds rose from 3,000 (1955) to 260,000 (1970).[42] Three model schools, employed as laboratories and also as standard-bearers of the new education, emerged in the early 1960's. These three schools—the Bac Ly school, the Cam Binh village school, and the Hoa Binh socialist labor youth school—overcame notorious poverty through the exaltation of productive labor and through "preserving and developing oneself through one's own efforts" (*tu luc canh sinh,* a common East Asian phrase used by the Chinese communists also and by village development programs in Meiji Japan in the 1880s.) Pupils at the Hoa Binh school planted manioc and maize crops, for example, and made their own contributions to the state treasury every year, rather than drawing revenues from it. Unlike China, however, none of northern Vietnam's model schools in the early 1970s were urban schools. The new education was closely associated with politics: every school had its "management cadres" (the school principal and assistant principal, the party cell secretary, and the youth federation cell secretary) whose tasks were to "lead" the teachers and to serve as a "general staff" on educational work to party committees and to local governments. Yet in the early 1970s there were still challenging, "difficult" areas for the new schools—the cities, the industrial zones, the lowland Catholic regions, and the very high mountain areas.[43]

The mountain areas, where hundreds of thousands of non-Vietnamese highland peoples live, would of course be regarded as "difficult" regions by almost any lowlands-based Southeast Asian state. There have been interesting contrasts in the approaches which different Southeast Asian states have made to this problem, although the subject is far too complex to be discussed adequately here. Governments of Thailand, beginning in the reign of King Chulalongkorn (1868–1910) and continuing into the late 1960s, have employed Buddhist monks on missions to the hill peoples of northern Thailand, hoping to use the Theravada Buddhism of the Thai state church as a means of promoting national integration and of strengthening the links of minority peoples to Bangkok. In the contest, widespread throughout Southeast Asia, to make border minority societies the shop windows of the larger, more modern Southeast Asian nation-states which attempt to control them, Hanoi has not relied upon Buddhism. It has relied instead upon the expansion of literary education into the highlands. The Hanoi government has encouraged highland peoples to change from the production of group oral literature to individual written literature, in emulation of the example of trailblazing modern highlander writers like

Nong Quoc Chan. And it has taken proud notice of the fact that groups like the Thai minorities of northwestern Vietnam, while related to Thai-Lao peoples elsewhere in Southeast Asia, have adopted, and converted into literature of their own, many of the famous literary tales which are popular among the Vietnamese people. The common taste in literature guarantees a common taste for one nationhood, it is hoped, even though some of these literary tales are actually Chinese in origin: they include the novels "Romance of the Three Kingdoms" and "Ch'ien-lung Travels to Kiangnan." But if difficulties in spreading the new education into the non-Vietnamese highlands were not unexpected, what accounts for the difficulties of the new educational system in the cities?

In communist fashion, the blame for the shortcomings of revolutionary education in northern cities is not placed upon the appearance of new phenomena in Vietnamese society since 1954. (These might include a natural tendency on the part of some members of the revolutionary elite to want to enjoy, after their victory, some of the perquisites and privileges that were once reserved for the foreign colonialists: the chief of the central educational curriculum commission in Hanoi charged in 1971 that in many localities scarce building materials had been diverted from school construction to cadre housing.)[44] Apart from American bombing, they are attributed entirely to "negative influences" still surviving from the past, especially the influences of the old mandarin perspective upon education, a perspective which refuses to recognize the role of education in community economic development. Far too many primary school teachers in northern schools still subscribe to the "erroneous belief" that "a good harvest of labor means a bad harvest of literature." How can the old intelligentsia—and the younger generation—be brought to play more effective, predictable parts in the industrialization process?

Revolution and Legal Organization

In March 1973, Le Duan, the secretary-general of the communist party, published in Hanoi a long analysis of problems concerning cadres and organization in a socialist revolution. He praised the importance of a law-oriented society: "to speak of the state is to speak of the legal system," law is the organizational tool of the state which carries out party policy, cadres who fear the pervasiveness of legal forms and statutes as a "heavy burden" upon themselves may be guilty of indulging in either "despotism" or anarchy.[45] This pronouncement was a significant one. For at the time it was made the DRV, like China, did not possess a single modern law code, either in criminal law or in civil law, unless its marriage and family laws could be regarded as a partial code. For a quarter of a century it had been depending upon a miscellaneous collection of statutes of an uncoordinated nature which sometimes even "contradicted" each other.[46]

Once again, East Asian historians would be apt to see lurking, behind this tale of two East Asian communist regimes without law codes, the spirit of traditional China and Vietnam. The two traditional societies never worshiped the universal mystique of written laws as fervently as societies in the West. Le Duan's declaration was a clear signal, however, that a battle was being fought in the north between the conception of revolutionary participation guaranteed and compelled by law, and the conception of social mobilization based upon regimented exhalations of personal virtue, almost a modernized Confucianism. Previously, Le Duan admitted in 1973, party policies had been implemented among the masses by means of propaganda and small-group organization, person by person, group by group. But now there was need for "large-scale organizational reforms" which required the existence of state laws applicable to "tens of millions" of citizens. Here was yet another side to the question of community building.

It has been stated that the Vietnamese revolution developed in an environment with little legal consciousness. Revolutionaries who have come to power find such an environment inimical to the institutionalization of their revolution. In Hanoi a modern legal system is regarded, among other things, as an economic coordinating mechanism. To put the matter more specifically, in a society that wishes to undergo rapid industrialization, a modern legal system that clearly stipulates the rights and responsibilities of individuals—and their roles in the production process—is believed to be a prerequisite. As a DRV legal research cadre wrote in 1971, weakness of law, and of popular knowledge of law, is nothing but another manifestation of the anarchical, undisciplined "small-producer" mentality of the feudal past.[47] The desirability of law is associated with the desirability of economic standardization, and with hopes for the successful implementation of complicated state planning. In the DRV, "violations of the law" and overt "crimes" are two separate categories. "Violations of the law" constitute a vast realm which includes failure to execute, strictly, regulations governing the management of shops and stores; failure to observe rules governing economic contracts and the management of capital; failure to distribute cooperative profits and rations equitably; or deliberately making false reports to superiors. Hoang Quoc Viet, a veteran revolutionary who presided over the People's Supreme Control Organ in Hanoi in the early 1970s, observed pessimistically in 1971 that the achievement in Vietnam of a crime-free society (a belief in the possibility of this is mandatory) would be a long way off, because, of course, of the surviving "remnants" of the old society and of the old mode of production.[48]

But the question is really more complex, and the content of the struggle much more interesting. How are universally accepted, predictable guidelines for the attribution of responsibility for such violations to be established? What has commonly happened is that individuals in northern Vietnam have "mistakenly" sought to transfer responsibility for their own shortcomings to their organization or collectivity.[49] And here is a supreme instance of how the process of industrial modernization may facilitate the expansion of old reflexes of social behavior, not their contraction. Hanoi administrators have had to watch, helplessly, as the traditional Vietnamese principle of joint responsibility has been turned *against* the revolutionary state, encouraged by the new context of collectivism (which creates more organizations, and hence more opportunities for dissembling individual defects)—a reversal of the situation when the principle of joint responsibility was enforced *by* the dynastic state against the villages, as it was in the early 1800s by a Vietnamese court which cared far less about individual types of control. The new Vietnamese state, indeed, seeks two breaks with the past: the collectivization of the economy, and the creation of legally described individual responsibilities within this collectivization. Sometimes it experiences a cultural rip tide.

By the early 1970s, Hanoi legal cadres had become concerned with the development of effective labor obligation laws, directed against "laziness" or the desertion of labor assignments in Vietnamese factories. (Military obligation laws in the north dated back to 1960.) In preparation for the codification of labor obligation laws, even Cuban labor obligation legislation of March 1971 was studied in Hanoi for inspiration.[50] This was revealing: the most highly organized state in Southeast Asia, one which had astonished the world with its cohesiveness under the severest pressures, lacked legal methods of compelling work performances after nearly two decades of existence, and was forced to look at the Cuban legal system for references. Could it be inferred that the very success of the Vietnamese communists' apotheosis of nationalism, and of a cult of collective will-power, had led to certain institution-building deficiencies? Could it be inferred that the disadvantage of a revolution of the spirit was that sometimes the allocation of political energies and talents to less glamorous kinds of institutions themselves was weak?

Probably these inferences are premature. But it is clear that written laws now enjoy a rising importance in northern life, perhaps as part of a "routinization of revolution." Rudimentary "limited material liability" laws—of the kind which compel violators of labor discipline to make financial reimbursement for damage to factory or cooperative property, the maximum level of reimbursement not to exceed three months' salary—made their appearance in Hanoi in 1968.[51] (They preceded by only a few years a movement in Vietnamese factories away from the collective management systems of Chinese factories and toward the more concentrated one-man management systems of Russian factories: the 1970 reforms in the Tran Hung Dao machinery factory in Hanoi were portents.)[52] The DRV government appears more anxious than ever to want to develop a legal system as the matrix of a predictable economic management system. Vietnamese villagers, for their part, preserve much of their ancient attitude of suspicion of codified law—which they associate with esoteric learning, a heavy penal emphasis, and the costs and harassments of old-style litigation in the district magistrate's yamen.

Moreover, this conflict between the ideal new community of laws and the ideal old community of moral goodness through indoctrination and virtuous example is ubiquitous. It is prominent even in the people's army, where, as part of Giap's desire to build a "regular," "contemporary" army, a modern legal apparatus is again believed to be a necessity. In 1962, for example, as the second Indochina war intensified, a campaign was waged within the army against two kinds of officers whose habits were all too traditional: those who had a "psychology of hesitating to be implicated" in legal matters or in legal organs, thereby ignoring crimes, and those who used the law as a "bogey," getting results by threatening to take soldiers to the public security offices.[53] This revolution—the revolution of the routinization and organization of political and economic change through law—may indeed become the most elusive, or the most challenging, the Vietnamese communist movement has ever undertaken.

8

Social Groups and Organizational Dilemmas in the South

Political Ferment and Colonial Myths

The "National Liberation Front" (NLF), which continued the communist struggle in southern Vietnam in the 1960s against a succession of Saigon governments and American military power, has been much better studied than the Viet Minh but represented few radical departures from its predecessor. Its intention was to put together the largest "united front" of all in a history of "united fronts" which ran back more than two and a half decades. All classes, peoples, parties, groups, and religions which believed in "independence leading to reunification" were invited to join it; and it assembled around it more than twenty subsidiary organizations. Its strategy was to combine military struggle with political struggle, as expressed in its slogan of December 1960 of "attack from three points" (*ba mui giap cong*)—from the political side; from the military side; and from the side of carrying out agitation among the soldiers of the Saigon army (*binh van*), another Viet Minh idea dating back to the 1940s. (The formal unification of the NLF army, from local armed guerrilla units, occurred in February 1961.) NLF mobilization appeals based themselves upon much the same pantheon of national heroes the Viet Minh had discovered in the early 1940s: Truong Dinh, Phan Dinh Phung, Hoang Hoa Tham. For obvious reasons NLF exploitation of this pantheon became particularly potent when more than half a million American troops flooded the country. And NLF claims to the leadership mantle of an outraged Vietnamese nationalism were carried throughout the south by an NLF broadcasting service and by some thirty clandestine NLF journals, some in non-Vietnamese languages, which spread a flow of political news from an NLF "Liberation News Agency."[1]

In other words, this was hardly the primitive guerrilla movement it was sometimes described as being in the West. Like the Viet Minh, it preached the satisfaction of social discontents as well as those of nationalism; and it developed strong local organizations based upon landless or land-poor social elements. Indeed it claimed to have redistributed more than 1.6 million hectares of land to its own indigent supporters or potential supporters between 1960 and 1970; if this claim is true, it would imply a land reform scheme almost twice as great, in terms of quantities of land transferred, as that of the DRV in the 1950s. The manpower of successive Saigon governments usually concentrated itself at district and provincial levels. The NLF, on the other hand, mustered its own political workers much more densely in the villages and hamlets. (But it should be noted that this famous manpower distribution policy was more characteristic, although not exclusively characteristic, of a revolutionary force that had not yet come to power. By the 1960s Hanoi was having to "transfer" thousands of cadres—some three thousand in 1962 alone—from central state organs to rural areas, to prevent a deadly gravitation of power seekers to posts remote from the villages.)[2] Only the enormous firepower of the NLF's American enemy, employed in MacBeth-like progressions from one act of destruction to another, and the obstacle of a strong residual (and sometimes defensible) hatred of communism among important segments of the southern population—such as members of the Hoa Hao movement—prevented the NLF from coming to power between 1960 and 1973. By the early summer of 1969 the NLF had created a "provisional revolutionary government" for the south, whose nominal head was the architect Huynh Tan Phat.

What was striking about many of the Saigon governments which came and went between 1954 and the late 1960s was their urban outlooks and their confinement to the cities. This was in part a colonial legacy which such governments failed conspicuously to overcome—unlike their rival in the north. Colonial governments in Southeast Asia had been characterized by urban-based power structures. On the purely technical side, the French colonial regime had not bequeathed to Ngo Dinh Diem, in 1954, any modern administrative framework or machinery for controlling Vietnamese villages, let alone creating new arrangements of social forces in them as the NLF were to try to do. One of the big differences—and there are many—between the guerrilla war of the late 1940s and early 1950s in Malaya and the partially guerrilla war of the 1960s in southern Vietnam was that in Malaya there was already in being, when the war broke out, an extremely efficient police administration (over seventy thousand policemen, principally Malays) capable of repressing rural insurrection. There was no such police administration in the countryside (as opposed to the cities and towns) in southern Vietnam in 1954, or in 1960.

This, of course, hardly begins to do justice to the subject. Decay, not growth, of the few modern central government institutions in the southern provinces was the rule in a number of important spheres after 1954. As an instance, the Indochina Foods and Grains Office, created in 1920 with sixteen centers for rice crop research, was actually shut down in 1960,[3] presaging the later collapse of the rice export economy. Urban-centered bureaucratic status criteria were applied constantly to questions of rural leadership. In 1967, the government's central committee for village reconstruction, located in Saigon, issued an order stipulating that all provincial detachment chiefs engaged in this program had to have university diplomas, and that all ordinary section chiefs working in the villages had to have at least middle school diplomas. The far from obvious relationship between the diplomas and the rural revolution was not even explained, but taken for granted.[4] The Saigon National Film Center's anticommunist propaganda film "Eleven Thirty," produced by Le Hoang Hoa and released in 1967, was aimed at Vietnamese peasant audiences but filled with middle-class urban cultural forms, like multi-story houses, jazz music, dancing, and cars.

The American allies of this heavily urbanized southern elite prided themselves upon being village conscious. They took with them to the villages members of the Vietnamese service class of clerks and interpreters with whom they were constantly in contact, and who now saw, or thought they saw, a very precise morphology of American penetrations of their society. One Vietnamese interpreter to an American military adviser in the villages published an account of his experiences with his American boss which became something of a Saigon bestseller in 1969. It remained unknown to most Americans, however. In his book the Vietnamese interpreter sardonically summarized for a Vietnamese audience his American army captain's attempts to persuade Vietnamese officials and contractors at the county level that a Protestant church should be built in their county, followed by a school, through which American aid programs might be channelled:

> The American captain showed difficulty, not knowing which words to use. What he planned to say was that building the church was for the morale of Vietnamese Protestants, but they were very few in number, if not to say non-existent. . . . I thought that the captain adviser could have said: "A Protestant church is very necessary because it is there that we will disseminate little by little the civilization, culture, and way of life of Americans. In one small, impoverished county·one quiet, simple, clean Protestant church will be able to embrace many American agencies, agencies which on the outside have a social and philanthropic character, like English language

classes . . . but about whose inner realities no one knows." The Vietnamese contractor turned to me and said in Vietnamese: "That
bunch of Americans is like that, everywhere they go they want to
build a church before they build a school. . . . I've contracted many
jobs and I know. They keep starting out with a soldiers' barracks,
then a church, and only then do other things follow." I said:
"Surely they must all be Protestants?" He replied: "The Protestant-
ism of these Americans now is exactly like the Catholicism of those
Frenchmen before. But in the previous period the Frenchmen had
few churches and they were situated only in provincial capitals,
whereas with the Americans now they spread their churches down to
the county and then even to the village level."[5]

Was this portrayal of the American army captain, oblivious to the critical
Vietnamese dialogue of his own interpreters and contractors and armed
with his own alien citadel mentality at the very moment when he thought
he was seeking to change the villages, a completely accurate one? In most
cases, probably. Was this picture of the American army captain also tinged,
slightly, by the shame of a member of the Vietnamese service class which
had itself become alienated from the peasantry? Possibly. What was
profoundly true was that the Americans had arrived in a formerly colonial
society whose colonial myths—including the myth of Western superiority—
were now withering. This could be noticed in many small things, such as
the tendency of Vietnamese urbanites to refer to the Americans as
inferiors (as "youths," *thang*) rather than by the more elevated pronoun
they had had to use only a few decades earlier to refer to Frenchmen ("mister," *ong*). Fighting between young Vietnamese, and American soldiers in
Saigon bars, was another sign of the decline of the whole atmosphere of
colonial indoctrination and deference. Young Vietnamese urban males of
the early 1930s, dressed in their white suits and shuffling wooden clogs,
would have vented their frustrations less overtly and spontaneously.

And yet, had all the colonial myths really withered?

Traditional Forms of Integration and Their Failure
to Disappear

To some extent, the dominant institutions and groups in the south, in the
1950s and 1960s, rested upon a social and cultural bedrock which contained postcolonial, colonial, and precolonial elements in a curious mixture. As an example of this mixture, one of the eighteen slates of ten
people who were nominated to run for the Saigon upper house in elections
held in 1970, the "Fish In Water" slate, presented an interesting profile of
certain hegemonic anticommunist social and professional interests. The
slate was a loose assortment of Dai Viet party politicians, their associates,
and friendly intellectuals. But it included a law professor who was serving

as the dean of the school of advanced studies of politics and business at Dalat University; a Montreal-trained polytechnical engineer who was head of the Saigon Vietnam-Canada Association; a northern-born businessman who had graduated from the University of Tennessee in banking and agriculture; and an industrialist who was the assistant head of the General Association of Confucian Studies (*Tong hoi Khong hoc*) in Saigon.[6] Missing from the slate (with the possible, strained exception of Tran Ngoc Nhuan, chairman of the upper-house armed forces committee and onetime director of the army school report) were people linked to the most powerful social and occupational group of all, the army. And yet the southern army itself harbored important tendencies from the past.

On the surface, the army looked modern, perhaps too modern. Tran Ngoc Nhuan, who has just been mentioned, described the self-defeating essence of its modernity particularly effectively. In a debate on the army budget in the upper house in 1969 he commented that the army had many leadership weaknesses, untalented commanders, confused management, and "slovenly" organization, but that to remedy this by reducing its size and relying more heavily upon village self-defense forces (which would also be more economical) was impossible: a large regular army had to be preserved because only such an army could receive and use the "most modern" American weapons, including tanks and airplanes.[7] Officers in this extravagant army were graduates of foreign French and American military training programs, or of the Dalat Military Academy, a colonial period institution which remained staffed with French officers until 1954. From such programs they had received good technical training but not training in political leadership, since, as one Vietnamese writer noted, in the American army officers were regarded merely as "fighting specialists."[8] Despite its modern and foreign features, therefore, the army entered a highly political war with policies and predispositions many of which could be easily traced back to the seemingly extinct Confucian bureaucratic state.

The army was not a major channel in the south for satisfying nationalist aspirations. But it was a major channel for satisfying upward-mobility aspirations, especially (as a study of the background of its generals shows) the career dreams of sons of the landowner and bureaucratic classes. Ambitious regiment commanders, for example, looked forward to becoming province chiefs. Indeed, as a result of the peculiar militarization of upward mobility, certain "army families" began to emerge in southern society in a manner reminiscent of the emergence of civil service gentry families whose sons had won examination system degrees in clusters back in the precolonial period. A stunning example of this was provided in the winter of 1970–1971: Colonel Le Van Tu, the province chief of Long An province, was replaced in this post by his younger brother, Colonel Le Van Nam, when Colonel Tu was transferred to become province chief of Gia Dinh. Army-serving families in the south viewed the collection of such positions as a contribution to the family honor—and this reflex was a very old one in Vietnam, even if it had been almost profanely transposed from nineteenth-century mandarins to twentieth-century military officers.

The army had other special reasons for functioning, at times, as a gigantic shelter of fossilized, debased Confucian social philosophies, with their stress upon the ethics of family solidarity. Shortly before he was killed in a helicopter crash during the southern army's incursion into Laos in the spring of 1971, General Do Cao Tri gave an interview to Vietnamese reporters (not American ones) in Tan An. During the interview, he discussed his own career in the army, and the way he saw his future. He was quoted as having said:

> I still have a year and a half more to serve, and then I will ask to be released from the army so that I can worry about my family affairs, because now my children have grown up and it is not easy for their mother to attend to them as it was in the time when they were still suckling infants. I grew up in a well-to-do family with some education and then was promoted from second lieutenant [eventually] to general, always because of activities on the battlefront; I mean that I created a proper position for myself, I am not like all the others who sat there playing with their fingers yet who were also promoted consistently from their ranks as sergeants in the French colonial period. . . .[9]

All the details of this oral autobiography may not have been true. But even as a deliberately fabricated myth General Tri's self-analysis shed an immense amount of light upon the state of mind of officers in the southern army. It revealed the Confucian theme of periodic retirement as a moral gesture to manage family problems; it disclosed the common memory of service as inferior sergeants in the Indochina colonial army under the French, and the desire to compensate for this memory, after 1954, by rapid promotion and by the acquisition of an ennobling if entirely spurious Confucian mystique; and it displayed a defensive consciousness that upward mobility in the post-1954 army could be, for many, relatively unearned, or unnaturally rapid, compared to the other occupational sectors of southern society.

What fossilized Confucianism did exist within the army existed as part of a narrow, defensive professional ideology, not as part of a moral code which army officers necessarily believed to be of society-wide relevance. The generals, unlike traditional emperors, were not bound by the precedents set by dynastic predecessors or by the fear of a withdrawal of loyalty by their civil servants. Hence there was the paradox that a general like Do Cao Tri could talk about his own Confucian-style retirement, but function as part of a military machine which crushed such traditions whenever they guaranteed the rights of people outside the army. The paradox was vividly illustrated by such episodes as the army's "pacification" of Hoi Son village in Dinh Tuong province, in 1969. This village, which was more than a century old, was subdivided into five hamlets. Each of its five hamlets (Hoi Nhon, Hoi Nghia, Hoi Le, Hoi Tri, and Hoi Tin) was named after one of the "five constant virtues" (*ngu thuong*)—benevolence, right conduct, politeness, knowledgeability, and sincerity—which had been enshrined (in this precise sequence) for at least nineteen centuries in East Asian classical philosophy. The Thieu government announced in 1969 that in order to improve military security in the region, Hoi Son village would have to be merged with a larger village, and the number of its hamlets would therefore have to be reduced from five to two. The villagers wrote an anguished petition to Saigon newspapers, appealing to public opinion by calling this reduction of the number of their hamlets "spiritual destruction," since it meant the symbolic elimination of three of the "five constant virtues." In traditional Vietnam, the Confucian monarchy had been forced to respect this kind of guarantee of limited group identity and freedom, which was based upon the imitation of semisacred patterns in classical ideology and not, as in Europe, upon written legal documents such as village or municipal charters. The Saigon army, contemptuous of the persistence of classical patterns in associational life outside its own professional sphere, did not hesitate to attack what Vietnamese emperors would not have dared to attack.[10]

To many southerners, the omnipotence of the army (and of its American allies) meant the same thing as the French omnipotence: the stultification of the creation of really significant new forms of "organized communities" that could, in turn, be capable of revitalizing and reforming Vietnamese society. And without far-ranging organizational experimentation, chances of catching up with the West and of ending the reign of "the ideology of any way we do it just so long as it's done" in southern life were slim. The journalist Nguyen Vy had founded an anticolonial newspaper in Hanoi as far back as 1937. He published a satirical poem in Saigon in 1967 in which he conveyed the fatalistic belief that all honest social groups and classes (which he represented in his poem, in typical Vietnamese fashion, in zoological terms) had now become so fatally weak that their combinations and organizations among themselves were useless. Only a national leader of enormous strength who could combine with such groups against the forces which threatened them could rescue the situation. (For the sake of better understanding, this poem was a reconstruction of a famous attack by a Buddhist nun upon General Thieu, first elected president of the south in 1967, for going fishing with visiting American politicians at Vung Tau while the war was raging. The expression "the little shrimps and prawns" can be a byword in Vietnamese for "the common people," a little like the American expression "John Q. Public"; and the fabulous roc, a mythical bird which is supposed to be able to fly ten thousand miles, is the ironic symbol of a politician who has attained office too quickly and abnormally.) Pretending to be the nun, Vy wrote:

. . . Mister Thieu, oh mister Thieu, I the nun Huyen do not approve of your fishing. Fish have a predestined affinity with the water, living in it and swimming in it freely. . . . You who are in a position to sound drums and to wave banners, to inspire awe and to preserve the borders of the homeland, how can you have the heart to kill unjustly the small shrimps, the little prawns, the tiny crabs? I the female Huyen earnestly beg you to have compassion for the ocean fish, the river fish, the thousand birds, and not to hunt them or shoot them cruelly, lest the killing beget hatreds and resentments that flood the entire country. As for the various kinds of tigers and leopards, of fierce, cruel animals, of sharks and eels, of tenacious leeches, of snakes and vipers, of wolves and foxes and rats and gigantic worms and flies and mosquitoes that fly everywhere, oh mister Thieu you may kill them all, kill them so that our household will be rid of their stinking odors. . . . Not until then will I admire you. . . . Even if you . . . ride a golden horse into the jungle and shoot a pair of fabulous rocs, I will not venture to praise you; I love the birds and the fish, oh how cruel, mister Thieu![11]

Vy's attack was also aimed, obviously enough, at the fact that the Thieu regime was the client government of a foreign power. But its equally obvious frustration at the organizational weakness of the "small shrimps" and "little prawns" in their own right raised, once again, the recurrent "organization question" in modern Vietnamese history.

In the countryside, Saigon regimes, like traditional dynasties and French colonialism but unlike the Viet Minh, habitually cherished a fear of permitting any profusion of intermediate organizations. What few peasant unions and cooperatives there were languished, at least until the late 1960s. The ineffective Office of the General Commission of Cooperatives and Agricultural Credit, an agency created by the Diem government to "guide" peasant cooperatives, was dissolved after the November 1963 coup against Diem; and its legacy of ineffectiveness was magnified by the fact that after 1963 cooperatives and peasant unions were to be treated as competing enterprises, under the aegis of different Saigon ministries. The "Central Farmers' Union" (*Hiep hoi nong dan Trung uong*) which emerged in Saigon in the 1960s filled its management board not with representatives of the floundering farmers' unions, but with Saigon politicians who used its resources for the private profit of their own friends and factions.[12] As if the fear of too many uncontrollable rural organizations, the pervasion of corruption, and the inferiority complex some Saigon administrators felt with regard to communist organizational techniques were not enough in the way of disadvantages, the biases of the urban-based colonial successor state imposed one more. Out of a general population of fifty thousand university-level students in the south, in 1973, only about one thousand of these students had enough rudimentary knowledge of agricultural technology to be able to supply specialized help to a village cooperatives movement—far fewer than in the north.[13]

The "small shrimps" and "little prawns" did not make their homes entirely in the rural areas. Crowds of refugees, uprooted from their village homes by bombing, swelled the populations of southern cities. Here they were frequently forced to depend upon the most instinctively tradition-alistic forms of group life to survive. Modern institutions in the cities were certainly inadequate to help them. For one thing, there were the social consequences of the anachronistic administrative classifications of south-ern cities. These classifications had mainly evolved between 1952 and 1956 and had then remained static during the population shifts of the 1960s; under them, a community like Dalat was labelled a "township" (*thi xa*) whereas cities which had become much more populous than Dalat by the late 1960s—Nha Trang, Qui Nhon, and Phan Thiet are instances—were still officially regarded as "villages" (*xa*). The distinction was an important one. A "township" like Dalat enjoyed the privileges of being subdivided into counties and numbered street districts; of being governed by a variety of specialized offices (public works, construction, finance, elementary educa-tion) which could provide modern services; and of acquiring appropriate urban institutions like hospitals and technical high schools. A "village" like Nha Trang (with a population of about 200,000 in its general vicinity by 1967) was denied such facilities and administrative specialization, merely being divided into "hamlets" like its smaller rural counterparts.[14]

For another thing, there was the stagnation of the southern labor union movement. Noncommunist labor unions were not allowed to germinate in the south until 1952. In that year, with the Viet Minh approaching victory, the Bao Dai government belatedly produced a 386-article labor law code and attempted to stimulate the growth of "Christian" unions that would not preach class conflict. By this time, the illegal communist labor unions had made the Saigon-Cholon area one of their main centers of gravity. Having enjoyed an almost competition-free environment for decades as a result of their opponents' prejudices against popular organizations, the communists were hardly put out of business by the abrupt legitimation of nation-wide rival unions in 1952. They merely intensified their talismanic "small-group" approach in southern factories and shops in the early 1950s, stressing the creation of innocent-looking mutual savings and loan groups and newspaper reading groups which increased the sense of personal participation of the workers involved and prepared them for membership in higher, more secret organizations.[15] Furthermore, the Bao Dai labor code was born among the corruptions of a collapsing colony. Thus it had little effect upon those islands of social and economic power, created by the French, which had always remained above any recognizable rule of law. In the last days of the colony, rubber plantation owners were empow-ered to command the French soldiers stationed on their plantations to prevent Vietnamese workers from deserting. Such plantation owners simply ignored articles in the law code which did not favor them; and the legal Vietnamese rubber workers' union was little more than a paper organization.[16]

Two decades later, the noncommunist labor world in the south resembled the political world there: it was a medley of pasteboard confederations and coalitions whose leaders practiced highly oligarchical organizational politics. The similarity between southern labor unions and southern political parties was, of course, too extreme to be accidental. As Vietnam entered the 1970s, there were four main labor union confederations to which workers in southern labor unions could belong: the Confederation of Workers (*Tong Lien Doan Cong Nhan*) led by To Thanh Tuyen; the Confederation of Vietnamese Laborers (*Tong Lien Doan Lao Dong Viet-Nam*) led by Phan Van Chi; the Freedom Federation of Labor Unions (*Tong Cong Doan Tu Do*) led by Bui Luong; and the Confederation of Christian Labor (*Tong Lien Doan Lao Cong*) led by Tran Quoc Buu. Many of the leaders of these unions had married their destinies to the destiny of the anticommunist cause in Vietnam when that cause was still almost indistinguishable from colonialism. Tran Quoc Buu had been the head of the Confederation of Christian Labor in 1952, when it first sponsored dozens of anticommunist unions, and Bui Luong had served as general secretary of this confederation under him. Even more unchanging than the leaders were the laws. In 1972 the basic document which established the rules and regulations for the creation of unions under the Saigon regime was still the Bao Dai government directive of 1952.

This does not mean that new policies of managing urban labor had not emerged in the south in the two decades after the end of French colonialism. Had they not emerged, communist ferment in the towns, based—as orthodoxy demanded—upon a small but growing proletariat, might well have occurred in a far more explosive form, and have made the existence of an unstable stalemate in the second Indochina war impossible for Saigon governments and their American allies to maintain as late as 1973. The Diem government dramatically introduced collective contract bargaining into a number of crucial industries, such as the rubber industry, in 1960. This did not much improve the rubber workers' economic lot, but the claim was made that it did bring them into contact with their employers in a more egalitarian way than had been fashionable under the colonial regime. From 1959, proclaiming a doctrine of "reconciling the social classes," the Diem government also created "triangular committees" (*uy ban tam giac*) to solve disagreements in the labor world: these committees included representatives of the government, of businessmen, and of workers.

The Thieu government continued this practice of softening dangerous social acrimonies by the application of the "triangular principle" of consultation. Indeed it extended the reach of this principle, on an institutional basis, by developing labor inspection offices, labor tribunals, and arbitration councils. Apolitical labor unions were obviously useful as bulwarks against the triumph of a communist-dominated labor movement. In one of the least well studied activities of the second Indochina war, representatives of world Catholic labor unions and of the largest American labor unions (which strongly supported the American war machine in Vietnam) visited Saigon frequently and sponsored training classes for southern labor union cadres, after 1956. Considerable amounts of foreign-aid money (from the United States, West Germany, and elsewhere) were diverted to the funds of the principal leaders of the south's unions—how great these amounts were soon became a controversial question in Saigon politics. It was clear that the NLF had been prevented from quickly capturing the loyalties of the south's urban work force. But it was also clear that southern labor unions themselves—some 400, with a membership of 300,000 people, according to 1967 estimates—had not made an organizational breakthrough.

The leaders of southern labor union confederations practiced what some people called an aloof "notification" or "circulars" (*thong tu*) style of appealing to rank-and-file labor union members. More modern leadership styles, based upon populist impulses of either an authoritarian or a democratic kind, were not displayed. Southern labor unions did not really pioneer democratic methods of conducting labor conflicts, and they did not introduce and make comprehensible, like their northern counterparts, many new economic roles. Labor struggles, it was true, remained fragmented. They often took the form of relatively isolated battles for wage raises: the wage structures of southern industries had undergone no rationalization between 1954 and 1972, and labor contracts lacked guarantees that wages would be based upon the spiralling cost of living. At the same time, the oligarchical leaders of the labor unions sent their haughty "circulars" to workers many of whom had long traditions of activism.

Transport workers in particular had been among the first workers to be radicalized in both modern China and modern Vietnam. Possibly this was partly because secret societies and politically volatile religious fraternities had been entrenched among China's Grand Canal junk coolies and their Vietnamese counterparts for centuries. In Saigon, one of the most famous of all colonial period strikes had been the strike of the "tombstone cart" drivers in November 1935. More than one thousand drivers of the matchbox-shaped horse carriages which the Vietnamese called "tombstone carts"—horse carriages which played a vital role in transporting goods and passengers between Saigon and Cholon—had stopped work to protest the discriminatory behavior of a French police chief. Significantly, the strike was centered in the northwestern area of Saigon, which the French had begun to call the city's "red belt" as early as 1930.[17] In December 1936, the Saigon autobus drivers had staged another famous strike, in order to demand a nine-hour work day from the French company which employed them.

Thirty-three years later, in the winter of 1969–1970, the Capital City Coalition of Labor Unions in Saigon ordered a general strike to support the city's indomitable autobus workers, who were now demanding increased allowances to enable them to avoid "starvation," as well as guarantees against unemployment. At the last moment the top of the union polity ordered the general strike halted. The Capital City Coalition had received a directive from Tran Quoc Buu: it stipulated that the strike was to be suspended because he was having contacts with "political personalities," and the unions must therefore show "maximum good will" toward the colonel serving as Saigon city chief who had agreed to receive a union delegation. The results of this sudden reversal were revealing. Half the workers in the Saigon water works, commercial port facilities, electric power plant, and oil company workers' union went to work, and half of them stayed at home: for half of them did not receive the directive ordering the cessation of the strike, just as many of them, earlier, had not received the directive ordering its commencement.[18] The "autobus affair" was a typical mixture of elitist self-indulgence, poor coordination, layers of coalitions and federations, embattled transport workers, and grievances ripe for exploitation by populist revolutionaries, against whom the only barriers were the workers' social fragmentation and the government police.

Like the labor movement, the noncommunist political movement through much of this period was characterized by neoclassical personal loyalties, oligarchical secrets, and ideological stagnation. Fragmentation in politics and among organized religions was, perhaps, worse. At the time of the 1971 presidential elections, won by General Thieu without opposition, Vietnamese Buddhism was divided into some five blocs: the An Quang bloc, strong in central Vietnam; the Vinh Nghiem bloc, strong among northern refugees; the National Temple bloc; the General Congregation bloc; and the Old Monastery bloc. Catholics were divided into two blocs: that of the "northern refugees" of the mid-1950s had actually almost tripled its membership between 1954 and 1971. The Hoa Hao movement was divided into seven blocs (*khoi*): the Congregation bloc, the Huynh Van Nhiem bloc, the Precious Mountain Miraculous Fragrance bloc, the Four Blessings Buddhism bloc, two Social Democracy blocs, and the Community of Former Hoa Hao Warriors bloc. And the Cao Dai movement was scattered among five politicized blocs: the Former Heaven bloc, the Tay Ninh-Ben Tre-Can Tho-Da Nang bloc, the Minh Tan bloc, the Van Thanh Cao–Nguyen Van Thanh bloc, and the Bui Van Set bloc.

What remained of the once proud Vietnamese Nationalist Party had crumbled into three main fragments: the United Vietnam Nationalist Party, whose supporters might be found in strength in Quang Nam-Quang Tin; the Southern Region Vietnam Nationalist Party; and the Centralized Vietnam Nationalist Party. And what remained of the almost equally proud Dai Viet Party, which dated back to 1940, was dissipated among four important offshoots: the Great Vietnam Revolution Party, the

National Rapid Advance Movement, the Vietnamese Democratic Force, and the Democratic Freedom Force. Five political parties were regarded as "Catholic" vehicles, and three were regarded as Cao Dai progeny.[19]

What could be made of the bankruptcy of so many of these organizations, in politics, religion, and labor? Many of their members, as highly intelligent, patriotic men, desired change. But they could not find wholly comfortable models for such change in the Vietnamese tradition, which suggested religious faith-healing movements and secret societies. And they were in a blind alley because they could not consistently use foreign models either. These were either too culturally idiosyncratic (for example, the British model) or too suggestive of external dependence (the French and American models). As for the Marxist-Leninist model, it had already been appropriated, not just by the Vietnamese communists but, in a homeopathic fashion, by the army-dominated government in Saigon. In 1973 President Thieu became the leader of a new political organization, the "Democratic Party" (*Dang dan chu*), which made unashamed use of such features as a party central, cadres, propaganda transmission teams, and internal revitalization campaigns,[20] and gave no indication that it would accept the equally unrestrained use of such features by competitors. Political party leaders, and labor union leaders, could therefore not break out of their slough of despond by means of cross-cultural equations with their counterparts in other countries. Such cross-cultural equations, even when jail sentences were not their reward, were too ambiguous and too doubtful, with the result that Vietnamese organization leaders might make an explicit identifying connection with leaders in another country one minute, and refuse to do so, for reasons of nationalism and cultural uniqueness, the next. Such fluctuations and bogus changes contributed to an organizational stalemate.

Meanwhile, more makeshift social groups arose within the no-man's-land between the communist forces and the Saigon government. The war's destruction of the Vietnamese social order made the dimensions of this no-man's-land shockingly extravagant ones: by 1972 it was estimated that the south was burdened not merely by 300,000 prostitutes but also by 300,000 "vagabonds."[21] Vagabond "parties" sprang up, composed of teenagers, discharged soldiers, and military deserters. The city of Quang Tri, which was to suffer the full fury of the war in the spring of 1972, had six identifiable vagabond "parties" (*dang,* the same word used for political parties) operating within its precincts by the summer of 1971, specializing in smuggling and in pickpocket raids. The city of Hue, for its part, had at least eight. Local government in the two central provinces of Thua Thien and Quang Tri had decayed in 1971 to the point that it had to tolerate the depredations of at least three of these "parties"—the "Bat Man party," which plundered the highway between Hue and Da Nang, the "Love Without Condition party," and the "Devote Oneself to Freedom party."[22] Since these vagabond "parties" included among their members the delinquent children of government functionaries, they demonstrated the symptoms of traditional dynastic breakdown in more than just their successful challenge of the organs of local government. The secession of even the most youthful and undisciplined members of elite families from the existing political establishments could be regarded, for example, as the modern urban equivalent of the gentry who withdrew to build up local family fortunes, scrupulously or unscrupulously, at the end of a dynastic cycle.

But the absence of satisfying official organizational frameworks in the south that could embrace everyone led to more than the creation of secret counterorganizations by vagabonds, or by Saigon shoeshine boys. It led to an unlicensed recurrence, in numerous underworlds if not on the surface of society, of the most traditional East Asian organizational and moral prototypes: the prototype, especially, of a monarchy and ministers. Duyen Anh, a southern novelist of the late 1960s who wrote about various members of the Saigon lower classes—porters, coolies, chauffeurs, shoeshine boys—was remarkable for the colloquial pathos with which he described the superficial Americanization of Saigon adolescents, those members of the street population who gave themselves pseudo-American names like Chau Kool (Joe Cool) and Hoang Guitar. In one semidocumentary novel, however, he focused upon the Saigon lepers: a very real community, and the group most outside regular society, since their families avoided them and their villages expelled them. Excluded from normal life, such outcasts faced the most compelling need of any group in the southern urban whirlpool to create their own social organizations. Duyen Anh explains how the lepers not only fabricated their own political parties but obeyed deep-rooted classical instincts, by evolving from "parties" to their own royal court, complete with leper king and leper ministers:

> The history of Leper Nine was the history of a living man waiting for death. His family, his neighbors, his friends had ostracized him from the time they discovered the uncontrollable germs lying deep in his marrow . . . people locked him up in ward ten of the Cholon hospital. Here he met many young men [lepers] of his own age. Confidential stories were exchanged. And a lump of resentment swelled up. Leper Nine was satisfied to have found refuge in ward ten. He organized his brothers and then commanded them. By day he scattered his "party members" outside to engage in "finances." By night the party of lepers withdrew into the ward. . . . Gradually the band of Leper Nine became famous in the outlaw world. . . . The lepers became an arrogant court in the middle of Saigon. Every morning the king of the lepers assembled his ministers and gave them their assignments. Group after group of lepers received their assignments and went out. One group went to the Ong Lanh bridge and stole wallets. One group went up to the center of Saigon to beg. . . . When vehicles carrying American goods came to a stop, two "suicide

squad" boys climbed up the sides of the trucks and threw goods
down. Boys who were waiting underneath took the goods and carried them away. When policemen nabbed them, they would expose
their pus-filled wounds, and smile and say, "We are leper people,
don't you see, so we are not afraid of Chi Hoa prison." And they
won all the time, because of the saying, "Who is so stupid as to stand
near a leper." Financial capital was relatively abundant, and the leper
court added to its activities the stealing of dogs and chickens and
ducks. They opened a store, and sold dog meat and duck and
chicken congee. Not long ago, the leper court purchased Hondas and
Suzukis in order to offer taxi services to the Americans, and to go on
special missions stealing American goods at the docks. . . .[23]

It was one kind of commentary on southern society in the 1960s that
leper parties and leper courts on the margin of society might be viewed as
being more capable of performing fundamental social services—like the
redistributing of material goods—than the more normal political "parties"
of the National Assembly. That it could also be suggested that the hope
still lived in many Vietnamese that the old non-Western, Confucian society
of emperors and loyal officials was only asleep, and that the proper
hero—even if he were only an energetic leper—could awaken it, showed
how weak the modern organizational initiatives were which had appeared
in the south since 1954.

The Educated Classes and the Hangovers
of Colonialism

Urban intellectuals in the south responded to the American intervention in
Vietnam with both hostility and war weariness. But there was no publicly
overwhelming gravitation of the intellectuals to the NLF cause. (Secret
sympathies, which were safer, would be more difficult to measure.)
Indeed, the disillusioned pessimism of many southern writers was resented
and criticized in communist periodicals for its lack of affection for the
communist alternatives. Under Diem, leftward-leaning intellectuals concentrated their efforts upon demanding freedom of the press and the
general use of the Vietnamese language (rather than French) in university
classrooms. Student nationalism accelerated, understandably, after 1962.
At the beginning of the last year of the Diem regime it was estimated that
only about three thousand of more than twenty thousand university students in the south were members of the national General Association of
Vietnamese Students,[24] but by 1967 student organizations had become a
vanguard of the nationalist reaction to the American-sponsored presidential
elections of that year.

In Saigon, a "Force For the Preservation of National Culture" had
formed itself by 1966–1967. It was an amalgam of many "movements"
which recruited writers and some university teachers. Under its umbrella

appeared publishing companies like the one named after the nineteenth-century patriot poet Nguyen Dinh Chieu, and pointed essays in literary criticism like Vu Hanh's study of the great nineteenth-century Vietnamese national poem *The Tale of Kieu*. (In his preface to this book on *The Tale of Kieu*, written in October 1966, Vu Hanh directly compared the tragic situation the poem described to the current situation in southern Vietnam.) The journal "The Great National People" (*Dai dan toc*), an organ of the new nationalist ferment precipitated by the Americanization of Saigon, commented that "literature and the arts are a roar from within the iron curtain of an oppressed life." Saigon itself became both the nursery and the clearinghouse for the nationalism of the intelligentsia. Students, journalists, and teachers in other cities, responding to Saigon stimuli, might create "committees for the preservation of the national culture" in their own localities; and Hue intellectuals especially distinguished themselves in 1967 with their movement (which, once again, had an anti-American flavor) to organize study groups, publications, and celebrations revolving around the hundredth anniversary of the birthday of Phan Boi Chau.[25] Even Hue intellectuals, however, were affected by the "brain drain" to Saigon. Hue university was usually starved by inadequate budgets, and teachers serving on its staff were forced to go to Saigon to get additional "moonlighting" employment to make ends meet.[26] This concentration of dissatisfied intellectuals in Saigon all shared a justified fear of American destruction of Vietnamese culture. Apart from sporadic repression, and the distaste for communism which some of them possessed, what factors inhibited and limited their protests?

The educated classes in the south suffered from at least three different sets of dilemmas. To begin with, all of them were trapped in a situation which met the needs neither of nationalism nor of individual liberty (unlike their counterparts in the north, whose situation did meet the needs of nationalism).

Their situation did not fill the needs of nationalism because many of them were tormentedly aware that their existence, and the institutions which had created and sanctioned them, did not serve the people. Southern middle schools and universities were still "prefabricated frameworks" imported from Europe and America,[27] which ignored domestic Vietnamese problems and failed to produce the public health cadres or the electrical engineers which Vietnamese society demanded. (In the summer of 1972 the south had an estimated 425 government medical doctors and 1,403 private doctors, meaning one publicly employed doctor for every 40,000 people and one private doctor for every 10,000 people.)[28] Education and national economic development remained disconnected from each other. Vietnamese graduates of American engineering schools returned to the south to teach English, science bachelors of arts taught French, law school graduates founded laundries. The schools themselves rarely ventilated such difficult issues of public policy, and in fact evaded consideration of even far more obvious nationalist themes. It was sourly observed in 1969 that southern middle school classes stopped their study of Vietnamese literature at 1940, carefully paying no attention to the novels and poetry Vietnamese writers had produced about the struggle against the French between 1945 and 1954.[29]

As for individual liberty, it could be enjoyed only spasmodically. The organs of journalism were repeatedly censored or suppressed: one controversial journalist, Chu Tu, could complain that within a relatively short period in the late 1960s the Saigon Information Ministry had shut down five daily newspapers and two weekly journals which he had either edited or written for.[30] In universities, anti-American students and faculty members were confronted by opponents who were either sincere defenders of the status quo or, more ominously, government plants. In 1969, for example, a major conflict engulfed the law school faculty of Saigon University. The two antagonists were a "Clearing Away Faction" (*nhom Khai Pha*), which published two newspapers of its own, carried on the work of a defunct faculty executive committee some of whose members had been arrested and sentenced to hard labor, and distributed some four thousand applications for military deferment to incoming students, and a progovernment "Participation Faction" (*nhom Nhap Cuoc*), which attacked the "foggy" position of its rival on communism and also published its own faction newspaper. Intermediate factions hovered between these two major ones. Faction leaders were regularly beaten up by their enemies.[31]

The second set of dilemmas affected those members of the educated classes who were formally involved in the political party movement. The activities of the colonial secret police had very naturally imposed an obsession with secrecy upon politically engaged Vietnamese intellectuals during the period of French rule. This blocked the development of experienced, explicit associationism among many Vietnamese politicians, and also prevented political party leaders from acquiring the habit of publicly ascertaining the wishes of a large popular constituency about practical social and economic issues. (This factor could not be the complete explanation for their failures, by any means, as the success of the communists, who were also affected by it, attests.) Even after 1945, and 1954, the secret political parties of the colonial period could not "completely reveal themselves," as one of their more astute veterans has observed;[32] they had to remain partly secret. Politicized intellectuals who had a taste for the same ideas, and recipes for the future, could not get to know each other, or combine into one bloc; instead, they were scattered into a number of unrelated mutually distrusting groups. The cult of secrecy turned politics into a kind of inorganic pantomime. And the horrors of the second Indochina war did very little to tame the demons of political fragmentation: in the early 1970s the south possessed some twenty-four "legitimate" political parties.

A third dilemma for the south's educated classes (with the exception of some, but not all, of the leaders of the religious movements) was their excessive confinement to the cities and towns. Members of the political parties themselves faced two obstacles here. One was that they lacked the financial resources to spread their parties into the provinces. The second was that they were inevitably opposed in such efforts by provincial officials, who feared that the rise of strong political parties in their jurisdictions would reduce their own "prestige," and who accordingly used convenient general mobilization laws to sweep up young activists in the provinces—those who might make effective political party cadres—into the army or into the civil service.[33] The traditional "Son of Heaven" pattern—the pattern of the Chinese or Vietnamese ruler who could not accept the idea of a legitimate opposition, because it implied that his monopoly of virtue, which had supposedly earned him his position, was somehow imperfect—was not just confined to Saigon presidents, beginning with Ngo Dinh Diem, but had left its mark upon provincial bureaucrats as well.

Even without these two obstacles, noncommunist party politicians seemed incapable of doing what the communists had been doing since the 1930s: practicing revolutionary parochialism, introducing new issues and stimulating new wants within the idiomatic but not inflexible contexts of old, and previously more self-contained, communities. Indeed, many noncommunist southern politicians did not depend upon precise political programs at all, but turned instead to oral jingles, symbols, and inspired "prophecies" which reinforced the boundaries of existing social and religious groups but did not pull these groups toward new policies of social and political transformation. In the elections that were held for village, town, city, and provincial councils in the south in the spring of 1965, for example, Buddhist candidates were elected heavily to the township councils of Hue and Da Nang and to the provincial councils of Phu Yen, Thua Thien, and Quang Tri, not so much because of new programs as because they chose a series of related symbols—lotus flowers, lotus leaves, and the roots, leaves, and fruits of assorted trees—as the ballot decorations by which they wished the voters passively to identify them. In Lam Dong province, in a more extreme example, although only 35 percent of the population professed to be Catholic, Catholic candidates won four out of six seats on the provincial council in 1965 by orally repeating the jingle "a bow, a branch, a house, a bird" (*cai cung, canh tra, cai nha, con chim*) which was alliterative in Vietnamese. Villagers remembered this jingle and looked for its symbols, which Catholic candidates were of course using, on the ballots.[34] Slates of candidates for the National Assembly competed with each other for the right to use the same vague, utopian language. In the 1967 upper-house elections, slate two called itself "The Great Unity of the Nation" slate, slate three was named the "Unity in Order to Advance" slate, slate eight called itself "The Great Unity" slate, and slate forty-three had the title "The Unity of the People."[35] All this was a far cry from the discussion and promotion of specific change or of the redistribution of resources in Vietnamese society—which rural NLF cadres were even then attempting to dramatize in ways peasants could understand.

What was the connection between this relative political stagnation and the educated classes? A very rough tabulation of the occupational backgrounds of the 180 men and women who declared themselves as candidates for the 1970 upper-house elections in the south (and this tabulation cannot avoid arbitrariness, because some candidates were engaged in several occupations, and must be assigned to just one) showed 30 teachers of the middle school level or below; 23 active or retired military officers; 20 active or recently retired civil servants; 13 university professors; 13 currently serving senators without announced outside occupations; 12 businessmen; 9 lawyers; 7 "industrialists" (this term usually refers to, say, owners of small rice mills or printing presses or fish sauce factories or brick kilns); 7 journalists; 6 judges or judicial figures (like court prosecutors); 6 highland people functionaries; 5 doctors and dentists; 5 currently serving lower-house representatives without announced outside occupations; 4 pharmacists; 4 engineers; 4 ex-cabinet ministers; 2 office managers; 2 Cambodian community leaders; 2 "retired scholars" (*cu si*, Buddhist devotionalists); 2 bankers; 1 newspaper company director; 1 independently employed economist; 1 Buddhist monk; and 1 Hoa Hao veterans' association chairman.[36] Here were the educated classes with a vengeance.

Teachers and professors, along with civil servants and military officers, dominated southern Vietnamese electoral politics—unlike elections for the American congress and the Canadian and British parliaments, which habitually attract the ambitions of lawyers more readily than those of other occupation holders. Of course the category of "teacher" was shapeless and deceptive. It remained an occupational refuge for ex-ministers and aging politicians. But the old Vietnamese village teacher-who-becomes-court-official tradition had survived, however awkwardly, and had metamorphosed into the middle school teacher-who-hopes-to-become-senator theme of 1970. Many Vietnamese teachers still saw themselves as preordained to play important parts in politics, and as waiting in the wings for a summons from some movement or modernized equivalent of a "dragon countenance." Their prominence in politics—if not in the actual enjoyment and exercise of power, which was reserved to the armed forces—makes it appropriate to look at their general position in society.

The role of the teacher has always been defined much more expansively and totalistically in East Asia than in the West. Nguyen Van Trung, a Catholic nationalist, hardly did more than demonstrate this ancient fact in a modern way when he wrote in 1967 that southern Vietnamese university professors should not just lecture to their students, but should endow them with "political consciousness" and "national consciousness."[37] More vivid evidence of the survival of the south as a shell-shocked gallery of mandarin vanities, not all of them decadent, was provided in 1970 by an engineer, Tran Van Tri. He informed a meeting of Vietnamese educators in

Saigon that the "virtue" of the teacher had an "eternal value," and that when the current wave of materialism threatening the country caused heaven to react, a courageous new class of men would arise, acting as heaven's agents, who would be filled with morality imparted to them by their teachers.[38] These claims obviously reflected Confucius and Mencius much more than the more impersonal, technocratic American "nation-building" whimsies which were still being aggressively if superficially circulated in Saigon.

But despite these brave claims, the actual condition of southern teachers was not a happy one. In a society polarized between peasants and military bureaucrats, the teachers were in limbo. Living in cities and towns, their salaries did not keep pace with inflation, yet teachers were ineligible for the benefits of "land reform," whether from the NLF or from President Thieu. Living in the villages, teachers were at the mercy of militarized local governments which confused them with ordinary civil service underlings, denied them highly respected statuses, and ignored the Confucian stipulation that gentlemen were not "tools": during elections, for example, teachers were compelled to perform menial tasks like counting ballots. Yet the real problems of southern teachers stemmed from certain holdover features of the French colonial period which Saigon governments, after 1954, had significantly failed to liquidate.

When the colonial regime created "superior schools" and university-level institutions in Vietnam, its intention was to produce servants, not leaders—to produce competent Vietnamese subordinates who could serve the colonial system and the French administrators who controlled it. Partly because of the service mentality of many of the Vietnamese who remained inside these institutions, the most original contributions to Vietnamese cultural life in the 1920s and 1930s were usually made by men outside them: university-level teachers themselves, a small group, failed to play the role of creative intellectuals. After 1954, university teachers did become more active politically and culturally. But the ghosts of the monopoly exercised over Vietnamese economic development by foreign colonial administrators remained unexorcised. In 1973 it was calculated that the worst manpower shortage of all which the south suffered from was the shortage of effective indigenous economic administrators, those who could lead rather than obey. Indeed the entire southern work force remained, in 1973, a colonial work force dependent upon imported technical specialists: middle-level and high-level Vietnamese technical specialists of any kind occupied only about 3.6 percent of an industrial work force of more than one million people.[39]

Unlike the Chinese overseas student movement, which at least began as part of a national strategy by the Chinese state, in the 1870s, to master foreign knowledge in self-defense, the Vietnamese overseas student movement of the colonial period did not express any national strategy or plan at all. Instead it represented the climax of hundreds of family stratagems by the heads of rich households, who sent their children to France to acquire French degrees for the sake of individual and family advancement, not for the sake of endowing the Vietnamese nation with real leaders who could challenge the West. More nationalistic motives did come into play to some extent after 1954. But it might not be too cruelly unfair to suggest the persistence, throughout the war years of the 1960s, of a southern upper class, effectively detached from both science and manual labor, whose children continued the diploma-hunting individualism of the upper-class families of the colonial period. In the decade 1962–1972, of some 9,000 students in the south who were "accepted" for overseas study, 7500 were "self-sufficient" financially—evidence of the still unchecked overseas migrations of the rich.[40]

A second holdover from the French colonial period was certainly a generalized obsequiousness to foreign standards. This quality is of course difficult to evaluate, since Vietnam, like every modern nation (including the United States) is faced with very real necessities for cultural borrowing. But consider the southern medical world. Higher education in the south in the 1960s dedicated itself to the creation of only about one hundred new doctors every year, partly in order to prove to the world that Vietnamese medical faculties still had the same high regard for quality as the Paris medical faculty. This occurred against the background of the existence of the peasant world beyond the gates of Saigon, a peasant world which had an immediate need for thousands of doctors and tens of thousands of public health assistants. When Minh Duc university offered to open an "Eastern medicine faculty" in 1971 to fill these needs, by training "half-way" medical men who could utilize inexpensive traditional Vietnamese drugs and healing arts as a replacement for the Western-style medical facilities and resources Vietnam could not immediately afford, the oligarchy of foreign-trained Vietnamese doctors employed such "large knife and big hammer language" against the project that the Education Ministry opposed it.[41] According to Nguyen Van Trung, the 1966 Saigon university student directory showed the presence at the university of more than three hundred "lecturers" (*nhan vien giang huan*) but only about thirty full "professors." A reason for this was that professors could not apparently be produced in southern Vietnam itself. All professors required French diplomas, for the French-educated Vietnamese who had gained control of higher education in Saigon after 1954 had insisted upon the perpetuation of French diploma worship in order to preserve their own power and limit their numbers.[42]

The American invasion of Vietnamese society hardly terminated this connection between upward mobility and "cultural emigration" from Vietnam. On the contrary, it gave it two competing foci and injected new tensions into the colonial hangover from which Vietnamese intellectuals suffered. Southern institutions like the National Technology Center were undergoing a severe crisis in the early 1970s partly because they were racked by "discreditable individualistic movements" which included disputes between specialists who had been trained in America and those who had been trained in France. The curricula of such institutions were designed to imitate French and American curricula, whether or not these had much relevance to Vietnamese interests.[43] The fetish of overseas study nevertheless was given priority over the domestication of technical education in Vietnam itself: the 1969 government budget for financing overseas study was more than six times the 1969 government budget for the one National Technology Center on Vietnamese soil.[44] The real domestication of experimental technical education, on a large scale, might have threatened what remained of the old mandarin society. Overseas study, on the contrary, was sometimes an outside escape hatch which helped to postpone that society's collapse. Only in 1973, when the power of the world technological revolution could no longer be denied, did the Saigon government announce the birth of the Thu Duc polytechnical university—to be modeled after the Massachusetts Institute of Technology.

The third holdover from the past which inhibited the educated classes of the south was their isolation from the lower classes and, accompanying this, an inability to plan and organize practical social change. Nguyen Van Trung, a Catholic himself, is surely right to emphasize the historical "upper-class drift" of Catholic schools in Vietnam as a symbol of this. Many Catholic schools and hospitals, originally designed to help the lower classes, in line with the fertile idealisms of Jean Baptiste de la Salle and of Vincent de Paul, drifted away from the proximity to the lower classes they enjoyed in the 1800s and eventually became captured by those segments of the upper classes who were the colonial regime's clients.[45] The social revolution of the 1880s and 1890s, which, at its most extreme, could turn Catholic coolies and kitchen boys into interpreters and bureaucrats, began the process. In the 1960s southern Vietnam still maintained a dual educational system: there were the French-speaking private schools, attended mainly by the children of the urban rich, and the Vietnamese public and private schools, attended by the children of small businessmen, clerks, workers, and peasants. This duality, which represented a gulf between classes, seemed self-prolonging. Unlike French *lycées* in other countries, the French schools in southern Vietnam, after 1954 as before 1954, were connected to the central social-mobility channels of the society. For their graduates were conspicuously more successful at winning entry to foreign and Vietnamese universities.

What was striking about the situation, however, was that even the Catholic schools' sectarian competitors were prisoners to some extent of an urban universe which might fail to accommodate the ideas or problems of the Vietnamese peasantry. In 1970, southern Vietnam had more Buddhist middle school students (36,462) than Buddhist primary school pupils (34,539).[46] Although its population was at least three times the size of Cambodia's, the south had less than twice as many Buddhist primary schools as its neighbor: one hundred to sixty-one.[47] In other words, even Buddhist education in the south was more of a force in the towns (where most of the middle schools were) than it was in the villages, unlike Buddhist education in Cambodia.

A keynote of the world of the educated classes in the south was the acquisition of individual statuses. These classes were not, in a sense, even organized to serve themselves in group terms, as a social bloc or community, let alone to serve others. The struggle of so many Vietnamese revolutionaries to find new forms of organized communities had passed them by, or had not been permitted to develop among them. Nothing attested this more clearly than the strange lack of "white collar unions" among teachers and civil servants in the south, some twenty years after the colonial labor legislation of 1952 had permitted such unions to be formed. The labor laws of 1952, still in effect in 1972, did have a dark ambiguity: they forbade "political" or religious activity by unions, without defining satisfactorily what "political" meant. The nondevelopment of teachers' unions, to which there was ostensibly no legal bar and for which catastrophic inflation rates alone provided a substantial motive, had a number of other possible causes. One was the obstacle of the army as a new if temporary dynasty, making sure that competing forces and intermediate organizations would remain weak. Another was the stumbling block of teachers who still dreamed of mandarin statuses rather than of revolution, and who therefore had recourse to a paralyzing moral camouflage, shunning unions—and "struggle"—as an indignity. The irony was that other groups of teachers—the mandarin proletarians of the Viet Minh, for example—had made the Vietnamese revolution, by overcoming their distaste for bread-and-butter "struggle" organizations through their discovery of a transcendental "righteous cause" (*chinh nghia*).

Had teachers' unions materialized in Saigon between 1952 and 1972, they might have been the strongest unions in the south, no matter how fragmented by region and by religion. By 1972 there were perhaps 100,000 teachers, from primary schools to universities, in the public and private sectors, who could have joined such unions[48] (as opposed to some 180,000 primary school teachers alone in the DRV by 1971—at least according to official claims). Quite apart from this, such teachers could have mobilized the support of many of their pupils and of their pupils' adult relatives. Did the existence of this tradition of intense moral-social networks of support for teachers in Vietnamese life by itself make their continuing occupational nonorganization a necessity for nervous Saigon governments? The political parties, which were organized, did not often fight for specific group rights or for "full rice pots"—for meaningful material goals. And organizations which could and would fight for group ambitions and for easier living conditions, even among the urban middle classes—teachers' unions, judges' unions, engineers' unions, secretaries' unions—remained mysteriously absent from the landscape. Southern society continued to revolve around its agrarian and military-bureaucratic poles; and collective organization by urban white collar groups, despite the traumatic growth of the cities, amounted to even less in 1972 than the lingering laws of the colonial period permitted.

Epilogue: The Vietnamese Revolution Reviewed

Vietnamese communist revolutionaries required a mere twenty-seven months, after the withdrawal of American armed forces from Vietnam at the end of January 1973, to conquer the southern part of their country. By the end of April 1975, a communist military government had been installed in Saigon. In that month the old Saigon government army was routed, and American helicopters evacuated, to American warships waiting off the Vietnamese coast, pro-American South Vietnamese military officers laden with gold bars and bottles of cognac, as well as many more humble and more honest Vietnamese participants in the short-lived Americanization of Vietnamese life. The century of Western colonialism in Indochina had ended.

In January 1973, the Saigon government of General Nguyen Van Thieu entered the final phase of its losing struggle with the Vietnamese communist revolution with a number of illusory assets. It had an army of more than 1,000,000 men; a police force of 122,000; some 300,000 national cadres to engage in political warfare; and a prized elite force of 10,000 officer students, graduated from the National Military Training College, the Nha Trang Non-Commissioned Officers School, the Quang-trung Training Center University, and the Political Struggle University, who were to be sent out in waves to the villages to disseminate propaganda and inhibit communist infiltration.

All this represented the absolute climax of decades of defensive creation of the forms of revolution by various southern governments, as a means of frustrating a real revolutionary enemy. That these forms lacked much coherent substance and were animated by few positive national dreams or ambitions, apart from anticommunism, was obscured by the fact that in southern Vietnam, as in no other society, fighting a revolution had now become an all-consuming, all-embracing profession, with its own professional—as opposed to nationalist—rewards. In addition, as the famous economist Vu Quoc Thuc claimed in January 1973, the South enjoyed enormous economic advantages over the North. It was richer in natural resources, it was receiving more foreign aid, it had more foreign investment capital to draw upon, and it could count upon more intimate economic and political relationships with its Southeast Asian neighbors.[1]

The lesson of the Vietnamese revolution is that none of these things really had much value. Political authoritarianism, however inventive, did not by itself have a decisive worth either. Even before the Paris peace agreements, President Thieu had tightened his Saigon dictatorship by forbidding all workers to go on strike (a law of July 15, 1972); by authorizing the arrest and detainment of people without any court judgment or examination of the process (a law of November 25, 1972); and by forcing even anticommunist political parties to withdraw from public activity (a law of December 27, 1972). Having carried out a ruthless and instinctive suppression of opposition, Thieu poured the varieties of military and bureaucratic manpower which he controlled into the villages, hoping at last to correct what he himself called South Vietnam's "huge head and small buttocks" polity—that is, the old Cochin China colonial polity, in which most significant administrative power had been concentrated in the cities and in the central government rather than in the localities.

This meant, in practice, an effort to militarize the administration of southern villages and, through such increased militarization, to control them more vigorously. In April 1974, each village supposedly received its own "branch zone chief" (*phan chi khu truong*), an army lieutenant or captain who was to wrest command of village self-defense units and policemen from the village chiefs, and who was also to be given the powers of assistant village chiefs to control and inspect the wealth and the manpower of the villages, by means of the collection of family declarations. The available evidence suggests that the young soldiers who were inserted into unfamiliar villages as branch zone chiefs in 1974 became trapped in debilitating power struggles with the old Vietnamese village elites, who were elected to office but who often managed to buy success in such elections by means of the revenues from joint enterprises in corruption with county chiefs.[2] The very appearance of the branch zone chief system in the last year of the war demonstrated the continuing unreliability of existing village chiefs and notables; the Saigon government's faith in the army and in military methods as the solution to village problems; and the Saigon government's determination to penetrate the villages without reforming them, by matching rather than replacing corrupt county and village chiefs with its own officers.

But without any positive universal or national ideology, the Saigon army itself was doomed to decay. The exact extent of its decay on the eve of March 1975 will always remain controversial. Military inspectors of the Saigon general staff discovered in 1974 that south of Saigon, in military zone four alone, some 24,000 of the soldiers on the army payrolls were "ghost soldiers" (*linh ma*) and 12,000 more of the soldiers on the same payrolls were "potted-tree soldiers" (*linh kieng*). Ghost soldiers were soldiers who had been killed or who had deserted to the enemy. Their names remained in the registers, and they were therefore still paid monthly salaries, which various officers secretly collected. Potted-tree soldiers were living soldiers nominally registered in front-line units, who were in fact working at peaceful jobs many miles from the battle areas, or even performing menial services in the homes of high-ranking officers, in which they had been planted in return for their military salaries. This highly traditional form of corruption had been common to Vietnamese dynastic armies in decline. But one of the functions of American technology was to make the facts of such corruption much more elusive than they would have been in the nineteenth century. For American helicopters were lavishly used to fly soldiers from other sections of the army to fill depleted front-line units undergoing random inspections.[3] Advanced technology is not necessarily an aid to, or a catalyst of, political and social change and reform.

Extraordinary corruption is not something that drops inexplicably out of the sky. It is a political symptom. As an innately counterrevolutionary group, the Saigon officer corps and many of the civilians whom it tried to protect obviously did not possess a sufficiently high level of revolutionary nationalism to withstand serious corruption. It did not have enough consistent faith in the long-term durability and desirability of the cause or the larger community it was fighting for, to make personal sacrifices equal to those of its opponents. Many of its members therefore turned to other purposes, such as the magnification of their own families' economic interests, through legitimate or through corrupt means. They dissociated their families' interests from those of the relatively bogus southern Vietnamese national community which foreign power maneuverings had helped to create in 1954. And once enough of them had made, even slightly, this fatal dissociation—between their families or themselves, and the political community which employed them—flagrant corruption and military defeat became inevitable as the outcomes of conditional national loyalties. The victors in the Vietnamese revolution were those whose loyalties were unconditional in the most self-sacrificial Confucian sense; and the development of such unconditional loyalties must be explained in historical as much as in ideological terms.

It does not slander the political contributions of one of the most hardworking and resourceful peasantries in all Asia, to point out again that the Vietnamese revolution was led for the most part by the sons of the traditional intelligentsia, and that this was the section of Vietnamese society which found itself earliest and most often in demeaning circumstances of cultural and political conflict with the colonial power. The peasantry were also exploited by the colonial power, and cherished extensive memories of a national tradition of resistance to outside aggression. But peasants did not have to make enormous immediate cultural concessions to the French colonialists in order to survive: they did not have to learn to speak the invaders' language and adopt the invaders' clothes merely in order to occupy the same echelons of society, with the same dignity and power, that their fathers and grandfathers had occupied. Why did some members of the intelligentsia "collaborate," while others became revolutionaries? To this question it is impossible to give dogmatic answers. Forced cultural change, on the scale which the Vietnamese upper class experienced it after 1884, multiplies options and the needs for choosing them much more rapidly than any human society can tolerate in a stable manner. Uniform behavior on the part of the intelligentsia would therefore have been surprising. What was far less surprising was that some Vietnamese intellectuals should ultimately seek to marry the cloistered, priestly cosmopolitanism of the Marxist-Leninist church to the generous, capacious parochialisms of the Vietnamese national tradition in order to throw the invaders out.

There are many dissimilarities between the French revolution, as Alexis de Tocqueville saw it, and the Vietnamese revolution. Vietnamese popular discontent most certainly did not run highest in times or regions in which economic improvement was occurring, as de Tocqueville claims it did in France,[4] nor were revolutionary Vietnamese politics seriously affected by the aggrandizing pull of a gigantic metropolis like Paris. One can, however, notice in colonial Vietnam at least one of the important trends which de Tocqueville perceived in eighteenth-century France: a separation between the literate members of society who shaped public opinion (by writing iconoclastic novels and political and social tracts), and the literate members of society who shaped public affairs (in the Vietnamese case, by serving as colonial administrative subordinates). The split between the two groups, which meant a permanent juxtaposition in the popular imagination between visions of an ideal free Vietnam and appreciations of a contradictory colonial reality, came perhaps no later than the "Eastern Travel" movement and the Tonkin Free School.

Into the whirlpool of revolution, Vietnamese intellectuals not unnaturally carried with them many social and ideological elements and predispositions from traditional Vietnam. Not all the old turned out to be incompatible with the new. If one considers only the Vietnamese communists, one might conclude that they have now combined the belief in the indivisibility of politics and ethics enunciated by generations of East Asian Confucian philosophers with the belief in the indivisibility of politics and economics so characteristic of the modern West. Furthermore, their Marxist-Leninist emphasis upon the "latent power" of the people—an emphasis harboring the thought that obstacles to progress are caused by defective institutions or "remnants" from the prerevolutionary past or defective class relationships, but not by original sin or by impacted inner psychological tendencies—coincides to some extent with the doctrine of man's "natural goodness" which centuries of Vietnamese schoolboys were taught by the writings of Mencius.

What is dramatically new is the effort to abolish distinctions between

mental and manual workers. Here Marxism does not coincide with Vietnamese traditions but does show its capacity to be a synopsis, however
excessive its own claims, of a number of dynamic European philosophies
which Vietnamese revolutionaries now desire to import. It is worth noting
that the original social value of this crusade to break down the barriers
between the intelligentsia and the workers and peasants, in the eyes of
such revolutionaries, did not lie in the stimulating effects it might be
believed to have upon mobilization for economic development. It lay
instead in the unprecedented powers of cohesion it was believed to lend to
newly created revolutionary communities. Some writers have argued that
the great motive force of communism is entrepreneurship—the promotion
of industrialization—by means of crash programs characterized by dictatorial rule, consumer austerity, the reeducation of peasants, and the transformation of preindustrial cultures. But Vietnamese communism did not
show much sign of becoming "entrepreneurial" or "developmental"
communism until relatively late in its history. It did not, for example,
even create its own banking apparatus until the spring of 1951—much
later than its Chinese counterparts. By that time its leaders had been
conscientiously "proletarianizing" themselves, as part of their drive to link
themselves to mass constituencies which could successfully fight colonialism, for several decades.

Has the role of the intelligentsia in the Vietnamese revolution diminished
much since the days of Phan Boi Chau or of the Nghe-Tinh soviets? To
take one crude, perhaps too crude, index, there is the membership composition of the Vietnamese Communist Party, known in the north, since
1951, as the Vietnam Labor Party (*Dang Lao-dong Viet-Nam*). Has
"labor" really supplanted patriotic mandarins as the primary force of this
movement? "The majority of all our cadres take their origins from petty
bourgeois elements," noted one party theorist in 1963,[5] and a decade later
the situation had not dramatically changed. The crucial testing ground was
the city of Haiphong, which was, with Hanoi, the industrial capital of the
north and the one place (apart from the mines) where the party might
have easily recruited and received an influx of genuine worker members.
Yet as of May 1971, only 15 percent of the members of party cells and
party committees in Haiphong could be described by the regime as
"workers."[6] This was about the same as the *national* percentage of workers in the Chinese Communist Party a decade earlier,[7] and it was also
actually less than the *national* percentage of workers in northern Vietnamese society as a whole, which was about 16 percent in 1968.[8] Needless to
say, such statistics also fell vastly below the percentages of worker
members which European communist parties officially claimed.

Behind this superficial rip tide of doctrines and realities, the intellectuals
who continued to dominate Vietnamese revolutionary politics did so as
the bearers of a magnificent but unique cultural heritage. Revolutionaries
are usually evangelists, people who wish to communicate their revolu-

tionary vision to outsiders as well as to the members of their own society. But if the revolutionary vision they wish to communicate is a vision that has been molded and inspired by peculiarly national factors, its international attractiveness, its capacity to flourish outside the boundaries of its one national culture, will obviously be weakened. The quantities of history-dependent cultural nationalism which have appeared in Vietnamese revolutionary thinking—cultural nationalism which celebrates centuries-old movements of resistance to foreign invaders, centuries-old familial loyalties, centuries-old village rituals, centuries-old patterns of communalism— are very great. Sometimes they are so great that they make the meaning of the Vietnamese revolution, apart from its resources of courage and tenacity, difficult to export or to expound to foreigners.

When the American literary critic Susan Sontag returned from a visit to Hanoi in 1968, she published an account of her travels (*Trip to Hanoi*) in which she stated that however much she admired her hosts, no American had any way of incorporating Vietnam into his or her consciousness. It is not well known in the United States that Susan Sontag's book was extensively reviewed by Hanoi literary journals about two years later (1970), and all her reactions to that part of the Vietnamese revolution represented by the communists were carefully scrutinized. The Vietnamese national poem *The Tale of Kieu,* written in the early 1800s—and discussed by Susan Sontag in her book—soon occupied the heart of the controversy over the intelligibility of the Vietnamese revolution to outsiders, even sympathetic ones. In this masterpiece of literature, the heroine, Kieu, abandons the man she loves and to whom she is betrothed, in order to rescue her imprisoned father, an undertaking that eventually leads her into prostitution and concubinage, all for the sake of filial piety. After many vicissitudes, Kieu is reunited with her mandarin fiancé, but she refuses to become the mother of his children on the grounds that her previous experiences had cost her her purity and her reputation. The poem ends with her lover married to her younger sister, and with Kieu herself living close by as her former fiancé's friend but not as his full conjugal partner. Susan Sontag found the ending of this famous poem disappointing by Western standards. With the full self-assurance of the New York literary world, she wrote in her book that Western readers would have preferred to see Kieu die from tuberculosis in the arms of her lover, after being reunited with him, rather than be rewarded with a strange, self-denying communal life with him and her sister as well.[9]

Would revolutionary intellectuals in Hanoi accept this Western verdict about a poem which had, after all, been written in the feudal period, and whose themes presumably did not have much in common with the proper ethics or behavior of a modern revolutionary state? The answer was never in doubt. Nor was it ambiguous. The opinions of Susan Sontag, it was judged by Hanoi literary critics, reflected the taste of a person who represented centuries of development of the Western "individualist ethic."

Susan Sontag did not understand the "limitless richness" of the Vietnamese soul, nor did she understand the necessary paramountcy of a society of communal sharing, no matter what the individual hardships.[10]

The Vietnamese revolution's quest for new forms of organized communities had brought it, by the 1970s, back to an acceptance of some of the most feudal of its own national traditions. Even the communists were not as immune to their attractions as they had once thought. The contents of these traditions were, indeed, most difficult for even well-meaning foreigners to assimilate; and their implications for individual liberty were almost certainly quite unacceptable to most Westerners. On the other hand, could the inhabitants of American cities, confronting their own situation of intimate neighborhoods smashed by expressways and high-rise apartment developments, afford to agree with Susan Sontag that the decades-old Vietnamese search for a more effective sense of community offered them no lessons at all?

Notes

Chapter 1

1. To Hoai, "Chuyen Ong Giang: kich phim hoat hoa" ("The story of Ong Giang: an animated cartoon film"), *Van Nghe* [Literature and the Arts], Hanoi, October 30, 1964, p. 10.
2. Nhat Linh, *Di Tay* [A Journey to France] (1935; reprint ed., Saigon, 1960), pp. 20–21.
3. "Chuong trinh toi thieu ve cuoc tuyen cu cua cac doan the Mat tran Binh Dan" ("The minimum program for the election enterprises of the Popular Front groups"), *Ngay nay* [Nowadays], Hanoi, July 3, 1938, p. 9.
4. Thanh Lang, "Bao chi Viet-Nam va 100 nam xay dung van hoa" ("Vietnamese newspapers and a hundred years of cultural construction"), *Van but* [Letters], Saigon, November 1971, p. 7.
5. Pham Quynh, "Chu nghia quoc gia" ("Nationalism"), *Nam phong* [The Vietnamese Ethos], Hanoi, December 1925, pp. 402–403.
6. "Bon muoi nam hoat dong cua Dang" ("Forty years of activities of the Party"), *Nhan dan* [The People], Hanoi, January 14, 1970, p. 3.
7. Nguyen Van Trung, *Nhan dinh IV: Chien tranh, cach mang, hoa binh* [Realizations, vol. 4, Conflict, Revolution, Peace] (Saigon, 1966), pp. 106–107, 133.
8. Yamaguchi Ichirō, *Gendai Chūgoku shisō shi* [A History of Contemporary Chinese Thought] (Tokyo, 1969), p. 216.
9. Milton E. Osborne, *The French Presence in Cochinchina and Cambodia* (Ithaca, 1969), pp. 39, 59.
10. Nguyen Van Phong, *La Société Vietnamienne de 1882 a 1902 d'après les écrits des auteurs français* (Paris, 1971), p. 251.
11. Quoted in Pham Van Son, *Viet su tan bien: Viet-Nam khang Phap su* [A New Compilation of Vietnamese History: A History of Vietnam's Resistance to France] (Saigon, 1962), p. 276.
12. Phong, *La Société Vietnamienne*, p. 255.
13. Son, *Viet-Nam khang Phap su*, pp. 277–278.
14. Ibid., pp. 278–279.
15. Phong, *La Société Vietnamienne*, pp. 255–256.

16. Ibid., pp. 229–230.
17. Son, *Viet-Nam khang Phap su*, pp. 278–279.
18. Phong, *La Société Vietnamienne*, pp. 88–89; Kieu Oanh Mau, *Ban trieu ban nghich liet truyen* [Official Biographies of the Rebels of this Dynasty], trans. into modern Vietnamese by Tran Khai Van, (Saigon, 1963 edition), p. 123.
19. Phong, *La Société Vietnamienne*, p. 89.
20. Ienaga Saburō, *Nihon kindai shisō shi kenkyū* [Research into the History of Japanese Modern Thought] (Tokyo, 1961), pp. 283–292.
21. Son, *Viet-Nam khang Phap su*, p. 280.
22. Pham Quynh, "Chan chinh quan-truong" ("The improvement of officialdom"), *Nam phong*, Hanoi, March 1926, pp. 108–112.
23. "Van-te nguoi chet duoi trong phong trao chong thue o mien Trung nam 1908" ("A funeral oration for the people who were drowned in the tax resistance movement in central Vietnam in the year 1908"), in Thai Bach, comp., *Thi van quoc cam thoi thuoc Phap* [Forbidden National Literature of the French Colonial Period] (Saigon, 1968), pp. 280–285.
24. Pham Quynh, "Chan chinh quan-truong," pp. 109–110.
25. *Dai Nam thuc luc chinh bien* [Primary Compilation of the Veritable Records of Imperial Vietnam], 2 (Minh-mang reign), 207: 4ff.
26. D.N., "Dieu tran ve hien tinh o nha que" ("A statement concerning present conditions in the countryside"), *Nam phong*, Hanoi, April 1926, pp. 258–259.
27. Pham Quynh, "Chan chinh quan-truong," pp. 111–112.
28. Khai Hung, *Gia dinh* [The Family] (Saigon, 1959), p. 50.
29. Julio Cotler, "The Mechanics of Internal Domination and Social Change in Peru," I. L. Horowitz, ed., *Masses In Latin America* (New York: Oxford University Press, 1970), p. 428.
30. G. H. Camerlynck, "Le mariage entre Français et Annamites," *La Revue Indochinoise Juridique et Economique*, Hanoi, 1937, pp. 51–95.
31. See the discussion in John T. McAlister, Jr., *Vietnam: The Origins of Revolution* (New York: Doubleday Anchorbooks, 1971), pp, 65–66.
32. Lang Nhan, "Ong Tay Annam" ("Mister Annamese Frenchman"), in his *Chuyen vo ly* [Irrational Tales] (Saigon, 1962), pp. 11–13.
33. Pham Quynh, "Tong luan ve luat hoc" ("A general discussion of legal studies"), *Thuong-chi van tap* [A Collection of the Writings of Thuong-chi] (Saigon, 1962), 5: 135–160.
34. *Dai Nam thuc luc chinh bien*, 2, 116: 25b–26b; and 2, 40: 18b–19.
35. Paul Couzinet, "La structure juridique de l'Union Indochinoise," *La Revue Indochinoise Juridique et Economique*, Hanoi, 1939, pp. 329–354.
36. Tu Ly, "Dan que va luat" ("The people of the countryside and the laws"), *Phong hoa* [Customs], Hanoi, March 30, 1934, pp. 1–2. My italics.

310 / *Notes*

37. Huynh Thuc Khang, "Dien van doc truoc vien dan bieu Trung-ky ngay 1–10–1928" ("Speech read before the Annam council of representatives on October 1, 1928"), in Thai Bach, *Thi van quoc cam thoi thuoc Phap,* pp. 486–497.

38. Raden Adjeng Kartini, *Letters of a Javanese Princess,* trans. Agnes Louise Symmers (New York: W. W. Norton and Co., 1964), pp. 60–61.

39. Ly Chanh Trung, "Ong toan quyen va dan Giao chi" ("Mister governor-general and the people of Vietnam"), *Dai dan toc* [The Great People], Saigon, June 14–20, 1970, p. 4.

Chapter 2

1. Hai Au, "Vi sao nguoi minh thieu cai quan-niem quoc-gia?" ("Why do our own people lack the nation-state concept?"), *Tieng dan* [Voice of the People], Hue, January 9, 1932, 1, 4.

2. Truong Buu Lam, *Patterns of Vietnamese Response to Foreign Intervention 1858–1900,* Southeast Asia Series (New Haven: Yale University 1967), p. 71.

3. David G. Marr, *Vietnamese Anticolonialism 1885–1925* (Berkeley: University of California Press, 1971), p. 96.

4. Cf. Liang Ch'i-ch'ao's own penetrating analysis, in *Che-hsüeh* [Philosophy], Peking, April 1922, p. 546ff.

5. Trinh Van Thanh, *Giang luan Viet van* [Lectures on Vietnamese Literature] (Saigon, 1962), p. 391.

6. R. B. Smith, "The Development of Opposition to French Rule in Southern Vietnam 1880–1940," *Past and Present,* Oxford, February 1972, p. 127.

7. T'ao Ch'eng-chang, "Chiao Hui yüan-liu k'ao" ("An Examination of the Origins and History of the Religions and the Societies"), in Lo Erh-kang, *T'ien-ti-hui wen-hsien lu* [Recorded Literary Offerings about the Triad Society] (Shanghai, 1947), pp. 61–74; and Suzuki Chūsei, *Shinchō chūki shi kenkyū* [Research into the History of the Middle Period of the Ch'ing Court] (Tokyo, 1952), p. 104.

8. Marr, *Vietnamese Anticolonialism,* pp. 222–223; Smith, "The Development of Opposition to French Rule," pp. 104–107; and Shōji Kichinosuke, "Yonaoshi ikki oboegaki" ("Notes on world reformation insurrections"), *Rekishi hyōron* [Historical Review], Tokyo, October 1, 1967, pp. 33–40.

9. T'ao Ch'eng-chang, "Chiao Hui yüan-liu k'ao," pp. 71–72.

10. Tran Huy Lieu, *Lich su tam muoi nam chong Phap* [A History of Eighty Years of Resistance to the French] (Hanoi, 1957), 1: 178–180.

11. "Vu Nguyen An Ninh dem ra giua toa phuc an Saigon" ("The Nguyen An Ninh case is brought out into the Saigon appeals court"), *Than chung,* Saigon, July 18, 1929, p. 1.

12. Phan Van Hum, *Ngoi tu kham lon* [A Stay in the Great Prison]

(1929; reprint ed., Saigon, 1957), p. 101.

13. Marr, *Vietnamese Anticolonialism*, p. 84.

14. Georges Boudarel, "Mémoires de Phan Boi Chau," *France-Asie*, Paris, 1968, 3–4, pp. 306–309.

15. Ibid., pp. 391–394.

16. Phan Chu Trinh, *Giai nhan ky ngo* [Rare Encounters with Beautiful Personages] (Saigon, 1958), pp. 5–8 (of poetry text).

17. Phan Chu Trinh, "Quan tri chu nghia va dan tri chu nghia" ("The ideology of monarchical rule and the ideology of rule by the people"), in Thai Bach, *Thi van quoc cam thoi thuoc Phap*, pp. 456–482.

18. Ibid., p. 463.

19. Thanh Lang, *Bang luoc do van hoc Viet-Nam* [A Summary Roster of Vietnamese Literature] (Saigon, 1967), 2: 94–95. "Tonkin Free School" is, to be frank, a most inadequate translation into English of the Vietnamese term, which refers to the names of Hanoi and Tokyo (both "Eastern Capitals," the meaning of Dong Kinh) in a pun designed to symbolize East Asian solidarity; but a better translation that is not burdensome to the English-speaking reader is hard to find.

20. Lam Giang, *Giang luan ve Phan Boi Chau* [Lectures on Phan Boi Chau] (Saigon, 1959), p. 104.

21. Ch'ien Mu, *Chung-kuo li-tai cheng-chih te-shih* [The Achievements and Failures of Successive Generations of Chinese Governments] (Hong Kong, 1959), pp. 40–41.

22. Phan Chu Trinh, "Quan tri chu nghia," pp. 457–458.

23. Ch'ai Te-keng et al., *Hsin-hai ko-ming* [The Revolution of 1911] (Shanghai, 1957), 2: 333.

24. Tsou Lu, "Chung-kuo t'ung-meng-hui" ("The United League of China"), in Ch'ai Te-keng et al., *Hsin-hai ko-ming*, 2: 67.

25. Chuong Thau, "Moi quan he giua Ton Trung-son va cach-mang Viet-Nam dau the ky XX" ("The relations between Sun Yat-sen and the Vietnamese revolution at the beginning of the twentieth century"), *Nghien cuu lich su* [Historical Researches], Hanoi, October 1966, pp. 22–23.

26. Chien Po-tsan et al., *Wu-hsü pien-fa* [The Reforms of 1898] (Shanghai, 1953), 2: 236–237.

27. Ibid., p. 230–233.

28. Ibid., 4: 439–441.

29. Phan Chu Trinh, "Quan tri chu nghia," p. 471.

30. Liang Ch'i-ch'ao, "K'ang Yu-wei ch'üan" ("A Chronicle of K'ang Yu-wei"), in Chien Po-tsan, *Wu-hsü pien-fa*, 4: 5–47.

31. "Tay Ho Phan Chu Trinh" ("Tay Ho Phan Chu Trinh"), *Phu nu tan van* [Women's News], Saigon, March 20, 1930, pp. 9–13.

32. K'ang Yu-wei, "Fa-kuo ko-ming shih lun" ("A discussion of the history of the French Revolution"), in Chang Nan and Wang Jen-chih, comp., *Hsin-hai ko-ming ch'ien-shih-nien-chien shih-lun hsüan-chi* [A Selected

Collection of Discussions of the Times from the Decade before the 1911 Revolution] (Hong Kong, 1962), Two, 1:295–308.

33. Liang Ch'i-ch'ao, "Chung-kuo li-shih-shang ko-ming chih yen-chiu" ("A study of revolution from the standpoint of Chinese history"), in Chang Nan and Wang Jen-chih, *Hsin-hai ko-ming ch'ien-shih-nien-chien shih-lun hsüan-chi,* One, 2:803–812.

34. Stuart Schram, *Political Leaders of the Twentieth Century: Mao Tse-tung* (Baltimore: Penguin Books, 1967), p. 27.

35. Marr, *Vietnamese Anticolonialism,* p. 153.

36. Ibid., p. 117.

37. Hao Chang, *Liang Ch'i-ch'ao and Intellectual Transition in China 1890–1907* (Cambridge: Harvard University Press, 1971), p. 95ff.

38. Hayashi Megumi, "Hōyaku 'shakai' kō" ("A study of the translation into Japanese of 'society'"), *Hikaku bunka kenkyūshō kiyō* [Bulletin of the Institute of Comparative Studies of Culture], Tokyo, June 1966, p. 65ff.

39. Jung Meng-yüan, "Hsin-hai ko-ming ch'ien Chung-kuo shu-k'an-shang tui Ma-k'o-ssu chu-i ti chieh-shao" ("The introduction of Marxism from the standpoint of Chinese books and publications before the 1911 Revolution"), *Hsin Chien-she* [New Construction], Peking, 1953, 3, pp. 5–11.

40. Thach Lan, "Cac giai cap" ("The social classes"), *Phu nu tan van,* Saigon, April 10, 1930, pp. 13–14.

41. Chang Ping-lin, "Ko-ming chih tao-te" ("Revolutionary morality"), Chang Nan and Wang Jen-chih, *Hsin-hai ko-ming ch'ien-shih-nien-chien shih-lun hsüan-chi,* Two, I, 509–520.

42. Nguyen Truong, "Nhan thuc cua Phan Boi Chau ve vai tro quan chung trong su nghiep dau tranh giai phong dan toc" ("Realizations by Phan Boi Chau of the role of the masses in the work of struggling to emancipate the people"), *Nghien cuu lich su,* Hanoi, March–April 1972, p. 36.

43. Nhuong Tong, *Nguyen Thai Hoc 1902–1930* [Nguyen Thai Hoc, 1902–1930] (Saigon, 1956), p. 23.

44. Ibid., p. 63.

45. Hoang Van Dao, *Viet-Nam Quoc Dan Dang, lich su dau tranh can dai 1927–1954* [The Vietnamese Nationalist Party, A History of its Modern Struggle 1927–1954] (Saigon, 1964), p. 452.

46. Nhuong Tong, *Nguyen Thai Hoc,* 13.

47. Hoang Van Dao, *Viet-Nam Quoc Dan Dang,* p. 33; Nhuong Tong, *Nguyen Thai Hoc,* pp. 24–26.

48. Nhuong Tong, *Nguyen Thai Hoc,* p. 46.

49. Hoang Van Dao, *Viet-Nam Quoc Dan Dang,* p. 43.

50. Ibid., pp. 53–79.

51. Tran Huy Lieu, *Lich su tam muoi nam chong Phap,* 1: 285–286.

52. E. Daufès, *La Garde Indigène de l'Indochine de sa Création à nos jours* (Avignon, 1933), I, iii–vi.

53. *Luc tinh tan van,* [News of the Six Provinces], Saigon, October 26, 1936, p. 1.
54. Nhuong Tong, *Nguyen Thai Hoc,* p. 45; McAlister, *Vietnam: The Origins of Revolution,* p. 81.
55. Hoang Van Dao, *Viet-Nam Quoc Dan Dang,* p. 79.
56. "Tuong thuat vu Viet-Nam Quoc Dan Dang" ("A report on the Vietnamese Nationalist Party case"), *Than chung,* Saigon, July 12, 1929, p. 1.
57. Nhuong Tong, *Nguyen Thai Hoc,* p. 21.
58. "Tuong thuat vu Viet-Nam Quoc Dan Dang," *Than chung,* July 17, 1929, p. 1.
59. Ibid., July 19, 1929, p. 2.
60. Thach Lan, "Cac giai cap," *Phu nu tan van,* April 10, 1930, pp. 13–14.
61. Li Han-sheng, comp., *Pa-i-ch'i Yüeh-nan Hai-fang ts'an-sha Hua-ch'iao an-chi* [Records of Cases of the August 17 Vietnamese Haiphong cruel massacres of the overseas Chinese] (Canton, 1927), p. 5.
62. Nhuong Tong, *Nguyen Thai Hoc,* pp. 31–32.

Chapter 3

1. Trinh Van Thanh, *Giang luan Viet van,* p. 242.
2. Goto Hiroyuki, "Masu rōgu no naritachi ni tsuite no kōsatsu" ("An inquiry concerning the achievement of oral communication with large crowds"), *Shakaigaku hyōron* [Sociological Review], Tokyo, January 1972, 63–69.
3. Duong Ba Trac, "Chuc trach si-luu trong xa-hoi ta ngay nay" ("The functions and responsibilities of the scholar class in our society now"), reprinted in Duong Quang Ham, *Van hoc Viet-Nam* [Vietnamese Literature] (Hanoi, 1939; Saigon, 1968), pp. 189–192.
4. Fu Ssu-nien, "Chung-kuo hsüeh-shu ssu-hsiang chieh chih chi-pen wu-miu" ("The basic errors of the world of Chinese scholarly thought"), *Hsin Ch'ing-nien* [New Youth], Shanghai, April 15, 1918, pp. 328–336.
5. Phan Khoi, "Canh cao cac nha hoc phiet" ("An admonition against the intelligentsia cliques"), *Phu nu tan van,* Saigon, July 24, 1930, pp. 9–12.
6. Pham Van Dieu, *Viet-Nam van hoc giang binh* [Critical Lectures on Vietnamese Literature] (Saigon, 1961), pp. 381–382.
7. Nguyen Duy Thanh, "Y cua toi ve tieng Viet-Nam" ("My opinions on the Vietnamese language"), *Phu nu tan van,* Saigon, February 18, 1932, pp. 5–10.
8. Phan Khoi, "Su dung chu Tau trong tieng Viet-Nam" ("The use of Chinese words in the Vietnamese language"), *Phu nu tan van,* Saigon, March 3, 1932, pp. 5–7.
9. Pham Van Khoa, "Mot nen dien anh cach mang da ra doi" ("A basis

for revolutionary films has already been born"), *Tap chi van hoc* [Journal of Literary Studies], Hanoi, May 1970, pp. 38–51.

10. Osborne, *The French Presence in Cochinchina and Cambodia,* pp. 89–93.

11. *Tieng dan,* Hue, March 1, 1930, p. 3.

12. Van Tan, "Tran Huy Lieu, nha bao va nha van cach mang" ("Tran Huy Lieu, journalist and revolutionary writer"), *Tap chi van hoc,* Hanoi, October 1969, pp. 32–43.

13. Feng Ai-ch'ün, *Chung-kuo hsin-wen shih* [A History of Chinese Newspapers] (Taipei, 1967), p. 227.

14. Thanh Lang, "Bao chi Viet-Nam va 100 nam xay dung van hoa," *Van but,* Saigon, November 1971, p. 8.

15. Ogi Shinzō, *Showa shonin bunka shi* [A Cultural History of the Common People of the Showa Period] (Tokyo, 1970), 1: 28–32.

16. Viet Sinh, "Mot cai lam to" ("A big error"), *Phong hoa,* Hanoi, February 17, 1933, 1. Thach Lam is the author.

17. Auguste Rivoalen, "L'oeuvre française d'enseignement au Vietnam," *France-Asie,* October-November-December 1956, pp. 401–418.

18. Thuong Chi, "Mot cai chuong-trinh cai-cach su hoc o nuoc ta" ("An educational reform program in our country"), *Nam phong,* May 1926, pp. 315–320.

19. Ly Chanh Trung, *Tim ve dan toc* [Searching for a Return to the People] (Saigon, 1967), pp. 30–31.

20. Ts'ai Yüan-p'ei et al., *Wan Ch'ing san-shih-wu nien lai ti Chung-kuo chiao-yü* [Chinese education over the past thirty-five years since the late Ch'ing] (Shanghai, 1931), pp. 26–35.

21. Ch'iao Ch'i-ming, *Chung-kuo nung-ts'un she-hui ching-chi hsüeh* [The Economics of Chinese Village Society] (Shanghai, 1946), p. 293.

22. *Luc tinh tan van,* Saigon, October 15, 1936, pp. 1, 6.

23. Thuong Chi, "Mot cai chuong-trinh cai-cach su hoc o nuoc ta," pp. 316–317.

24. Pham The Ngu, *Viet Nam van hoc su: van hoc hien dai 1862–1945* [A History of Vietnamese Literature: Contemporary Literature, 1862–1945] (Saigon, 1965), pp. 284–285.

25. Vu Ngoc Phan, *Nha van hien dai* [Contemporary Writers] (reprint ed., Saigon, 1959), I, 55–59.

26. The Lu, *Mai Huong va Le Phong* [Mai Huong and Le Phong] (reprint ed., Saigon, 1962), p. 30.

27. Ibid., p. 77.

28. Pham Quynh, "Chu nghia quoc gia," *Nam phong,* December 1925, pp. 401–405.

29. Le Van Truong, *Trong ao tu truong gia* [In the Stagnant Pond of High Society] (reprint ed., Saigon, 1961), pp. 19–21.

30. Ton Quang Phiet et al., "Du luan ve thanh nien" ("Opinions on youth"), *Nam phong,* Hanoi, January 1925, pp. 70–73.

31. Hoang Dao, *Tieng dan* [The Sound of the Guitar] (reprint ed., Saigon, 1964), pp. 14–17.

32. *Dai Nam chinh bien liet truyen so tap* [First Collection of the Primary Compilation of Biographies of Imperial Vietnam], 1841, 29: 1b–2.

33. Ngo Quang Huy, "Tinh canh nguoi du hoc" ("The situation of people who study abroad"), *Than chung*, Saigon, January 8, 1929, p. 4.

34. Nhat Linh, *Doan tuyet* [A Severance of Ties] (reprint ed., Saigon, 1967), pp. 181–183.

35. Phan Van Gia, "Dau oc tay va dau oc annam" ("The French mentality and the Vietnamese mentality"), *Than chung*, Saigon, July 1, 1929, p. 2.

36. Ch'in Shang-chih, *Chung-kuo fa-chih chi fa-lü ssu-hsiang shih chiang-hua* [Discussions of the History of Chinese Legal Systems and of Chinese Legal Thought] (Taipei, 1966), p. 146.

37. Nguyen Trai, *Gia Huan Ca* [Songs of Family Exhortation] (Saigon, 1953), prepared and edited by Dinh Gia Thuyet, pp. 16–17.

38. Thuy An, "Chi em lay chong" ("Girls acquire husbands"), *Phong hoa*, Hanoi, January 13, 1933, p. 13.

39. Bui Quang Huy, "Gia dinh giao duc" ("Family education"), *Nam phong*, September 1925, pp. 209–217.

40. Phan Khoi, "Doc cuon 'Nho giao' cua ong Tran Trong Kim" ("Reading the book 'The Confucian Teaching' of Mister Tran Trong Kim"), *Phu nu tan van*, Saigon, May 29, 1930, pp. 11–15.

41. Pham The Ngu, *Viet Nam van hoc su . . . 1862–1945*, pp. 298–301.

42. Phan Khoi, "Doc cuon 'Nho giao,'" *Phu nu tan van*, May 29, 1930, pp. 11–15.

43. Nomura Kōichi, "Kindai Nihon ni okeru Jukyō shisō no hensen ni tsuite no oboegaki" ("Notes concerning the transitions of Confucian thought in modern Japan"), *Kindai Chūgoku kenkyū* [Researches on Modern China] (Tokyo, 1959), 3: 233–270.

44. Pham Quynh, "Van de tien hoa cac dan toc" ("The problem of the evolution of peoples"), in Pham Quynh, *Thuong Chi van tap*, 3: 41–43.

Chapter 4

1. Jerome Blum, "The Internal Structure and Polity of the European Village Community from the Fifteenth to the Nineteenth Century," *Journal of Modern History*, December 1971, pp. 541–576.

2. Nguyen Tuan, *Vang bong mot thoi* [The Reflections of a Moment in Time] (reprint ed., Saigon, 1962), pp. 169–170.

3. Tran Khai Van, trans., *Le trieu giao-hoa dieu luat* [The Local Moral Teaching Regulations of the Le Court] (Saigon, 1962), p. 48.

4. Alexander Barton Woodside, *Vietnam and the Chinese Model* (Cambridge: Harvard University Press, 1971), pp. 134–135.

5. *Dai Nam liet truyen chinh bien so tap*, 13: 7ff.

6. Phan Ke Binh, *Viet Nam phong tuc* [Vietnamese Customs] (reprint ed., Saigon, 1970), pp. 112–114.

7. Ibid., pp. 95–96.

8. Tran Khai Van, trans., *Le trieu giao-hoa dieu luat,* pp. 26, 38.

9. Ibid., pp. 39–40.

10. Phan Khoang, "Luoc su che do xa-thon o Viet-Nam" ("A summary history of the village-hamlet system in Vietnam"), *Su Dia* [History and Geography], Saigon, 1, 1966, pp. 34–51.

11. Nguyen Thanh Nha, *Tableau économique du Vietnam aux XVIIe et XVIIIe Siècles* (Paris, 1970), p. 67.

12. Phan Huy Le, "Ban them may van de ve phong trao nong dan Tay-son" ("Supplementary remarks upon some problems related to the Tay-son peasant movement"), *Nghien cuu lich su,* Hanoi, April 1963, p. 23.

13. M. Villa, trans., "La révolte et la guerre des Tayson d'après les Franciscains Espagnols de Cochinchine," *Bulletin de la Société des Etudes Indochinoises,* Saigon, XV, 3–4, 1940, 75.

14. Aoki Kōji, *Hyakushō ikki no nenjiteki kenkyū* [A Yearly Sequences Study of the Insurrections of the Common People] (Tokyo, 1966), pp. 90, 97.

15. Pierre Gourou, *Les paysans du delta Tonkinois* (Paris, 1936), pp. 214–217.

16. "Le paysan se meurt sous le joug du capitalisme," *La Lutte,* Saigon, February 4, 1936, p. 1.

17. Thai Bach, *Thi van quoc cam thoi thuoc Phap,* pp. 70–75.

18. Pham Cao Duong, *Thuc trang cua gioi nong dan Viet Nam duoi thoi Phap thuoc* [The Situation of the Vietnamese Peasantry under French Colonialism] (Saigon, 1966), p. 166.

19. *Dai Nam thuc luc chinh bien,* 2, 209: 24bff.

20. Tran Ngoc Dinh, "Che do so huu ruong dat lon o Nam-bo trong thoi de quoc Phap thong tri" ("The big landed estate ownership system in Cochinchina in the period of French imperial domination"), *Nghien cuu lich su,* Hanoi, May-June 1970, pp. 81–90.

21. Ngo Vinh Long, "Before the Revolution: The Living Conditions of Vietnamese Peasants under the French," unpublished mss., pp. 18–24.

22. "Quan thong-doc voi phong canh-nong Nam Ky" ("The governor with the Cochinchina chamber of agriculture"), *Luc tinh tan van,* Saigon, July 3, 1934, p. 1.

23. "Nong dan ta can biet: cach khan dat quoc-gia duoi muoi mau" ("Our peasants need to know: ways of clearing national lands that are under ten acres"), *Luc tinh tan van,* Saigon, January 12, 1939, p. 1.

24. Lang Nhan, *Chuyen vo ly,* pp. 48–49.

25. *Duoc Nha Nam* [The Torch of the Southern Homeland], Saigon, July 29, 1931, p. 1.

26. "Loi thinh cau cua cac vi dien-chu o Hau-giang voi quan thong-doc" ("Words of petition of the Back River landowners with regard to the governor"), *Luc tinh tan van,* Saigon, July 5, 1934, p. 1.

27. Bui Quang Chieu, "Noi lo ngai cho nen nong nghiep" ("Surfacing anxieties for the agricultural foundations"), *Luc tinh tan van,* Saigon, January 9, 1939, p. 1.

28. James C. Scott, "The Erosion of Patron-Client Bonds and Social Change in Rural Southeast Asia," *Journal of Asian Studies,* November 1972, pp. 5–37.

29. Ly Chanh Trung, *Tim ve dan toc,* pp. 28–29.

30. Khai Hung, *Gia dinh,* pp. 25–27.

31. Charles Robequain, *The Economic Development of French Indochina* (New York: Oxford University Press, 1944), p. 82.

32. Nghiem Xuan Yem, "Van de canh nong o Bac Ky: thanh nien tri thuc voi nghe nong o xu nha" ("The agricultural problem in Tonkin: intellectual youth and the profession of agriculture in our region"), *Thanh nghi* [Clear Counsel], Hanoi, April 16, 1943, pp. 6–10.

33. Yem, "Van de canh nong o Bac Ky," *Thanh nghi,* April 16, 1943, pp. 6–10.

34. Nguyen Tuan, *Vang bong mot thoi,* pp. 140–141.

35. Yem, "Van de canh nong o Bac Ky," *Thanh nghi,* April 16, 1943, pp. 6–10.

36. Vu Dinh Hoe, "Viec hoc thanh nien trong khi tan cu" ("The work of youthful education in a period of dispersion"), *Thanh nghi,* Hanoi, March 11, 1944, pp. 3–4.

37. Charles Robequain, *Le Thanh Hoa: Etude géographique d'une province Annamite* (Paris, 1929), 1: 101–102.

38. Nguyen Van To, "Thanh nien doi voi viec lang" ("Youth with regard to the work of the village"), *Thanh nghi,* March 1, 1943, pp. 21–22.

39. Philippe Preschez, *Essai sur la Democratie au Cambodge* (Paris, 1961), pp. 7–8.

40. Ngo Vinh Long, "Before the Revolution," unpublished mss., pp. 148, 176.

41. Duong Cong Nhuong, "Thay giao lang voi huong chuc lang" ("The village teachers with regard to the village functionaries"), *Luc tinh tan van,* Saigon, January 17, 1924, p. 5.

42. Nguyen Nhu Dang, "Giao lang voi chuc viec lang" ("The village teachers with regard to the village functionaries"), *Luc tinh tan van,* Saigon, January 10, 1924, p. 1.

43. Toan Anh, *Lang xom Viet-Nam* [Vietnamese Villages] (Saigon, 1968), pp. 116–119.

44. *Tieng dan,* Hue, January 1, 1936, p. 5.

45. Ibid., January 8, 1936, p. 5.

46. Ibid., January 1, 1936, p. 5.

47. Tran Thieu Tue, "Khuyen ai bot viec tranh dua" ("An exhortation to everyone to decrease their competition"), *Luc tinh tan van,* Saigon, August 31, 1925, p. 1.

48. *Tieng dan,* Hue, February 4, 1936, p. 4.

49. Ibid., March 12, 1936, p. 4.

50. Toan Anh, *Lang xom Viet-Nam,* pp. 97–106.

51. Nguyen Thanh Nhan, "Noi kho cua huong-chuc lang" ("The miserable plight of the village functionaries"), *Luc tinh tan van,* Saigon, January 10, 1939, pp. 1, 6.

52. Toan Anh, *Lang xom Viet-Nam,* pp. 108–112.

53. N.D.P., "Dieu tra ve tinh-trang huong-thon" (An investigation of the situation of the villages"), *Nam phong,* Hanoi, January 1927, pp. 41–48.

54. Tan Phong, "Viec cai-luong huong-chinh o Bac Ky" ("The work of reforming village administration in Tonkin"), *Thanh nghi,* Hanoi, August 1941, pp. 5–6.

55. Van Tao, "Vai net ve qua trinh xay dung va phat trien cua nha nuoc cach mang Viet Nam 20 nam qua" ("A few lines on the process of construction and development of the revolutionary Vietnamese nation over the past 20 years"), *Nghien cuu lich su,* Hanoi, August 1965, p. 23.

56. Tan Phong, "Van de ngoi thu o huong-thon va du ngay 23 Mai 1941" ("The question of rank in the villages and the edict of May 23 1941"), *Thanh nghi,* Hanoi, September 1941, pp. 6, 15.

57. Tan Phong, "Viec cai-luong," *Thanh nghi,* August 1941, pp. 5–6.

58. Kurt Steiner, *Local Government in Japan* (Stanford: Stanford University Press, 1965), p. 35.

59. Ōno Takeo, *Kindai Nihon nōson hattatsu shiron* [A Discussion of the History of the Development of Modern Japanese Villages] (Tokyo, 1950), pp. 100–101.

60. Ibid., p. 105.

61. Andō Seiichi, *Edo jidai no nōmin* [The Peasants of the Edo Period] (Tokyo, 1959), pp. 230–238.

62. Okutani Matsuji, *Nihon nōgyō kyōdō kumiai shi* [A History of Japanese Agriculture Cooperative Associations] (Tokyo, 1961), p. 270.

63. Ch'en Kuo-fu, "Shih nien lai ti Chung-kuo ho-tso yün-tung" ("The Chinese cooperative movement in the last ten years"), in *Shih nien lai ti Chung-kuo* [China in the Last Ten Years] (Shanghai, 1937), p. 457.

64. Hoang Dao, *Muoi dieu tam niem* [A Sequence of Ten Fundamental Concepts] (reprint ed., Saigon, 1964), pp. 31–34.

65. "To phuc-trinh cua ban tri-su hoi Canh-nong tuong-te tinh Tra Vinh" ("The report of the board of managers of the Tra Vinh mutual help agricultural association"), *Luc tinh tan van,* Saigon, January 24, 1938, p. 6.

66. "Viec truyen ba ve sinh o cac lang" ("The work of disseminating hygiene in the villages"), *Thanh nghi,* Hanoi, March 16, 1943, p. 28.

67. Nguyen Van To, "Thanh nien doi voi viec lang," *Thanh nghi,* March 1, 1943, pp. 21–22.

68. Tran Huy Lieu, *Lich su tam muoi nam chong Phap,* II: 1, 111–112.

69. Lam Dien, "Trai thanh nien hoc sinh Tam Dao hay la doi song cua trai trang lang Tran Quoc Toan" ("The Tam Dao student youth farm or the life of the youth of Tran Quoc Toan village"), *Thanh nghi,* Hanoi, July 22, 1944, pp. 19–22. Tam Dao is now the location of a communist state farm.

70. Phan My, "Buoc hung vong cua mot tieu cong nghe: phao Binh Da" ("The upward and downward steps of a handicraft industry: the firecrackers of Binh Da"), *Thanh nghi,* Hanoi, March 4, 1944, pp. 16–20.

71. Nghiem Xuan Yem, "Dieu tra nho: nhung tieu don dien" ("Micro-investigations: the small concessions"), *Thanh nghi,* Hanoi, April 22, 1944, pp. 7–10.

72. Nghiem Xuan Yem, "Nghe chan nuoi trau bo o xu ta" ("The occupation of raising water buffaloes and oxen in our region"), *Thanh nghi,* Hanoi, May 13, 1944, pp. 11–13.

73. Tran Huy Lieu and Van Tao, eds., *Tong khoi nghia thang tam* [The August General Uprising] (Hanoi, 1957), pp. 40–43.

74. V.H., "Dieu tra nho: mot don dien lon o Thai Nguyen" ("Micro-investigations: a large plantation in Thai Nguyen"), *Thanh nghi,* Hanoi, September 16, 1944, pp. 4–6, 24–25.

75. V.H., "Dieu tra nho: mot don dien ca-phe o Son Tay" ("Micro-investigations: a coffee plantation in Son Tay"), *Thanh nghi,* Hanoi, November 11, 1944, pp. 7–8, 22.

76. Vu Dinh Hoe, "Gia thoc phai nop cho nha nuoc" ("The value of the unhusked paddy that must be delivered to the state"), reprinted in Thai Bach, *Thi van quoc cam thoi thuoc Phap,* pp. 506–517. The most famous contemporary study of rural taxes at the end of the colonial period.

77. Ngo Vinh Long, "Before The Revolution," p. 241.

Chapter 5

1. Erh-shih-pa hua sheng, "T'i-yü chih yen-chiu" ("The study of physical training"), *Hsin Ch'ing-nien,* Shanghai, April 1, 1917, pp. 1–11.

2. Nguyen Trong Thu, "Xa Nam Lien va lang Kim Lien: que huong cua Ho Chu tich" ("The village of Nam Lien and the hamlet of Kim Lien: the homeland of Chairman Ho"), *Nghien cuu lich su,* Hanoi, May 1965, p. 7.

3. Furuta Hikaru et al., *Kindai Nihon shakai shisō shi* [A History of Modern Japanese Social Thought] (Tokyo, 1968), 1: 17ff.

4. Nguyen Duc Van and Kieu Thu Hoach, transl., *Hoang Le nhat thong chi* [A Chronicle of the Polity of the Imperial Le] (Hanoi, 1970), p. 7.

5. Le Si Thang, "Ho Chu tich va su nghiep truyen ba chu nghia Mac-Lenin vao Viet-Nam" ("Chairman Ho and the work of spreading Marxism-Leninism into Vietnam"), *Nghien cuu lich su,* Hanoi, May–June 1972, pp. 12–23.

6. Nguyen Hai Ha, "Ho Chu tich va mot so tac pham van hoc Nga-Xoviet" ("Chairman Ho and some Russian-Soviet literary works"), *Tap chi van hoc,* September–October 1972, pp. 105–106.

7. "Cach mang Thang Tam" ("The August Revolution"), 1, *Nhan dan,* Hanoi, August 27, 1970, p. 3.

8. Trung Chinh, "Ho Chu tich da tiep thu chu nghia Le-nin va truyen ba vao Viet-Nam nhu the nao?" ("How did Chairman Ho adopt Leninism and transmit it to Vietnam?"), *Nghien cuu lich su,* Hanoi, May–June 1970, p. 51.

9. Ibid., pp. 52–53.

10. Tran Huy Lieu, *Lich su tam muoi nam chong Phap,* 1: 277–278.

11. Cf. the reprinted excerpt from this text, complete with eccentric spelling, in *Nhan dan,* January 1, 1970, p. 1.

12. Jean Lacouture, *Ho Chi Minh: A Political Biography* (New York: Vintage Books, 1968), p. 45.

13. Ho Chi Minh, *Selected Works,* (Hanoi, 1960), 1: 66–69. My italics.

14. Le Quoc Su, "Vai y kien gop ve bai hoc: kheo ket hop cac hinh thuc dau tranh chinh tri va vu trang trong cach mang thang Tam" ("Some opinions on the lessons of skilfully combining the forms of political struggle and armed struggle in the August Revolution"), *Nghien cuu lich su,* Hanoi, May 1963, pp. 14–15.

15. Le Si Thang, "Ho Chu tich va su nghiep truyen ba," *Nghien cuu lich su,* May–June 1972, p. 22.

16. Ho Chi Minh, *Selected Works,* 1: 62.

17. Tran Phu, "Luan cuong chanh tri cua Dang Cong san Dong Duong" ("The Political General Theoretical Summation of the Indochina Communist Party"), *Nhan dan,* January 15, 1970. Originally published October 1930.

18. Do Duc Hieu, "Tac pham 'Ban an che do thuc dan Phap' cua Ho Chu tich va van hoc hien dai" ("The work 'The Trial of the French Colonial System' of Chairman Ho and contemporary literature"), *Tap chi van hoc,* Hanoi, July–August 1971, p. 4.

19. Ho Chi Minh, *Selected Works,* 1: 45–47.

20. Ilpyong J. Kim, "Mass mobilization policies and techniques developed in the period of the Chinese Soviet Republic," in A. Doak Barnett, ed., *Chinese Communist Politics In Action* (Seattle: University of Washington Press, 1969), p. 79.

21. Tran Huy Lieu, *Lich su tam muoi nam chong Phap,* II, 1, 66, 60–61.

22. Ibid., p. 70.

23. An eloquent exposition of these local themes may be found in Dao Duy Anh's book *Khao luan ve Kim Van Kieu* [A Study and Discussion of the Kim Van Kieu], which was published in Hue in 1943.

24. Dang Huy Van, "Them mot so tai lieu ve cuoc khoi nghia nam Giap Tuat (1874) o Nghe An va Ha Tinh" ("An additional number of mater-

ials on the 1874 uprising in Nghe An and Ha Tinh"), *Nghien cuu lich su,* Hanoi, June 1965, pp. 16–17, 11–12; Tran Huy Lieu, *Lich su tam muoi nam chong Phap,* II, 1, 65–66.

25. Tran Huy Lieu, *Lich su tam muoi nam chong Phap,* II, 1, 67, 76–77.
26. Ts'ao Po-i, *Chiang-hsi su-wei-ai chih chien-li chi ch'i peng-hui* [The Construction of the Kiangsi Soviet and Its Collapse and Destruction], (Taipei, 1969), pp. 288–289.
27. Tran Huy Lieu, *Lich su tam muoi nam chong Phap,* II, 1, 67–68, 80.
28. Tran Van Giau, *Giai cap cong nhan Viet-Nam* [The Vietnamese Worker Class], (Hanoi, 1962), 1: 154–155.
29. Ibid., pp. 126–129.
30. Quach Tan, *Nuoc non Binh Dinh* [The Homeland of Binh Dinh] (Saigon, 1967), pp. 456–457.
31. Phan Ngoc Lien and Nguyen Van Duc, "Cong xa Pa-ri voi cach mang Viet-Nam" ("The Paris commune with regard to the Vietnamese revolution"), *Nghien cuu lich su,* Hanoi, March–April 1971, p. 6.
32. Nguyen Trai, *Gia huan ca,* pp. 36–37.
33. Nguyen Dang Manh, "Vai net gioi thieu van tho xo-viet Nghe-Tinh" ("Some lines introducing the Nghe-Tinh soviet prose and poetry"), *Tap chi van hoc,* Hanoi, October 1966, p. 66.
34. Pi K'o et al., "P'ing-chia-li jen-min ti ko-ming tou-cheng" ("The revolutionary struggle of the people of P'ing-chia-li"), *Li-shih yen-chiu* [Historical Researches], Peking, 5, 1965, pp. 14–15.
35. R. B. Smith, "An introduction to Caodaism: origins and early history," *Bulletin of the School of Oriental and African Studies,* London, 33, part 2, 1970, 339.
36. Hiroaki Kani, " 'Fu-luan' zakki: minshū Dōkyō no shūhen" ("Miscellaneous notes on sand-writing divination: the peripheries of popular Taoism"), *Shigaku* [Historical Studies] Tokyo, September 1972, pp. 57–88.
37. Nguyen Trai, *Gia huan ca,* p. 24.
38. Sakai Tadao, *Kindai Shina ni okeru shūkyō kessha no kenkyū* [A Research Study of Religious Associations in Modern China] (Tokyo, 1943), p. 61.
39. Ch'en Tu-hsiu, *Tu-hsiu wen-ts'un* [Preserved Writings of Ch'en Tu-hsiu] (Hong Kong, 1965), 3: 289.
40. Dong Tan, *Lich su Cao Dai dai dao tam ky pho do* [A History of the Great Third Period of Universal Passage Cao Dai Religion] (Saigon, 1967), 1: 108–110.
41. Smith, "An introduction to Caodaism: origins and early history," p. 341.
42. Dong Tan, *Lich su Cao Dai,* 1: 44–46.
43. Toan Anh, *Nep cu: tin nguong Viet-Nam* [The Old Way of Life: Vietnamese Creeds] (Saigon, 1967), p. 428.

44. Quach Tan, *Nuoc non Binh Dinh*, p. 482.
45. Sakai Tadao, *Kindai Shina ni okeru shūkyō kessha*, p. 147.
46. Nguyen Van Hau, *Nhan thuc Phat giao Hoa Hao* [Becoming Acquainted with Hoa Hao Buddhism] (Saigon, 1968), pp. 8–15; Hue Tam Ho Tai, "Vietnamese Folk Buddhism and Its Chinese Origins," unpublished mss., pp. 35–40.
47. Nguyen Van Hau, *Nhan thuc Phat giao Hoa Hao*, p. 269.
48. Hoa Hao statement in *Chinh luan*, Saigon, February 21–22, 1971, p. 3.
49. Toan Anh, *Nep cu: tin nguong Viet-Nam*, pp. 406–407.
50. Stuart Schram, *Mao Tse-tung*, p. 201.
51. Nguyen Van Hau, *Nhan thuc Phat giao Hoa Hao*, p. 137.
52. Alexander Woodside, "Ideology and Integration in Postcolonial Vietnamese Nationalism," *Pacific Affairs*, Winter 1971–1972, p. 490.
53. Holmes Welch, *The Buddhist Revival in China* (Cambridge: Harvard University Press, 1968), p. 16.
54. Tran Van Giau, "Phong trao Chan hung Phat giao . . . I" ("The Buddhist Restoration Movement . . . I"), *Nghien cuu lich su*, Hanoi, July–August 1971, pp. 8–10.
55. Nguyen Manh Nhu, "Mot y kien muon trinh bay cung Hoi Phat giao Trung-uong Bac Ky" ("An opinion that I wish to present to the Central Tonkin Buddhist Association"), *Duoc tue* [The Torch of Enlightenment], Hanoi, November 1, 1939, pp. 3–5.
56. Tran Van Giau, "Phong trao Chan hung Phat giao . . . II," *Nghien cuu lich su*, September–October 1971, pp. 7–19.
57. D.N.T., "Pha ba dieu nhan lam giao ly cua Dao Phat" ("Demolish the three mistaken realizations of the doctrinal principles of Buddhism"), *Duoc tue*, Hanoi, July 1, 1937, pp. 4–8.
58. Nguyen Trong Thuat, "Nghia binh dang cua Dao Phat, I" ("The meaning of equality of Buddhism, I"), *Duoc tue*, Hanoi, August 1, 1937, pp. 6–12.
59. Nguyen Trong Thuat, "Nghia binh dang cua Dao Phat, II," *Duoc tue*, August 15, 1937, pp. 3–10.
60. David Thomson, "The Problem of Equality," in William T. Blackstone, ed., *The Concept of Equality* (Minneapolis: Burgess Publishing Co., 1969), p. 11.
61. Nguyen Van Hau, *Nhan thuc Phat giao Hoa Hao*, pp. 127–128.
62. Nguyen Hue Quang, "Chanh tri doi voi Phat giao trong xu ta" ("The government's relations with Buddhism in our region"), *Luc tinh tan van*, Saigon, December 21, 1936, p. 1. The author was editor of a Buddhist journal.
63. Van Quang Thuy, "Phep tu tinh do" ("The ways of cultivating the Pure Land"), *Duoc tue*, Hanoi, April 1, 1940, pp. 3–12.
64. Phan Van Hum, *Ngoi tu kham lon*, pp. 135–137.

Chapter 6

1. Tran Van Giau, *Giai cap cong nhan Viet-Nam*, 2: 61–63.
2. Ibid., pp. 70–71.
3. Ho Chi Minh, *Selected Works*, 2: 149–150.
4. See his biography in *Nhan dan*, January 11, 1970, p. 1.
5. Tran Van Giau, *Giai cap cong nhan Viet-Nam*, 2: 80–81.
6. Duc Thuan, "Su menh lich su cua giai cap cong nhan doi voi cach mang giai phong dan toc Viet-Nam: thoi ky truoc nam 1930" ("The historical mission of the working class with regard to the liberation revolution of the Vietnamese people: the period before the year 1930"), *Nghien cuu lich su*, Hanoi, March–April 1970, pp. 13–14.
7. K. Tokumo, "Goshi undō to Shanhai rōdōsha" ("The May Fourth Movement and Shanghai Workers"), *Shigaku kenkyū* [Historical Studies Research], Hiroshima, April 1971, pp. 21–37.
8. G. D. H. Cole, *A Short History of the British Working Class Movement* (New York: Macmillan Co., 1927), p. 30.
9. Tran Van Giau, *Giai cap cong nhan Viet-Nam*, 2: 246.
10. *Luc tinh tan van*, Saigon, July 19, 1941, p. 1.
11. Duc Thuan, "Su menh lich su cua giai cap cong nhan," *Nghien cuu lich su*, March–April 1970, pp. 9–18.
12. Tran Van Giau, *Giai cap cong nhan Viet-Nam*, 1: 139.
13. Suehiro Izutarō, *Nihon rōdō kumiai undō shi* [A History of the Japanese Labor Unions Movement] (Tokyo, 1950), pp. 80–81.
14. Nakayama Ichirō and Ōkōchi Kazuo, *Nihon no rōshi kankei to rōdō kumiai* [Japan's Labor Unions and Relations between Laborers and Employers] (Tokyo, 1959), pp. 84–86.
15. Suehiro Izutarō, *Nihon rōdō kumiai undō shi*, pp. 85–86.
16. Ibid., p. 90.
17. Tran Van Giau, *Giai cap cong nhan Viet-Nam*, 2: 112–113.
18. "Les marchands d'hommes à Cholon: comment les jauniers dépouillent les coolies," *La Lutte*, Saigon, January 21, 1936, pp. 1, 4.
19. Diep Lien Anh, *Mau trang mau dao: doi song doa day cua phu cao su mien dat do* [White Blood and Peach Blood: The Brutalized Life of the Rubber Coolies of the Red Earth Region] (Saigon, 1965), p. 23.
20. Diep Lien Anh, *Mau trang mau dao*, pp. 61–66.
21. Ibid., pp. 43–45.
22. "Loi phan tranh lang may, lang tao" ("Styles of conflict between your village, my village"), *Luc tinh tan van*, Saigon, January 16, 1937, p. 1.
23. Jeffrey Race, *War Comes to Long An: Revolutionary Conflict in a Vietnamese Province* (Berkeley: University of California Press, 1972), pp. 179, 206.
24. The Tap, "Bao Thanh Nien va su truyen ba chu nghia Mac-Le-nin vao Viet-Nam" ("The journal 'Youth' and the dissemination of Marxism-

Leninism into Vietnam"), *Hoc tap* [Study and Practice], Hanoi, March 1973, p. 83.

25. "Relatively" should be emphasized. Before the French Popular Front government came to power, *La Lutte* estimated (January 14, 1936, p. 1) that only about four thousand out of eighty thousand Vietnamese inhabitants of Saigon could vote.

26. Trung Chinh, "Nguyen Van Cu, mot can bo lanh dao dang trong thoi ky 1938–1940" ("Nguyen Van Cu, a party leader cadre in the period 1938–1940"), *Nghien cuu lich su*, Hanoi, July–August 1972, pp. 7–17.

27. Tran Van Giau, *Giai cap cong nhan Viet-Nam*, 2: 440–442.

28. "Cach mang thang tam," *Nhan dan*, August 27, 1970, p. 1.

29. Ibid., pp. 1–3.

30. Philippe Devillers, *Histoire du Vietnam de 1940 à 1952* (Paris, 1952), pp. 88–89.

31. Ibid., p. 85.

32. "Cach mang thang tam," *Nhan dan*, August 27, 1970, pp. 1–3.

33. Phan Ngoc Lien, "Tim hieu ve cong tac van dong, giao duc quan chung cua Ho Chu tich trong thoi gian Nguoi o Pac Bo" ("Toward an understanding of the work of mass agitation and education of Chairman Ho in the period he lived in Pac Bo"), *Nghien cuu lich su*, Hanoi, March–April 1973, p. 13.

34. *Dai Nam thuc luc chinh bien*, 1, 45: 11b.

35. Phan Ngoc Lien, "Tim hieu ve cong tac van dong," *Nghien cuu lich su*, March–April 1973, p. 15.

36. Dang Thai Mai, "Mot bai van suoi cua Lo Tan" ("A prose text by Lu Hsün"), *Thanh nghi*, Hanoi, February 1943, pp. 27–29.

37. Phan Ngoc Lien, "Tim hieu ve cong tac van dong," *Nghien cuu lich su*, March-April 1973, pp. 14, 17.

38. Nong Thi Trung, "Bac gioi thieu toi vao dang" ("Uncle introduces me to the party"), *Nhan dan*, Hanoi, May 17, 1965, p. 2.

39. Phan Trong Binh, "Nho lai lop huan luyen dau tien" ("Recalling the first training classes"), *Nhan dan*, January 10, 1970, p. 2.

40. Bertrand Russell, "Dialectical materialism," in Patrick Gardiner, ed., *Theories of History* (Glencoe, Ill.: The Free Press, 1959), pp. 288, 293.

41. "Cach mang thang tam II," *Nhan dan*, August 28, 1970, pp. 3–4.

42. Hoang Nhu Mai, *Van hoc Viet-Nam hien dai 1945–1960* [Contemporary Vietnamese Literature, 1945–1960] (Hanoi, 1961), pp. 106–107.

43. Phan Ngoc Lien, "Tim hieu ve cong tac van dong," *Nghien cuu lich su*, March–April 1973, p. 15.

44. Tran Huy Lieu, *Lich su tam muoi nam chong Phap*, II, 1, 34–37.

45. "Cach mang thang tam," *Nhan dan*, August 27, 1970, pp. 1–3.

46. Pham Khac Hoe, "Su ra doi cua nha nuoc dan chu nhan dan Viet-Nam" ("The birth of the Vietnamese people's democratic state"), in *Mot so van de ve nha nuoc va phap luat Viet-Nam* [A Few Problems concerning the Government and Laws of Vietnam] (Hanoi, 1972), pp. 37–38.

47. Ho Hai, "Mot vai y kien ve moi quan he giua nong thon va thanh thi nuoc ta trong thoi ky 1939–1945" ("A few opinions on the relationships between the villages and the cities of our country in the period 1939–1945"), *Nghien cuu lich su,* Hanoi, July 1963, pp. 12–19.
48. The fascinating story is told best by King Chen, *Vietnam and China 1938–1954* (Princeton: Princeton University Press, 1969).
49. "Cach mang thang tam, II," *Nhan dan,* August 28, 1970, pp. 3–4.
50. Tran Trong Kim, *Mot con gio bui* [A Tempest] (Saigon, 1969), pp. 49–51.
51. Kim, *Mot con gio bui,* pp. 57–58.
52. Ibid., p. 68.
53. "Cach mang thang tam," *Nhan dan,* August 29, 1970.
54. Ibid.
55. "Cach mang thang tam," *Nhan dan,* August 30, 1970.
56. "Cach mang thang tam," *Nhan dan,* August 31, 1970.
57. Ibid.
58. "Ho Chu tich viet tuyen ngon doc lap" ("Chairman Ho writes the declaration of independence"), *Nhan dan,* August 29, 1970, p. 3.
59. Huy Can, "Vao Hue: nhan su thoai vi cua Bao-dai, hoi ky" ("Going into Hue: Receiving the Abdication of Bao-dai, a memoir"), *Nhan dan,* August 30, 1970, p. 3.
60. Roland Mousnier, *Fureurs paysannes: les paysans dans les révoltes du XVIIe siècle, France, Russie, Chine* (Paris, 1967), p. 314.
61. "Nghi quyet cua hoi nghi quan su cach mang Bac Ky (15–20 thang 4 nam 1945)" ("The resolution of the Tonkin revolutionary military affairs conference, April 15–20 1945"), reprinted in *Nhan dan,* August 25, 1970, pp. 1–4.
62. "Cach mang thang tam," *Nhan dan,* August 29, 1970.
63. "Cach mang thang tam," *Nhan dan,* August 31, 1970.
64. "Cach mang thang tam," *Nhan dan,* August 28, 1970.
65. Franz Schurmann, *Ideology and Organization in Communist China* (Berkeley: University of California Press, 1968), p. 129.
66. Ton Quang Duyet, "Mot vai y kien bo sung ve lich su hai dong chi Tran Phu va Nguyen Thi Minh Khai" ("A few supplementary opinions on the history of the two comrades Tran Phu and Nguyen Thi Minh Khai"), *Nghien cuu lich su,* Hanoi, July–August 1971, pp. 22–29.
67. Karl Mannheim, *Ideology and Utopia: An Introduction to the Sociology of Knowledge* (New York: Harvest Books edition, 1936), pp. 156–159.
68. Tran Van Giau, *Giai cap cong nhan Viet-Nam,* 1: 135–136.
69. Cf. James J. Y. Liu, *The Chinese Knight Errant* (London: Routledge and Kegan Paul, 1967).
70. Alexander Woodside, "The Development of Social Organizations in Vietnamese Cities in the Late Colonial Period," *Pacific Affairs,* Spring 1971, p. 55.

71. Tran Van Giau, *Giai cap cong nhan Viet-Nam*, 1: 139–141.
72. Nguyen Tai, "May mau chuyen ve cu Dang Thuc Hua" ("A few anecdotes about the elder Dang Thuc Hua"), *Nghien cuu lich su*, Hanoi, November 1965, p. 45.
73. T'ang Chen, "Wu hsing" ("Five forms"), quoted in Hou Wai-lu, *Chung-kuo ssu-hsiang t'ung-shih* [A Comprehensive History of Chinese Thought] (Peking, 1956), 5: 313.
74. Yamaguchi Ichirō, *Gendai Chūgoku shisō shi*, pp. 78–80.
75. Ibid., pp. 73–86.
76. Such as the *Tay-son bang-giao tap* [Historical Collection on Tay-son Interstate Relations]. Cf. Van Tien Dung, "Duoi ngon co cua Dang: nghe thuat quan su Viet-Nam khong ngung phat trien va chien thang" ("Under the flag of the Party: Vietnamese military art will not stop developing and being victorious"), *Hoc tap*, Hanoi, December 1969, pp. 89–115.
77. Vo Nguyen Giap, "Duong loi quan su cua Dang la ngon co tram tran tram thang cua chien tranh nhan dan o nuoc ta" ("The military path of the Party is the flag of one hundred battles and one hundred victories of the people's war in our country"), *Hoc tap*, Hanoi, December 1969, pp. 62–70.
78. Giap's own statistics, given in 1957: Van Tao, "Vai net ve qua trinh xay dung va phat trien," *Nghien cuu lich su*, August 1965, p. 22.
79. Nguyen Luong Bich and Pham Ngoc Phung, *Tim hieu thien tai quan su cua Nguyen Hue* [Toward an Understanding of the Military Genius of Nguyen Hue] (Hanoi, 1971), p. 294.
80. Nguyen Khac Dam, "Thu ban lai mot diem ve van de hanh quan chop nhoang cua Nguyen Hue" ("Supplementary discussion of a point about the problem of the lightning speed military operations of Nguyen Hue"), *Nghien cuu lich su*, Hanoi, March 1964, pp. 35–38.
81. Vo Nguyen Giap, "Su sang tao cua Dang ta va nhan dan ta trong viec vu trang quan chung cach mang va xay dung quan doi nhan dan" ("The creations of our Party and our people in the work of arming the revolutionary masses and constructing a people's army"), *Hoc tap*, Hanoi, April 1972, pp. 14–17.
82. Vo Nguyen Giap, "Vu trang quan chung cach mang xay dung quan doi nhan dan" ("Arming the revolutionary masses and building people's armies"), *Hoc tap*, Hanoi, January 1972, pp. 17–19.
83. Ibid., p. 15.
84. Van Tao, "Vai net ve qua trinh xay dung va phat trien," *Nghien cuu lich su*, August 1965, p. 22.

Chapter 7

1. Pham Van Dong, *Nha nuoc dan chu nhan dan Viet-Nam* [The Democratic Republic of the People of Vietnam] (Hanoi, 1964), p. 73.
2. Translated and quoted in Alexander Woodside, "The Development of

Social Organizations in Vietnamese Cities," *Pacific Affairs*, Spring 1971, pp. 41–42.

3. Woodside, "The Development of Social Organizations in Vietnamese Cities," *Pacific Affairs*, Spring 1971, p. 40.

4. Van Tao, "Vai net ve qua trinh xay dung va phat trien," *Nghien cuu lich su*, August 1965, pp. 20–21.

5. Alexander Woodside, "Decolonization and Agricultural Reform in Northern Vietnam," *Asian Survey*, August 1970, p. 708.

6. "Bon muoi nam hoat dong cua Dang" ("Forty years of activity of the Party"), *Nhan dan*, January 17, 1970, p. 3.

7. Pham Van Dong, *Nha nuoc dan chu nhan dan Viet-Nam*, p. 87.

8. Ibid., p. 80.

9. Trinh Van Thinh, "May van de kinh te ki thuat ve phat trien chan nuoi trau bo" ("A few economic technology problems concerning the development of the animal husbandry of water buffaloes and oxen"), *Tap chi hoat dong khoa hoc* [Journal of Scientific Activities] Hanoi, April 1972, pp. 12–20.

10. Vu Van Hoan, "Qua trinh xay dung che do hoi dong nhan dan va van de tang cuong hoat dong, phat huy tac dung cua hoi dong nhan dan cac cap" ("The process of establishing the system of people's councils and the problem of strengthening the activities and developing the functions of the people's councils of the various levels"), *Mot so van de ve nha nuoc va phap luat*, p. 180.

11. Pham Van Dong, *Nha nuoc dan chu nhan dan Viet-Nam*, pp. 109–110.

12. Ibid., p. 110; Vu Van Hoan, "Qua trinh xay dung," *Mot so van de ve nha nuoc va phap luat*, p. 183.

13. Vu Van Hoan, "Qua trinh xay dung," *Mot so van de ve nha nuoc va phap luat*, pp. 184–190.

14. "Cac van de: xa vien, dai hoi xa vien va dai hoi dai bieu xa vien, co quan quan ly hop tac xa" ("Problems: cooperative members, cooperative members' congresses and congresses of cooperative members' representatives, cooperative management agencies"), *Nhan dan*, October 13, 1969, p. 2; Nguyen Dieu, "Viec hoc van hoa cua cac can bo chu chot o xa Dong-la" ("The culture-studying work of the key cadres in Dong-la village"), *Hoc tap*, Hanoi, August 1973, p. 75.

15. Dao The Tuan, "Phuong huong giai quyet giong cay luong thuc tren the gioi va mot so i kien giai quyet van de nay o nuoc ta" ("Orientations in the solving of food supply plant strains in the world and a number of opinions about solving this problem in our country"), *Tap chi hoat dong khoa hoc*, Hanoi, May 1971, pp. 6–13.

16. Nguyen Thanh Nha, *Tableau économique du Vietnam*, pp. 58–59.

17. *Nhan dan*, December 6, 1970, p. 2.

18. Le Loc, "Hoan thanh viec phan vung va quy hoach nong nghiep" ("Perfect the work of regionalizing and planning agriculture"), *Nhan dan*, August 29, 1969, p. 2.

19. Ta Hoang Co, "Coi viec gui tien tiet kiem nhu nghia vu cua moi cong

dan" ("Regard the work of sending thrift money as the duty of every citizen"), *Nhan dan,* November 18, 1970, p. 2.

20. Tran Huyen Kieu, "Tuoi vang tuoi bac" ("Golden ages and silver ages"), *Van hoa nghe thuat* [Culture and the Arts] Hanoi, January 1973, pp. 47–49.

21. Tran Khai Van, trans., *Le trieu giao-hoa dieu luat,* p. 42.

22. Lu Giang, "Phong cach Quynh Hong" ("The Quynh Hong style"), *Van hoa nghe thuat,* Hanoi, August 1971, pp. 44–46. It should be added that a minority of Catholic peasants did participate in the soviet movement.

23. Editorial in *Nhan dan,* July 11, 1971.

24. "Tang cuong cong tac quan ly ruong dat" ("Reinforce the work of managing farm land"), *Nhan dan,* July 11, 1971, p. 1.

25. Nghiem Van Thai, "Mot vai net ve cong nhan mien Bac trong 10 nam dau xay dung chu nghia xa hoi 1955–1965" ("A few points about the workers of the north in the first ten years of establishing socialism, 1955–1965"), *Nghien cuu lich su,* Hanoi, March–April 1970, pp. 34–37.

26. Ibid., pp. 37–39.

27. Luu Van Trac, "Tinh hinh giai cap cong nhan mien Bac xa hoi chu nghia trong giai doan danh bai cuoc chien tranh pha hoai cua de quoc My 1965–1968" ("The situation of the working class of the socialist north in the period of defeating the war of destruction of American imperialism, 1965–1968"), *Nghien cuu lich su,* Hanoi, June 1970, p. 102.

28. Ibid., pp. 98–100.

29. Nguyen Van Phung, "Mot so y kien ve nep lao dong moi o Hai Phong" ("Some opinions on the new labor habits in Haiphong"), *Van hoa nghe thuat,* Hanoi, August 1971, p. 10.

30. Nguyen Lan, "Nep song trong gia dinh cua thanh thieu nien" ("The manners of living in the family of youths and adolescents"), *Van hoa nghe thuat,* Hanoi, May 1971, p. 42.

31. Nguyen Van Phung, "Mot so y kien," *Van hoa nghe thuat,* August 1971, p. 10.

32. Vu Dinh Khoa, "Lam gi de duy tri va phat trien phong trao cau lac bo" ("What do we do to preserve and develop the clubs movement"), *Van hoa nghe thuat,* Hanoi, January 1973, pp. 56–59.

33. Survey of Ninh Binh literature and arts movement in *Nhan dan,* July 19, 1970, p. 3.

34. Tran Bang, "Mot so van de trong nghe thuat kich hat dan toc" ("Some problems in the art of singing plays of the people"), *Nhan dan,* Hanoi, October 18, 1970, p. 2.

35. U Thein Han, "A Study of the Rise of the Burmese Novel," *Journal of the Burma Research Society,* Rangoon, June 1968, pp. 1–7.

36. Van Tao, "Vai net ve qua trinh xay dung," *Nghien cuu lich su,* August 1965, p. 18.

37. Do Duc Duc, "Ve tieu thuyet hien thuc phe phan phuong Tay the ky

XIX" ("On Western critical realist novels of the nineteenth century"), *Tap chi van hoc,* Hanoi, April 1970, p. 44.

38. To Huu, "Nam vung duong loi cua Dang, hoc tap cac truong hoc tien tien, dua su nghiep giao duc tien len manh me, vung chac" ("Maintain firmly the line of the Party, study and practice the advanced schools, carry educational enterprises forward to strength and stability"), *Hoc tap,* Hanoi, August 1971, p. 23.

39. Text in *Nhan dan,* March 1, 1970, pp. 1–2.

40. Pham Ke, "Nhung ky su nong nghiep tuong lai" ("Agricultural engineers of the future"), *Nhan dan,* January 20, 1970, p. 2.

41. Nguyen Khanh Toan et al., *Tieng Viet va day dai hoc bang tieng Viet* [The Vietnamese Language and University Teaching in the Vietnamese Language] (Hanoi, 1967), pp. 46–47.

42. To Huu, "Nam vung duong loi," *Hoc tap,* August 1971, pp. 11–12.

43. Ibid., p. 29.

44. Ibid., p. 26.

45. Le Duan, "May van de ve can bo va ve to chuc trong cach mang xa hoi chu nghia" ("A few problems concerning cadres and organization in the socialist revolution"), *Nhan dan,* March 15, 1973, p. 2.

46. Ta Nhu Khue, "He thong phap luat Viet-Nam: dac diem, trien vong" ("The Vietnamese legal system: special features, prospects"), in *Mot so van de ve nha nuoc va phap luat,* p. 252.

47. Do Xuan Sang, "Phan khoi cua mot can bo phap ly" ("The enthusiasm of a legal cadre"), *To quoc* [Ancestral Land] Hanoi, May 1971, pp. 15–16.

48. Hoang Quoc Viet, "Tang cuong phap che xa hoi chu nghia de phuc vu tot cong tac quan ly kinh te" ("Strengthen the socialist legal system in order to serve well the work of economic management"), *Hoc tap,* Hanoi, November 1971, p. 34.

49. Ibid., p. 35.

50. Do Xuan Sang, "Phan khoi cua mot can bo," *To quoc,* May 1971, pp. 15–16.

51. Hoang Quoc Viet, "Tang cuong phap che," *Hoc tap,* November 1971, p. 34.

52. Cf. article by Nguyen Huu Dat in *Hoc tap,* Hanoi, July 1971, pp. 54–64.

53. Vu Thuy, "Nhan ro vai tro luat phap trong xay dung quan doi, cung co quoc phong" ("Recognizing clearly the role of law in the construction of the army and the strengthening of national defence"), *Quan doi nhan dan* [The People's Army] Hanoi, July 3, 1962, p. 3.

Chapter 8

1. On page 86 of his comprehensive study *Viet Cong* (Cambridge: The MIT Press, 1966), Douglas Pike states that to the Viet Minh, *binh van* had had a different meaning, namely propaganda action among their

own troops. This is at least partly incorrect, as a study of the text of the resolution of the Tonkin revolutionary military affairs conference of April 15–20, 1945, will show. On the extensive propaganda facilities of the NLF, see Phan Lac Tuyen, article in *Mot so van de ve nha nuoc va phap luat,* p. 313.

2. Le Tat Dac, "Day manh hon nua cong tac cai tien to chuc va le loi lam viec trong cac co quan nha nuoc" ("Strengthen further the work of reform of organizations and of procedures of doing work in state organs"), *Hoc tap,* Hanoi, March 1963, pp. 27–30.

3. Ton That Trinh, "Nuoc nha can mot chinh sach lua gao" ("The nation needs a rice policy"), *Chinh luan,* Saigon, December 1, 1972, p. 2.

4. Article by Truong Loc on village reconstruction in *Chinh luan,* Saigon, December 12, 1967.

5. Thai Lang, *Nhat ky cua nguoi chung* [The Diary of a Witness] (Saigon, 1969), p. 46.

6. Tran Trieu Viet, "Ve 180 ong, ba chay dua vao Thuong Vien" ("On the 180 men and women running in competition to enter the upper house"), *Chinh luan,* Saigon, July 19–20, 1970, p. 2.

7. Reported in *Cong luan,* Saigon, December 31, 1969, p. 1.

8. Trinh Pho, "Tap the quan nhan trong cuoc can quet moi" ("The military collectivity in the new mopping up enterprise"), *Quan chung* [The Masses], Saigon, September 5, 1969, pp. 79–84. Cf. John Prados, "Generals and Politics in South Vietnam," *Indochina Chronicle,* Washington, July 17, 1973.

9. *Hoa binh,* Saigon, January 17, 1971, p. 3.

10. "Tieng khoc nong thon" ("The weeping cries of the villages"), *Cong luan,* Saigon, August 20, 1969, p. 2.

11. Nguyen Tan Long and Nguyen Huu Trong, *Viet-Nam thi nhan tien chien* [Vietnamese Poets in the Van of the Struggle] (Saigon, 1968), 1: 493–495.

12. Nguyen Van Hao, *Dong gop 1: lanh vuc kinh te 1965–1972* [One Contribution: The Economic Sector, 1965–1972] (Saigon, 1972), pp. 179–182.

13. Tran Ngoc Cu, "Van de nhan dung tai Viet-Nam" ("The problem of manpower use in Vietnam"), *Chinh luan,* Saigon, March 8, 1973, p. 2.

14. Article by Hoang Minh in *Chinh luan,* Saigon, November 9, 1967, pp. 4–5.

15. Pham Quang Toan, "Phong trao cong nhan Viet-Nam vung tam bi chiem trong thoi ky khang chien 1945–1954" ("The Vietnamese workers' movement in the temporarily occupied zones in the period of resistance 1945–1954"), *Nghien cuu lich su,* Hanoi, May 1965, p. 56.

16. Diep Lien Anh, *Mau trang mau dao,* pp. 108–110.

17. Tran Van Giau, *Giai cap cong nhan Viet-Nam,* I, 175.

18. *Chinh luan,* Saigon, January 9, 1970, p. 3.

19. Viet Son, "Phan tich 'the nhan dan' cua 3 lien danh Thieu, Minh, Ky"

("Analyzing the popular influence of the three name-slates Thieu, Minh, Ky"), *Chinh luan,* Saigon, August 15–18, 1971, p. 2.

20. *Chinh luan,* March 30, 1973, p. 3.
21. Bui Quang Diem, "Van de phat trien" ("The development problem"), *Tap chi Minh Duc* [Minh Duc Journal], Saigon, June–July 1972, p. 24.
22. *Hoa binh,* Saigon, July 25, 1971, p. 3.
23. Duyen Anh, *Vet thu han tren lung con ngua hoang* [The Marks of Hostility on the Backs of the Untamed Horses] (Saigon, 1968), pp. 56–57.
24. Phan Kim Thinh, "Van de cua chung ta" ("Our problems"), *Van hoc* [Literature], Saigon, November 1962, p. 27.
25. Cf. Le Van Hao, "Ve cong cuoc dau tranh bao ve nen van hoa dan toc o mien Nam" ("On the work of struggling to preserve our people's cultural foundations in the south"), *Van hoa nghe thuat,* Hanoi, July 1971, pp. 10–12.
26. *Chinh luan,* Saigon, January 25, 1969, p. 3.
27. The phrase of Tran Van Nghiem, in *Chinh luan,* April 10, 1971, p. 2.
28. Bui Quang Diem, "Van de phat trien," *Tap chi Minh Duc,* June–July 1972, p. 24.
29. Nguyen Van Sam, "Vai sai lam trong chuong trinh trung hoc hien tai" ("Some errors in the present-day middle school program"), *Cap tien* [Rapid Advance], Saigon, May 1969, p. 63.
30. *Cong luan,* Saigon, August 23, 1969, p. 3.
31. *Chinh luan,* Saigon, January 25, 1969, p. 3.
32. Nguyen Ngoc Huy, "Chanh dang o Viet-Nam" ("Legitimate political parties in Vietnam"), *Cap tien,* Saigon, November–December 1970, pp. 4–5.
33. Nguyen Ngoc Huy, "Chanh dang o Viet-Nam," *Cap tien,* November–December 1970, p. 11.
34. Tran Van Duong, "Gop y kien ve the thuc bau cu thuong nghi vien" ("Contributing opinions on ways of electing the upper chamber"), *Chinh luan,* Saigon, June 4–5, 1967, p. 4.
35. *Chinh luan,* September 10–11, 1967.
36. Tran Trieu Viet, "Ve 180 ong, ba," *Chinh luan,* July 17, 18, 19–20, 21, and 22, 1970. My tabulation.
37. Nguyen Van Trung, *Gop phan phe phan giao duc va dai hoc* [A Contributed Share of Criticism of Education and Higher Education] (Saigon, 1967), p. 102.
38. *Chinh luan,* July 21, 1970, p. 3.
39. Tran Ngoc Cu, "Van de nhan dung," *Chinh luan,* March 8, 1973, p. 2.
40. *Chinh luan,* Saigon, November 9, 1972, p. 3.
41. *Duoc Nha Nam,* Saigon, February 8, 1971, p. 1.
42. Nguyen Van Trung, *Gop phan phe phan giao duc,* pp. 102–103.
43. Hoang Huan Dinh et al., "Dat lai van de trung tam quoc gia ky thuat va giao duc ky thuat" ("Restating the problems of the national tech-

nology center and technical education"), *Chinh luan*, March 15, 1972, p. 2.

44. Hoang Huan Dinh et al., "Dat lai van de," *Chinh luan*, March 17, 1972, p. 2.

45. Nguyen Van Trung, *Gop phan phe phan giao duc*, pp. 148–149.

46. *Chinh luan*, July 19–20, 1970, p. 3.

47. *Etudes Cambodgiennes*, Phnom Penh, October–December 1966, p. 9.

48. Ha Minh Ly, "Ban ve viec thanh lap cac nghiep doan giao duc" ("A discussion of the work of creating educational labor unions"), *Chinh luan*, March 18, 19–20, 1972, p. 2.

Epilogue

1. Quoted in *Chinh luan*, January 27, 1973, p. 3.

2. See the article by Tran Tuan in *Chinh luan*, October 17, 1974, p. 2.

3. Described by Viet Tuan in *Chinh luan*, November 2, 1974, 2.

4. Alexis de Tocqueville, *The Old Regime and the French Revolution*, trans. Stuart Gilbert (New York: Doubleday Anchorbooks, 1955), pp. 176–177.

5. Dao Duy Tung, "May y kien ve van de boi duong, nang cao trinh do ly luan, nghiep vu va van hoa cua can bo ta" ("Some opinions on the problem of reinforcing and raising high the levels of theory, specialized duties, and culture of our cadres"), *Hoc tap*, Hanoi, March 1963, pp. 40–47.

6. Tran Kien, "Ket nap dang vien lop Ho Chi Minh o Hai Phong" ("The admission of the Ho Chi Minh class of party members in Haiphong"), *Nhan dan*, May 7, 1971, p. 2.

7. J. M. H. Lindbeck, "Transformations in the Chinese Communist Party," in Donald W. Treadgold, ed., *Soviet and Chinese Communism: Similarities and Differences* (Seattle: University of Washington Press, 1967), p. 89.

8. Van Tao, "Ve chat luong cua giai cap cong nhan" ("On the substance of the worker class"), *Nghien cuu lich su*, Hanoi, May–June 1972, p. 36.

9. Susan Sontag, *Trip to Hanoi* (New York: Farrar, Straus, and Giroux, 1968), p. 51.

10. Nguyen Duc Nam, "Con nguoi Viet-Nam hien dai trong nhan thuc cua nha van My Xu-dan Xon-tac" ("The contemporary Vietnamese people in the realizations of the American writer Susan Sontag"), *Tap chi van hoc*, Hanoi, April 1970, pp. 6–16.

Suggestions for Further Reading

What follows is a brief list—sometimes amplified by my comments—of published Western-language books which I have found useful, either because of their great merits or their provocative prejudices, in my own study of the Vietnamese revolution. I have also included one or two journal articles and some specimens of my own previous work.

1 Colonialism and the Vietnamese Community

Buttinger, Joseph. *The Smaller Dragon: A Political History of Vietnam.* New York: Praeger Publishers, 1958.

——. *Vietnam: A Dragon Embattled.* 2 vols. New York: Praeger, 1967.

Cadière, Léopold. *Croyances et pratiques réligieuses des Vietnamiens.* Saigon: Imprimerie nouvelle d'Extrême-Orient, 1958.

DeBary, William T., ed. *Sources of Chinese Tradition.* New York: Columbia University Press, 1960.
For readers wholly unfamiliar with the fundamental philosophies and religions of East Asian classical civilization—the ideas of Confucius, Mencius, the Taoists, and the various schools of Mahayana Buddhism which modern Vietnam, as well as modern China, inherited—this book is an excellent and balanced introduction.

Le Thanh Khoi. *Le Viet-Nam: histoire et civilisation.* Paris, Editions de Minuit, 1955.

Nguyen Du. *The Tale of Kieu.* Translated and annotated by Huynh Sanh Thong. New York: Random House, 1973.
The most formidable introduction, in poetry, to many of the most enduring themes in the high classical civilization of Vietnam. These themes—loyalty, filial piety, the appropriateness of rebellion under certain conditions, individual fortitude and self-denial in a time of troubles—have also governed, and continue to govern, the thought of many modern Vietnamese revolutionaries. The author of this verse novel, a brilliant classical scholar, died in 1820.

Nguyen Thanh Nha. *Tableau économique du Vietnam aux XVIIe et XVIIIe Siècles.* Paris: Editions Cujas, 1970.
An excellent study of social and economic change in Vietnam in the seventeenth and eighteenth centuries.

Nguyen Van Phong. *La société vietnamienne de 1882 à 1902.* Paris: Presses Universitaires de France, 1971.
This study offers cogent summaries of the social upheavals which attended the French conquest of Vietnam, as seen through the eyes of French observers whom business, curiosity, or wanderlust attracted to the colony in its early years.

Smith, Ralph. *Vietnam and the West.* London: Heinemann Educational Books, 1968.

Steinberg, David Joel, et al. *In Search of Southeast Asia: A Modern History.* New York: Praeger Publishers, 1971.

Woodside, Alexander Barton. *Vietnam and the Chinese Model.* Cambridge, Mass.: Harvard University Press, 1971.

2 The Early Nationalists' Search for a New Community

Chang Hao. *Liang Ch'i-ch'ao and Intellectual Transition in China, 1890–1907.* Cambridge, Mass.: Harvard University Press, 1971.

Duiker, William J. "Hanoi Scrutinizes the Past: The Marxist Evaluation of Phan Boi Chau and Phan Chu Trinh." *Southeast Asia* 1 (Summer 1971), 243–254.

Marr, David G. *Vietnamese Anticolonialism 1885–1925.* Berkeley: University of California Press, 1971.

Nguyen Khac Vien. "Confucianisme et marxisme au Vietnam." In his *Expériences vietnamiennes,* pp. 201–232. Paris: Editions sociales, 1970.
The author is an eloquent spokesman for Vietnamese Marxism. He asserts that traditional Vietnam harbored two currents of Confucian thought: the current of court or bureaucratic Confucianism, and the current of popular Confucianism as expressed by iconoclastic village school teachers. In the 1800s, while court mandarins remained supine, these village literati "saved the honor" of Confucianism by fighting the French invaders. The first Marxist militants in Vietnam are shown to have continued the traditions of these "revolutionary literati" of the past. Moreover, Vien claims that an intellectual "kinship" existed between Marxists and "authentic Confucians" in Vietnam, which facilitated a bond between the two doctrines: in defining man by the totality of his social relations, Marxism is supposed not to have disconcerted Confucian intellectuals who assumed that the supreme goal of man was the fulfillment of social obligations. Any Chinese Marxist who suggested, in 1973, that "kinship" might exist between revolutionary egalitarian communism and a monarchy-supporting, hierarchy-promoting Confucianism would be much criticized in Mao's China. That a Vietnamese Marxist advances such views indicates the gulf between the two East Asian revolutions, and the greater force of romantic traditionalism in the Vietnamese one.

Truong Buu Lam. *Patterns of Vietnamese Response to Foreign Intervention, 1858–1900.* Southeast Asia Studies, Monograph Series No. 11. New Haven: Yale University, 1967.
On the basis of the impressive documentation which he has collected and translated, and which ranges back to the eleventh century, the author argues that there were vigorous traditions of resistance to foreign aggression in Vietnam in the medieval period and in the nineteenth century with which twentieth-century revolutionaries could associate themselves. Emphasis is placed upon the emotional continuities of the modern revolution.

3 The Intellectuals and the Problem of Social Organization

Osborne, Milton E. *The French Presence in Cochinchina and Cambodia: Rule and Response, 1859–1905.* Ithaca: Cornell University Press, 1969.
This book, while dealing with other matters too, discusses the emergence of the colonial educational system in southern Vietnam at least, as well as the spread of the use of romanized Vietnamese writing in place of Chinese characters.

Pham Thi Ngoan. "Introduction au Nam Phong." *Bulletin de la Société des Etudes Indochinoises* (Saigon), New Series, 48 (1973), 175–473.
A detailed dissection of one of the two most famous Vietnamese periodicals of the interwar period, the journal which was the platform of Pham Quynh and of several other intellectuals mentioned in this chapter.

Vella, Walter F., ed. *Aspects of Vietnamese History.* Honolulu: Asian Studies at Hawaii 8, The University Press of Hawaii, 1973.
A collection of essays which includes one of the rare surveys in English of the development of modern Vietnamese literature (by Hoang Ngoc Thanh).

Woodside, Alexander. "The Development of Social Organizations in Vietnamese Cities in the Late Colonial Period." *Pacific Affairs* 44 (Spring 1971), 39–64.
This article looks briefly and far from exhaustively at several of the nurseries of the colonial Vietnamese intelligentsia—the Indochina law schools and medical schools—and at the characteristic difficulties of newfangled Vietnamese organizations, like regional fellowship societies and urban consumers' cooperatives, under the colonial regime.

4 Colonialism and Premonitions of Revolution in the Countryside

Gourou, Pierre. *Les Paysans du delta tonkinois: étude de géographie humaine.* Paris: Les éditions d'art et d'histoire, 1936; Mouton, 1965.
——. *L'utilisation du sol en Indochine Française.* Paris: P. Hartmann, 1940.

Hickey, Gerald C. *Village in Vietnam.* New Haven: Yale University Press, 1964.
This pioneering English-language study of life in a southern village was based upon anthropological field work of the late 1950s and early 1960s. But the usefulness of its descriptions often extends back to the French colonial period.

McAlister, John T., Jr. and Mus, Paul. *The Vietnamese and Their Revolution.* New York: Harper Torchbooks, 1970.
This book presents the views of a distinguished French Indochina scholar, Paul Mus, who wrote about Vietnamese village life, and the ways in which the colonial system was disrupting it, with an oracular reverence that is difficult to duplicate. Mus knew northern villages better than southern ones, and was inclined to emphasize the "autonomy" of the villagers and the superficiality of their dealings with the traditional Vietnamese monarchy. But the crucial element missing from the Mus picture of precolonial villages is the influence of the civil service examination system. Since most village elite families passionately wanted their sons to win degrees (and bureaucratic positions) through the examinations, which were controlled by the emperors above the village, village "autonomy" was more hollow than Mus supposed.

Ngo Vinh Long. *Before The Revolution: The Vietnamese Peasants under the French.* Cambridge, Mass.: The MIT Press, 1973.
This forcefully written work taps previously unexploited Vietnamese journalistic and literary sources. It also includes translations of important Vietnamese writings in the colonial period which depicted growing rural decadence, or what the authors translated (Phi Van, Ngo Tat To, Hoang Dao, Nguyen Cong Hoan, Tran Van Mai) plainly regarded as the decay of village life.

Robequain, Charles. *The Economic Development of French Indochina.* Translated by Isabel A. Ward. New York: Oxford University Press, 1944.

Scott, James C. "The Erosion of Patron-Client Bonds and Social Change in Rural Southeast Asia." *Journal of Asian Studies* 32 (November 1972), 5-37.

Vu Quoc Thuc. *L'économie communaliste du Viet-Nam.* Hanoi: Presses universitaires du Viet-Nam, 1951.

5 The Origins and Expansion of Communist Power

Ho Chi Minh. *Selected Works.* 4 vols. Hanoi: Foreign Languages Publishing House, 1960-1962.
——. *On Revolution: Selected Writings, 1920-1966.* Edited and introduced by Bernard Fall. New York: Praeger Publishers, 1967.

Lacouture, Jean. *Ho Chi Minh: A Political Biography.* Translated by Peter Wiles. New York: Random House, 1968.
This is the most serviceable biography of Ho Chi Minh in existence in the West. It was written by a French journalist who has had extensive experience in Indochina and who has personally interviewed Ho and other revolutionaries. Nevertheless, this book is not based upon any of the growing body of Vietnamese language documentation and memoirs about Ho's career, and consequently remains somewhat shallow. There is a most pressing need, still to be filled, for a first-rate scholarly biography of Ho Chi Minh.

Nguyen Khac Huyen. *Vision Accomplished? The Enigma of Ho Chi Minh.* New York: Macmillan, 1971.

Nguyen Tran Huan. "Histoire d'une secte religieuse au Vietnam: Le Caodaisme." In J. Chesneaux, G. Boudarel, and D. Hemery, *Tradition et révolution au Vietnam,* pp. 189-214. Paris: Editions Anthropos, 1971.

Smith, R. B. "An Introduction to Caodaism." *Bulletin of the School of Oriental and African Studies* (London) 33, Part 2 (1970), 335-349; and Part 3 (1970), 573-589.

Thich Nhat Hanh. *Vietnam: Lotus in a Sea of Fire.* New York: Hill and Wang, 1967.
Satisfying descriptions and discussions of Vietnamese Buddhism are extremely rare in Western languages. This book, written by a Buddhist intellectual in the 1960s primarily in an effort to change American policies of intervention in Vietnam, nonetheless has about thirty pages of analysis of Vietnamese Buddhists' political and religious heritage, and of the Buddhist revival movement from the 1920s. For Buddhism in general, perhaps the most masterful brief survey is that of Edward Conze, *Buddhism: Its Essence and Development* (New York: Harper Torchbooks, 1959).

6 The Mandarin Proletarians and the Redemption of the Past

Chen, King C. *Vietnam and China, 1938-1954.* Princeton, N.J.: Princeton University Press, 1969.
The Vietnamese communist movement especially as viewed through the eyes, and the documents, of important Chinese politicians and military men who dealt with Ho Chi Minh during World War II.

Devillers, Philippe. *Histoire du Vietnam de 1940 à 1952.* Paris: Editions du Seuil, 1952.

Hammer, Ellen J. *The Struggle for Indochina 1940-1955: Vietnam and the French Experience.* Stanford: Stanford University Press, 1955.
This pioneering book is still useful as a diplomatic and political history of the Indochina crisis in the 1940s and early 1950s.

Huynh Kim Khanh. "The Vietnamese August Revolution Reinterpreted." *Journal of Asian Studies* 30 (August 1971) 761-782.

McAlister, John T., Jr. *Vietnam: The Origins of Revolution.* New York: Alfred A. Knopf, 1969.
This book, which covers the Vietnamese revolution from the 1880s to 1946, relies heavily upon its author's use of French army archives, and emphasizes the politics of the period of Indochina's occupation by the Japanese.

Truong Chinh. *The August Revolution.* Hanoi: Foreign Languages Publishing House, 1958.
One of its architects speaks.

Vo Nguyen Giap. *People's War People's Army.* Hanoi Foreign Languages Publishing House translation. New York: Praeger Publishers, 1962.
This English version of the work has a classic cold war polemical introduction by Roger Hilsman, who describes Giap's writings as "less ambitious" than, but comparable to, Hitler's *Mein Kampf.* However, once the reader has passed beyond the shop-worn anticommunist pieties of the early Kennedy administration, he will discover, in the Giap text, such things as an exposition of the battle of Dien Bien Phu from the communist side.

7 Revolution and the New Organizational Ethic

Chaliand, Gérard. *The Peasants of North Vietnam.* Translated by Peter Wiles. Baltimore: Penguin Books, 1969.
Life in rural northern Vietnam—especially the provinces of Hung Yen, Thai Binh, Ha Tay, and Ninh Binh—during the American air assault in 1967. Interesting data on village life, presented by an admirer of the Hanoi regime.

Fall, Bernard. *The Two Vietnams: A Political and Military Analysis.* rev. ed. New York: Praeger Publishers, 1967.

Hoang Van Chi. *From Colonialism to Communism: A Case History of North Vietnam.* New York: Praeger Publishers, 1964.
A hostile description of land reform and thought control in the north after 1954, by a former member of the Viet Minh, whose personal experiences and feelings deserve more respect than his far from reliable statistics.

Le Duan. *The Vietnamese Revolution.* New York: International Publishers, 1971.

A 1970 report by Le Duan, the first secretary of the Vietnamese Communist Party; it discusses the party's hopes, plans, and achievements in industry and agriculture in the north.

"Symposium on Vietnamese Communism." *Asian Survey* 12 (September 1972).
Includes articles by William S. Turley on the role of women in the communist revolution, and by Phan Thien Chau on changes in party leadership.

Woodside, Alexander. "Decolonization and Agricultural Reform in Northern Vietnam." *Asian Survey* 10 (August 1970), 705–723.

———. "Ideology and Integration in Postcolonial Vietnamese Nationalism." *Pacific Affairs* 44 (Winter 1971–1972), 487–510.
Among other things, this article examines the "localization" of education in the north, and partial southern imitations of such "localization."

8 Social Groups and Organizational Dilemmas in the South

Duncanson, Dennis J. *Government and Revolution in Vietnam.* London: Oxford University Press, 1968.

Fitzgerald, Frances. *Fire in the Lake: The Vietnamese and the Americans in Vietnam.* Boston: Little, Brown and Co., 1972.
A highly acclaimed, well-written study of the American military and political intervention in Vietnam. Some of its critics (on the right) have accused it of romanticizing communist repressiveness; others of its critics (on the left) have felt that it lacked a broad understanding of the use of Marxist-Leninist theories in Vietnam; Vietnamese specialists of all persuasions undoubtedly feel that its efforts to present psychological explanations of Vietnamese behavior, especially collective behavior, are a bit rash. Its provocativeness as well as its eloquence make it worth reading.
The pithiest review of it known to me is by Nguyen Khac Vien, "Myths and Realities," available in *Bulletin of Concerned Asian Scholars* 5 San Francisco (December 1973), 56–63.

Goodman, Allan E. *Politics in War: The Bases of Political Community in South Vietnam.* Cambridge, Mass.: Harvard University Press, 1973.

Kahin, George M. and Lewis, John W. *The United States in Vietnam.* New York: Dell Publishing Co., 1967.

Pike, Douglas. *Viet Cong: The Organization and Techniques of the National Liberation Front of South Vietnam.* Cambridge, Mass.: The MIT Press, 1966.
Written with an intense (and unconcealed) anticommunist bias, this book is still a most impressive repository of information in English on NLF politics and organization, and is even quoted as a reference in northern Vietnamese historical journals by writers like Nguyen Hoai.

Race, Jeffrey. *War Comes to Long An: Revolutionary Conflict in a Vietnamese Province.* Berkeley, University of California Press, 1972.
A vivid, persuasively written study of how, in the early 1960s, in one province, the NLF revolutionaries gained the advantage over a Saigon government far too remote from village life and far too dependent upon imported weapons. Purists might argue that the book is too schematic to do justice to the rich heterogeneities of Vietnamese village life. This could be said about almost any book about Vietnam, it must be ruefully admitted; here the schematization is unusually compelling.

Sansom, Robert L. *The Economics of Insurgency in the Mekong Delta of Vietnam.* Cambridge, Mass.: The MIT Press, 1970.

Scigliano, Robert. *South Vietnam: Nation under Stress.* Boston: Houghton Mifflin Co., 1963.

Senator Gravel Edition, The. *The Pentagon Papers: The Defense Department History of United States Decisionmaking on Vietnam.* 5 vols. Boston: Beacon Press, 1972.

The documents of this famous work, as most readers are no doubt aware, present a picture of the Vietnam War as it was seen by Washington decision-makers, not by the Vietnamese people.

Shaplen, Robert. *The Lost Revolution: The U.S. in Vietnam, 1946–1966.* New York: Harper and Row, 1966.

Index